Betrayal and Treason

CRIME & SOCIETY

Series Editor John Hagan
Northwestern University

Betrayal and Treason: Violations of Trust and Loyalty, Nachman Ben-Yehuda

*Breaking Away from Broken Windows: Baltimore Evidence and the Nationwide Fight Against
Crime, Grime, Fear, and Decline,* Ralph B. Taylor

Costs and Benefits of Preventing Crime, Brandon C. Welsh,
David P. Farrington, and Lawrence W. Sherman

Losing Legitimacy: Street Crime and the Decline of Social Institutions in America, Gary LaFree

Public Opinion, Crime, and Criminal Justice, Julian V. Roberts
and Loretta Stalans

Power, Politics and Crime, William J. Chambliss

The Community Justice Ideal, Todd Clear and David Karp

*Whistleblowing at Work: Tough Choices in Exposing Fraud, Waste, and
Abuse on the Job,* Terance D. Miethe

Casualties of Community Disorder: Women's Careers in Violent Crime,
Deborah R. Baskin and Ira B. Sommers

Poverty, Ethnicity, and Violent Crime, James F. Short

Great Pretenders: Pursuits and Careers of Persistent Thieves, Neal Shover

Crime and Public Policy: Putting Theory to Work, edited by Hugh D. Barlow

Control Balance: Toward a General Theory of Deviance, Charles R. Tittle

Rape and Society: Readings on the Problems of Sexual Assault,
edited by Patricia Searles and Ronald J. Berger

Inequality, Crime, and Social Control, George S. Bridges
and Martha A. Myers

Forthcoming
Latino Homicide: A Five-City Study, Ramiro Martinez

Betrayal and Treason

Violations of Trust and Loyalty

Nachman Ben-Yehuda

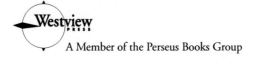

Westview
PRESS

A Member of the Perseus Books Group

Crime and Society

Copyright © 2001 by Westview Press, A Member of the Perseus Books Group

Westview Press books are available at special discounts for bulk purchases in the United States by corporations, institutions, and other organizations. For more information, please contact the Special Markets Department at the Perseus Books Group, 11 Cambridge Center, Cambridge MA 02142, or call (617) 252-5298.

Published in 2001 in the United States of America by Westview Press, 5500 Central Avenue, Boulder, Colorado 80301-2877, and in the United Kingdom by Westview Press, 12 Hid's Copse Road, Cumnor Hill, Oxford OX2 9JJ

Find us on the World Wide Web at www.westviewpress.com

Library of Congress Cataloging-in-Publication Data
Ben-Yehuda, Nachman.
   Betrayal and treason: violations of trust and loyalty/ Nachman Ben-Yehuda.
      p. cm. — (Crime and society)
   Includes bibliographical reference and index.
   ISBN 0-8133-9776-6
      1. Betrayal. 2. Treason. I. Title. II. Crime & society.

BJ1500.B47 B46 2000
179'.8—dc21
                                                          00-043985
                                                                CIP

The paper used in this publication meets the requirements of the American National Standard for Permanence of Paper for Printed Library Materials Z39.48–1984.

10   9   8   7   6   5   4   3   2   1

To
Caroline and Jean Wittenberg and
Beatrice and Abraham Heilbruun
whose friendship I have learned
to cherish dearly

"I Did Not Betray"

—Note written by Uri Illan, an Israeli paratrooper who was captured by the Syrians in 1955, while on an intelligence mission, and tortured. He hid a few notes with the above statement on his body prior to committing suicide in the Syrian prison.

Contents

Illustrations

Acknowledgments

The beginning of this project is clear in my mind. It was during a university faculty strike in 1994 when one faculty member lost his nerve and decided to break the strike shortly before it ended anyway. His own statement that the rest of the faculty may view him as a "Quisling" prompted me to start readings on this topic (the incident is recorded in fuller detail in Chapter 3). There were a few other incentives. Preceding this incident was my involvement in politics and deviance (1989) and my project on political assassinations by Jews (1993) where so many of the cases of assassination were in the context of accusations of "betrayal." What fueled my quest even more was the 1995 assassination of Israeli premier Yitzhak Rabin (discussed in Chapter 11), again in the context of his being accused by so many people from the Israeli right and religious right as being a "traitor." The instigation against Rabin and his government in the context of betrayal was ominous. My previous interests in constructionism, power, and politics made studying betrayal a natural extension of my work. As is usually the case, the road from plunging into the project to its end was a long one. It is time to express my gratitude to all those who gave a helping hand along the way.

My first gratitude is to Etti, Tzach, and Guy, whose love, devotion, and dedication enabled me to transform this project from an idea into a book.

The Israeli-Canada exchange program enabled my research in the library of the University of Toronto on Benedict Arnold (Israeli libraries had *nothing* on this man). The London School of Economics, Department of Sociology, enabled me to spend two wonderful summers (1996–1997) in London collecting data about various cases of betrayal and treason. I am particularly grateful to Eileen Barker, Paul Rock, and Stanley Cohen, whose help and support were crucial. I especially appreciate Paul Rock's many practical and essential comments on an earlier draft. In London, I enjoyed the generous, courteous, and very effective assistance of librarians and staff from the Wiener Library, the British Library, and particularly the Imperial War Museum.

As I was spending large amounts of time in both libraries, I learned to appreciate the different entrances to both. At that time, entry to the British Library was through the British Museum. That entry meant passing near the Rosetta Stone. Entry to the Imperial War Museum meant passing by two huge sixteen-inch naval guns. Although I could never decide which was more impressive (a symbolic dilemma for a person who faced daily dilemmas of deciding what was and what was not treason), I eventually discovered that I preferred the Rosetta Stone after all.

Einat Usant, Vered Vinitzky-Seroussi, Iris Wolf, Dalit Rudner, Avi Shoshana, and Michal Laron helped at various stages of this lengthy project as research assistants. I am very grateful to them all for their dedicated and indispensable help.

Barbara Weinstein was extremely helpful in putting me in touch with Ross Hassig. Without his penetrating critical work, my understanding of the Malinche case would have been less than desired. I am very grateful to both.

Uzi Amit-Kohn, Gershon Ben-Shachar, Stanly Cohen, Martin Gladman, Marianna Bar, Adam Seligman, and John Simpson volunteered many insightful comments and assistance, which helped to crystallize the approach presented in this volume. Barry Schwartz, John Simpson, and Erich Goode kindly provided useful and pointed comments as to how to proceed with this project at some crucial moments in the summer of 1997. I am also grateful to Jennifer B. Swearingen, whose editorial suggestions and comments were very helpful in preparing the manuscript for publication.

Last, but certainly not least, it is a genuine pleasure to acknowledge my deepest gratitude to an outstanding criminologist, John Hagan, without whose professional support and guidance this book would not have been possible. I am also very grateful to Ron Gillis, Erich Goode, Simon Singer, and—again—John Hagan, whose constructive review provided productive comments and suggestions. Their indispensable assistance most certainly made this book significantly better. It is indeed an honor and a pleasure to have had the privilege of benefiting from the insights of such outstanding colleagues.

Nachman Ben-Yehuda

Part One

1

Introduction:
Violating Trust and Loyalty

In this book we shall acquaint ourselves with a dazzling spectrum of behaviors that qualify for the dubious title of "betrayal." We shall try to develop an understanding of the essence of this fascinating form of behavior and examine whether behind its many varied manifestations there is
a common analytical and empirical core. Are there such acts that, when
committed, increase significantly the probability of being branded as
"betrayal"? As we shall see, betrayal does indeed present a universal
structure.

The actual behaviors that fall into the "betrayal" category form a fascinating spectrum. Outlining this spectrum requires some vivid and powerful illustrations. Hence, I have tried to invoke as many illustrations as
possible. This is a good place to start. I have deliberately chosen somewhat problematic cases to whet the appetite for what follows.

The Yehuda Gil Affair.   During December 1997 and January 1998, the
Israeli public was amazed to learn that a Mossad (Israeli foreign secret intelligence service) operative called Yehuda Gil, who was in charge of collecting and processing information about Syria, was suspected of fabri-
cating sources and falsifying his reports. The general implication was that
he made Syria appear much more threatening, with belligerent intentions, than it actually was. His reports made it appear as if Syrian President Hafez Al-Assad was planning another war against Israel. Gil was
probably effective in helping to create a false impression in the summer of
1996 by telling Mossad that Syria was planning a surprise, but limited,
ground attack in the Golan Heights, which supposedly aimed at seizing
some territory. Part of his deception was based on reports of threatening
movements by Syrian army units. This falsified information might have
caused great harm if Israel had acted on it. Luckily that did not happen,
as other checks and balances were operating.[1]

In March 1999, a Tel Aviv district court convicted Gil on charges of providing false information, intending to harm the state's security, and stealing tens of thousands of dollars from Mossad. He was given a five-year prison sentence.

The Bus No. 300 Affair.   On April 12, 1984, four Palestinians boarded Israel's Egged bus no. 300 in Tel Aviv. The bus was heading to Ashkelon, a southern Israeli town on the Mediterranean coast. Along the way, the Palestinians hijacked it. Later, Israeli soldiers stormed the bus and released the passengers. Two of the Palestinians were killed during the action. Two others were taken prisoner, interrogated by SHABAC (Israel's domestic secret security service), and later killed.

In what was probably the most spectacular (and nasty) cover-up operation in the history of the Israeli secret services, SHABAC initially denied that its people were ordered to, and did indeed, kill the two Palestinians. Civil servants in SHABAC lied and manipulated other civil servants (including, among other things, an attempt to falsely implicate Brigadier General Yitzhak Mordechai, later Israel's minister of defense). Eventually, this cover-up was exposed (by some SHABAC whistle-blowers).[2]

In both cases, the same violation of values and norms occurred. Although Gil's motives were complex (he held a personal grudge for not being promoted, a political inclination to the right, and a problematic personality), it can be easily argued that Gil violated in the most fundamental way both the trust invested in him by Mossad and his loyalty to be truthful to the organization of which he was a member for many years. In the case of bus no. 300, there can hardly be a doubt that the chiefs of SHABAC and those who participated in the cover-up betrayed the trust and loyalty invested in their positions in the most fundamental way.

The Puzzle

Social life, the very essence of sociological inquiries, is a complicated issue. On the one hand, cultures and societies are "out there," as if they constitute separate entities that we can talk about, orient ourselves toward, and study. On the other hand, these entities are "there" because we construct them to "be" there. That is, without us and our language, they have no existence. For a sociologist this problem is magnified because, clearly, the terms we have devised to describe and analyze cultures and societies are abstractions. They form what C. Wright Mills called "the sociological imagination"—a sort of consciousness based on a particular perception that is shaped by the abstractions we use, not unlike one of those stories involving Baron Munchhausen, or perhaps Alice's Wonderland. People's social life may appear quite chaotic, but with a good conceptual apparatus, its inner workings and order can be made clear.

Taking a long and critical look at cultures easily yields one basic observation. Most people in any one particular culture would agree about certain aspects of their life, such as facts, which they take for granted. Furthermore, we can get more refined agreements regarding these facts if we consult the relevant experts. However, when we demand to know the meaning of these facts—the way they are interpreted and contextualized—then we very quickly encounter a problem referred to as the social construction of reality. That is, different people and experts, as well as their reference groups, create a dazzling, fantastically complicated, and fascinating kaleidoscope of varying definitions (and constructions) of reality. If we are not careful, we can easily get lost in a myriad of symbolic moral universes of meaning with Wonderland's Cheshire cat's partially materialized smiling mouth chuckling at us from different corners.

I shall examine very closely one particular aspect of social life—the puzzle involving the violation of trust and loyalty, which is referred to as "betrayal." I shall explore the nature of trust and loyalty, the different empirical manifestations of their violations, and their meanings. A major focus of this inquiry is on one particular form of violation of trust and loyalty—treason. This form of social behavior provides us with some interesting and important insights about the ways in which we construct realities and create meaning.

Some of the more interesting and instructive aspects of cultures are to be found in contrasts. Among the more enchanting contrasts are those between truth and that which is not truth, between loyalty and its betrayal, between good and evil, between right and wrong, and between trust and lack of it. Studying these contrasts brings one, first, to the issue of social and moral boundaries[3] and, second, to issues of power. Moreover, by focusing on the Hegelian concept of antithesis, this book can be thought of as raising the age-old Hobbesian question, How is social order possible? This general plot is occasioned by directing attention to how, why, where, and when challenges to the status quo emerge and function as catalysts for processes of social change or stability. Concepts of deviance and conformity are endemic to such an inquiry, as well as the concept of truth.

Trust, Loyalty, and Their Violations

In exploring the nature of these concepts, we shall have an interesting opportunity to examine culturally created contrasts. We shall look at conformity, loyalty, and trust, as well as deviance. When we focus on treason, the relevance of these topics to processes of social change and stability, to moral boundaries and the way they are formed and changed, and to the power behind these processes will become clearer. With loyalty, the important question is that of "loyalty to who" or "to what." Loyalty is something we negotiate. Trust is not. Trust, loyalty, and their violation touch some very profound and powerful feelings we all have about the moral nature of our cultures, what is right and what not, and how violators should be treated. That is, the nature of the societal reaction to deviants becomes an issue, too. Moreover, the results of examining violations of trust and loyalty can be surprising and are not always morally pleasant. The materialization of a double violation is the analytical heart of betrayal. It also involves significant, but different levels of, threat potential.

Violations of loyalty and trust can appear in such varied and different contexts as religion, politics, science, the military, industry, commerce, and personal relations. These violations often involve using deceptive techniques such as lying. Thus, discussing violations of trust usually involves examining truth and its subversion. Hence, in some profound sense, discussions about trust and its violations assume that there are some parameters of reality that we all accept as true, as genuine, as authentic. Constructions of reality are woven on this shared and accepted foundational framework.

Trust involves a particular type of relationship, where the participants perceive that a genuine, authentic, and truthful interaction exists. Violating that trust and subverting that truth typically involves lying, cheating, concealment, and deception. Loyalty, first and foremost, involves fidelity. Violating these moral codes invokes strong emotional responses because feelings of trust and loyalty are typically constructed as deep and profound.

To achieve a better understanding of these concepts, I shall rely on a contextual constructionist interpretation (Ben-Yehuda 1995:20–21), and then continue with looking at the characteristics of trust and loyalty.

Contextual Constructionism and Culture

In recent years a theoretical distinction (whose antecedents can be traced to Schutz, Mead, James, and others) has emerged between the so-called objective and constructionist views. The objective view is a variant of the positivist approach, which is closely related to functionalism. It assumes that deviance (or more generally, social issues and problems) constitutes an objective and measurable reality and, in particular, that it consists of objective conditions and harm. On the other hand, there is the constructionist approach (also referred to as subjective or relativist). This approach maintains that deviance and social issues and problems do *not* present the characteristics of a so-called objective reality and that they are the result of collective social definitions of what some organized members of a culture view as a problematic, harmful, or dangerous condition(s). That is, the nature of what is, and what is not, defined as reality is not a result of some objective condition but rather is a social construction. As Goode puts it, "to the subjectivist, a given condition need not even exist in the objective sense to be defined as a social problem" (1989:328).

Both Best (1989, 1995) and Goode (1989, 1997:58–61) point out that there are two variants of the constructionist perspective. First, there is strict constructionism (for example, see Best 1993), and second, there is contextual constructionism. As Goode (1989:328–329) notes, the first variant argues that the expert or scientific evaluation of, for example, deviance, social problems, or other issues represents simply one "claim-making" activity out of many such activities. This view argues that scientific claims are socially constructed, as are other claims, and can be studied as such. This view negates the existence of an objective dimension of reality and argues that there are different versions of reality, each one just as valid as another, including this statement itself. Obviously, postmodernism's influence can be easily detected here.

The second variant argues that although such phenomena as deviance and social problems are the results of "claim-making" activities, the so-called objective dimension can be assessed and evaluated by relevant experts on the basis of scientific evidence. This view accepts that in a given time and place, it is possible to use empirical facts to reach a consensus (even a temporary one) about the nature of reality. This perspective implies that although there may indeed be different versions of reality, they should not be accepted as equal. Contextual constructionism attempts to find out and substantiate which version is more empirically valid. Works that utilize this theoretical perspective typically contrast the "objective" with the "constructed" versions of reality and utilize empirical evidence as a basis for evaluating different constructions.

It is important to note that contextual constructionism does not claim to know the absolute "truth" or to be absolutely "objective." Rather, it bypasses the epistemological problematics involved in deciding on "objectivity" by establishing a consensus of relevant experts. The goal of contextual constructionists is to collect empirical evidence and make informed and intelligent choices based on the relevant and important facts for specified narratives (or versions). Although this agreed-upon, fact-based consensus is temporary and relative, it provides a powerful baseline with which we can evaluate a variety of claim-making activities.

Specific cases of treason and betrayal exist within specific moral and cultural contexts. One observation that must be made immediately is that this is typically not the case in betrayal between individuals. The context of such cases is such that in most (if not all) of them, interpreting who violated whose trust and loyalty is not too difficult to establish. The context (and therefore the interpretation) of betrayal on the collective level is much less clear. However, although the specific context and interpretation of different cases may sometimes be unclear, the social structure of the cases is not. The very structure of betrayal means that it always involves essential violations of both trust and loyalty. Thus, the conceptualization that I utilize takes the factual level of each case and examines the way in which these facts are socially constructed and interpreted vis-à-vis violations of trust and loyalty. This is a genuine exercise in examining the facts as opposed to the social construction of those facts—that is, a contextual constructionist approach.

Essence and Constructionism

This book attempts to combine two perspectives. On the one hand, I assume that the label "betrayal" will be universally invoked whenever both trust and loyalty are violated. This is an essential statement. It implies that these violations can be objectively described and measured. On the other hand, the content and meaning of these violations are always (and necessarily) contextual and, thus, highly susceptible to social constructions. It is this level that yields the statement that "betrayal lies in the eyes of the beholder," a paraphrase on Becker's (1963) classical work on deviance. To some extent, betrayal does lie in the observer's eyes, but not completely. The construction of betrayal is limited by a universal structure of violations. It is possible that such structures underlie and limit the generalizability of Becker's argument about other forms of deviance as well. Contextual constructionism enables us to bridge these two perspectives: essential and constructionist. However, there will always be tension between these two levels of analysis.

Culture and Betrayal

What are the basic characteristics of culture that make betrayal possible? On the personal level, it requires at least two characteristics: the ability to deceive or lie or manipulate and the specific motivation to do so. The two criteria can be easily met. We are quite capable of both lying and developing devious motivations. Still, we must remember that the overwhelming majority of people are not involved constantly in behavior labeled by their respective cultures as "treacherous." However, once these two criteria are met, we are still left with the question of the "cultural why," which goes beyond specific personal motivation. The answer for that, I believe, can be found in a major cultural facet: socially constructed moral boundaries. This cultural aspect is composed of both power and morality.

Culture can be conceptualized as being composed of a number of symbolic moral universes,[4] each of which competes with the others for symbolic resources (support, recognition, influence) as well as economic resources. In fact, this structure is intrinsic to a pluralistic society. The problem is that morality in such a society becomes a complicated and negotiated issue. Moreover, the problem becomes immensely more complex once we allow into this conceptualization the existence of different, sometimes antagonistic, societies. Viewing cultural structure from this perspective will enable us to better understand betrayal at both the collective and the personal level.

In the past decade the topic of trust has captured the attention of quite a few scholars. Since trust is based on both personal acquaintance and the convergence of interests, it is very likely that trust is influenced by social structures and societal institutions. The conditions under which societal trust increases or decreases, as well the type and distribution of trust in different societies, have increasingly occupied the attention of various scholars.[5]

Deviance, as so many have pointed out, is void of meaning without considering what is *not* deviant—that is, conformity and conventional morality. The conformist conventional morality that lies at the base of this study consists of trust and loyalty. Thus, before we delve into examining different types and cases of violations of trust and loyalty, we need first to examine how trust and loyalty are conceptualized.

Betrayal is dangerous. When trust and loyalty are violated, the threat potential for interpersonal relations or for state integrity (especially during periods of conflict) is profound.

Characterizations of Trust and Loyalty

Trust

Defining trust is not an easy undertaking, and the literature presents quite a few approaches. In some cases, the definition of the term blends with the consequences of the presence (or lack) of trust.

Luhmann (1988) and Johnson-George and Swap (1982) define trust as a behavior, or attitude, that permits risk-taking behavior. Similarly, Gambetta (1988) and Kee and Knox (1970) suggest that trust is inversely related to the willingness to become vulnerable to the actions of another person or group. This approach is focused on expectations, and Gambetta, for example, does not even distinguish between trust and cooperation (although cooperation can be easily conceptualized as resulting from trust). Luhmann (1988) and Cook and Wall (1980) center their definition around the concept of confidence; Dasgupta (1988) and Good (1988) focus on predictability; and Mayer, Davis, and Schoorman (1995) concentrate on the characteristics of the trustor and trustee. Oliver (1997) chose to focus on the mechanisms of trust within the context of organizations, preferring to examine how trust actually works. The very process through which trust is socially constructed and maintained is an interesting topic. Luhmann (1988) and Kramer, Brewer, and Hanna (1996) chart some of the possibilities (for example, a process that follows Baysian principles).

Coleman's influential work (1990) discusses the issue of trust as a particular form of relations and focuses on systems of trust ranging from the micro-level between individual trustor and trustee to the macro-level of society. Coleman states that trust involves expressions of confidence within a specified set of relations. Establishing this confidence, particularly in close and intimate relations, requires time, and there are sets of behaviors and verbal expressions that can strengthen or weaken this trust. Thus, "the trustee may engage in actions explicitly designed to lead the potential trustor to place trust" (p. 96). At the most basic level, Coleman—like others—points out that trust involves behavior that takes into consideration the element of risk. One interesting issue is what happens when the trustee breaks the trust.

Trust, says Coleman, permeates society. The much earlier works of Durkheim (1933) and Simmel (1950) implied that transactions involving trust range from personal, intimate relations to monetary loans, trade, politics, science, the arts, medicine, law, and so forth. Trustless societies will find that existence is very problematic.

Seligman's recent work (1997) distinguishes between trust and confidence. Confidence refers to a situation where roles are clear and one knows what to expect; that is, confidence is based on clear expectations. Trust is what one needs when one does not have confidence. Seligman makes the insightful point that the general erosion of trust in contemporary cultures creates some very serious problems in the integration of those cultures. Seligman feels that the decline of the integrative power of trust is due to the new perception of individuals, in which the individual is reduced to a sum total of group identities and an abstract matrix of rules. This erosion of trust accompanies the decline of personal integrity, responsibility, and sense of belonging. According to Seligman, the modern crisis in identity formation and maintenance translates into a crisis in trust. The problem is not one of extremes, but of degrees. "The general question of what is the optimum level of norms, laws, and sanctions to maintain trustworthiness on the part of trustees is a complex one" (Coleman 1990:114).

Aware of the problems involved in defining trust, Friedrichs (1996:11–12) is right in pointing out that although trust is a central cultural notion, there is no single meaning for the term. "It has referred both to property of individuals and organizations and to expectations defining various types of relationships" (p. 11).

There can hardly be a doubt that trust involves relationships based on confidence, predictability, and the willingness to take risks (that is, the deliberate suspension of suspicion). The trust relationship is based, in the most fundamental way, on deliberately avoiding lies, deception, and manipulation.

Ekman (1992), whose work focuses on lies and deceptions, does not fail to notice that deception can easily ruin trust:

> No important relationship survives if trust is totally lost. If you discover your friend has betrayed you, lied to you repeatedly for his own advantage, that friendship cannot continue. Neither can a marriage be more than a shambles if one spouse learns that the other, not once but many times, has again and again been a deceiver. I doubt any form of government can long survive except by using force to oppress its own people, if the people believe its leaders always lie. (1992:324)

The Importance of Trust

What is so culturally important about trust, and why? Seligman (1997) (and earlier, Misztal 1996) has pointed out that trust contributes to the cohesiveness and integration of cultures. Seligman's work tends to mark a distinctive sociological (as opposed to psychological) meaning of trust. Giddens's sociological approach (1991) suggests that in modern societies trust is increasingly shifted from the individual level of friendship to abstract expert systems in the public domain. Thus, the creation and processing of trust is removed to a detached and anonymous cultural level. Let me continue this by suggesting that two lines of reasoning can be followed here.

The first is functional. As posited by exchange theory, trust enables exchange; without it no social exchange is possible. Trust invokes the concepts of reliability, faithfulness, and responsibility. Trust is one of the elements that Durkheim (1933) refers to in his discussion of the "pre-contractual" elements that are absolutely required for social cohesion and solidarity to exist. As such, trust has acquired a quality of sacredness. Undoubtedly, trust is an essential integrative ingredient of the cultural "collective conscience," that is, of the central and core value system, and it lies at the foundation of consensual social constructions of symbolic moral universes. The argument here can be easily made more complex if we remember that we expect, indeed even hope, that some cultural roles may involve deliberate violations of trust in the form of deceiving and lying. For example, diplomats are expected to lie, and it is difficult to imagine the survival of politicians without their involvement in some form of concealment or manipulation of the truth. Nevertheless, lower levels of social and personal trust may mean that social disintegration is occurring and that holding the culture together may require using more force and formal rules. Because trust is considered to be sacred, the violation of trust is interpreted and reacted to emotionally.

This conceptualization, which is focused on examining cultures from their moral point of view, exemplifies the major issue facing us. In a morally monochromatic society, one that is dominated by one symbolic moral universe, the demarcation of moral boundaries is nonproblematic, and moral meanings are simple and easy to grasp. However, when societies are composed of diverse and competing symbolic moral universes, the meaning of moral codes can become very problematic. As I have shown elsewhere (1985), such societies are prone, by the very nature of their moral structure, to experience repeated moral crusades aimed at redefining their moral boundaries. Living in a multimorality society is far from simple, and people who search for the elusive comfort that lies in certainty (deceptive and shallow as it may be) have a tendency to turn uncertainty into certainty.[6]

Thus, although the meaning of trust is rather straightforward in a monochromatically moral society, it is far from that in a society characterized by a multiplicity of symbolic moral universes. The meaning of many forms of betrayal in such societies is contested. The main reason is that the base value of trust becomes unclear. Such questions as trust in who? in what? are crucial issues in these multicultural societies. Moreover, if we choose to leave one society and look at its moral structure from the outside, making comparisons between different societies, the meaning of many forms of betrayal (for example, treason, whistle-blowing, collaboration) becomes immensely complex. Indeed, betrayal will always involve violation of trust. But the *specific meaning* of that violation is context dependent. Hence, although the construction of the specific cultural category of violating trust, in its various forms, is universal, the specific meaning of that category is not.

For example, Friedrichs (like a few others) feels that the central characteristic of white-collar criminality is the violation of trust (1996:11), and he titled his book *Trusted Criminals*. In this respect, one may indeed find some common analytical parallels between white-collar criminals and traitors. Moreover, Friedrichs points out that when levels of societal distrust increase, people tend to become distrustful and cynical (1996:12).

The second line of reasoning is more ethnomethodological. What are the underlying assumptions of the social relationship called trust, whose violation causes such a harsh reaction? Trust assumes such social relationships as loyalty,[7] friendship, faith, and belief. It also assumes that there is an implicit quality of such social relationship as primary relationship and, to some degree, perhaps even intimacy. These qualities constitute both necessary and sufficient conditions for the social construction of reality itself. Without these, no such constructions would be possible because it would not be feasible to maintain consistency, persistence, and prediction of social relationships. Faithfulness, as implied by trust and loyalty, is an essential and vital ingredient of social life. Without it, "society could simply not exist . . . for any length of time" (Simmel, in Wolff 1950:379). Violation of trust shatters what actors view as the "natural order of things" because it destroys the perception of reality constructions. Moreover, violation of trust tends to involve deception and lying, which, according to Simmel, are among the most destructive forces in social interactions (Wolff 1950:312–316).

However, it needs to be stated that *some* lying may be absolutely necessary for a successful, ongoing social relationship. Social interaction cannot survive without some measure of deception. If we were honest all the time, about everything and everyone, social interaction—as we know it— would probably not be possible because societies and cultures would disintegrate into chaos. Very few people, if any, can—or want to—experience the complete, unadulterated truth. Lying and deception, therefore, are continuous variables. Deception can range from simply putting on makeup and other cosmetics to deceptive infidelity. Some lies and deceptions are socially accepted; others are not. And, again, we are faced here with a contextual variable. In a way, some lies may be used to affirm trust. They may be used to show how much we care about our interacting partners. We may hide from them unpleasant truths and construct a more comfortable reality. This view supports the constructionist approach taken here, and it does not contradict the statement about the common conceptual core. However, examining deception contextually as a continuous variable implies that the continuum has ends and extremes. Simmel's observation that deception has a high potential to ruin cultures must be interpreted in this context.

Violation of trust disrupts the perception, or illusion, of consensual reality constructions. However, the thing that is denied and shattered in treason, for example, is not only a social relationship but another fundamental facet of the human existence: the social self. In this sense, Luhmann's (1995:127–129) observation that the opposite of trust is not distrust but a sense of dread or even anomie and a state of anxiety producing normlessness fits well.

Hence, the violation of trust tends to elicit a strong emotional reaction in the form of severely hurt feelings. For example, the invocation of a charge of treason necessitates showing an *intention* to systematically betray, deceive, and lie to the victim/s. Thus, traitors are typically punished severely because treason always elicits the motivation for revenge or, its Western equivalent, justice.

Loyalty

The element that accompanies trust in our analysis is loyalty. This element introduces a tone of uncertainty into violations of trust. Although it is difficult to circumvent the issue of trust, loyalty requires a directional definition—loyalty to whom, or to what. It is not too difficult to see that we can trust and not be loyal (for example, having a bank account). It is much more difficult to be loyal and distrustful. However, some people defined as traitors have maintained that they were loyal to a specific country but mistrusted its specific form of government, such as loyal Germans who distrusted Hitler. Let us examine two illustrative cases.

The Case of Mordechai Va'anunu.   Israel's policy regarding its nuclear weapons program has been crystallized in the statement, "Israel shall not be the first one to use nuclear weapons." This policy on nuclear weapons has been characterized as being "deliberately opaque" (see Avner Cohen 1998). Va'anunu disagreed and thought that full disclosure was a better policy.

Born in 1954 to a Jewish orthodox family, Va'anunu studied at Ben-Gurion university in the Israeli Negev. Needing some source of income, he began to work in January 1977 as a technician in the Israeli nuclear reactor near Dimona. Va'anunu was trained in 1976 for the job and signed an agreement in which he agreed to keep his knowledge secret and confidential. After about eight years, he left his job (according to some sources he was laid off). In the early 1980s, Va'anunu began to be politically active and demonstrated affinities with the Israeli left. Moreover, he was also disillusioned with the Jewish faith. In January 1986 he left Israel for Australia, where he converted to Christianity. From there he continued his voyage to London where he told the *Sunday Times* (August 1986) that Israel had an arsenal of about 200 nuclear weapons (way above what most experts thought the country actually had). He was rewarded quite nicely by the newspaper (some sources state that he was paid US$100,000). In September 1986, just a few days before the *Sunday Times* published the story, agents of the Israeli secret service (Mossad) used a "honey trap" (an agent called "Cindy") to lure Va'anunu into leaving London and traveling to Rome. There he was kidnapped by agents of the Mossad, brought to Israel, charged with espionage and treason, and in 1988 sentenced to seventeen years in prison.[8] For reasons that are not entirely clear, he was kept in solitary confinement for about twelve years (some say for security reasons, others maintain that this was a measure of revenge aimed to drive him crazy). He was let out of solitary confinement in 1998. In a self-serving interview that he gave to the *Sunday Times* on April 19, 1998, he stated that he would not hesitate to do what he did again because he had acted under a deep conviction and belief in the appropriateness of his actions, acting courageously alone against the entire Israeli security establishment. Va'anunu was quick to point out that his revelations were made out of a genuine concern for Israeli society, despite the fact that Israel has come to view him as public enemy number one.[9]

There is, of course, nothing unique about Va'anunu's account. Many whistle-blowers, or spies, have given similar accounts expressing loyalty to their country (or organization) but distrust toward specific governments (or executives), policies, or regimes.

The Case of Nachum Manbar.   A somewhat similar case came to its culmination on July 16, 1998, when three Israeli judges convicted fifty-two-year-old Nachum Manbar of betraying Israel by supplying Iran (during 1992–1994) with materials required to manufacture agents for chemical warfare for a hefty profit. Specifically, Manbar was found guilty of aiding, and attempting to aid, the enemy (Iran) in its conflict with Israel and giving the enemy information intended to damage Israel's national security. Manbar, an ex-Kibbutznik and ex-paratrooper in the Israeli army, was sentenced to sixteen years in prison. His act of treason was stated as "worse than that of Va'anunu,"[10] and Israel's prime minister—Binyamin Netanyahu—stated that Manbar "sold his soul to the devil."[11] Manbar, of course, denied the charges and claimed that the state of Israel allowed other Israelis to trade with Iran and that, therefore, what he did was not so deviant. The prosecution responded by stating, first, that the state authorized many activities that independent individuals were not allowed to do and second, that Manbar was never allowed to sell chemicals to Iran that could be used in chemical warfare. Manbar's accounts were rejected by the court.

Within a military context, the main association of trust is with dependability, reliability, but most of all of with loyalty and hence with honor. In a boundary defining paper, Captain Ormerod (U.S. Marine Corps Reserve) writes that:

> loyalty is defined as faithfulness to commitments or obligations, or an adherence to a sovereign, a government, a cause, or the like. It connotes sentiment and the feeling of devotion that one holds for one's country, creed, family, and friends. In the military sense, loyalty is defined by the Marine Corps . . .

as 'the quality of rendering faithful and willing service, while accepting one's duties and responsibilities with selflessness. This evaluation is a measure of loyalty to the unit, the Marine Corps, and the Nation, not just to seniors. (1997:55)

Pincher, who discusses treason within the framework of loyalty (1987:1–14), states that loyalty means "constancy in a trust or obligation" (p. 1). Thus, even the definition of loyalty invokes trust. But the two can, and should, be separated analytically and linguistically. Loyalty means constancy in a relationship, dependency, and long-term faithfulness between (or among) the parties involved; and treason means that "loyalty" becomes negotiated, broken, or questionable.

One can be loyal to many things—to one's friend, country, religion, territory, political system, and so on. An interesting conflict may emerge when one is faced with incommensurable loyalties: between one's country and one's friends; between one's country and family (for example, the case of the Walker spy ring); between one's country and one's political views; or between one's political and professional views. When Daniel Ellsberg revealed to the *New York Times* what has become known as the Pentagon Papers, he clearly showed his preferred moral loyalty: Stopping the war in Vietnam took precedence over his obligations to his employers in the Defense Department. When Va'anunu revealed the scope and magnitude of Israel's nuclear weapon program he too opted for loyalty to his ideas about peace rather than to his previous employer in the Israeli nuclear program. The history of religions clearly provide us with some spectacular examples: Thomas à Becket, Jeanne d'Arc, Jesus, and many others.

An important distinction Pincher makes is between major and minor loyalties. Not every loyalty is characterized by the same degree of importance, moral weight, or impact. Thus, Pincher argues that it is not only possible but warranted to stratify one's loyalties by criteria of importance. Pincher does not spell out who exactly is to perform this stratification of loyalties or how it can be accomplished. His suggestion is related to the issue of value incommensurability discussed in 1991 by Cohen and Ben-Ari. The problem, simply put, is that many situations are characterized by incommensurability of values, as individuals tend to rank and stratify their values. Loyalty is indeed a value, and incommensurability between loyalties may rise, for example, between the loyalty to one's country versus the loyalty to one's friends. What Pincher fails to tell us is that loyalties are stratified according to the prevailing cultural moralities adhered to by a specific individual or group.

Fletcher (1993) advocates returning to loyalty to one's country as a central remedy for many modern ills. Combining loyalty to one's country and increased national trust as main ingredients of modern identities may, in fact, pave the way for renewal in nationalism (and hence, in renewed definitions of treason).

Loyalty is a more complex variable than trust. Furthermore, in a pluralistic society, where any one person occupies a set of roles and possibly holds a number of loyalties, it may not be uncommon to face a painful dilemma of incommensurability. The "enemy" (Aho 1994) in such societies may be difficult to define. And yet societies and cultures have to define their moral boundaries, thereby creating and contextualizing their "strangers" and "enemies." Excluding both different individuals and categories of people enables the construction of collective feelings of cohesive togetherness and identity. The case of Marlene Dietrich (discussed in detail later in this book) is a good illustration for the first case, and the exclusion of Jews by Nazism (or more generally, anti-Semitism) is an illustration for the second. Inability to do that may mean social disintegration, loss of local and cohesive cultures, and—possibly—the formation of a new cultural order. A global one perhaps. However, even such new boundaries will exclude some and include others. The "enemy" will still be there, in a different format and context. Betrayal may actually be one of those social categories that will survive even globalization.

Violations of Trust and Loyalty

Trust and loyalty are fundamental facets of cultures. When they fail, chaos follows. The violation of trust and loyalty is typically characterized by one of the many forms of betrayal, for example, treason. It is important to note that invoking the term "treason," in turn, elicits a set of concepts associated with it, such as revolt, sedition, insurrection, disobedience, mutiny, uprising, and subversion. Similar terms are associated with other forms of betrayal, such as treachery, deception, trickery, perfidy, and infidelity. It is thus obvious that any one particular form of betrayal is associated with complex cognitions and emotions. In the next chapter I shall chart the different forms of betrayal, and in Chapter 3, I will explore each form in depth.

Cultural Perception of Violating Trust and Loyalty

Individuals and groups do not take lightly violations of trust and loyalty. However, the distinction between betraying one's country and betraying one's close friend, lover, or family is significant. Treason has frequently elicited the death penalty. In fact, in both Israel and the United Kingdom, where the death penalty does not exist for regular criminal behavior, treason is nevertheless punishable by death. Not so for personal betrayal.

Even the terms are different: Treason is used primarily within the political context and betrayal in the personal context.

Moreover, acts of betrayal seem to be constructed as main cultural tales. The theme of betrayal of trust and loyalty is strong and powerful and lies at the very core of many cultures. Let us examine some illustrations.

Accounts of Betrayal from Ancient Greece

Reading the history of both ancient Greece and imperial Rome reveals numerous accounts of betrayal. Ancient Greece provides us with an era and a location rife with narratives involving changing loyalties and supposed treason, especially as Greeks moved their loyalties from one side to another. Two illustrations are presented here.

The first illustration is the "last stand" battle staged by King Leonidas and his three hundred Spartans at the pass of Thermopylae (in August or September 480 B.C.). That battle turned against the Spartans when a Greek renegade named Ephialtes informed the attacking Persians of a passage through the hills. Utilizing that passage the Persians could bring a significant number of soldiers behind the Spartans. That done, the fate of the battle was doomed, against the Spartans. Thus, the activities of one Greek who sided with the Persians against the Greeks helped the Persians win a decisive battle (Dupuy and Dupuy 1970:26; Philip 1994:12).

The second illustration is focused on the activities of Alcibiades, a statesman and warrior, in the fifth century B.C. His actions, and the context, are too complicated to be described here in detail, but let me just give a general and brief outline. Alcibiades was active during the Peloponnesian Wars. He kept switching from Athens to Sparta and vice versa, maneuvering in a very complex political and military situation. While he led Athenian forces to battle, a campaign against him had been raging in Athens. He was smart enough to escape to Sparta as an Athenian court sentenced him to death. In Sparta, he gave the Spartans some crucial advice on how to win their conflict with Athens. Eventually, Alcibiades lost his base of power in Sparta, too, and he again fled to Tissaphernes. From there, he tried to pave a possible comeback to Athens, and in fact, he returned and later headed the Athenian fleet to battle. He returned from his battles to a hero's welcome and was elected as strategos for 407–406 B.C. and appointed as the chief commander of all Athenian forces. Following a failed naval battle in Notium (spring of 406 B.C.), his opponents were able to elect new commanders, and Alcibiades had to flee again. That was the beginning of his end. Although he tried to find a new asylum in Asia, when Lysandros demanded that he be given to him, an order was given to kill him. Reading the history of Alcibiades, in its relevant context, simply leaves one gasping with a fast-spinning head.[12] If the situated and contextual meaning of treason can be obfuscated and made totally context dependent, then the adventures of Alcibiades illustrate it. Moreover, the city of Athens once saw him as a hero, then passed a death sentence against him as a traitor, then welcomed him again as a hero. The changing configurations of power and moralities, as reflected in his public image and his actions, are simply staggering.

Judas Iscariot

Perhaps the most salient cultural construction that comes to mind is the prototypical betrayal of Judas Iscariot. According to the prevalent Christian version, Judas betrayed Christ by exposing his movements and selling that information to the chief priests and elders for thirty pieces of silver. They provided the armed guard brought to the Garden of Gethsemane near Jerusalem to arrest Christ, who went there to pray with the Apostles following the Last Supper. Moreover, it was Judas who identified Christ by a kiss, addressing him as "master." Thus, Judas, appearing close to Christ, kissing him and addressing him with an hierarchical term, was the one who, underneath that facade of friendship, trust, and loyalty, betrayed him.

The traitor in this narrative plays a powerful cultural script. While he appears to be a close and loyal friend, he is deceitful. Although Judas's motives aren't entirely clear, he is constructed as an archetypical traitor. The man who pretends to be trustworthy, one of "us," and loyal actually embodies the opposite traits. He is not loyal to the group but to that inanimate object called money; he is engaged in deliberately misleading behavior, which projects loyalty and love, while in fact, he is very hostile. All the major elements of betrayal can be found in this narrative: violation of trust, loyalty, and commitment, coupled with a fundamental deception. Indeed, the name of Judas Iscariot has become a cultural icon. It is interesting to note that Nazi ideology used the term "Judas-Jude" to create a connection and identification between "Jew" and "traitor" (Snyder 1976:184).

Other Biblical Illustrations

The Bible provides us with some other intriguing illustrations. How about Samson and Delilah?[13] Around the year 1161 B.C. the Israelites found themselves under the domination of the Philistines. One of the Israelite judges was Samson, born at the supposed intervention of an angel to a mother who was married for many years but had been barren. The angel told her that this divine intervention would yield a boy who would be dedicated to God and who would rid the Israelites of the Philistines' yoke. Samson grew to have an amazing physical strength. Eventually he married a Philistine girl, but the marriage did not work. Samson then turned his superior physical strength against the Philistines, killing many of their people.

The critical moment came when Samson met Delilah. Whether she was actually sent to him by the Philistines or used by them after she got involved with Samson is not known. In any event, it is clear that Delilah acted as an agent of the Philistines, charged with the task of finding out the secret of his strength. Samson must have been aware of the treacherous nature of Delilah because at first he evaded her questions. Eventually, however, she won him over, and he told her the secret of his strength—his hair. That was his end. Once she cut his hair, the powerless Samson was arrested and ridiculed. His death—like his life—was violent. With his bare hands he tore down the Philistine temple, destroying himself along with his enemies.

Delilah was awarded eleven hundred pieces of silver for her successful mission. It is clear that Samson's trust in Delilah was betrayed. Was Delilah a traitor? This is not an easy question to answer. Clearly, her loyalties, like those of Judas, lay with money and with the Philistines. Obviously, Samson should have not trusted her.

Another Biblical story involves Jael, Heber Hakeini's wife, who assassinated Sisera (who had oppressed the people of Israel cruelly for twenty years). After his defeat in the battle against Barak,[14] Sisera came to Jael's tent to rest, trusting that he was in a safe place and in the company of a loyal woman. But Jael, acting loyally to her own people, violated Sisera's trust and murdered him in his sleep.

Contemporary Cultural Fiction

The theme of betrayal is also very powerful in contemporary cultural fiction. One of the most successful science fiction books, *Dune*, by Frank Herbert (made into a movie in 1984), has treason at its root (Dr. Yue betrays the trust of the Duke, causing his downfall and death). Many science fiction and adventure movies have betrayal as a main theme. The first *Star Wars* trilogy has treachery as a major theme (Darth Vader moves to the Dark Side of the Force); *Indiana Jones and the Temple of Doom* (1984) has Indiana Jones tell the head of the Kali cult that "you betrayed Shiva"; *Fahrenheit 451* (1967) has a "firefighter" betray his assigned employers; *Forbidden Planet* (1956) has Dr. Morbeus betraying everyone, even himself; *2001—A Space Odyssey* (1968) deals with a betrayal by a computer; and *The Matrix* (1999) has its own traitor. The eighteenth James Bond movie, *Golden Eye* (1995) has treason at its center. War movies frequently have traitors and betrayal at their center as well. *The Bridge on the River Kwai* (1957), *A Bridge at Remagen* (1969), *Apocalypse Now* (1979), *Battle of the*

Bulge (1965), *The Counterfeit Traitor* (1962), *The Guns of Navarone* (1961), *Stalag 17* (1963) are all first-rate war movies involving betrayal as a main theme. Major action adventure movies released in the late 1990s have betrayal as a central theme: Arnold Schwarzenegger's 1996 movie *Eraser* has treason as a main theme; both *The Net* (1996) and *Braveheart* (1995) also have treason at their center. Other popular movies, such as *Air Force 1*, play on the theme of betrayal as well. One could easily write a decent-sized work on the theme of betrayal and treason in movies alone.

The cry "traitor" or "treason" invokes powerful cultural icons. It tends to unite people against the traitor and requires that they exercise power through their ability to define specific contextual forms of behavior as trust violations and disloyalty. This process requires the reexamination of moral boundaries and the definition of who is to be trusted and why. The punishment of a traitor strengthens the cohesion and integration of a culture's moral perceptions. The history of the British monarchs is full of tales of treason. The Tower of London even has a "Traitor's Gate." We need not go far to remind ourselves of such famous traitors as Thomas à Becket and Thomas More. But treacherous behavior was quite prevalent in the 1970s–1990s, too. Let us examine some illustrations.

Contemporary Examples of Violations of Trust and Loyalty

Charges of Betrayal in the Philippines. For almost a quarter of a century, the conflict between the Christian majority and the Muslim minority in the southern Philippines has torn that country apart. In September 1996 a ceremony took place in Malacañang Palace in Manila for the signing of a peace treaty between then President Fidel Ramos and Muslim rebel leader Nur Misuari. The ceremony was supposed to continue in Mindanao, home for most of the Philippines' 6 million Muslims. However, many of the Christians in Mindanao were unwilling to accept the peace treaty. Anyone watching television news could hear people stating their disbelief in this peace and see the signs of protest in processions of Christians accusing Ramos of betrayal.[15]

Betrayal in the Church. In England, a more personal scandal took place in September 1996. The BBC and daily newspapers reported that a Roman Catholic bishop had disappeared. The fifty-six-year-old Bishop of Argyll and the Isles, the Rt. Rev. Roderick Wright, had disappeared on Monday, September 9, 1996. Concern about his disappearance prompted calls in the media by church officials for the bishop to show signs of life, and prayers were said for him. Then, on September 16, the vanishing bishop did send a sign of life. As time passed, it became clear that the bishop had probably disappeared with a forty-one-year-old divorcée—

Kathleen MacPhee—with whom he had had a long-standing friendship and who had consulted with him about her divorce. This revelation created a heated debate about the celibacy rule for Roman Catholic priests. At this point, the disappearing bishop was portrayed as a good and honest man, very well-liked by his parish, who had just fallen in love.[16]

However, the atmosphere changed dramatically when another woman, Joanna Whibley, appeared on television and told stunned viewers that she and Bishop Wright had had a romantic affair fifteen years earlier, the result of which was the birth of her son Kevin Whibley. Fifteen-year-old Kevin appeared on television, too, and made some unflattering statements about his absent father. This opened the floodgates for other women to come forward and confess about their relationships with priests. For example, Mrs. Adrianna Alsworth told astonished audiences that her two children were fathered by a parish priest. Bishop Wright now was portrayed more as a dishonest, deceiving, and manipulative man. His resignation was accepted.

Leading figures in the Catholic Church labeled the runaway bishop a traitor,[17] describing his acts as betrayal. The Bishop was never really the man he pretended to be. In other words, Bishop Wright was accused of violating trust and loyalty. That this violation involved a monumental deception only added fuel to the burning furnace of rage against him.[18]

On September 22, 1996, *News of the World* published an extensive interview with Bishop Wright.[19] In it, the runaway bishop admitted that sixteen years earlier, he had indeed had a relationship with Ms. Whibley, and he asked for her and Kevin's forgiveness. He also admitted that at the time of the interview, he was romantically involved with Kathleen MacPhee, a divorced mother of three children, and in a joint interview, both lovers talked about their illicit love. It is interesting to note that the couple found it important to state that they did not have sex.[20] Responding to a question in the televised interview, the Bishop added that he accepted the responsibility for his betrayal of the church. His clarification was that he understood betrayal to mean that he had left the church,[21] which was a very different "understanding" than the one provided earlier by the leaders of the church.

These dramatic events created a great deal of discussion in the media about celibacy and the fact that there were many cases of priests having such relationships with women. The charge of betrayal in these cases is obvious: It is a betrayal of a commitment. Moreover, because of the nature of this violation of trust, it is typically done in secret and definitely involves deception (certainly at the beginning).

It is interesting that the issue of sexual standards for the clergy has remained a focus of public discussion (Woodward 1997). In this case, an act of deviance helped to launch a public debate about moral boundaries.

Betrayal in Hong Kong.   In July 1997, Hong Kong became part of China, and Britain's last governor of Hong Kong, Chris Patten, left the country. The nonviolent event received generous global coverage and was celebrated lavishly by the Chinese. During the few years leading up to the move, a debate had raged. Was nondemocratic China going to tolerate a more democratic Hong Kong? Governor Patten certainly tried to introduce a number of democratic measures before his departure, but that was not to China's liking. Jonathan Dimbleby's book *The Last Governor* leaves little doubt regarding the nature of Patten's accusations against some of the top administrators in Britain. Jenkins (1997) and Heald (1997), both reviewers of the book, were quick to grasp it—treason.

The implications of Governor Patten's thoughts are profound in the sense that what he experienced was fierce objection from a series of British high officials who seemed to have done their utmost to appease China's antidemocratic inclinations by blocking every step toward democracy taken by Patten. Patten's experience also implies that his opponents deceived the British political democracy in order to keep millions of inhabitants in Hong Kong in the darkness of nondemocracy. As Jenkins states, Patten's accusations suggest that he was betrayed by opposing British officials. In other words, treason on the British side is insinuated. Moreover, in July 1997, six Hong Kong police officers resigned over plans to use tough new steps against democracy activists. These new steps were viewed by China as new laws against treason.[22] Of course, Patten's critics would give a different version of events, perhaps focused on principles of realpolitik.

Reflexivity and Morality

Betrayal as a socially constructed phenomenon constitutes a complicated subject. However, at its very core lies an essential main structure and a process. To begin with, betrayal can be accomplished only by those who are members of the group that they betray. This issue of "membership" is of crucial importance. Without it, charges of betrayal may sound hollow. Thus, the charge of Newnham (1978) that New Zealand could be viewed as a "treasonous" state because of its relationship with South Africa during apartheid requires a very liberal view of what membership means.

Although membership is a necessary condition, it is not sufficient. A structure composed of two major violations needs to materialize if we are to invoke the label of betrayal. One violation is of trust, the other of loyalty. When a member of a group is engaged in a process of violating both trust and loyalty, the invocation of the term "traitor" to characterize the behavior of that individual is not far behind. However, there are several important factors to consider when making such a characterization. Did the behavior occur in the open or in stealth? What are the reasons given by the individual for the behavior? There are different types and degrees of betrayal. Was the betrayal a discrete event or an ongoing activity? Were the violations of trust and loyalty carried out by one person or by a group? What was the social status of the individual or group? The context in which the betrayal occurs is of crucial importance.

In pluralistic cultures the meaning of "membership" in a collective can become extremely problematic. These problems are complicated further by the meaning one attaches to "loyalty" and to "trust." Although individuals from two opposing symbolic moral universes may agree that betrayal involves issues of membership and violations of trust and loyalty, their application of these concepts will probably be entirely different. To push this argument to its extreme, a Nazi and a Jew may agree that my argument regarding the nature of betrayal is valid, but they may choose entirely different cases and may even interpret them in a contradictory manner, rendering their initial agreement irrelevant. In other words, it is not enough to establish some principles and then apply them in an undifferentiated matter. There are qualitative differences between cases, and we need to pay attention to the relevant context or else we may end up with some absurdities. What are these differences? One major factor is morality.

What this argument implies is that it may be impractical, perhaps even futile, to discuss "betrayal" without being judgmental at the same time. "Judgmental" in this case simply means a contextual ethical and moral evaluation of the case, the selection of cases, and the language used. Thus, I agree with Goode (1997) that, first and foremost, we need to get our facts straight. However, once we do that, there is nothing wrong with attributing moral values to the facts when that evaluation seems necessary and appropriate. For example, it is difficult, even wrong, to describe and interpret a concentration/death camp in completely neutral terms.

Even if the tone of a presentation seems neutral, the very act of selecting cases and illustrations, as well as the choice of words to describe these cases, forms a judgmental process. It may thus be advantageous to be open about the position from which one makes evaluative statements, selects cases, and chooses words.

The fact that we do not have, for example, the account of Judas Iscariot for his actions makes it very easy for us to brand him as a traitor. However, knowing much more about such traitors as Benedict Arnold, Vidkun Quisling, Roger Casement, Lord Haw-Haw, Malinali Tenepal, Ozaki Hotsumi, and others discussed in the chapters of this book, makes the decision in their cases much more difficult. I will take their designations as traitors by the dominant cultures in which they lived as given and will explore why they were treated as such. Furthermore, I will use the cases to test the hypothesis that in each case violations of trust and loyalty occurred. However, in asking such questions as "whose loyalty and trust were breached?" and "what was the meaning of those breaches?" we shall quickly reach issues of moral boundaries and incommensurability of values, as well as deciphering the specific context of the cases. At that point, it will be wise to make a moral stand on these issues; not only will it enhance the interpretation and make it more understandable, but it is unavoidable (see Klausner 1998).

In summary, this book seeks to expose the elementary forms of betrayal and the common core that characterizes all acts of betrayal. It is this common core that permits me to examine the different cases as instances of a configuration or syndrome that not only is definitionally unified but also has common dynamics. The combination of this core and the cases requires laying out a typology of betrayal. Together, this core and typology will enable us to examine infidelity and espionage as forms of the same general phenomenon. This approach compels us to view betrayal as a continuum or spectrum rather than an either-or proposition. Moreover, this approach implies that the characterization of a given act as an instance of betrayal is inherently problematic. Finally, I examine betrayal as a type of deviant behavior and, as such, as amenable to the sorts of analysis to which sociologists have subjected more traditional forms of deviance. In this respect, this book continues my previous work, which examined deviance in science, witchcraft, science fiction (1985), politics (1990), assassination (1993) and myth (1995).

Plan of the Book

The first three chapters form Part 1. This part provides the conceptual framework (Chapter 1), a typology of betrayal (Chapter 2), and an in-depth exploration of different types of betrayal (Chapter 3). Having acquainted ourselves with the conceptual framework, I then focus on one particular form of treachery—treason. In this particular form, the issues of membership, power, morality, and moral boundaries—as well as those of violating trust and loyalty—are very salient. Part 2 first gives a historical and conceptual review of treason (Chapter 4) and then delves into quite a few cases of treason, across time and countries, utilizing the conceptual framework laid out in Part 1. I examine the various cases involved in World War II (Chapters 5 and 6), the cases of radio traitors Lord Haw-Haw and Tokyo Rose (Chapter 7), the cases of Ezra Pound and Knut Hamsun (Chapter 8), the case of King Edward VIII as a possible traitor (Chapter 9), the case of Malinche (during the Spanish conquest of Mexico—Chapter 10), and some cases of treason in Judaism and Israel (Chapter 11). The Conclusion presents a summary of the book's main ideas and findings.

2

Violating Trust and Loyalty: A Typology

The Analytical and Structural Nature of Violating Trust and Loyalty

The behavior that evokes the label of betrayal consists of a universal structure in which violating moral boundaries of two important values takes place: those of trust and loyalty. These violations tend to involve different levels of threat potentials, both for the interpersonal level (for example, infidelity) and the state level (for example, sedition, treason). The traitor is a person who pretends to be very close, even intimately so, loyal, and trustworthy to specified individuals and/or collectives, but in reality he or she is as far as one can be from the above pretense. "Far," however, is an innocent term. The traitor is diametrically opposed, even hostile, to the essence/person/collective being betrayed. Sometimes, at the basis of betrayal there may lurk a sizeable lie and deception. Both espionage "moles" and infidel spouses illustrate this. That lie is typically of a person who pretends to be friendly and manages to deceive the relevant audience into believing that his or her falsified presentation of self is genuinely true. It is a lie of a disloyal person who pretends to be loyal. A lie of a person who pretends to be honest and interested, but is in fact manipulative, uninterested, and dishonest. Emotionally, this is a rather explosive combination. The lie and deception seem to be clearer when the act of betrayal is on the personal level than on the national, or state, level.

This interpretation makes it clear that often an act of betrayal violates, on the personal level, an imagined consensus regarding shared interests and personal identities and, on the collective level, a sense of an imagined community (Anderson 1991) and of collective memories and national identities. Betrayal, therefore, breaches the symbolic moral boundaries of some of the values we cherish the most—those we consider to be very high in our moral hierarchies and priorities. The challenge created by betrayal on the boundaries of any symbolic moral universe is formidable.

At the very heart of the various manifestations of betrayal lies a violation, a deviance from trust and loyalty. It is the systematic, planned (sometimes concealed) violation of these values that invokes the cultural label of "treason" or "betrayal." This is the hallmark and the most important distinctive characteristic of betrayal. The construction of the degree of severity of the betrayal is typically proportional to the constructed degree of the violation. There must also be the perception that the one referred to as "traitor" is "one of us," that is, an assumption of loyalty. If not, the label "traitor" may become problematic. Thus, a spy who was "planted" in a different culture than his or her own can earn the trust of those around him, but he or she is not genuinely part of that culture. That is, the direction of loyalty is different. Being a bona fide member of a group is a precondition of betrayal of that group. Without such a genuine membership, there can be no meaning to betrayal. For example, the claim that William Joyce (Lord Haw-Haw) was American and not English casts a shadow on his betrayal of loyalty. Regardless of the legal subtleties involved, the fact is that he defined himself as English. In that sense, his insistence on a self-adopted English identity made his breach of loyalty to the English an interesting issue.

Betrayal involves the issue of morality in the most intimate way: It touches issues of trust, loyalty, honesty, and commitment. However, morality is not the only issue here. Another major ingredient is power. First, the power to betray; second, the power to decide who betrayed who or what. The salience of these two elements—power and morality—in cases of treason constitutes the main reason for my decision to focus on treason on the collective level in the second part of the book.

As Akerstrom (1991) pointed out, one of the major differences between a hero and a traitor is whether the person in question has a collectivity supporting him. As an opening illustration we can use the case of Benedict Arnold, who was most certainly viewed as a bona fide traitor by the Americans, but not so by the British. The case of Nathan Hale provides an inverse example.

Benedict Arnold

Arnold was born January 14, 1741, in Norwich, Connecticut. When he was fourteen years old, he ran away from home to participate in the French and Indian War of 1756–1763. On April 9, 1775, at the age of thirty-four, he joined the Continental Army as a captain serving with Colonel Ethan Allen and participated in a command position in the successful at-

PHOTO 2.1 Benedict Arnold. Engraving by I. Fielding, 1783, from a drawing by Pierre Eugene du Simitière, c. 1777.

SOURCE: *Reprinted from Clare Brandt,* The Man and the Mirror: A Life of Benedict Arnold *(New York: Random House, 1994).* Photo from The Collection of the New York Historical Society, 40979.

tack on the British-held Fort Ticonderoga (New York) in May 1775. He was later promoted to the rank of a colonel. In the fall of 1775, Arnold was appointed by General George Washington to lead a military force of about 700 men to capture Montreal. Despite a remarkable land march through the Maine wilderness, the attack on the city (December 31, 1775, in the middle of a snowstorm) failed. During that military operation Arnold suffered serious injuries. Later, Arnold took part in a few actions, the most notable of which was the October 11, 1776, battle of Valcour Island. There, having constructed a flotilla on Lake Champlain, the force he commanded managed to inflict some major damage on a much superior enemy fleet.

In February of 1777, Arnold was passed over for promotion to major general by Congress. The bitterness caused by this incident must have been profound for Arnold.

In April 1777 British forces raided Danbury. Arnold (who was visiting his family in New Haven at the time) got himself very quickly involved in a fight against those British forces (together with General David Wooster). Arnold's combat conduct won him much appreciation—and his much sought after promotion to the rank of major general. However, his promotion did not restore his seniority over those who were promoted before him. During September and October of that year, the Battles of Saratoga took place. During those battles he was wounded in his leg. Washington acknowledged Arnold's courageous role in Saratoga and showered him with precious gifts. In October 1777 he was cited as the victor of the Battles of Saratoga. His battle conduct forced Congress to restore his seniority. At this point, it appears that Washington considered Arnold to be his best field commander and one of his most trusted and reliable military men. Unquestionably, Arnold was an able and dedicated military commander. He is considered by many to have been one of the most capable generals of the American Revolutionary War.

Arnold's wounds prevented him from going back to an active field command, and he was appointed military governor of Philadelphia following the British evacuation of that city in June 1778. There he immersed himself in the pleasures of city life and embarked on some commercial ventures. In June he also met Margaret (Peggy) Shippen, who was to have a major influence on his life.

The following year (1779) proved to be a stormy year for Arnold. While he was the military governor of Philadelphia, he was suspected of violations in raising funds (February) to support an extravagant lifestyle. Despite Arnold's protests, Congress ordered in April that he be court-martialed. The trial began in June and ended in January 1780 with Arnold being cleared of all charges except one.[1] The sentence that the court recommended was an "official public reprimand from the commander in chief." Congress confirmed the verdict on February 12, 1780.[2] Even that was too much for Arnold, for he expected to be fully acquitted.

At this point in his life, Arnold must have felt pretty annoyed. Despite his distinguished military record, his career path was not smooth and was riddled with some very unpleasant events. His promotion to the rank of major general had been delayed, and when he finally won his promotion, his seniority was officially recognized only later. He had to experience the unpleasant (and humiliating) event of facing charges of corruption in a court-martial, and he was found guilty on one charge. He must have felt mistreated, frustrated, and upset, and his bitterness must have been growing throughout 1779. Brandt suggests that Arnold must have felt abandoned and betrayed by his country, so that

> if the Congress—if America—had truly abandoned him, perhaps he should return the favor; if the country in whose cause he had suffered so much was

truly incapable of appreciating his talents and granting his heart's desires—a secure fortune and a secure status in a secure society—then perhaps he should offer his services to a country that could. (1994:175)

Certainly, his military record stood in contradiction to the other humiliating events that occurred to him.

Another major event helped to fuel his discontent—his April marriage to Peggy (his previous wife, Margaret Mansfield, had died in June 1775), who was a young woman of Loyalist sympathies. The connection between the two was to prove very significant for Arnold. Peggy was about twenty years younger than Arnold, and she came from a pro-British family. Brandt (1994:175) suggests that Arnold's idea of betraying the Americans was supported by Peggy and that they both emerged from their honeymoon (April 1779) with some mature ideas about shifting their loyalties to the British. It is well worth noting that during the previous British occupation of Philadelphia, Peggy had cultivated a good relationship with a British officer, Major John André. It is thus rather obvious that 1779 must have been a year when Arnold was in a very high degree of dissonance, an emotional state that was not alleviated by Peggy's political sympathies.

In May 1779 he began to develop contacts with the British. His technical contact (through correspondence) was, not surprisingly, John André. However, the person he was dealing with on the British side was Sir Henry Clinton. Arnold provided the British with valuable intelligence regarding America's military situations. For example, he gave Clinton precious information about American capabilities regarding the defense of Charleston (South Carolina), which led to a successful British siege of the city. General Henry Clinton captured it by assault on May 12. In May 1780, Arnold proposed to the British the capture of a major military installation for a fee of £10,000 in cash and a command of a battalion in the British Army. The British answer was not forthcoming (Brandt 1994:190).

The military installation Arnold had in mind must have been West Point. And, indeed, during the months of March–June 1780 Arnold intensified his efforts to make sure he became the commander of West Point. He began by lobbying General Philip Schuyler for the appointment. Meanwhile, Arnold received a letter from Washington (June 4, 1780) from which it could be inferred that the Americans were considering the invasion of Canada. Arnold passed this secret and crucial information to the British (Brandt 1994:191–192). Later, he made an effort to learn about the actual operational invasion plans, which he also sent to General Clinton. Although General Clinton acted according to this information and changed his operational plans, the whole idea of invading Canada was a pure fabrication that was meant to help Washington and Lafayette hide their true goal—a major attack in New York against Clinton's forces

(Brandt 1994:193). When Arnold learned about the true plan, he tried to send a warning to Clinton, but that warning arrived too late.

Eventually, Arnold's pressure worked, and on August 3, 1780, he was awarded the command of West Point (and some areas around it). He arrived there on August 5. In that year Arnold negotiated with the British the surrender of West Point forts and territories (and possibly George Washington as well)[3] for a hefty sum of £20,000 plus an equal rank in the British Army—a very clear act of betrayal, both of trust and loyalty. On September 22, 1780, Arnold and his British contact, Major John André, met to further discuss Arnold's betrayal plans. The next day André was captured by the Americans. This fluke occurrence foiled this interesting plot of betrayal. The exposure of Arnold was now just a matter of time.

Major André served in the 54th Foot in the British Army as adjutant general to General Sir Henry Clinton, British commander of New York. André was corresponding with Arnold in 1779 and was involved in the 1780 negotiations with him regarding the surrender of the West Point territory and fortifications to the British. Having met Arnold on September 22, 1780, André was trying to return to British lines. On September 23 he was caught by three Americans (who were later awarded with special medals and some cash rewards), and this led to the surrender of Arnold's treacherous plan. When Arnold found out about the capture of André, he realized that his time was up. He fled as quickly as he could and reached New York on September 26. Although the British tried to negotiate the release of André, it did not succeed because General George Washington demanded that Arnold be exchanged for André. André was tried as a spy and executed by hanging on October 2, 1780, at Tappan, New York. His remains were reinterred in Westminster Abbey in London on November 28, 1821.[4]

Arnold was made a general in the British Army and received £6,315 for his efforts. He formed a regiment of British troops and was effective in leading raids against the colonies along the Chesapeake Bay (December 1780) and in New London, Connecticut.

On December 1781, Arnold left the United States, never to return, and went to England. He involved himself in some business enterprises, which were not very successful.

In May 1792, James Maitland, Earl of Lauderdale, made a remark at the House of Lords that General Arnold was guilty of apostasy from principles. Arnold could not let that just pass. He spent years of his life making the point that he was *not* an apostate, a turncoat, or a traitor. He demanded that the earl make a public apology. The request was complied with, but in language that Arnold thought was insufficient. He thus challenged the earl to a duel, which took place on July 1, 1792. Arnold shot first but missed. Lauderdale refused to fire, claiming that he had no bad feelings toward Arnold. Although at first he refused to re-apologize, eventually an apology was made and the conflict ended.

During the wars of the French Revolution, Arnold was unable to procure a military commission. In the spring of 1794 he sailed on a trading ship to the West Indies and arrived in Guadeloupe a short time before it was reoccupied by the French fleet. Captured by the French, he was questioned aboard a French ship. Fearing for his life, Arnold did not identify himself and gave his French interrogator false information about himself, including a false name. During the night Arnold managed to escape and reached the British fleet, which was anchored near another part of the island. At that time, Arnold offered his services as an adviser to the British commander—Sir Charles Grey—and as a volunteer quartermaster for the British force that fought the French in the West Indies during 1794–1795. Arnold returned to England in July of 1795.

However, Arnold was not yet at peace with himself and the world. In December 1796 he submitted to British prime minister Pitt a plan to "liberate Chile, Peru, and both Mexicos" from Spanish influence. This plan called for an expedition commanded by Arnold. He never received a reply. Only one year later, in January 1798, fearing a threat of invasion from Napoleon Bonaparte, Arnold proposed to the First Lord of Admiralty a command of fire ships in the English Channel. The proposal was rejected.

From this point on, Arnold tried again to involve himself in commercial enterprises, an area in which he typically failed almost consistently, which is what occurred this time, too. He died in London, in relative anonymity, after a short and agonizing illness, on June 14, 1801, leaving behind a debt of a few thousand pounds. Peggy died on August 24, 1804.[5]

There can hardly be a doubt about Arnold's exceptional characteristics and personal history. He was a courageous military man but a very poorly performing merchant. Was he a hero or a traitor? First, it must be stated clearly that by all criteria he betrayed the Americans. He pretended to be loyal to them, but he was not. He most certainly also betrayed the trust vested in him by the Americans. All of this deception was done in extreme secrecy. Had it not been for the random capture of André, Arnold's treason would have had some dire consequences for the Americans. Thus, in terms of damage, the potential was enormous. Brandt (1994), as well as a host of others, tends to attribute the motivation for this betrayal to personal motivation. However, this personal motivation (for example, the expectation that his military achievements be properly recognized) was in itself formulated and expressed in terms of a military and revolutionary code of the culture in which he lived.

Not discounting this personal motivation, both Randall (1990; see also Wauck 1991) and Wright (1986) rightly point out that the dilemma of choosing between loyalty to the British and to the Americans at the time of the Revolution was a genuine and painful one. Regardless of Arnold's personal motivation, the issue of which country to trust, which to be loyal to—England or the new emerging and crystallizing United States—was neither simple nor easy. Furthermore, examining the demonization of Arnold, Ducharme and Fine (1995) point out that because the question of loyalty was so painful and because

> so many Americans had engaged in acts contrary to those espoused during the rage militaire, it was necessary to emphasize that Arnold was totally different, to magnify his greed and make it exceptional. Rather than igniting a witch-hunt against the numerous minor traitors in their midst . . . the colonists singled out the hero of Quebec and Saratoga as uniquely unpatriotic, and collectively ostracized him, providing him a permanent place in their history. (p. 1315)

The major tools in that demonization process were (1) biography and (2) motive. Ducharme and Fine (1995) point out that there is a tendency to portray Arnold as "a self-centered, glory-seeking madman," whose "actions were consistent with his character" (p. 1317) and that his actions were best explained by three main motives: a stormy relationship with an unappreciative Congress, a distaste for the affiliation with the French, and a belief that he could end the revolution (for example, that giving West Point to the British could serve as a turning point). Greed is typically added to these. In addition, his courageous and outstanding military performance for the revolution prior to his treason is neutralized.

Benedict Arnold was a courageous man with significant combat skills. He was not a coward. However, after his move to the British, he was never regarded as a hero. For the Americans, prior to Arnold's defection, he was the hero of the battle at Fort Ticonderoga, the siege of Montreal, the battle at Valcour Island, and the Saratoga battles. And yet his name was also associated with administrative corruption and abuse of his rank. Although eventually Arnold was considered a major traitor by the Americans, he was not viewed so scornfully by the British.

In contrast to the stigmatization and demonization of Arnold, others who engaged in espionage were glorified. One was Major André, Arnold's British contact, whom history has portrayed as having been deserted and betrayed by Arnold and hung by the Americans as a spy. Another contemporary figure who is glorified is the spy Nathan Hale.

Nathan Hale

Details about Hale's enigmatic figure, mission, and capture are subjects on which historians disagree. However, it is plausible to assume that

PHOTO 2.2   Statue of Nathan Hale in front of the
Chicago Tribune building in Chicago. Photo by author.

since British headquarters were at New York, General Washington was interested in finding out about these headquarters, the size of the military force there, its supplies, weapons, and logistics. Why Hale was chosen for an intelligence mission is unclear. Moreover, there was no contemporary mention of Hale, or his mission, until Hannah Adam published *The History of New England* in 1799.

The standard account states that Hale was born in 1755 in Coventry, Connecticut. He graduated from Yale in 1773 and taught in schools in New London and East Haddam, Connecticut, for two years prior to enlisting in the Connecticut militia in June 1775 at the rank of lieutenant. The unit in which he served took part in the siege of Boston during the summer of 1775, and following that he became an officer in the newly established Continental Army. Promoted to the rank of captain in January 1776, he arrived in New York with his unit in April 1776. Hale took part in the capture of the British warship *Asia* (mid-May).

On September 10, General Washington asked Colonel Knowlton to find a volunteer for an espionage mission in New York. Hale agreed to spy on the British and provide the information that General George Washington required. One historical version states that he embarked on his mission on September 12. Wearing civilian cloths, Hale used a small boat (the *Schuyler*, a sloop piloted by Charles Pond) to sail from Connecticut to Huntington, Long Island. He passed British lines in Manhattan and used his profession as a teacher for a cover. Having spent a few days gathering information about the British in Brooklyn, he tried to return to the American side, but his attempt was unsuccessful, and he was caught on September 21.

On one thing there is no disagreement—his end. The commander in chief of the British forces in North America, Sir William Howe, ordered Hale's execution on charges of espionage and treason, without a trial. Hale was not allowed the privilege of a clergyman or a Bible, and on September 22, 1776, he was hanged. Standing on the scaffold he is reputed to have said the following eternal statement: "I only regret that I have but one life to lose for my country" (or "I only regret that I have one life to give for my country"). Hale's last words, revealed by a British officer years after the execution, were suppressed and his last letters destroyed because the British had no intention of helping this man become a martyr. Yale University has a statue of Hale (put there in 1914), and a copy of this statue (made in 1973) stands near the entrance to CIA headquarters in Langley. These statues portray an interesting fictional image because no portrait of Hale is in existence. Hale became an official hero of the state of Connecticut in 1985.[6]

Other figures I discuss in detail later fall into the same category. Vidkun Quisling and Lord Haw-Haw were certainly not considered traitors by the Nazis, but Norway and England respectively executed them on charges of treason after World War II. The famous poet Ezra Pound came very close to being put on trial for treason but was spared from that by his incarceration in a mental hospital. Although fascist Italy did not see him as a traitor, the United States almost did. Jonathan Pollard was certainly viewed by Americans as a traitor, but not by Israelis. Aldrich Ames was viewed as a traitor by Americans, and Kim Philby was viewed in that way in the United Kingdom, but neither of them was perceived as such by the former Soviet Union.

Toward a Typology of Betrayal

The antagonistic violation of trust and loyalty, and hence the crossing of moral boundaries by a genuine member in the collective or dyad, is interpreted as betrayal. It can range from the personal level to the level of an organization, such as a nation-state.

It is important to note that despite the universal structure that distinguishes betrayal from other forms of behavior, betrayal has the characteristics of a continuous (or multidimensional) variable rather than a discrete one. Several dimensions supplement the basic structure of betrayal and can alter its construction. For example, was the violation done in secret or not? Was concealment involved? Was an actual and overt turncoating involved or not? As we shall see later, violating trust and loyalty in a deceptive manner and concealing an actual turncoating tends to be perceived differently than when such violations are committed openly. Also, the issue of personal or national betrayal is important. One can, of course, choose one or more dimensions to focus on in interpreting betrayal. In this text, violations of trust and loyalty are perceived to be the important ones. I shall use other dimensions when the context demands that. For example, the classification of betrayal here utilizes the dimension of membership as a main criteria.

There is a major cultural difference between the insider who changes sides, a so-called "turncoat," and the outsider who pretends to be an insider (mostly, a "spy"). Membership in a group, and thus the acquisition of an identity that depends on membership in a particular group or dyad, is a powerful and important variable. Being part of a group or a collective creates not only a strong sense of genuine belonging but also a strong distinction between those in the in-group and those in the out-group, which is directly related to who is to be trusted and who is not. This sense of cultural belonging can serve as a robust criterion for a classification scheme, as we shall see below.

Violating trust and loyalty are not single-variable issues. They involve a variety of problems and are thus multidimensional and complex topics. First, there is the issue of whether the violator is a bona fide member of a group. Second, there is the issue of who is the target of the treacherous scheme, an individual or a group. Third, the question of whether the violation of trust and loyalty was done in secret is an important one. Fourth, the motivation of the betrayer is a significant issue. Fifth, the damage from the betrayal needs to be assessed. Sixth, the societal reaction to the betrayer needs to be addressed. In any given case, the specific name and meaning assigned to a particular violation of trust and loyalty depends on the distinctive combination of the above issues.

Some of the issues tend to gain prominence over others. The first three variables seem to be dominant. We can create an interesting and empirically useful typology for different forms of violating trust and loyalty by cross-tabulating membership in a group against the target/victim. This typology creates distinct cells in a table that unites different types of betrayal into a coherent unity (see Table 2.1).

TABLE 2.1   A Typology of Betrayal

Target/Victim	In-Group	Out-Group
Personal	Infidelity, adultery Informing Mutiny	Con artistry Private investigation Professional betrayal
Collective (general)	Collaboration Defectors & desertion Espionage Treason Internatioal betrayal State-sponsored terror Human rights violations Mutiny	Espionage Surveillance
Collective (the in-group)	Whistle-blowing Political turncoating Conversion Strikebreaking Assassination	

It must be noted that the meaning of membership here is on the level of perception and construction and that the specific content of membership in groups can be a complicated and thorny issue. For example, to what group exactly did the pre–World War II Sudeten Germans belong, and who has the legitimacy to provide an answer? Likewise, the specific content of target/victim may have different meanings. In addition, categories of betrayal may have different interpretations. For example, mutiny, which appears in two places in the table, may be interpreted as members of a group acting against individual targets, as in naval mutiny, or it could be interpreted as a collective act of insurgence.

Table 2.1 charts the major types of betrayal that our classification yields. The typology allows us to convene under one theoretical umbrella an interesting spectrum of what may look like different phenomena.

We must note that the "Personal" and "In-group" cell may have subdivisions based on such different variables as motivation, structure, or context (for example, between a romantic dimension and a nonromantic friendship). Treason appears on the left side of the table, in the "In-group" column. The reason for that is that violating trust is not enough to win any person the dubious title of traitor. After all, trust can be violated by formal organizations, through white-collar crime, and the like. The added element here is that not only is trust violated, but the assumptions of commitment and loyalty are broken as well.

In the illustrative case of personal betrayal in a romantic relationship, the assumption of sexual exclusivity is violated in addition to trust. Hence, betrayal in this category implies that a quality characteristic of primary relationships, referred to as gemeinschaft, was violated, often in a deliberately deceitful manner.

Moreover, some of the other categories in the table may have subdivisions, too. For example, one ends up with very different types of spies, if one examines such cases as Judas, Pollard, and Hale (for example, see Hagan 1989, 1997).

Dimensions of Betrayal

Secrecy

An underlying and important dimension in the typology is the dichotomy between secret and nonsecret violations of trust. Following Simmel (see Wolff 1950:330–376), Scheppele's landmark study on the sociology of secrecy (1988:3–23) defines a secret as "a piece of information that is intentionally withheld by one or more social actor(s) from one or more other social actor(s)" (1988:12). Secret violations of trust (for example, infidelity, some forms of espionage, con artistry, informing) always involve, in an explicit manner, a major form of deception where the betrayer possesses information crucial to the betrayed. Indeed, Scheppele points out that secrecy and deception are two sides of the same reality (1988:22, n. 29). Nonsecret violations of trust (for example, political turncoating and some forms of collaboration and treason) are more problematic. Although there may be little or no deception, these cases involve a violation of trust of members in the in-group, and the perception is that the violator has acted in a manner contrary to the interests of the collective. The thorny point, of course, is who defines or interprets these interests and who can enforce this interpretation. In such cases, the betrayal can be conceptualized as crossing moral boundaries between hostile organizations or collective identities. In this sense, it is possible to claim that there is some form of deception behind nonsecret violations of trust as well (see also Ku 1998).

Deception

Deception here is focused on definitions of moral commitment and interest. The violator may argue that his (or her) crossing of moral boundaries was not a betrayal at all but an embodiment of the true interests and moral commitments of the collective. Thus, the violator of trust and loyalty may be perceived by members of the betrayed collective as involved in activities that not only betrayed them but that were presented deceptively, as if they were in their best interests. The perpetrator of what appears to be a nonsecret betrayal is in fact engaged in a huge deception by pretending to be what he (or she) is not and by presenting a harmful behavior to the collective as a helpful behavior. The deception lies in the warping of reality à la Orwell's *1984* doublethink. Viewed in this way, deception indeed lies behind violations of trust and loyalty.

Introducing the element of deception in this fashion raises the issue of the manipulation of constructions of reality. Violations of trust and loyalty, secret or not, always involve such manipulations. The degree of manipulation and lying in secret violations by far exceeds those of nonsecret violations. However, even the nonsecret cases share a decent amount of subversion. Consequently, discussions of trust and loyalty and their violation require some understanding of deception as well.

There are many studies and works on deception. One of the better and more thoughtful definitions of, and approaches to, lies and deceptions was developed by Ekman (1992). He states that a lie or deceit occurs when "one person intends to mislead another, doing so deliberately, without prior notification of this purpose, and without having been explicitly asked to do so by the target." He then distinguishes between two forms of lie: concealment—when a "liar withholds some information without actually saying anything untrue," and falsification—when the liar not only withholds information but "presents false information as if it were true" (1992:28).

Although concealment may seem to be less disreputable because it may not involve inventing untrue accounts, it is quite capable of leading audiences to believe in a reality that is based on false assumptions and information.

Ekman bases his inclusive definition on a few elements. First, an *intent* to deceive must exist. This element is mentioned by almost everyone who has done work in this area. Second, this intention implies that the deceiver or liar made a *choice* (to lie rather than not). Third, the target of a lie or a deception did not give his or her *consent* to be misled, and the liar did not give any *prior notification* of the intent to make a false presentation. This is an important point because, for example, no one considers calling actors in movies or theaters "liars" despite the fact that they, by choice and intent, make a false presentation. Finally, the distinction between concealment and falsification is indeed illuminating. As Ekman points out, given a choice, liars will always choose concealment rather than falsification. The main reason is that concealment is much easier to accomplish, and liars tend to assume that it is less reprehensible than falsification (1992:29).

Ekman notes that there are many social situations where we need to conceal—for example, poker and other similar games, and commercial and political negotiations. Furthermore, Ekman points out that in some situations concealment is essential for survival. For example, Jews had to conceal their identities under Nazi rule or occupation. "Marranos" or "Anusim" were Jews who were forced to convert to Christianity and pretended to do so, while keeping parts of their Jewish identity in secret, during the early and later Middle Ages in Spain. When the term "deception" is used in this book, it is very much in accordance with Ekman's approach.

Motivation

A significant dimension in understanding betrayal is the motivation of the person involved in that act. Motivation in the psychological sense is a complicated issue to base conclusions on and—in my view—provides rather shaky ground for generalizations. How is one to infer motivation? From behavior? From statements given by the one accused of betrayal? From both? Clearly, when information elicited from both behavior and personal statements is congruent, one's confidence in that information as explaining the betrayal increases. However, what if the information is inconsistent? What if one wishes to discuss, for example, "patriotic traitors" (such as those described by Littlejohn's 1972 work, or Marlene Dietrich and Willy Brandt)? Is that an oxymoron?

A crucial factor is the source of our information regarding the motivation. Confessions elicited during arrest and trial are clearly suspect and problematic. Autobiographies written after the fact frequently have an ax to grind. Nevertheless, motivation in the cultural sense is something we need to pay some attention to, that is, motivation as expressed and understood within the cultural context in which it is formed. This particular angle also ties us to C. Wright Mills's idea that biographies and accounts are to be understood within their particular contexts and not in the abstract.

The solution to this problem, I believe, is to combine the perspectives. The issue of betrayal should be taken at face value. That is, we need to ask ourselves, in each case, whose trust and loyalty was violated. This question will always involve us in discussing morality and symbolic moral universes. Power will come next—the power to betray and to decide who betrayed (and sometimes to prosecute and execute a punishment). However, it is also useful to be inquisitive (carefully) about the "why," that is, about motivation.

Personal and Collective

One important distinction that the table projects is provided by the division between the "Personal" and the "Collective." Although sometimes the distinction may be blurred, it is nevertheless a powerful one. A significant difference exists between a specific person as the target of betrayal and a collective group as the target of betrayal. The treason of men like Vidkun Quisling, Anthony Blunt, and Jonathan Pollard was not aimed at any one particular person, although specific people were victimized by it. On the other hand, a police informer directs his or her acts against very specific targets. The same would hold true for a prisoner of war in a camp providing his captors with reliable information regarding what is going on in the barracks, thus reducing even further the limited independence of other POWs who trust that informer and believe that he is loyal to them.

The categories included in the "Personal" row of Table 2.1 are, obviously, very interesting. Infidelity tales make their way regularly onto the front pages of tabloids and respected newspapers alike. Con artists and private eyes are frequently made into popular cultural heroes in novels, movies, television series, and other symbolic cultural products. However, the categories included in the "Collective" sections of Table 2.1 are the ones I shall focus on. Questions of morality, power, and motivation are much more salient there and thus make these types of betrayal more relevant for studying deviance and morality.

The different cells presented in Table 2.1 refer to various socially constructed types of behaviors where the issues of trust and loyalty and their violations are central subjects. Although these categories are analytically distinct, they are not completely alien to one another. In Chapter 3, I shall discuss in more depth each one of the cells and the types included in them.

3

Violating Trust and Loyalty:
Categories and Cases

In this chapter I shall discuss at some length the different manifestations of violating trust and loyalty that were outlined in the typology of the previous chapter. In this way, we shall acquaint ourselves more thoroughly with each of these different manifestations. The different cells in Table 2.1 portray distinct types of betrayals. In this chapter, these distinct types will be brought to life by examining empirical cases representative of them. Selecting the illustrative cases was not an easy task because there are so many of them. I finally chose cases that seemed intrinsically interesting. I could have—just as easily—selected other cases. My only limitation was, simply put, the size of this book.

Infidelity, Adultery, Informing, and Mutiny

The first cell I shall focus on includes acts of betrayal committed by a member of a group or dyad in which the violation of trust and loyalty is aimed at a person. Typically, the threat potential for the relationship in such cases is high.

Infidelity and Adultery

This type of betrayal refers to violations of trust by individuals who view themselves, or are viewed by others, as either close or very close to one another. The term "infidelity" usually refers to people who are romantically involved; the term "adultery" is used to describe violations of trust and loyalty between married people; and the term "betrayal" is used to refer to people who are close friends, but not romantically or sexually involved (although adultery can be constructed as betrayal as well). There is, of course, a qualitative difference between the two because the type of assumed trust and loyalty that is broken is qualitatively judged to be different. Obviously, there is much more professional literature about infidelity. However, history and fiction contain numerous accounts of events that have been presented as "betrayal" (for example, the stormy relationship between Thomas à Becket and King Henry II). Although this book is not focused on infidelity and adultery, the context of this study makes it important to look at it, even briefly.

Adultery is a very interesting topic. One can look at worldwide trends and statistics of adultery,[1] or combine a study of prevalence together with interviews, and thus gain a deeper understanding and insight.[2] Here I examine some of the main conclusions from various studies about infidelity and adultery.

Nature of Infidelity.   Many works have been written about adultery. However, Lawson (1988) provides some of the more interesting insights into its nature. As her work shows, historically speaking, the nature and meaning of adultery are not simple. In the narrower sense of the term, a married man or woman who has sex with other than his wife, or her husband, may be considered an adulterer. Simple enough, no? In keeping with the academic reputation of making the "simple" "complex," let us ask a few more questions. For example, who is the partner? Is that partner a prostitute? Another married person? Is the extramarital "affair" a short one-night stand or a longtime romance? How about a lover or a mistress? What if the betrayed spouse knows and agrees to the affair? Is the partner (any partner) also guilty of adultery? It does not take too long to realize that characterizing adultery can give one a headache. It may be worthwhile to point out that betrayed partners may reduce the complexity above to such rather simple issues as, "Did you do it or didn't you?" thus reconstructing the issue in a different manner. Although I present infidelity in terms of qualitatively different categories, those involved may present it in terms of differences of degree. Moreover, the dual standard in adultery within some orthodox cultures (for example, some religious fundamentalists believe that a married man can commit adultery only with a married woman) provides support for the contextual constructionism of betrayal.

At the basis of extramarital affairs lies a violation of both trust and loyalty (not included are extramarital affairs with mutual consent, such as mate swapping, group sex, or swinging). Sexual exclusivity is the foundation of marriage, or an equivalent (perhaps preparatory) relationship. That is, the partners are committed to having sex only with one another and are forbidden from having sex with others. Trust, faith, and fidelity between the partners are supposed to ensure that this exclusivity is maintained. Some cultures (for example, orthodox Judaism, fundamentalist Islam) exercise such a stringent system of social control that even those who are tempted to violate this trust find it very difficult to do so. Other cultures are much more tolerant. In any event, this particular violation of trust and loyalty frequently brings a complete disintegration of the relationship. Indeed, it is estimated that infidelity and adultery are the primary cause of divorce in both Europe and North America. These violations of trust and loyalty are also major motives for domestic violence.[3] Because these violations are so difficult to characterize, there are different names given to this particular breach of trust, ranging from "adultery" and "infidelity" to "unfaithful spouse" and "affair" to the much more neutral term "extramarital affair."

Lawson (1988) notes that adultery is typically perceived as posing a grave threat. It is portrayed as having the potential to ruin a marriage (or relationship) altogether. Indeed, a 1974 survey by the National Opinion Research Center (NORC) based at the University of Chicago found that those favoring the view that having an extramarital affair is always wrong "won a majority in every age group," with the smallest majority among the 18–29-year-old group (59 percent agreed with the statement).[4] And in 1994, the very same age group condemned adultery in an even clearer voice. Lawson found that among her respondents

> it was the most traditional men—those most strongly adhering to the myth of Romantic Marriage—who spoke of their liaisons in this way. In other words, "casual affairs" were what highly permissive women but highly traditional men, recalling their feelings when they married, had. They indicate the continuing greater breach implied by a wife's adultery compared with that of a husband; she commits adultery generally only when her feelings are deeply involved or likely to become so—the risks are too great for her to play as he can—while he is entitled to his "bit on the side." (Lawson 1988:38–39)

However, Lawson does not indicate whether this threat is equally valid in situations where the partner knows about the infidelity, as opposed to having no knowledge of the affair.

Another persistent cultural image of adultery is adultery as theft, implying that a man steals another man's property: "He 'possesses' what is not his to 'take,' even if the woman 'gives' herself to him, for she does not own her own self, not even her body. . . . [Her husband] owns her and can—indeed, sometimes must—punish her, even kill her" (Lawson 1988:41). A second image is of adultery as threatening the lineage. This image implies that wives are "the property of men and so were children" (p. 45).

Lawson also describes three prevalent types of adultery. The first is *parallel adultery:*

> An affair at any historical period, with a concubine or a mistress whose relationship to the husband is well known and even accepted by the wife—as in the case of Nelson and Lady Hamilton; or "the king's whore" (as Nell Gwynn called herself) and her royal sponsor, Charles II; or a later king, Edward VII and Mrs. Keppel, who was invited, so it is said, by Queen Alexandra to the king's bedside before he died. . . . Similar examples in America are the well-known and accepted or condoned relationships of many presidents from F. D. Roosevelt to L. B. Johnson, whose wife, Lady Bird, is reported as saying, "My husband loved all people, and half the world's people are women." (p. 52)

The second type is *traditional adultery*, "where the relationship . . . *is* considered a breach of the marriage" (pp. 52–53). Typically, this relationship is kept secret, with a significant effort to prevent the spouse from learning about it (typically, friends and relatives often possess knowledge of this damaging information).

The last form of adultery is *recreational adultery*, a relationship that

> satisfies a desire to play. . . . It is, as its name implies, lighthearted, not serious or committed, but for *fun, joie de vivre*, filling empty moments rather than hours, time away from normal family and working environments, a leisure activity like an excellent meal with a good bottle of wine, a hedonistic adventure of the flesh rather than of the spirit, though it is the spirit that may be enhanced. (p. 54)

One can expand the level of generalization of this category and add to it such practices as group sex. As Lawson rightly points out, this type of adultery can be transformed into the first or second type.

To make things somewhat more complicated, let us think of a strong emotional involvement between heterosexual individuals married to others. If no sex is involved, should we still view it as adultery? Probably not. But the noninvolved spouse will probably not like this relationship because it is on the verge of violating both trust and loyalty. Let me use a few illustrative cases.

It is not insignificant that in the case of the romantic involvement of Bishop Roderick Wright with divorcée Mrs. Kathleen MacPhee, an affair that shook the United Kingdom in the summer of 1996,[5] the romantically involved couple felt it was important to state, in public, that they had no sexual relations.

Cultural fiction, in the forms of books and movies, reinforce this point as well. For example, in the 1970 war movie *Hell Boats*, which takes place on the island of Malta during World War II, actress Elizabeth Shepherd plays a woman married to naval officer Ronald Allen. She is in despair about the miserable state of her marriage, which seems to be in bad need of love and affection but is immersed instead in rejection and bitterness and—for all practical purposes—going down the drain. In her despair, she betrays her husband and finds much-needed comfort in another officer's arms (played by James Franciscus). However, it is clear that despite the fact that she initiated the affair with her new lover, the sex she is involved in is distant, alienated, and frozen. In other words, the scriptwriter and director portray an emotionless affair. That portrayal is what enables her to return to her husband at the end of the movie (after he saves, heroically, the life of her lover in a daring and suicidal operation against U-boat pens in Sicily). This is an important point because an emotional involvement would probably mean she would have to be "killed" at the end of the movie.

What about sex without emotional involvement (for example, with a prostitute) or with a very minimal level of such involvement? In the summer of 1996, the powerful political consultant to President Bill Clinton, Dick Morris (married to Connecticut lawyer Eileen McGann) lost his position following a public disclosure in a tabloid that he had a year-long affair with a $200-an-hour call girl Sherry Rowlands.[6] *Newsweek*, which used this story in a larger report about adultery, points out that there is a new understanding of adultery: "It is a sin of the heart and mind as much as—or even more than—the body." Morris's relationship with Sherry Rowlands, according to this new understanding (consistent with the atmosphere of "political correctness"), is that "he carried on a long-term relationship with another woman that went beyond sex into the realm of intimacy."[7] The magazine's extensive report quotes psychiatrist Dr. Frank Pittman as noting that most infidelity is done on the telephone rather than in bed. According to Pittman, the "essence of an affair . . . is in establishing a secret intimacy with someone. . . . Infidelity isn't about whom you lie with. It's whom you lie to."[8]

An additional element that needs to be considered is motivation. What about a married couple whose relations are not too great, sex is dull and infrequent, and then one of the partners finds a lover? Or what if one of the partners is temporarily, or permanently, prevented from having sex (for example, due to an incapacitating condition or illness of a spouse)? Should we take into consideration the factor of motivation? Should we give it a prominent place in the analysis? The moral problem here is that if we do so, we may risk providing an indirect justification for violating the partners' loyalty and the trust in the sexual exclusivity of marriage.

As is becoming clear, even the relatively simple category of adultery is far from simple. The so deceptively simple violation of marital exclusive sexual rules is turning into a rather complex issue. To make this point even more interesting, Lawson (1988) points out that in a number of her cases,[9] the affair severed the old relationship and opened the door to a new relationship:

> While over 70 percent of the faithful remained married to their original spouse, this was true of just over half of the adulterous; and the more liaisons a person had, the more likely it was that they would not remain married to the first spouse. If they did divorce, only 10 percent . . . married their lovers. (p. 287)

The rate of remarriage for women having an affair in order to separate from their husbands was much higher than those of men.

Glass (1998) has isolated three main factors that characterize an extramarital affair: (1) the existence of secrecy (for example, they meet without telling others about it), (2) emotional intimacy (for example, they disclose inner feelings and information to one another that they do not disclose to their married partners), and (3) sexual chemistry (i.e., physical attraction). Glass's findings led her to conclude that although males tend to have extramarital affairs that are based on sexual attraction, females tend to conduct such affairs on the basis of emotional involvement.[10]

Prevalence and Its Meaning.   One very important question regards the prevalence of infidelity for males and females, in different cultures, and in different time periods. This is an important issue because it can give us some significant clues not only about sexual behavior but also about how people in everyday reality behave in terms of loyalty and trust.

Although there is little in the way of reliable cross-cultural and longitudinal information about the magnitude of infidelity, the few available studies are suggestive. It is generally estimated that in about 50 percent of marriages—internationally—one partner will be unfaithful.[11]

In January 2000 British electronic and print media disclosed some amazing facts. Summaries of routine DNA examinations done in the previous year in several laboratories (some of which performed thousands of such examinations) revealed that the father of every seventh (or tenth, depending on the laboratory) child is not his biological father. These findings should not really surprise us because if the rate of marital infidelity is around 50 percent, then it stands to reason that at least some of these affairs may end in pregnancy and childbirth (see Rogers 2000; Nachshon 2000).

Let us look more closely at some studies on this topic done in Israel. A study conducted in 1988 revealed that 63 percent of men and 50 percent of women admitted that they either had been disloyal to their partners or would have been if they had been given a chance to do so. Only 29 percent of the males and 41 percent of the females stated that they had never betrayed their partners. In another study, 60 percent of married women admitted that they had experienced extramarital sexual relations. Professionals who specialize in sex and marriage, estimate that in Israel 70 percent of married men and 50 percent of married women have had at least one extramarital affair. Younger couples, in the age range of 25–35, cite the discovery of an extramarital affair as a reason, or excuse, to initiate separation or divorce proceedings much more frequently than older couples (ages 36–55). It seems that as people grow older, they learn to compromise and be more flexible and are less willing to terminate relationships.[12]

In the context of Israeli culture, at least one important observation must be made. If the numbers quoted above indeed reflect reality, then this culture tolerates a rather high degree of infidelity. Since this culture is also characterized by a relative low level of divorce, one must assume that either most of these infidelities are effectively concealed from unsuspecting spouses or that they are absorbed and tolerated within existing arrangements.

In a sense, these findings suggest an explanation for a curious phenomenon. Mr. Binyamin Netanyahu ("Bibi") was elected Israeli prime minister in 1996. Netanyahu admitted, prior to his election, on public television (January 14, 1993), in a rather dramatic interview, that he had betrayed his third wife (Sarah) and that he had had an extramarital affair. It turned out that his affair was with marketing psychologist Ruth Bar, who was married to an ophthalmologist. The affair between Netanyahu and Mrs. Bar began prior to his marriage to Sarah and continued afterward.[13] This fact did not interfere with his election campaign and was not used by his political opponents against him. This phenomenon (probably not possible in American or British contexts) is quite understandable given the permissive practice of infidelity in Israeli culture.

The major conclusion from the studies of prevalence is, clearly, that infidelity and adultery are in fact common occurrences. Indeed, an interesting and theoretically challenging point of view is provided by Baker's (1996) evolutionary interpretation of betrayal. His sociobiological point of view holds that betrayal between partners is common because it provides an opportunity for increasing offspring.

Prevalence has moral meanings. In August 1998, *Newsweek* informed its readers that infidelity in China is "rampant" and that the Chinese authorities, alarmed by the increasing divorce rates (close to 25 percent), were seriously considering turning adultery into an illegal behavior, punishable by law (for example, forced labor). In a somewhat similar fashion, in

1998 Malaysia was in the process of defining extramarital sex as illegal and punishable by law.[14] Obviously, a deeper analysis of these cases would have to consider sociocultural factors, such as modernization, religious beliefs, fertility, and so forth. However, for our purposes the illustrative observation of a possible intervention of the law, that is, of the state, in adultery is instructive. In the main, it can be interpreted that the state does not view adultery as a private issue and feels that it has to use strong social control to regulate this behavior.

Some Culturally Famous Illustrations.   In the past decade, a few rather explosive cases of infidelity, involving famous international celebrities and politicians, were reported in the international media: Dick Morris, who was mentioned earlier (his wife remained with him); Princess Stephanie of Monaco, who was betrayed by her husband, Daniel Ducruet (she filed for divorce in October 1996); the public disclosure that François Mitterrand, president of France, had a longtime mistress, Anne Pingeot (and their daughter, Mazarine). Both Anne Pingeot and her daughter appeared at Mitterrand's funeral beside his wife and their children; Elizabeth Hurley, an actress and model for Estée Lauder cosmetics, who decided not to separate from Hugh Grant, who was arrested on June 27, 1995, in Hollywood with a female prostitute (a part-time actress and model who took the professional name "Divine" Brown).[15]

A late 1980s affair that still echoed in the mid-1990s was a double betrayal—between Prince Charles and Camilla Parker Bowles and between Princess Diana and James Hewitt. Indeed, in 1997 British commentator McDonaghin even suggested in public that "there's a place for an honest-to-God mistress," stating that Camilla Parker Bowles be Prince Charles's permanent mistress and lover.[16] It did not take the tabloids long to disclose to the public, using front page headlines, that Earl Charles Spencer, Princess Diana's brother, was not faithful to his wife and was involved in a number of extramarital affairs.[17] Earl Spencer denied the allegations.

A strong denial of the accusation that he was involved in an extramarital affair was also issued by forty-one-year-old British Parliament member Piers Merchant. However, in October 1997 his sexual involvement with a seventeen-year-old girl was exposed (with some rather sensational pictures) in public by the Sunday *Mirror*.

Each country has its own adultery tales of its famous citizens. In Israel, for example, some rather illustrious stories involve the famous Moshe Dayan, who is rumored to have experienced quite a few affairs and who ended one of them by leaving his wife, Ruth, and living with his lover, Rachel. Another tale involves him paying a large sum of money to one of his lovers—twenty-two-year-old Elisheva Chizis—to squelch the story;[18] Binyamin Netanyahu, who cheated on his third wife by having an affair (and admitted it on public television); Zalman Shazar, who was the president of Israel and was involved with both the famous romantic poet Rachel and with Golda Meir; Ben-Gurion, who seems to have had two lovers (Miriam Cohen and Doris May) while he was married to Pola; and ex-chief of staff, parliament member, and minister Rafael Eitan ("Raful"), who built an impressive house for his lover (later wife).[19]

The most famous case of infidelity during the last decade of the twentieth century undoubtedly is the affair that Bill Clinton, then president of the United States (married to Hillary, and in his fifties), had with Monica Lewinsky (a staff worker in the White House, single, and in her twenties).[20] Having denied the existence of the affair for a long time, on Monday, August 17, 1998, Clinton admitted publicly to actually having had the affair (following Ms. Lewinsky's testimony and the public allegation of the existence of a dress with incriminating DNA evidence on it). During the discussions on whether to impeach President Clinton in the House of Representatives in Washington, D.C., the Speaker of the House Bob Livingston announced (December 19, 1998) that he was resigning from Congress in view of his own infidelities. Considering the widespread prevalence of extramarital affairs, this should not really surprise us.

Identifying Adultery and Its Generalizability. A recent research effort aimed at finding out whether adulterers can be identified by telltale behavioral signs. A report by Norton and Hastings (1997) on Buss's research indicates that it may be possible to create a behavioral "guide" for determining whether a spouse is cheating.

A related issue regarding adultery is the generalizability of this particular form of violating trust and loyalty to other forms. For example, can a politician who violates his wife's trust and loyalty be trusted not to violate the loyalty and trust of those who elected him or her into office? Are these two manifestations of betrayal connected on the personal psychological level? This issue was raised in an editorial in London's widely circulated *Evening Standard*.[21] The commentator was responding to a debate between two British gentlemen. One (Sir Peregrine Worsthorne) had claimed that dishonest private life was associated with dishonest public life because it meant that deceit had become a way of life. His adversary, Claus von Bulow, had countered the argument by maintaining that adultery had nothing to do with deceit in public life.

In Summary. At the basis of adultery lies behavior that violates trust and loyalty and is deceitful. It is typically done in secret, using various deceptive techniques, and involves misleading and cheating a loyal and trusting partner. Even in cases of parallel adultery, it is clear that the spouse is the victim of these particular breaches of trust and loyalty. Although the nature of the victimization process is clear, its deconstruction reveals that as one delves into the different types of adultery, its history, and its motivations, the victimization argument is weakened considerably. Moreover, Lawson's 1988 work clearly points out that the weak position of women is at the root of their weakened bargaining position in cases of adultery.

A distinction not made by Lawson needs to be introduced here. One of the relevant questions is whether the threat potential of ruining a relationship exists when a disloyal partner is successful in deceiving the other partner that he or she is in fact loyal. Is sexual faithlessness inherently corrosive of a marriage, or does it become corrosive only when a spouse discovers the infidelity? Trust is a socially and interpersonally constructed phenomenon that can be built out of a diversity of materials. It is possible to conclude that if the deception is successful, it may not undermine a relationship or a social structure. However, the fact that its disintegrative nature emerges once it is discovered may mean that there is something corrosive about infidelity itself. Given the high prevalence of infidelity, this conclusion must have some validity. However, it may be the case that a social structure can tolerate and absorb a large volume of betrayal (or deviance) before it becomes threatened.

Based on interviews with prominent researchers and on published research, the September 30, 1996, *Newsweek* cover story about adultery claimed that as women were gaining more power, their tolerance for old-style adultery was disappearing. Moreover, this equalization of power means that adultery is more prevalent, because it allows more women to experience adultery, and this behavior is thus now spread more evenly between the sexes. Hence, although in the past more males were involved in adultery, today both males and females are involved in this behavior in similar ratios.

Newsweek quotes Lawson—a well-known authority on the subject—on the new meaning of adultery: "It is no longer acceptable for men to feel they own their women's bodies . . . so the commodity exchanged in romance is no longer sex, but intimacy. Today the deepest betrayal is not of the flesh but of the heart" (p. 44). Thus, the perception today of betrayal in the case of adultery may be not so much the violation of the exclusive sexual rule but the violation of intimacy—that is, emotional betrayal. If this is true, it is indeed an interesting twist because the underlying assumption is that married couples (or people in similar relationships) must keep not only their fidelity in terms of sexual exclusivity but in terms of emotional exclusivity as well.

These combined developments may imply that females have less tolerance for males' infidelity, that there is more infidelity on the part of females, and that there has been a redrawing of the boundaries of what adultery really means in the area of emotions. It is interesting to note that in a few rather publicized cases, for example, those of Dick Morris, François Mitterrand, Binyamin Netanyahu, Bill Clinton, and Hugh Grant, the pattern and the response reactions were of the old pattern/reaction and not what could be expected from the new. That is, despite the violation of sexual trust and loyalty, the spouses remained with their infidel partners. Their behavior seems to contradict the implications of the report in *Newsweek*.

Informing

The term "informing" applies to a variety of activities, ranging from simple informing on classmates (squealers) to police and intelligence informing. Tax authorities use informers as well. For example, Israeli income tax authorities used to have Malshinon (literally translated as "squealer"), which was a telephone service that anyone could call anonymously to report tax violations. Informers are sometimes identified with collaborators. Illustrations for informers can be found in many areas. For example, Akerstrom's book (1991) is focused on police informers.

Many individuals feel that "squealing" is morally ambiguous. For example, Knesset (Israeli parliament) members in the state of Israel tried to pass laws that would help protect whistle-blowers against persecution, but the president of Israel (Ezer Weitzmann) and the former chief of staff (Refael Eitan) objected because they felt that "squealers" should be not rewarded or supported.

An interesting case illustrates some the complexities of "squealing." According to Kalidman and Weston (1998), David Kaczynski helped the FBI capture his brother, Ted Kaczynski, suspected of being the Unabomber. Ted was suspected as the man behind a seventeen-year letter-bomb spree resulting in three deaths and twenty-three injured people. Was that squealing immoral? One brother squealed on another, but did he not prevent future terrible injuries?

This case had an interesting twist when David felt that *he* was betrayed. David expected the FBI to keep his role in the arrest of his brother secret and understood that the prosecution would not seek the death penalty. Both expectations were shattered. David's role in finding the Unabomber was revealed, and the prosecution did ask for the death penalty. In public statements, David made no secret of his claim that the FBI violated his trust and loyalty on these two issues and that he felt betrayed. As things turned out, David's brother did not receive a death sentence.

One other in-depth illustration for this issue is Knox's 1997 study. By focusing on a few figures, Knox's (1997) work contextualizes both heroes and informers in the late-eighteenth-century political struggle for Irish independence. Knox uses these Irish historical figures to understand who the rebels and heroes were, who the villains and collaborative informers were, what motivated them, and what conclusions can be drawn about Irish political and ideological culture. Through this process Knox is able to decipher the Irish cultural enigma, with its puzzling contradictions. His work portrays quite vividly those contradicting characteristics of the idealistic Irishmen: persistence, naiveté, determination, as well as their arrogance, ineptitude, and unrealistic utopian ideals—an explosive concoction that led eventually to tragedy, culminating in miserable deaths of tens of thousands of people.

Another interesting case of informing unfolded in 1996—the case of Sascha Anderson. Because of the political changes in Germany, the concealment and deception originally involved in the case were exposed, and the true facts were established.

Sascha Anderson was one of the most central figures in former East Germany's subversive movement. He was considered a dissident hero by those supporting resistance to the totalitarian East German political culture and was deeply immersed in networks of artists and underground dissidents in former East Berlin. When the Berlin Wall crumbled and East Germany ceased to exist in the early 1990s, documents from the Stasi (the East German secret service) revealed that, in fact, Anderson was one of their very best and most important informers. While pretending to be part of the movement against the East German regime, Anderson, from about the mid-1970s on, gave the totalitarian regime all the information he could gather (including some very personal impressions and evaluations) on members he met and knew among the resistance, betraying their trust and loyalty.

One interesting aspect of this case is that Charon Film Productions made a 1996 documentary about Anderson (for Channel 4 Television), in which he was confronted with some of his acts. At the time the documentary was made, he was hiding out in Rome. In one of the more tantalizing parts of the documentary, two of his previous Stasi operators were interviewed. One of them stated that Anderson was indeed concerned about the freedom of artistic expression and that no arrests were made within the dissident group about which Anderson was informing. Of course, it was not necessary. With such quality squealing provided by Anderson it was better to let those innocent dissidents continue their activities because they posed no real threat to the regime. The second operator stated that it was his impression that Anderson regarded the informing as a sort of a game in which he saw himself as an actor. That is, he did not see himself as really involved in the acts, denying the moral meaning of his informing. This explains Anderson's answer to the question of his intimate collaboration with the Stasi. He stated that although the Stasi believed he was working for them, he really was not. Certainly, a person who manages to convince himself that whatever he is doing is just a "game" might also believe that he really did not collaborate. After all, the "real" Anderson (whoever that was) was not involved in this dangerous "game." Anderson is indeed an interesting case of self-delusion.

In this particular context, "informing" and "collaboration" are not dissimilar. In both cases we have two opposing and clashing symbolic moral universes, where one tries to enlist "informers" or "collaborators" from the other to obtain an advantageous edge in the conflict. Whereas "collaboration" tends to be used more in war-like situations, "informing" tends to be used more in police work. One of the more fascinating cases, combining two such opposing universes against a third, is the "Luciano Project," where a legal military organization formed a collaborative alliance with an illegal and criminal organization.

The winter of 1942 was a difficult time. Nazi submarines were hitting ships off the east coast of the United States,[22] and rumors of sabotage were running wild. For example, the S.S. *Normandie*, a luxury liner that was being converted to a troop ship (to be christened *Lafayette*) and fast enough to outrun U-boats, suddenly burst into flames at her Hudson River pier while about 2,500 workers were involved in the conversion works (February 9). Attempts to squelch the fire caused the ship to capsize at the dock. Salvaging efforts failed, and she was sold for scrap in 1946. Although never proven, sabotage was suggested as the explanation for the sudden and unexpected fire.[23] This context produced one of the strangest partnerships between U.S. Naval Intelligence and the Mafia, morally two very different organizations.

The goal of this collaboration was to secure the port of New York from Nazi infiltrators. Such bosses as "Lucky" Luciano, Joe "Socks" Lanza, and Meyer Lansky were involved in this project, as well as more than 150 naval personnel. The U.S. Navy estimated that Luciano's contribution was "useful" but regarded the whole project as an embarrassing episode, better forgotten. Campbell, who provides the story of this project (1977), disagrees and feels that the U.S. Navy had nothing to be ashamed of. Indeed, if anything, "Project Luciano" provides one of the best illustrations of the old saying that wars create some rather strange bedfellows.

These examples illustrate that although many people despise informers, they sometimes provide information that helps society and saves lives.

Mutiny

Mutiny appears in our typology twice. Here the term is used to denote military insurrection. When a group of soldiers feel that their commanding officer no longer deserves their loyalty and trust, they move against that commander.

The most dramatic mutinies, and those that receive the most attention, have been aboard ships and at sea. The image of a crew revolting against the captain of a warship on the high seas is something that has captivated the imagination. Indeed, some classic books and movies have been created on this theme, such as Herman Wouk's Pulitzer Prize–winning novel *The Caine Mutiny* (made into a movie in 1954), the movie *The Mutiny on the Bounty* (1962 and 1984, based on an actual mutiny in 1806), and Sergei Eisenstein's 1925 Russian movie *Potemkin*, which was based on the 1905 revolutionary mutiny on the battleship *Potemkin*. As the works of Allen (1989), Hadfield (1979), and Guttridge (1992) reveal, naval insurrection has not been rare, and attempts to seize control of ships are part and parcel of the histories of many navies in the world.

There are several interesting cases of mutiny. One involves Force X, which was composed of British Royal Navy soldiers who were sent to assist American forces in the South Pacific during World War II. Their mutiny stemmed from "resentment against orders to a remote war zone considered principally someone else's province" (Guttridge 1992:223). Glenton (1986) and Bakeless (1998:318–327) describe the 1781 mutiny of the Pennsylvania line, which developed after incompetence and mishandling during the American Revolution. Another example is the 1743 mutiny of Lord Sempill's Highland Regiment (the so-called Black Watch Mutiny). The mutiny developed when the anxious soldiers of the regiment learned that they were to be sent abroad, contrary to their terms of recruitment (MacWilliam 1910).

A mutiny (naval or otherwise) basically means crossing the moral boundaries dictated by the military chain of command, using power to accomplish this crossing. By its very nature, a mutiny is an open, not secret, insurrection, however, the military can—and often does—censor information about such events.

Collaboration, Defection, Desertion, Espionage and Spying, International Betrayal, Mutiny, State-Sponsored Terror, and Human Rights Violations

The second cell we shall focus on includes acts of betrayal in which an in-member commits a violation of trust and loyalty against the general collective. The issue of whether the behavior in question was conducted in secret is of crucial importance. Although treason is part of this cell, I shall not discuss it here; I devote all of Chapter 4 to the topic.

Collaboration

The term "collaboration" connotes both positive and negative qualities. Collaboration between musicians, scientists, or physicians is typically assumed to be positive. In reference to war or conflict, the term connotes an altogether different and negative meaning, for example, collaborating with the enemy. There is a subtext to this negative meaning, and it is associated with treason. We shall delve into the issue, and cases, of collaboration more thoroughly in Chapters 5 and 6.

Defection

Defection refers to a situation where two adversarial groups are competing, or are locked in a conflict, and one or more members of one group shift their loyalties to the other and typically move from the territory of one group to that of the other. Defection can take place in secret (for example, when spies, or the military, are involved) or in public (for example, in politics). Moreover, defection—by definition—involves negotiated and changed loyalties and trust in the most straightforward way. The particular form of violation of trust and loyalty that we discuss here is perpetrated by a member of the in-group who changes his or her loyalty and is not aimed against anyone in particular, but against the group (although individual actors can, and frequently are, hurt). Although defection can be observed in a number of areas (for example, politics, religion, sport, commerce, industry, and even police work [Zilberberg 1997]), it does not invoke a unified societal reaction.

Illustrations for defection are numerous. The history of Czarist Russia and the Soviet Union has some fascinating tales about defectors, one of the most famous of which is the case of prince Andrey Mikhaylovich Kurbsky (1528–1583). Kurbsky was a military commander in Czar Ivan (the Terrible) IV's regime in the middle of the sixteenth century. He was liked by the czar and became one of his closest, most valued, and trusted associates. However, between 1563 and 1564 Kurbsky lost his special position with the czar, and in 1564 he defected to Poland and joined the forces of King Sigismund II Augustus of Poland-Lithuania, who was fighting against Russia. King Sigismund was generous both militarily and financially with Kurbsky. After his defection, Kurbsky wrote the czar a few letters, which serve as useful historical documents for the period. This defection clearly shook Ivan, who contemplated leaving his throne. Instead Ivan began suspecting conspiracies everywhere and ruthlessly moved to consolidate his power, resulting in a reign of terror (for example, see Keenan 1971).

In recent times, the term "defection" has been used most widely within the context of what has become known as the intelligence community, where officers of one country—typically in possession of some important information—move to a rival country.[24] Defection was very prominent within the intelligence community during the cold war between the West and the East.

Intelligence jargon differentiates between a "defector," who fits the above characterization, and a "defector in place," which refers to a potential defector who has denounced his or her country but has not left it. Such defectors typically continue their work and become "moles." Of course, moles can become defectors. Some examples include British spies such as Burgess, Maclean, and Philby (discussed below), and Arkady Shevchenko, a valuable Soviet mole in the service of the Americans who finally defected to the United States.[25] If a mole stays too long, he risks being caught.

Perhaps the most successful known American mole the Soviets ever had was Aldrich H. Ames (recruited in 1985), who caused severe damage to U.S. interests.[26] He was caught in 1994 while trying to flee and received a sentence of life in prison. A case of a Soviet mole working for the Americans was Dimitri Polyakov, who was operative for twenty years. Polyakov was betrayed by Ames and executed by the Soviets in 1986.[27]

Defectors may possess valuable assets (for example, information), and their defection can thus give the side they defect to some obvious intelligence and operational advantages. The first high-ranking Soviet intelligence officer to defect to the West was probably Schmeka Ginsberg.[28] Ginsberg was a former resident of the Soviet Union who joined the Soviet Military Intelligence (GRU) in 1923 and transferred to the NKVD (Stalin's secret police) in 1934, rising to the rank of major general there. He became disillusioned with Stalin and defected to the French in 1937. Ginsberg then traveled to Canada and from there to the United States. There he contacted the FBI, which helped to grant him alien resident status.[29] He later visited London and gave crucial intelligence information to the British as well. Unfortunately, the British failed to follow some of the important leads Ginsberg provided them and did not use all the information in an effective way. Ginsberg's body was found on February 10, 1941, in a Bellevue Hotel room in Washington, D.C., shot in the temple, with three suicide notes. Chances are that he was the victim of a successful assassination.[30]

Some famous defectors include the following: Afansy M. Shorokhov (alias Vladimir Petrov), who defected to Australia in 1954; Guy Burgess and Donald Maclean, two British diplomats who defected to the Soviet Union in 1951 (KGB moles for twenty years); Igor Gouzenko, a Soviet GRU agent stationed in Ottawa, Canada, who defected to the West in

September 1945; Polish secret service officer Michal Golienewski, who defected in December 1960 to the American CIA in West Berlin (actually a Soviet mole in the Polish secret service) and helped to expose and arrest George Blake (a Soviet spy in British MI6) and Harry Houghton (from the Portland spy ring, discussed later in this book); and KGB Major Anatoli Golitsin, who defected to the West from his Soviet post in Helsinki, Finland, in 1962.

Defectors may possess not only valuable information but also valuable and tangible assets, like a fighter plane. In the morning hours of August 16, 1966, an Iraqi fighter pilot, Munir Radfa, defected with his Soviet-made MiG-21 fighter plane to Israel. That operation took much effort from the Israeli secret service, but persuading Munir to steal that MiG-21 and defect to Israel was one of the most brilliant, useful, and valuable operations of the Israeli Mossad. The ability of the Israeli Air Force to examine, firsthand, what was then the first-line fighter plane of some of its Arab neighbors certainly gave them an obvious edge. Despite various efforts, Munir did not integrate into Israeli culture and experienced difficulties finding a job. Helped by Israeli authorities, Munir left the country to live elsewhere. He died in August 1998. Israeli authorities were asked to help in his burial and did so, far away from both Israel and Iraq (Black and Morris 1991:206–210; Dan 1998).

Whittaker Chambers and Alger Hiss.   One particularly notable case where facts and constructions are interesting to follow is the case of Whittaker Chambers (1901–1961), an editor for *Time* magazine. He was a dedicated American Communist who joined the party in 1924 and became a spy for the Soviets in 1933. Disillusioned with communism, he quit both the party and spying in 1937, that is, he shifted his loyalties to the Americans. In 1939, following the nonaggression pact signed by Nazi Germany and the Soviet Union, he warned the State Department about its penetration by Soviet agents. Specifically, he told Adolf Berle, assistant secretary of state, that Alger Hiss was a Communist and a spy. His warnings were ignored.[31] In 1942 he was in contact with the FBI but was hesitant about giving more names.[32] On August 3, 1948, he gave voluntary testimony to the House Un-American Activities Committee, in which he said that Alger Hiss was working for the Soviets. That was a significant piece of information. It started a case around Alger Hiss that to some extent is still puzzling even today.[33]

Alger Hiss was born in 1904 in Baltimore and developed an impressive career in different departments of the U.S. administration. In 1936 he entered the State Department where he served in some key roles, including advising President Roosevelt during the Yalta Conference (February 4–11,1945). Hiss quietly left the State Department to become the president of the Carnegie Endowment for International Peace in 1947. Following Chambers's statement in 1948, Hiss denied the charges and sued Chambers for libel. One member of the committee, Republican Richard M. Nixon, accused Hiss of lying and convinced Chambers to reveal some evidence he supposedly had against Hiss. Hiss continuously claimed that he was not a spy. The accusations made by Chambers and the denials and counteraccusations made by Hiss helped to produce two trials. Under the statute of limitations, Hiss could not be tried for espionage, and he was therefore indicted on two counts of perjury. In his first trial, in July 1949, the jurors could not come to a decision. Hiss's second trial began in November 1949. He was convicted on January 21, 1950, and sentenced to five years in prison (he actually served forty-four months).

For many years, the question of whether Hiss was really a spy haunted America.[34] As Polmar and Allen (1997) point out, this puzzling case was solved in the 1990s. First, in 1992 General Dmitri Volkogonov, a Russian historian in charge of the KGB and military intelligence archives, revealed that he had searched the relevant files, found nothing, and that therefore the accusations against Hiss had been "completely groundless."[35] However, Volkogonov admitted that he "could not rule out the possibility that some records had been overlooked or even destroyed."[36] Second, in 1993 a Hungarian historian doing research on the Hungarian secret police—Maria Schmidt—stated that she had discovered documents that indicated that Mr. Hiss was a Communist spy.[37] However, the most credible evidence was produced in 1996, the same year in which Hiss died. In that year, decrypted Soviet intelligence messages (code name "Venona") from the 1940s were released by the NSA (National Security Agency) and linked Hiss directly to espionage.[38] Specifically, one document, dated March 30, 1945, identified a Soviet spy in America code-named "Ales." The message identified "Ales" as working in the State Department and as the person who accompanied President Roosevelt to the 1945 Yalta Conference and then flew on to Moscow. There, "Ales" met Andrei Vyshinsky, then Soviet Commissar for Foreign Affairs, and was cited for his aid to the Soviets. We know that Hiss worked at the time of the Yalta Conference in the State Department and that he accompanied President Roosevelt to the Yalta Conference as an adviser.[39] Hiss himself admitted that he spent a night in Moscow after the Yalta Conference, but he denied that he was Ales. His version was that he went to Moscow to see the subway system.[40] Available evidence (Chambers's testimony and evidence, historian Maria Schmidt's statement, and the Venona files) thus seems to suggest that Hiss was indeed a Soviet spy and that throughout World War II he provided to the Soviets inside information that probably helped to undermine the policies of the United States government, which trusted him by allowing him to work in a sensitive role and to which he swore loyalty. The violations of trust and loyalty in this case are very obvious.

If indeed Hiss was a spy, he was very successful at creating a deceptive facade and managed to conceal his defection for a very long period of time. Not only did he damage U.S. national security, but his deception created a bitter and divisive national controversy—quite an achievement for a spy who was also a bona fide traitor. Hiss died on November 15, 1996, in New York City at age ninety-two.[41]

The Cold War.   The cold war saw quite a few spectacular cases of defection.[42] There were some famous defectors from the Soviet Union: Konstantin Volkov, Vladimir Petrov, Anatoly Golitsin, and Yuri Nosenko, among others. Three of the most famous defectors from the Soviet Union were Oleg Gordievsky, Igor Sergeievitch Gouzenko, and Oleg Penkovsky.

Oleg Gordievsky
Gordievsky was born in 1938 and developed a career in the KGB. Apparently, sometime in the 1970s (probably 1974) he began to work for British Intelligence (MI6). His motivation to spy for the West, supposedly, was fueled by the brutal Soviet invasion to Czechoslovakia in 1968. For more than a decade he was able to provide his British operators with valuable information. In 1985 his cover was blown by a double agent in the American CIA, and he defected to Britain. His defection was formally announced by the British Foreign Office in September 1985. Gordievsky paid a very high personal price for defection, as he left his wife and two daughters in the Soviet Union. His wife divorced him, and although in 1991 his family was allowed to leave the Soviet Union, the family did not reunite.[43]

Oleg Penkovsky
Penkovsky presents us with an altogether different case. Born in 1919, he took part in the Red Army's fight against the Nazi *Wehrmacht,* and after the war he was trained as an intelligence officer. He eventually became an officer with Soviet Military Intelligence (GRU). Like Gouzenko (discussed below), his first attempts at establishing contact with Western intelligence were rather frustrating. However, eventually he was successful in making such a contact with both the British and the Americans. From April 1961 until August 1962, he passed large volumes of vital classified information to the Americans and British. Some of this information proved quite important to President Kennedy during the Cuban missile crisis of October 1962 because it enabled the Americans to have a better assessment of Soviet intentions. Soviet intelligence was successful in exposing Penkovsky and arrested him on October 22, 1962. In a show trial in May 1963, he was

sentenced to death. On May 17, 1963, it was announced that he had been executed "by the method reserved for the Soviet Union's worst traitors: he was slowly fed into a live furnace, with some of his closest former colleagues forced to watch" (Volkman 1994:30). Clearly, Penkovsky was one of the best and most productive pro-West "defectors in place."[44]

Igor Sergeievitch Gouzenko

Gouzenko (1919–1982) is, perhaps, one of the more colorful cases of defection. Having been trained in military intelligence in Moscow in 1941, Gouzenko was sent in June 1943 to the Soviet embassy in Ottawa, Canada, as a cipher clerk (officially defined as a "civilian employee"). In September 1944 he received unexpected orders to return to the Soviet Union. Gouzenko and his wife decided that they were not going back. What happened next would be a good script for a Hollywood movie.

Gouzenko left the Soviet embassy on September 5, 1943, with a pile of classified documents, intending to defect to the Canadians on September 6, with his pregnant wife and son. Here was a man who possessed invaluable knowledge that was vital to the West's understanding of Soviet information-gathering methods. Was he received with joy and appreciation? Not at all. At first, Canadian officials refused to give him asylum. It was one of his neighbors, a sergeant in the Canadian Air Force, who actually gave him asylum. Only after a while, when the opaque Canadian authorities began to grasp the importance of the information Gouzenko possessed, and the fact that he was risking his life, did they decide to grant him official asylum.

The information Gouzenko brought revealed that the Soviets were operating a sizeable espionage organization in Canada. These revelations led to exposures and arrests of more then ten spies, all involved in an intensive effort to find information about atomic weapons and transfer it to the Soviet Union. It is noteworthy that Gouzenko also provided information (alas, inconclusive) that Alger Hiss was a Soviet spy.[45] A Canadian Royal Commission that investigated the Gouzenko affair submitted its report on June 1946, stating there that Gouzenko had "revealed the existence in Canada of a widespread conspiracy to obtain secret official information,"[46] and that the Soviets had tried to create a fifth column organization in Canada, whose goal it was to collect military, political, and general information.[47]

Two famous defectors from the West were Edward Lee Howard and Harold (Kim) Philby.

Edward L. Howard

Howard was born in 1951 in New Mexico. After an unsteady period of employment and moves within and outside the United States, he applied to the CIA and was contacted in 1980 (in Chicago). He was trained by the CIA for a variety of tasks and was eventually stationed in the American embassy in Moscow. Both he and his wife worked there as intelligence officers. Because Howard failed polygraph tests, his employment by the CIA was terminated in 1983 and he returned to the United States. In the mid-1980s Howard traveled a few times to Europe and was in contact with KGB officers in Vienna. In return for the information he gave them, he was given cash. The CIA caught on to his betrayal and in September 1985 was ready to arrest him. Howard was quicker, however, and by that time he was already on his way to Moscow (the last part of the journey, in the trunk of a Soviet embassy car).[48]

Harold (Kim) Philby

Philby is an altogether different, and much more complicated, case. The general context is that of the famous "Cambridge spy ring." The term refers to a group of British spies who were recruited by Soviet NKVD in the 1930s, and the name relates to the fact that the major figures were recruited at Cambridge University.[49] The core group consisted of Donald Maclean,[50] Guy Burgess,[51] Anthony Blunt,[52] Harold (Kim) Philby,[53] John Cairncross,[54] Alan Nunn May,[55] and Leo Long.[56] These spies were quite effective in causing significant damage to the West and were probably among the best-known spies of all time. In March 1951, as the British Scotland Yard was hot on their trail, Burgess and Maclean defected to the Soviet Union. Cairncross, Blunt, May, and Long remained in the West. Blunt and Long were promised immunity from punishment in exchange for information. Blunt eventually confessed and became socially isolated; Long was less prominent to begin with. May was caught and sentenced to ten years in prison in 1946 but was actually released in 1952. Philby defected and moved to Moscow.[57] Although the two most talked about spies from this group are Blunt and Philby, it is quite possible that the more effective and important spy was actually Maclean.

Philby must be viewed in the context of the ideological rivalries, World War II, and the sexual exchanges (as well as the heavy drinking of Maclean) among that group of spies. Philby was born in 1912 and in the 1930s attended Cambridge University, where he was recruited to Soviet intelligence. He left Cambridge in 1933 for a fascinating career as a spy. He managed to become a member of British MI5 (British Security Service in charge of domestic security and counterespionage activities in the United Kingdom) during World War I, and after leaving Cambridge he covered—as a journalist—the Spanish Civil War. After Spain, British MI6 (British security service in charge of espionage and foreign intelligence, also known as SIS) recruited him again. Philby developed quite a career in SIS and was given some of the most sensitive and classified positions there. He had no qualms passing all the information he considered valuable to his Soviet operator. As CIA suspicions against Philby were mounting in the early 1950s (as well as those of some of his British colleagues), he was forced to leave the British intelligence service.

His next assignment was as a reporter in the Middle East. Even there he was able to continue his espionage work. Philby's personal life was quite turbulent; he had a few affairs (some with wives of his associates), and as a spy, he was able to dodge rather successfully a few Soviet defectors who pointed their finger at him. But all good things come to an end. In 1963 British MI6 had enough evidence to confront Philby. In that confrontation, Philby was offered the same deal that Blunt and Long received: immunity from prosecution for information. Philby confessed but defected to the Soviet Union.[58]

Even after the end of the cold war, defections associated primarily with intelligence were rather common. One such example is the famous early August 1995 defection from Iraq to Jordan of Hussein Kamal Al-Hassan and General Saddam Kamal, both married to the daughters of Iraqi president Saddam Hussein. On August 12, 1995, Saddam Hussein, in a fiery speech, called them "traitors" and threatened to execute them. After spending time in Jordan, and accepting Saddam Hussein's later assertion that they would not be harmed if they returned to Iraq, they chose to believe him and returned to Iraq. Shortly after returning they were killed.

Another recent case occurred in September 1997 when Jang Sung Gil, North Korean ambassador to Egypt, and his wife defected in Cairo to CIA agents who rushed the couple to safety in the United States. As was the case with previous defections, the North Koreans reacted in anger, accusing the CIA of committing a hostile act. That anger may have been magnified because Jang was the axis around which Pyongyang's Middle East policy was turning. Obviously, the CIA hoped that ex-ambassador Jang's breadth of knowledge would be helpful in unveiling the mystery surrounding some suspected shady international transactions made by the North Koreans (for example, selling missiles to Syria, Libya, Iran, and Egypt).[59]

Intelligence-oriented defection is certainly an interesting form of betrayal. It involves the violation of trust and loyalty in betraying secrets to an alien and frequently hostile national adversary. This particular type of defection characteristically assumes a secret form.[60] Defectors are constructed differently by those they defect from and those they defect to.

Desertion

A category related to defection is desertion. In its most popular meaning, the term refers to the behavior of a soldier who leaves a military post without authorization, intending not to return. Such posts can be in trenches, tanks, naval forces, or an administrative position. Whereas defection means going to the other/opposite side of the conflict, desertion means walking away from a post, without changing sides. Much like defectors, deserters most certainly violate both trust invested in them and loyalty to their group. Indeed, desertion receives the severest of punishments (especially if done in the context of combat).

Desertion entails a larger category of behaviors associated with military duties that involve both loyalty and trust. Such behaviors include being AWOL (absence without leave), which has been treated frequently as betrayal. During World War II, both desertion and AWOL infractions took place among the various combatants. For example, one out of sixteen Soviet prisoners of war (POWs) were found to be deserters. Much of the Hungarian Army deserted to the Soviet Red Army. Mass desertion took place with the Burma National Army when it left the Japanese to fight with the British (March 1945). Despite the mythologies about them, Japanese soldiers deserted as well (especially as the war progressed). The U.S. Army had a total of 40,000 deserters. The *Wehrmacht* accused about 35,000 soldiers of desertion and sentenced to death close to 23,000, of whom at least 15,000 were actually executed. Because the U.S. Army tended to charge deserters with the lesser offense of AWOL, only one soldier was executed. More than 100,000 soldiers deserted from the British army.[61]

Many potential U.S. soldiers evaded the draft during the Vietnam War, many by leaving the country. In Israel, it became clear that during the Israeli invasion to Lebanon (which began in the summer of 1982) large numbers of soldiers (especially in the reserves) found ways to evade joining the war.

Conscientious objection to military service is not recognized as a legitimate moral and political category in a number of countries. In such situations this behavior is constructed as a violation of loyalty and trust. Thus, people who define themselves as such in these countries may face a grim and bitter dispute with drafting administrations and are often branded as traitors. Other countries are able to absorb such behavior without constructing it in such negative terms.

Deserters have played a role in quite a few fictional cultural creations, both as heroes and antiheroes. Perhaps one of the most memorable roles of a deserter is played by Marlon Brando in Francis Ford Coppola's 1979 violent, yet cryptic, Vietnam War movie *Apocalypse Now*.

A category close to desertion and defection, though in a very different context, is conversion, which is discussed later in this chapter.

Espionage and Spying

Not every spy is a traitor, and not every traitor is a spy. A spy that would qualify as a traitor must be a person that is a bona fide member of the in-group in a particular collective or organization, whose secrets that person gives ("betrays") to another, sometimes hostile, collective or organization. It is the trust, loyalty, and faithfulness that this member of the collective violates, which earns that person the label of traitor. Typically such acts are committed in secret and by using deception. The traitor, in such cases, needs to present a front that gives the impression of decency, loyalty, honesty, and commitment, but the underlying reality is the exact opposite of this false and deceptive impression.

A person who fakes membership in the group or the collective assumes—willingly and deliberately—a fake and deceptive identity. That person pretends to be a bona fide member of a collective but really is not. Such is the case with a transplanted spy with a fake identity. Such a person can hardly qualify for the term "traitor" because he or she does not violate any real trust or loyalty. Obviously, not classifying such a person as a bona fide traitor may become problematic if that person generates (deliberately so) feelings of trust and loyalty for many years, whereas his or her genuine loyalty is to an altogether different collective. However, members of the collective whose secrets the spy managed to disclose tend typically to express their feelings—once that spy is exposed—in a rhetoric of betrayal, no matter whether the spy's identity was fake or genuine.

There are numerous illustrations of people who hid their true identity and interests and pretended to be something else, thus gaining access to valuable information and damaging the group or collective, whose trust and loyalty they violated. Let us review a few illustrative cases.

The "Esek Bish" in Egypt.   In 1951 Israeli military intelligence organized a spy web in Cairo. Recruited members were sent for training to Israel and by 1953 all the members of the spy network were back in Cairo ready for action. These spies pretended to be trustful and loyal Egyptians, but they were not.

In 1954 the United States demanded that Britain evacuate the Suez Canal region. At that time, Israel was concerned about the growing American alienation toward Israel and felt that a continued British presence could be used to its advantage. Thus, Israel's military intelligence wanted to prevent, or at least stall, the British evacuation. They reasoned that hitting British targets in Egypt would achieve their desired goal by forcing the British government to reevaluate its willingness to comply with the American demand. Despite inner disputes in Israel regarding the wisdom of activating its Cairo spies against British targets, the decision was made, and the Israeli spies were ordered to spring into action.

The main strategy was to plant bombs in various places (on July 2 and 14). The activity on July 23 was fatal. One of the spies (Philip Natanson) was caught with a smoldering bomb when he entered the Rio cinema. It did not take long for the Egyptians to figure out what was going on, and within a matter of days all the members of the spy net were caught and arrested (with an additional nine members, plus one innocent Egyptian Jew—Yoseph Karmona, and Major Meir Binet, a representative of Israeli military intelligence who was indirectly associated with the net). The capture of the Israeli spy net was made public on July 26, 1954, and their trial began on December 11, 1954. Karmona either committed suicide or died while being tortured; Binet committed suicide; Dr. Moshe Marzuk and Shmuel Azar were sentenced to death (and hanged on January 31, 1955). Two were acquitted, and the rest were sentenced to spend long periods in prison.

In Israel, a political storm arose around the question of who exactly authorized the activation of the net in this amateurish way. The affair was never solved satisfactorily. It led, however, to the resignation of both Pinhas Lavon (minister of defense) and David Ben-Gurion (prime minister). Clearly, the fog around the authorization and orders to activate the net reflects the sad fact that those in charge were avoiding their responsibility to give truthful accounts. Thus, both trust and loyalty were compromised in a most significant way. The affair itself, referred to as "the Lavon affair" or more commonly as the "Esek Bish" (translated, perhaps, as the "fiasco"), eroded the foundations of the Israeli regime.[62]

Further insult accompanied the question of releasing the jailed members of the net. Two members were released after seven years, and four others were released only after the Six Day War (June 1967) in an exchange of prisoners agreement between Israel and Egypt. Thus, not only did members of the net feel betrayed by those who authorized their mission but refused to take full responsibility, but they also felt they were ignored and left to rot in prison when massive exchanges of prisoners took place between Israel and Egypt after the 1956 Sinai Campaign.

Betrayal in this case was a multiple issue: First, Egyptian citizens joined an espionage ring against their country; second, intelligence officers in Israeli military intelligence (and perhaps some politicians too) betrayed their spies by sending them on a risky and questionable operation and then refused full responsibility; third, the Israeli government did not aggressively pursue the release of the spies, particularly after the 1956 Sinai Campaign.

Tyler G. Kent. Cases of spying are abundant. The title of Knightley's illuminating 1986 book is indeed instructive: *The Second Oldest Profession.* One illustrative example is the case of Tyler G. Kent.[63] Born in 1911 in

Manchuria to American parents, Kent was an American who worked as a cipher clerk in the U.S. embassy in London from October 5, 1939. Affiliating himself, for ideological reasons, with a pro-Nazi network, he was able to leak to the Nazis much of the pre-war Churchill-Roosevelt cable correspondence. Eventually, MI5 exposed both him and his contacts. These individuals were charged in court and sentenced to various prison terms. Kent was released from prison in September 1945 and deported to the United States. There, he continued to express his racist and fascist views until he died in 1988. In reality, Kent was a Nazi sympathizer who pretended to be trustful and loyal, but who in fact caused his country much damage.

Aside from the instructive tales of spying in the Bible[64] and such actual cases as Mata Hari,[65] "Cicero,"[66] Harold (Kim) Philby, Whittaker Chambers, Richard Sorge, Aldrich Ames, Markus Wolf, and a host of others, it is interesting to note that some rather famous people of words were spies as well. These include Ernest Hemingway, Graham Greene, Somerset Maugham, clergyman Giovanni Montini,[67] and Daniel Defoe.[68] And a recent book claims that even William Wordsworth, one of the most acclaimed British poets, was spying in 1799 for the British against Germany, as part of an espionage network.[69]

Three rather famous cases in which Israel was involved are also worth exploring.

Jonathan Pollard.   Jonathan Pollard was an American citizen who betrayed his country's secrets to Israeli intelligence. Pollard began to work for the U.S. Navy in September 1979 as a civilian intelligence analyst. Around that time he made contact with a South African military attaché in Washington, D.C. U.S. counterintelligence discovered the liaison, and his security clearance was downgraded. In June 1984 his clearance was upgraded again when he was reassigned to intelligence work in the Anti-Terrorism Alert Center in the Naval Investigative Service. Pollard again used his privileged position to gain access to classified materials and gave classified information to an Australian naval officer and to a supporter of the rebel guerrillas in Afghanistan.

That, apparently, did not satisfy Pollard. He next made contact with an Israeli intelligence agent in New York. That began a relationship through which Pollard was paid tens of thousands of dollars by Israeli intelligence (for example, at the beginning, a monthly salary of $1,500, which was raised in 1985 to $2,500, and various gifts valued at $10,000–12,000). Pollard provided Israel with highly classified and valuable intelligence information. Becoming suspicious of Pollard's requests for huge amounts of data, his commanding officer ordered that he be watched closely. His cover began to crumble, and in November 1985 Pollard's betrayal became obvious. On Thursday, November 21, 1985, the Pollards, followed by FBI agents, drove to the Israeli embassy in Washington, D.C., asking for asylum. The Israelis refused, and as the Pollards left the embassy, they were arrested. Pleading guilty to charges of espionage, Jonathan Pollard was sentenced to life in prison, his wife was sentenced to five years in prison. Although Anne, his wife, was released in 1990 (they also divorced), Pollard remained—at the time of writing this book—in prison, despite a strong Israeli lobby to release him.

There is little doubt that Pollard violated both the trust and loyalty vested in him by his country and did it by way of deception. Pollard clearly fits every criteria of treachery and qualifies fully as a traitor.[70] Moreover, the literature reveals that Pollard may have been loyal to no one, making him a qualitatively different type of spy than, say, Arnold, Hale, or Kent.

Eli Cohen.   Born in Egypt in 1924, Cohen was an Arab linguist who immigrated to Israel in 1957; he was recruited by the Israeli secret service (Mossad) in May 1960. Assuming a false identity, he left Israel (leaving behind his wife and children) and arrived in Syria in 1962. He established himself in Damascus as a rich furniture and tapestry exporter and made many important friends. Cohen was highly successful in penetrating important political and military circles in Syria and provided Israeli intelligence with crucial information (among other things, about the Syrian fortifications in the Golan Heights). He was so popular that he was considered for the post of deputy defense minister. Eventually, Cohen's radio transmissions from Damascus were detected, and he was caught and arrested on January 18, 1965. He was tortured, interrogated, tried for espionage, sentenced to death, and hanged on May 18, 1965, in Damascus in Marjeh Square before a cheering crowd of more than 10,000 with full media coverage. Clearly, although Cohen was a spy, he was not a traitor.[71]

Israel Beer.   According to Israel Beer, following the Nazi takeover of Austria in 1938 (the so-called *Anschluss*), he fled from Vienna to Palestine. There he joined the Hagana (a prestate underground Jewish organization). He presented himself as an experienced guerrilla anti-Nazi fighter and as a person who took an active part in the fight against the fascists in the Spanish Civil War. Beer developed quite a military career.

During the 1948 Israeli War of Independence, he was deputy chief of operations of the general staff and, later, head of planning and operations. Following that war, he expected to be promoted to army deputy chief of staff. His expectation was not met, and he resigned from the army to become a military correspondent for a local newspaper. From 1953 on, he became close to David Ben-Gurion, as well as other defense officials, and Ben-Gurion appointed Beer to write the history of the 1948 war.

Despite that obvious trust, there were those who did not trust him. Those who were suspicious (for example, Moshe Dayan, army chief of staff, and Isser Harel, chief of the Israeli secret service) were correct. Beer was put under surveillance, and on March 30, 1961, he was caught passing information to a KGB officer (Victor Sokolow) in the Soviet embassy in Tel Aviv. Before that, he also tried to establish an unauthorized contact with Reinhard Gehlen (then head of West Germany's intelligence) in May 1960. That attempt may have been aimed to help him penetrate West German intelligence for his Soviet masters. Beer was arrested the next day, put on trial for espionage, and sentenced to fifteen years in prison. He died in prison in 1968.

At the time of his arrest, he held the chair of military history at Tel Aviv University and worked as a military commentator for the Israeli daily *Ha'aretz*. Beer remains an enigmatic figure, and there is still speculation about how much of his cover story was true. There are few answers for such basic questions of whether he was really Jewish, whether he was from Vienna, whether he fought in Spain or participated in any guerrilla warfare, and whether he held a legitimate Ph.D. degree. A thorough documentary made about him in February 1990 by Israeli television found that the unknown facts far exceed the known. Black and Morris point out that "Beer's impressive curriculum vitae turned out to be completely bogus. The colonel had never been in the Schutzbund, never fought in Spain, and had in fact been a lowly clerk in the Austrian Zionist Federation."[72] On one thing there seems to be no argument: He was a spy for the Soviets.

Beer was not the only spy planted in Israel during that time. Professor Kurt Sitta, from the Israeli Technion, was such a spy too (he was caught in June 1960 and sentenced to a five-year prison sentence).[73] Of course, neither qualifies as a traitor.

Beer was probably transplanted by the Soviets in Palestine just as Eli Cohen was transplanted by Israel in Damascus. Both acquired fake identities. One needs to be reminded that Soviet intelligence had a lot of experience in transplanting spies. The best-known example is Richard Sorge.[74] Sorge began working for Soviet intelligence in 1920 (in Germany), disguised as a teacher, and visited a number of countries in the late 1920s. Using a cover of German correspondent, Sorge worked as a Soviet spy in Japan beginning in 1933. He created a valuable and useful spy ring there and was able to pass his Soviet operators extremely valuable information about Japan. For example, in 1941 he was able to inform Stalin that Japan did not plan any aggression against the Soviets and that their focus was the south (the Dutch Indies and French Indochina). That information enabled Stalin to divert essential military forces from the Far East to the fight against the Nazi *Wehrmacht* (more on this case in Chapter 6).

Recent Books on Spies and Espionage.   Spies engage minds and imaginations. The number of books (fiction and nonfiction) and movies about them is staggering. Books about spies as traitors are published continuously; some even contain stunning revelations. These tend to capture the headlines, especially when they seem to suggest new discoveries that appear to reveal dark and hidden information. Three examples from 1999 illustrate the point. First is Allen Weinstein and Alexander Vassiliev's work about Soviet espionage in America during the Stalin era, *The Haunted Wood: Soviet Espionage in America—The Stalin Era* (New York: Random House). In some respects this book may have actually redefined the entire field of investigation in this area. The second book, *The Mitrokhin Archive: The KGB in Europe and the West* (London: Allen Lane, Penguin Press) is by Christopher Andrew and Vasili Mitrokhin. The revelations in this thick volume about the involvement of the Soviet KGB in a number of operations (including some interesting "honey traps") are breathtaking. Should Mitrokhin be considered a traitor for collecting all the damaging and discrediting information while he was working for the KGB? If his actions had been known to KGB, the consequences for Mitrokhin would certainly have been very dire. Finally, we have Mark Hollingsworth and Nick Fielding's somber and somewhat sad book, *Defending the Realms: MI5 and the Shayler Affair* (London: Deutch). Shayler was recruited by MI5 in an attempt to refresh and inject creativeness in the organization. Five years later, Shayler produced a scathing critique of MI5. Among other criticisms, he claimed that MI5 was incompetent and heavily bureaucratic and that many of its officers experience problems of excessive alcohol consumption. Should Shayler be considered a traitor for disclosing publicly all the damaging and discrediting information he collected about MI5? In a strange way, he may have actually helped Britain to revitalize and modernize MI5, which was the original reason for his hiring. The motivations of Mitrokhin and Shayler are—apparently—very different. However, both violated trust and loyalty, and thus both qualify for the title "traitor." All three books provide dramatic contrasts between factual truth vis-à-vis its construction in the complex and shady context of espionage and questionable loyalties.

The amount of literature about spies and espionage is indeed awesome.[75] The many resources spent on espionage reveal the importance attributed to "Humint" (human-collected intelligence, as opposed to "Elint," which is electronically collected intelligence). Contrary to theft by individuals, or even companies, theft of information in the form of espionage occupies the attention of nations. They pour money into research, bribing, and black-mailing in order to get information, as well as deceive others.

There is not a great deal of research on espionage from a social science point of view. However, one of the more interesting studies is by Frank Hagan (1989, 1997). Hagan views espionage as the secretive theft of information. His informative and insightful work focuses on examining espionage as a form of political crime, he has developed an empirical classification of spies based on their motivation. His typology consists of nine main categories and one miscellaneous category for the cases that do not fit the main categories. His typology classifies spies according to the following categories: mercenary (Aldrich Ames); ideological (Klaus Fuchs); alienated/egocentric (Edward Lee Howard); buccaneer/sport (Jonathan Pollard); professional (Rudolf Abel); compromised (Richard Miller); deceived (Edwin Wilson recruiting technique); quasi agent (Philip Agee), and finally, those who defect in order to avoid personal problems.

Hagan's typology is innovative and manages to surpass older typologies. For example, so-called sex espionage (using sex to gain access to information; see, for example, Bower 1990) can be broken into different and more generalized categories developed by Hagan. Other possible approaches could focus on a classificatory scheme based on the method utilized to gain intelligence information. This could include, for example, human data collection, electronic surveillance, data collection from open sources, and even schemes of espionage in cyberspace.[76]

Espionage has always been a hot topic for popular culture, and such spies as John Le Carré's Smiley and Ian Fleming's James Bond have become cultural heroes. Books and movies have glamorized the secret agent into mythical proportions.

Double Agents.   Double agent refers to an agent who works for two intelligence organizations, sometimes even without the agent's knowledge. Double agents push the boundaries between truth and deception to their farthest limits. For example, during World War II, MI5 (British internal counterespionage secret service) managed to capture every German agent sent to Britain by the Nazi German *Abwehr*[77] and turn them into double agents working for the British.

International Betrayal

International betrayal is a category of betrayal where both loyalty and trust are violated on the international level.[78] At least two salient possibilities exist here.

One possibility occurs when a state is being betrayed by another state(s). For example, the crisis created by Hitler in 1938 over Czechoslovakia was "solved" by the September 29–30, 1938, signing of the Munich Agreement. In this agreement, British premier Neville Chamberlain and French premier Edouard Daladier betrayed Czechoslovakia to Hitler for a questionable and flimsy hope of peace.

That was not the last time Czechoslovakia was betrayed. In 1968 Alexander Dubcek led Czechoslovakia into a freedom path that consisted of important reforms in freedom of speech and the economy. The "spring of Prague" did not last long. The Soviet Union, worried that other Eastern-bloc countries would follow this freedom trail, invaded Czechoslovakia with full military force in August 1968 and crushed the "spring" with an iron fist. Not one country in Eastern Europe moved to help Czechoslovakia resist or cope with this brutal conquest. Worse yet, some Eastern-bloc countries participated in the military invasion. For example, thousands of Polish soldiers took part in the first wave of invasion. No Western country helped either. The French prime minister, Michel Debre, made a "funny" remark about the invasion: "a traffic accident on the road to détente" (Ash 1994:280). Later, in the 1980s and early 1990s, the Polish Solidarity movement and the Mazowiecki government made public apologies to the Czech nation.

Certainly Czechoslovakia was not the only country that was betrayed like this. In 1956 the Hungarians revolted against the oppressive Soviet rule of the country. The Soviet army invaded Hungary, crushed the revolt, and reinstated an orthodox communist dictatorship. In this case, too, no country came to help the Hungarians.

Thus, in Czechoslovakia and Hungary, feelings of being internationally betrayed are not uncommon. However, those feelings, genuine and strong as they are, are based on the assumption that some Western or Eastern-bloc country could have intervened and stopped a Soviet-led invasion, a questionable assumption indeed.

A somewhat similar incident concerned the relationship between Italy and Nazi Germany. Fascist Italy and Nazi Germany signed a pact of cooperation. This "Pact of Steel," as Mussolini called it, was signed on May 22, 1939, in Berlin by the two countries' foreign ministers, Joachim von Ribbentrop of Germany and Count Galeazzo di Cortellazo Ciano of Italy. This pact continued the Rome-Berlin Axis treaty signed in 1936. Thus, one could view Nazi Germany and fascist Italy as two nations who—after 1937—saw their mutual interests eye to eye as genuine allies, in war and in peace. It is important to note that before this alliance was formed—particularly in 1934—the relations between these two countries had been strained, and points of conflict involved cultural and political differences.[79]

This alliance lasted until 1943. Following the major defeat of the Axis in the Mediterranean and the Allied strikes in Italy (for example, in Milan and Turin), the Italians faced the prospect of either continuing to fight a hopeless war or surrendering. Supported by the Italian army high command, and some of the fascist politicians, King Victor Emmanuel III called Mussolini to a conversation in which the king dismissed him from office. On July 23, 1943, upon leaving the palace, Mussolini was placed under house arrest. The fascist party and its apparatus were disbanded. From a Nazi German point of view, these events could certainly be interpreted as betrayal by Italy, that is, an act of international betrayal. It is interesting to note that these events occurred because of an inner structural tension within the Italian fascist movement—a dual loyalty to both the king and the Duce. Thus, this international treason could also be interpreted as treason within Italian fascism.[80]

This case had an interesting sequel involving other allegations of treason. On Hitler's commands, on September 12, 1943, Nazi airborne troops (headed by Major Otto Skorzeny) freed the Duce in a spectacularly dramatic raid and brought him to Germany. Hitler then appointed Mussolini as the puppet fascist head in control of German-occupied northern Italy (the Salo Republic). Mussolini used his position to put on trial, and execute, five of those who were involved in ousting him out from power, and whom he saw as traitors. One of those five was his son-in-law and foreign minister, signer of the "Pact of Steel," Count Ciano (January 11, 1944).

The second possibility for international betrayal occurs when a state betrays the loyalty and trust of a collective of sympathizers. Examples abound. The Yalta Conference (code-named "Argonaut") took place February 4–11, 1945, at Yalta in the Crimea and involved President Franklin D. Roosevelt, Premier Winston S. Churchill, and Premier Joseph Stalin. One of the agreements achieved there was the repatriation of all Soviet citizens. During the war, thousands of Soviets had fled their country. After the war ended, large numbers of Russians who were in areas under Western Allied control were forced, many at gunpoint, to board trains and return to Soviet-controlled areas, destined for incarceration, torture, and death.

> Particularly tragic was the experience of roughly 5.5 million Soviet citizens repatriated after the war, of whom 2.3 million were handed over on the basis of agreements concluded at the Yalta conference, often against their will. The core of the repatriated were 2.1 million *Ostarbeiter* ("labor from the east") and about a million prisoners-of-war. The *Ostarbeiter* had mostly not gone to Germany voluntarily. Nonetheless, half of all those repatriated were condemned to hard labor.[81]

There is little question that a very large number of those repatriated to Stalin's lethal and ruthless regime felt completely betrayed by the Western Allies.[82] After all, most of them were first forced to move from the So-

viet Union to Nazi-controlled regions, which must have been a most difficult experience. Many of those who survived trusted and were loyal to
the Western Allies. Most of them left a totalitarian regime to which they
never expected (or wanted) to be forcefully returned. One can easily interpret this nonselective act of repatriation as international betrayal. It is
important to note that among the prisoners were White Russians who
had never acknowledged the Soviet Union and who had lived outside the
country (more on this in Chapter 6), as well as groups of men who supported Nazi Germany.

A similar incident took place in post-1945 Poland. The instant recognition of the Soviet-sponsored government by the West was rightly interpreted by the Polish government-in-exile, and the legal opposition within
the country, as an act of international betrayal.[83]

There are cases where the two possibilities are mingled. An example is
the 1939 Molotov-Ribbentrop pact. Despite a very basic ideological in-
compatibility between Nazi Germany and the Stalin-led Soviet Union, in
August 1939, Nazi Germany's foreign minister—Joachim von Ribbentrop—and the Soviet Union's foreign minister—Vyacheslav Molotov—
signed a nonaggression pact that guaranteed the Soviet Union's borders
on its western and Baltic fronts and at the same time allowed Nazi Germany to invade Poland (and to risk war with both Britain and France, a
risk Hitler was willing to take).

The signing of this pact can easily be interpreted as an act of betrayal.
The Soviet Union clearly compromised Polish integrity as a state by enabling Hitler to attack Poland (on September 1, 1939) without much immediate risk for Nazi Germany. Moreover, the secret part of the pact divided large parts of Eastern Europe between Nazi Germany and the
Soviet Union and thus betrayed East European states and Communist individuals in the West, who found the pact indefensible. It is possible that
Soviet citizens under Stalin's regime also condemned the pact, but opposition to Stalin tended to evaporate rather swiftly, so that no strong voices
against the agreement were heard within the country.

Mutiny

Mutiny in this context refers to a collective insurrection not aimed at a personal or specific target. Some military insurrections (for example, against
poor living conditions or nourishment) can be thought of in this context
(for example, the mutiny of some 200 veterans of Montgomery's Eighth
Army in Salerno in 1943; see David 1995). However, the major and more
representative illustrations are those involving large-scale insurgencies
and their wars: the American Revolution (1775–1783), the French Revolution (1792–1800), the Russian Revolution (1917–1922); the great 1857

mutiny in India (Hibbert 1978; Dupuy and Dupuy 1970:858–860), the religious revolution in Iran; and the 1968 students revolts. As can be easily seen, some civil wars could be naturally classified into this category.

In all these cases, members from within the group get organized, develop distinct political consciousness, and engage in collective and direct action aimed at modifying part or all of a specific political regime. It thus should not surprise us to find that the rhetoric used in such conflicts frequently utilizes such terms as "rebel" and "traitor." Such internal conflicts, almost by definition, require the redrawing of moral boundaries and consequently redefinitions of loyalty and trust. In these situations, answering such questions as "are you with 'us' or against 'us'?" becomes a crucial issue, regardless of how that "us" is defined. Those engaged in mutiny tend to be described as "traitorous rebels" by those against whom they rise, and they are treated accordingly. From the point of view of those against whom the rebellion is directed, the rebels are indeed viewed as violating both trust and loyalty to the group by going against the status quo.

Social and political revolutions may elicit feelings and rhetoric typical of accusations of betrayal. For example, when young Jews in pre–World War II Europe joined the Zionist movement, orthodox families, from which many of them came, felt betrayed. Some even mourned their children as if they were gone. For some members of these families, the perception was that their children rebelled against tradition and violated their loyalty and trust in the "old ways" of orthodox Judaism. Unlike the Zionist revolution, insurgences need not always be successful. For example, Greenberg's 1987 work documents the successful counterinsurgency campaign (against the Communist-led peasant party) in the Philippines during 1946–1955. Success or failure of insurgences will certainly affect the relevant rhetoric of "betrayal."

The next category is similar to mutiny in that in both trust and loyalty of large numbers of individuals are violated. And in both cases, these violations are constructed differently by the betrayed and the betrayers.

State-Sponsored Terror and Human Rights Violations

Sometimes a state becomes involved in betrayals against its own individuals. When a regime is involved in executing large numbers of its own citizens, like Nazi Germany, Pol Pot and the Khmer Rouge in Cambodia, Stalin's purges and persecutions, one is tempted to invoke the term "betrayal." These regimes emerged from the same collective whose individuals it executed. The loyalty and trust of the victims in the state apparatus were thus violated in the most fundamental way. Consequently, one can use the term "betrayal of the state" in such cases.

A very close category is the use of paramilitary "death squads," such as those that existed in Brazil, South Africa, and Argentina. It can also be argued that states that violate human rights are betraying their citizens by violating their trust and loyalty. Human rights is a continuous, not discrete, variable, so the type and prevalence of those violations, as well as the context, are of crucial importance. The frequency of such violations is a genuine and worrisome issue, as various reports about violations of human rights indicate.

In all of these cases, those committing the violations have developed vocabularies of motives that help them to justify and ideologize those violations (or even ignore them; see Cohen 2000). One example is Stalin's reign of terror, when millions of Soviet citizens were accused of "counter-revolutionary" activities, of "betraying" the revolution. The victims were either deported or executed (sometimes after a mock trial and torture elicited "confessions") as "traitors" (for example, see Getty and Naumov 1999).

Another example is South Africa. Recent reports assert that during the power struggles of the 1980s within SWAPO (South West Africa People's Organization, formed in 1959 in today's Namibia to oppose South African rule), hundreds of its members were held against their will in SWAPO's camps, cruelly tortured, and interrogated on charges of betraying the organization. Thus, an organization that had the goal of releasing South Africa from the yoke of apartheid and freeing Namibia from South Africa's cruel regime directed some of its most torturous methods against its own members.[84]

States frequently justify their violations of human rights on the grounds of "security" or "public safety." They use the "ticking bomb" argument, which refers to a political situation that is extremely volatile, ready to "explode." Security agencies then make the case that in order to find, locate, and defuse the "bomb," they need to resort to methods of investigation that violate human rights (for example, torture).

Whistle-Blowing, Political Turncoating, Conversion, Strikebreaking, and Assassination

The third cell involves members of the in-group who violate the trust of, and loyalty invested in them by, other members of the in-group. The difference between this cell and the previous one, in which betrayals are committed against the general collective, lies in the level of sensitivity that these two separate cells provide. In all the cases cited here, members of the relevant group would typically regard such acts with scorn, and the violators of trust and loyalty would typically find it difficult to generate or recruit support for their actions.

Whistle-Blowing

In the early 1970s, the cargo doors of two different McDonnell Douglas DC-10's blew open in midair (in one case, causing the deaths of 350 passengers and crew members). An investigation discovered that a 1969 report that pointed out that there could be problems with that cargo door was not given to the Federal Aviation Authority.

In 1970 Ford launched a new subcompact car—the Pinto. Tests indicated that even a low-speed collision could result in a ruptured fuel tank. Having costs in mind, Ford did not change the faulty design. Despite warnings, the car went into production. By 1978, seventy-three people died in accidents resulting from Pinto fires. An engineer who warned about the faulty design was ignored and demoted, and he later resigned.

In 1986 the space shuttle Challenger was launched against warnings by a senior engineer that the seals in the rocket boosters would not hold because the temperature range was below the safety range for them. The Challenger exploded shortly after liftoff because of this problem. The engineer who revealed this fact and later testified against the management became isolated and eventually had to leave his job, and he found it difficult to acquire a new job.[85]

These dramatic cases illustrate the problems created by organizations when they fail to listen to warnings. In each case, the organization misrepresented or concealed important information. The literature on whistle-blowing is full of such cases.

At the simplest level, whistle-blowers are individuals who report to others within, or outside, an organization about various problems within the organization (incompetence, illegal and/or unethical activity, corruption, deceptive practices, etc.) in order to rectify and solve those problems. Obviously, this characterization is too broad, because organizations have quality controllers whose job is to do just that.

Whistle-blowing is characterized by the fact that key members in the organization disapprove of it. This disapproval is related to several factors; managers fear that the report may go to the "wrong people" or to the press, or it may be judged to be too harsh. Organizations tend to require full loyalty from their members and full mutual trust. A whistle-blower reveals information about an organization that contradicts the image that the organization tries to construct about itself. Moreover, whistle-blowers tend to have the trust of, and share loyalty to, the same organization. During their normal course of work they discover and acquire secrets and damaging information about the workings of that organization. Their choice at that point is to either stay loyal to the organization and keep quiet (or try to work on the problem from within the organization), or be loyal to other norms and "blow the whistle." Some decide that their genuine loyalty is to the truth, and they "blow the whistle." Managers and coworkers may view this whistle-blowing as an act of violating trust and loyalty (or as split loyalties), in other words, as an act of betrayal.

The organization sees whistle-blowing as betraying of the interests of the organization, violating the rules of hierarchy, bypassing authority, squealing, damaging the reputation of the organization, acting in a hostile manner toward the organization, poisoning the atmosphere, and supplanting cooperation with suspicion. Whistle-blowers, on the other hand, tend to justify their activities in such terms as doing one's job, being faithful to the community, revealing the truth, and doing something that is in the best interests of the organization.

Although both sides use the rhetoric of trust and loyalty, the interpretation of these terms, as well as their direction, is very different. Obviously, organizations do not like whistle-blowers. Research on whistle-blowing indicates that the road taken by whistle-blowers is difficult, with often very heavy social, psychological, and economic costs to the whistle-blower. O'Day (1974) points out that whistle-blowers risk isolation, increased criticism, defamation of character, being moved to an insignificant job, being fired, and being exposed to other degradation and harassment processes.[86] Glazer and Glazer point out that as in other cases of betrayal, one of the differentiating variables determining whether a whistle-blower will be awarded recognition and respect (and perhaps cast into the role of a cultural "hero") is whether the whistle-blower receives or generates the support of a collective of people, that is, mobilizes a significant amount of power.[87]

Because whistle-blowing is perceived by many as a "problem," many organizations (and states) have established specialized inner mechanisms that are supposed to critically examine organizations in a more or less routine manner. Organizations and state bureaucracies have created positions such as controller and ombudsman to deflect whistle-blowing. Although this may reflect a genuine desire to improve, it also coopts criticism and channels it in such a way that wrongdoing, corruption, mistakes, and the like are either ignored, buried for years in "investigations," or muddled in various conflicting and confusing "versions." The fact remains that despite these positions, whistle-blowing has not disappeared.

Some countries have instituted legal protections for whistle-blowers (for example, U.S. federal protection for whistle-blowers). The state of Israel has been trying, for quite some time, to pass legislation that would protect whistle-blowers but has encountered formidable opposition. One source of opposition has been the power of bureaucracy; there is a conflict among different authorities regarding who would be entrusted with enforcing the law. Others have expressed concern that such a law may encourage bogus complaints.[88] For example, the president of Israel, Mr. Ezer Weitzmann, stated in public that he refused to lend his support to a law that aimed to help and protect bona fide whistle-blowers because these people are "squealers."[89] Eventually, laws were amended (in 1992, 1994, and 1997) in such a way that whistle-blowers receive protection from their potential persecutors.[90] It remains to be seen how effective this legislation actually is.

Two analytical issues are associated with whistle-blowing. One is moral, and it concerns trust, loyalty, and concealment. The other issue concerns power.

Once a potential whistle-blower discovers that the organization for which he or she works is involved in such activities as sexual harassment, bullying, threats, cheating, concealment, or discrimination—conducted in a way that deceives the public and misrepresents the organization—a choice needs to be made. Either one must violate the trust relationships between the potential whistle-blower and the organization and publicly reveal the information or one must remain loyal and keep silent and try to solve the problem from within. This choice is not made in a vacuum. The issue of trust and loyalty here is much more complex, because maintaining loyalty to and trust in the organization is only one avenue among others. Loyalty to and trust in the truth, in the public interest, or in the law can easily dictate different courses of action. From the organization's point of view, there exists too a problem of who exactly the organization owes loyalty to, and what type of trust relationships exist between the organization and its environment. In addition, there are the issues of organizational misrepresentation, deception, and concealment. The problem of whistle-blowing thus involves primarily a moral dilemma centered around truth and the issues of loyalty, trust, and their violation.

However, there is another dimension involved here too—that of power. Typically, we have a powerful and resourceful organization facing a lone, powerless, and resourceless whistle-blower whose chances of coming out on top are not very promising. Studies show that in the end, power often trumps morality, as so many whistle-blowers have sadly found out.

Robinson describes five central moral features of whistle-blowing. First, there is a question of whose interests should be served (individual interests, organizational interests, or public interests). Second, lies and deception are involved in organizational cover-ups, often with profound negative consequences for the victims of those cover-ups. Third, whistle-blowers are exposed to psychological, social, and legal attempts to assassinate their character and delegitimize them. These attacks are sometimes physical, and there is a danger that the whistle-blower may slip into depression and attempt to commit suicide. Fourth, the organization receives negative exposure as corrupt or deceptive practices are revealed. Finally, what society does, or does not do, to protect whistle-blowers becomes an issue.[91]

It is imperative to point out that although whistle-blowers are frequently described as "traitors," it as just as likely that those being "whistled" about may themselves be implicated as "traitors," in the sense that they may have abused their power and position and violated the trust and loyalty invested in them. The illustrative cases with which we began this section exemplify this very well.

Political Turncoating

Politicians who are elected on the platform of one party and then change their loyalty to another party are referred to as "turncoats." Such an act involves issues of trust, loyalty, and their violation.

The term "political turncoating" connotes a negative judgment. However, like other cases of violation of trust and loyalty, these very same "turncoats" may be regarded by others as honorable, taking high risks by disregarding party politics. Turncoats may thus be viewed as loyalists (to themselves, to their principles) by one party and as traitors by other parties. Yet, it appears that most people hold loyalty to the party as the more important principle.[92] However, much depends on the context of the event.

As Leach points out, the personal experience involved in changing sides in the political arena is typically "uncomfortable and difficult."[93] It usually involves some soul-searching, new adjustments, confrontations with friends, and sometimes even a new identity and way of life. Let us examine a few illustrative cases from two countries: England and Israel.

In Hebrew, the colloquial term for political turncoating is Calanterism. In 1955 a man named Rachamim Calanter was elected to serve in the city council of Jerusalem as a representative of the National Religious Front (identified with the MAFDAL Jewish orthodox religious political party). During 1956, MAFDAL was involved in a municipal political conflict involving the authorization for a new school of archaeology in the same building where a Jewish Reformed synagogue was supposed to be built. One result of this conflict was that the MAFDAL decided to quit the municipal council coalition. That move left the municipal coalition without a majority vote. Interestingly, only one vote was required to reestablish the majority vote of the coalition. In return for promises and different favors, Calanter crossed the lines and remained in the coalition as an indepen-

dent member. Doing that meant that he left the MAFDAL, on whose list
he had originally been voted.[94]

Although quite a few politicians on the national level (for example,
Moshe Dayan), including members of the Israeli Knesset, as well as politicians on the local (mostly municipal) level, have either changed sides permanently or made such a move temporarily for specific issues without
permanently leaving their original party, Calanter was the first to do so.
His name has thus become synonymous with negative and stigmatized
political turncoating in Israel.

Leach provides a landmark study in this area. His 1995 work covered
turncoats in British politics from 1886 to the present. This is how he documents and describes some of the most famous British turncoats in his
study:

- Joseph Chamberlain, whose move from the Liberal Party to the
  Conservative Party won him the unsavory title of "archtraitor"
  and "Judas" (p. 57).
- Winston Churchill is perhaps the most famous turncoat. He "en-
  tered the Commons as a Conservative MP, crossed the floor to the
  Liberals in 1904, and eventually returned to his original party in
  1924 (effectively), providing an unusual example of a politician successfully defecting back to a party he had earlier deserted" (p. 85).
- Oswald Mosley is another famous politicians who changed sides:
  "He spent only ten years in Parliament, yet in that comparatively
  brief period sat under four labels—Conservative, Independent,
  Labour, and New Party. He was also for a time closely associated
  with the Liberals" (p. 116). Oswald Mosley also became Britain's
  most famous fascist leader. In fact, Leach states that fascism was
  the *only* ideology to which Mosley remained committed and loyal.
- Ramsay MacDonald, another famous turncoat, had a long political
  career that began in the early 1890s and ended in the mid-1930s.
  He was a member of Parliament and played a key role in the establishment and crystallization of the British Labour Party (1900), and
  he was appointed its leader more than once. In January 1924
  Britain elected its first Labour government, with MacDonald as
  prime minister. This government lasted only about nine months.
  The elections that followed spelled a major defeat for Labour. Following the May 1929 elections, MacDonald formed a new Labour-
  supported government and again became prime minister. Following the economic crisis, and faced by ministers who were not
  supportive of MacDonald's ideas, he resigned (August 24, 1931).
  The next day he formed a national government that was supported
  primarily by the Conservatives, the Liberals, and a few members

of Labour. The October 1931 elections awarded a major victory to MacDonald's coalition. This political structure lasted until 1935. However, this political "exercise" was perceived by other members of Labour as betrayal. "MacDonald occupies the prime place in the demonology of the Labour Party. Even now, over sixty years after the events of 1931, his treachery has neither been forgotten nor forgiven. Ramsay MacDonald is only remembered within the Labour Party, in so far as he is remembered at all, as the man who betrayed the movement" (p. 148).

- Enoch Powell provides "the most dramatic and sensational desertion of his party by a modern British politician" (p. 200). In 1974, he defected from the Conservative Party to the Labour Party in the middle of an election campaign, calling his followers to follow suit.
- Roy Jenkins "was an archturncoat. When he deserted the Labour Party to help found the SDP [Social Democratic Party], it involved a rendition of both his family background and his own long career in Labor politics" (p. 223) in a publicized controversy between 1979 and 1983. His desertion of Labour was "deliberate and premeditated" (p. 226) and not the result of some unexpected crisis.

The summer of 1997 saw another such turncoating by a British MP. According to *The Times*, just a few hours before the extremely popular newly elected British prime minister Tony Blair's visit to London's Uxbridge "a longtime Labor activist [announced] that he had decided to back the Tories. Michael Shrimpton, a party member since 1981, switched sides. . . . At a press conference with Lord Parkinson, the Conservative Party chairman, Mr. Shrimpton said he was 'appalled' at the way Labor had behaved since entering government."[95]

The issues Leach discusses regarding turncoating seem to be valid for similar discussions about betrayal: Where is the dividing line between genuine disagreement and passing to the opposition? When shall we call it "defection"? What are the personal costs to the turncoat? What is the impact of the defection?

Is there anything personally different about turncoats? Leach's very clear answer is negative. The issue of who becomes a turncoat, or a political defector, depends on a variety of factors, including opportunity, amount of identification with the original party, the political structure, and inducements offered. Leach points out that much of the current debate over the motivation for changing one's party loyalties is focused on a dichotomy between ambition and principle.

Political turncoating is most certainly not confined to Britain. In August 1997, Walter Felgate, one of the most important and influential leaders of the South African Zulu Inkatha Freedom Party (IFP), left his party and moved to the African National Congress (ANC). Obviously this caused much anguish, anxiety, and anger among IFP members, not to mention surprise among ANC members. Here is what Inkatha's leader, Mango-suthu Buthelezi, had to say about what was referred to as the "defection" of his former right-hand man, a person with whom he shared eighteen years of political and social activities: "This is an abject betrayal. . . . We, as human beings, had a friendship. For him to turn around and do this, it shakes right to the roots my confidence in human nature. You start wondering whom to trust."[96]

Conversion

Conversion is a category that resembles defection and desertion, but it differs in context and target. And conversion is not unlike political turn-coating. Ideological and religious conversions typically invoke the issue of betrayal.[97] A person who leaves one ideological or religious group to become committed to another stands a pretty good chance of being viewed by his or her preconversion symbolic moral universe as betraying that universe. Much depends, of course, on the manner in which this conversion is made, but the invocation of the term "betrayal" to describe that process always lurks in the background. The main reason is that members in the collective that is being left feel that the convert has betrayed their trust and loyalty. On December 13, 1999, *Newsweek* (pp. 34–35) published a report about ultra-Orthodox Jews who decide to become secular. The report was titled "Israel's New Defectors." The use of the word "defectors" is, obviously, revealing.

Basically, conversion means changing sides. There are many illustrations for conversion, some more famous and dramatic than others. Let us look at a few of them.

The Robert Hussein Affair. On July 6, 1996, *The Times*, reported on its front page:

> A Kuwaiti Islamic court has, in effect, sentenced a businessman to death for converting from Islam to Christianity, five years after Western soldiers rescued Kuwait from the clutches of Saddam Hussein.
>
> Robert Hussein, 44, has been forced to go into hiding after the court ruled that he is an apostate—a Muslim who has left the faith. . . . Mr. Hussein has been forced to move from safe house to safe house in Kuwait, his wife has been abducted and raped and forced by her family to leave him, he is forbidden to see his two children, and his building business is in ruins. . . . Mr. Hussein was sentenced on June 9 and given 28 days to appeal. . . . The court hearing lasted less than a minute and Mr. Hussein was declared an official

apostate from Islam. He is not allowed to use his passport so he cannot take refuge abroad.[98]

Although Kuwait is supposedly committed to "freedom of religion," Mr. Hussein was tried by a Shia court for apostasy, a serious crime under Sharia law.

The Jerusalem Mufti and Israeli Citizenship. The Arab Mufti of Jerusalem, Sheik Akrame Sabri, has warned, repeatedly, the Arab citizens of East Jerusalem not to take Israeli citizenship. He has stated clearly that doing so is treasonable. Sheik Sabri said that Islam did not allow Muslims to accept Israeli citizenship because they are asked to declare loyalty to the State of Israel. "Palestinians living in East Jerusalem are allowed, by law, to become Israeli citizens if they so wish. This is a direct result of the annexation of East Jerusalem to Israel in 1968. Since then and until the early 1990s very few East Jerusalem Arabs chose to become Israeli citizens. However, following the Madrid Conference in 1992, a sharp increase was recorded in the number of Palestinians asking Israeli citizenship."[99]

A similar example is that of the many Orthodox Jews in Europe whose family members converted to secular Zionism between 1925 and 1938. For many parents this conversion was a great tragedy, and many mourned their family members as if they had died.

Roger Casement. One of the better-known, and most tragic, cases of conversion, which ended with charges of treason and execution, was that of Sir Roger Casement. Born September 1, 1864, in County Dublin, Roger Casement developed an impressive and distinguished career as a British civil servant. He served as a diplomat, representing Great Britain, in such varied places as Portuguese East Africa (Mozambique 1895–1898), Angola (1898–1900), Congo Free State (1901–1904), and Brazil (1906–1911). Casement's work led him to expose the atrocities committed in the exploitation of natives by white traders in Africa (Congo) and South America (Peru). His 1904 report about the abuse of natives in the Congo won him international recognition and respect and brought about some profound changes in Belgian rule of the Congo. Casement was knighted following his 1912 report about the abuse of the natives in Peru.

Poor health forced Casement to quit his work, and he retired in Ireland in 1912. Despite a brilliant career and impeccable service to the Crown, Casement sympathized with Roman Catholic Irish nationalism. This was unusual, considering the fact that he came from a Protestant family. Pincher points out that Casement had been secretly baptized from Protestantism to Roman Catholicism, meaning that Casement experienced a religious conversion as well.[100]

It did not take long for Casement to harness his incredible abilities to the Irish cause. In 1913 he helped organize volunteers and in 1914 traveled to New York to solicit American support for an anti-British force. When World War I began in August 1914, Casement felt that it was a golden opportunity to seek German support for an independent Ireland. Specifically, he wanted to have tangible German support for anti-British activities. Casement was not a man to waste time; he immediately traveled to Berlin in November 1914. To his disappointment, German leaders made it clear that they were not going to risk an expeditionary force to Ireland. Moreover, Irish POWs refused Casement's proposal to join a brigade that he tried to organize to fight the British. He even failed to secure German minimal support for an Irish uprising planned for 1916.

Despite their refusal of Casement's proposal for a direct and forceful German intervention in Ireland, the Germans were interested in supporting the Irish national movement; Irish unrest would distract the British and divert their military resources. Thus, the Germans sent Casement back to Ireland, partly to help subdue the questionable 1916 revolt and partly to continue his agitation there. Casement made his trip to Ireland in a German U-19 submarine as a guest of its commander, Kapitanleutnant Weisbach. He landed in Tralee Bay on April 20 1916.[101] It did not take the British long to track Casement, and on April 24 he was arrested. Casement was taken to London where he was charged with treason, found guilty in court, convicted of treason on June 29, and sentenced to death. His glorious past and services to the British Empire did not do him much good, and appeals on his behalf were rejected. He was hanged on August 3, 1916, in Pentonville Prison.[102]

The contrast between the first half of his career and his end is most striking. It appears that Casement experienced conversion in two significant areas—the religious and the political. Casement was "the only Briton to be executed for espionage during World War I," and his "was the first execution in Britain for treason for more than a century."[103]

The Elli Geva Affair.   In June 1982, Israel began a military campaign in Lebanon, which included a massive invasion of ground forces into the country. In July, the Israeli military forces were circling Beirut, and politicians were debating the possibility of entering the city and occupying it. Colonel Elli Geva, a brigade commander, was outspoken in one of these discussions among the Israeli military commanders. He warned the chief of staff that such an entry was unwise. Later, in meetings with his superiors, he asked to be relieved of his command because he did not want to be one of the commanders that would order his troops to enter Beirut. Geva, however, agreed to remain in uniform as a tank driver. This did not happen. Following talks with Geva's direct commanders and political superiors, he was ordered not to return to Beirut, was fired from the army, and prevented even from having a proper farewell with his soldiers.[104] Moreover, he was refused a role, or command, in the Israeli army's reserve.[105]

Did Geva betray the trust invested in him as a commander and violate his loyalty? Many individuals feel he did and that he changed sides. By refusing to take command responsibility (but agreeing to participate in an invasion as a tank driver), his behavior could be interpreted as betraying his loyalty to his command and the trust they invested in him. The Colonel Geva who refused to order his troops to enter Beirut was not the same man as the one at the start of the war; his values were certainly changed. This is indeed a difficult case. On one hand, Geva was expected to obey orders given to him. On the other hand, he felt that orders to penetrate Beirut would cost numerous lives. He did not see the point to that, and this belief led him to state his objection. But Geva was no conscientious objector. Thus, the constructions of Geva and of his superiors are very different. He paid dearly, as his military career was shattered, and he disappeared from Israeli public life.

Strikebreaking

During the academic year 1994–1995, the senior academic staff at Israeli universities declared a full teaching strike due to a conflict over low salaries. It was the longest strike of academic staff in the history of the country, lasting seventy-six continuous days. As the strike continued, anger and feelings of frustration were building up. At the time of the strike, I was the chair of the department of sociology and anthropology, and I had to deal with all the administrative problems created by the continued strike. There really was not much one could do except wait for this labor dispute to end.

Toward the end of the strike, though no one knew at that time that the strike was going to end in one or two more weeks, one of the senior faculty members in the department—let us call him "Professor A"—asked to see me. When we met in my office, Professor A told me that he had had it with the strike. He was going to the president of Hebrew University to tell him that he personally was no longer on strike. He wanted his salary to be reinstated, and he was going to demand that the department's secretaries contact every one of his students and inform them that his classes were commencing. When I asked him whether he believed in the goals of the strike, he replied that he no longer believed that we—the strikers— could get what we wanted and that he had plans for the summer, which he did not want to be disturbed by the strike. Complying with his wish meant quite a bit of work for the administrative staff because his students had to be located (students had left campus during the strike), contacted, and told that his classes (and his classes only) were on.

I suggested that he speak to the dean of the faculty about his change of heart.[106] Despite my contempt for this despicable behavior at a very difficult moment, I felt that his wishes should be respected. He repeated his request to the dean, went to the president of Hebrew University and told him that he was a strike violator, and demanded that his salary be reinstated.[107] The departmental administrative staff made an effort to locate his students, sent them letters, and even called them. The result was that very few students came in. One must remember that the rest of Hebrew University was on full strike. Within two weeks or so, the strike ended when the Israeli state treasury agreed to respond positively to the overwhelming majority of our demands. These developments, obviously, put the treacherous behavior of Professor A in a rather ridiculous light. Moreover, he never approached anyone with an apology or stated that he was giving up the strike's economic gains.

From my point of view, one of the most interesting aspects of this situation occurred at the end of the first conversation with Professor A: He asked me to keep his request a secret. I pointed out to him that it would be utterly impossible because the dean, the president, a large administrative staff in the department, and the faculty, not to mention the students, would necessarily know about it. It was not possible to keep such an operation secret. He responded that once people learned about his behavior they would call him a "Quisling."

I was puzzled at that. I knew that Quisling was a name synonymous with treason around the days of World War II, but not more than that. Curious, I went to the library and picked up Hoidal's 1989 volume on Quisling. As I was reading it, two things occurred to me. First, Professor A was flattering himself. He had very little in common with Quisling. Although Quisling's treason is an open and difficult question, Professor A's betrayal of his colleagues, in one of their most difficult moments, was very obvious. Quisling's activities were motivated by a variety of motives, most important of which was ideological. Professor A was motivated by his egoism, his frustration, and his inability to forego his salary—two very different cases altogether. Of course, the self-aggrandizement of comparing himself to Quisling was perhaps typical of the person who breaks a strike, violates his colleagues' trust, and asks that this shameful act be kept secret. Second, it dawned on me that this issue of "treason" was well worth a study. The result of that incident is this book.

A labor strike is an interesting form of conflict. A typical strike has one group of laborers with a variety of demands facing a much smaller group of managers with different demands. A strike draws clear boundaries between "us" and "them," and each side is required to take a stand. Thus, a strike is not just a power struggle between laborers and management. The nature of the conflict is such that once the moral boundaries are drawn, a strong and emotional rhetoric emerges. The ability of both sides to achieve their goals depends, among other things, on the solidarity that each side presents. The erosion of this solidarity results in the loss of bargaining power by the collective.

Strikebreakers, obviously, are not liked or respected. Moreover, attitudes toward them differ according to whether they initially supported or opposed the strike. Breaking a strike after first consenting, like Professor A, is not viewed lightly. Breaking the solidarity of the group in this manner violates a moral code of trust and loyalty and can generate a very emotional response. This breach of moral boundaries and changing of sides justifies branding the strikebreaker as a traitor. Moreover, because a typical strike is a contest of power, a strikebreaker may tilt the balance. One of the more memorable definitions of this type of betrayal was constructed by the writer Jack London: "A strikebreaker is a traitor to his God, his country, his wife, his family, and his class."[108]

Before ending this section, a disclaimer is necessary. Strikes are meant to hurt. Without tangible threats and/or causing some damage, strikes are useless. The question remains, where is the boundary? In countries where physicians' salaries are state controlled (and paid), one must ask when does a physicians' strike become so life threatening to the population that it must be stopped? Does a teachers' strike threaten well-being and cause damage? It is possible to conceive that a strike could be so damaging that strikebreakers would be more than welcome. If this situation occurred, Jack London's "definition" would be rendered invalid. However, it must also be pointed out that deciding where the dividing line is between a legitimate strike and a strike that severely hurts the population in an intolerable fashion is itself a subject for debate between strikers and employers. The truck drivers' strike over fuel prices in Europe and England in 2000 is a good example. Drawing this line can sometimes be a difficult task.

Assassination

There is a specific form of assassination that involves betrayal in an interesting manner. It is well worth examining.[109]

The word "assassin" has an Arabic origin and refers to a particular pattern of killing that was practiced by an early Islamic Shiite religious cult called the Ismaili. The goal of the early Ismaili was to purify Islam through terrorism and killing corrupt and immoral officials.[110] The Ismailis, however, had no exclusive rights on this form of killing. There were earlier movements that used assassination as part of their struggle.

Well-known groups are the Thugs (who killed for Kali[111]) and the Sicarii (a group of Jews who practiced assassination in the Great Revolt of A.D. 66–73).[112] The order of Assassins, however, is probably the most famous of these groups.

Describing and analyzing the history of the order of Assassins has been accomplished by other scholars, and a full account of their history and activity is clearly beyond the scope of this work.[113] A brief account, however, is in order.

The death in A.D. 632 of the Islamic prophet, Mohammed, created a crisis. One result of that crisis was the creation of the caliphate, which institutionalized the Prophet's charisma. Abu Bakr became the caliph. However, there were those who disagreed and felt that Ali—the cousin and son-in-law of the Prophet—had a better and stronger claim than Abu Bakr. This particular dissenting group became known as the Shiatu Ali (Ali's party) and later as Shai. That early conflict gave birth to the most important cleavage in Islam.[114]

Around the year A.D. 760, a particular group broke away from Shiism. They called themselves Ismailis, after Ismail, son of Jafar al-Sadiq, great-grandson of Ali and Fatima. At the end of the eleventh century, a secret society of the Ismailite sect was founded in Persia by Hasan ibn al-Sabbah, who was born, at an unknown date, in the Persian city of Qumm and died in 1124. Hasan apparently traveled extensively in the Middle East, North Africa, and Egypt, winning converts. His goal was to disseminate heterodox doctrine and battle the Seljuq Empire.

Hasan needed a base, and by 1090 he had enough followers to help him conquer (1090–1091) the fortress of Alamut in the Elburz mountains (in northern Persia, south of the Caspian Sea). Alamut became the headquarters of Hasan's sect, and Hasan became known as the Old Man of the Mountain, or the Grand Master. Hasan, however, wanted to gain more converts and have more bases. He apparently felt that Islam could, and should, be purified by assassinating in a systematic way all of its major officials, whom he chose to define as corrupt. Hasan clearly aimed to unify Islam into one coherent and integrated community. Hasan and his sect thus developed the "art of assassination."

They were quite successful in spreading fear and terror (Rapoport 1984). Hasan's ruthlessness was justified on religious grounds. He chose young, intelligent, and able people, full of enthusiasm and faith. They were then trained and taught the principles of Hasan's interpretation of the faith and then sent on their deadly missions.

The groups of these young men were called Fidais. There are uncorroborated reports (traced to Marco Polo) that Hasan's young assassins at Alamut were led into a so-called garden of paradise where they consumed hashish. The purpose of this supposed ritual was to persuade the converts that paradise awaited them and that death in the course of carrying out their assassination plots would only hasten their entry to paradise. Hence the name *hashishin* became synonymous with Hasan's sect.

There are a few good reasons to suspect the validity and truthfulness of the story about the hashish consumption,[115] but the fact that it was socially constructed, told, and possibly believed created the dynamic of a self-fulfilling prophecy.

The Assassins, as they became known to the West by the Crusaders, were quite successful and gained almost full control of Syria. Because, in the Muslim context, the basis of power was personal, when a sultan, or an amir, was assassinated, his base of power disintegrated.[116] Assassinations within this cultural context were thus a powerful political and social weapon.

In the twelfth century, the Assassins were led by the last Grand Master, Rukh-al-Din Khurshah. The end of Rukh, and of the Assassins, came under the double assault of the Mongols and of the Mamluk sultan of Egypt, Baybars.

In 1256 the fortress of Alamut fell. Later, and throughout the 1270s, many other fortresses of the Assassins throughout the Middle East fell. Thousands of Assassins where killed. That was the end of the ruthless organization that had thrown an ugly shadow over the region for almost two centuries. Although the thirteenth century marked the virtual end of the Assassins as a sect, reports about them and their ideology and methods were carried into Europe by the Crusaders.[117]

The Assassins developed a policy of organized murder, which exhibited one of the most important features of political assassination: a specific target coupled with a carefully planned assassination plot. The pattern of assassination, however, was very interesting. The Assassins killed in a particularly vile manner—after they had befriended their victim.[118] Thus, an "assassin" was a person who won the trust and loyalty of his victim by deceit and then violated it in the most brutal way. This seems to qualify this form of killing as betrayal. The problem is that the "friendship" sought by the assassin was never genuine or sincere. In this respect, the assassins were like implanted spies,[119] pretending to be loyal and trustworthy members of a collective, but in fact the opposite.

One of the most famous modern illustrations of this technique is the assassination of Leon Trotsky on August 20, 1940. As Lentz points out, Ramón Mercader, disguising himself under the name of Frank Jackson, gained Trotsky's trust and loyalty and was able to breach the security of Trotsky's house near Mexico City.[120] Mercader then killed Trotsky with an alpine ax. He was caught, served twenty years in a Mexican prison, and was released in 1960. Before his death in 1978 in Havana, Cuba, he was pronounced a "hero of the Soviet Union."

As I have shown elsewhere,[121] the pattern of assassinations, cross-culturally, is such that in the majority of cases, the victim and the assassin seem to be from the same collective cultural group. However, contrary to the Assassins, in most cases, the assassin and his or her victim were not personally acquainted. Thus the issues of personal loyalty and trust, in most cases, are irrelevant.

There are many cases where people in prominent political positions were assassinated because their views were interpreted by assassins as treacherous and dangerous politically, ideologically, and/or socially. The November 4, 1995, assassination of Yitzhak Rabin in Tel Aviv is one such case (discussed in detail in Chapter 11).

Another example is the Irish politician Robert Erskine Childers. Born in England in 1870, Childers developed an interesting career as an author, a professional yachtsman, and an activist for Irish nationalism. His spy novel, *The Riddle of the Sands,* details a German plan to invade England.[122] Many take the book as a sort of a prophecy on Childers's part. Childers, opposed to anything other than republic status for Ireland, joined the Republican Army, and in the civil war in Ireland he fought against the forces of the Irish Free State. He was caught, tried, and executed by a firing squad of soldiers of the Irish Free State on November 24, 1922.[123]

Other prominent victims of political assassination include Abraham Lincoln (April 14, 1865), Irish activist Michael Collins[124] (August 22, 1922), Mohandas K. Gandhi (January 30, 1948), Rev. Dr. Martin Luther King Jr. (April 4, 1968), and Robert F. Kennedy (June 5, 1968).

Finally, there is one other form of assassination worth mentioning here, and that is tyrannicide. If a ruler is perceived to betray his own people, by violating their trust and loyalty to the point where the abuse of power becomes intolerable, subjects may resort to murder as a way of escaping oppression. This particular form of killing reminds us that betrayal can come from members of a ruling elite. Such cases as the assassinations of Julius Caesar (44 B.C.) and Caligula (A.D. 41), and the July 20, 1944, attempt on Hitler's life testify to this possibility.

Con Artistry, Private Investigation, Professional Betrayal, Surveillance, and Espionage

In the previous three parts I have discussed separately three of the cells that appear in our classificatory table. In this part, I shall discuss the final two cells together.

The first of these two cells comprises acts of betrayal committed by an outside member in such a way that the violations of trust and loyalty are aimed at the personal level. These include con artistry, private investigation, and professional betrayal.

Con Artistry

Con artists present an interesting combination of both deception and violation of trust and loyalty. In this respect, con artists are not dissimilar to implanted spies. Both engage in deception about their true identity and intentions. Contrary to implanted spies, who operate on the national level (and sometimes as industrial spies), con artists typically fall within the criminal jurisdiction. These individuals present themselves as something other than what they really are. A nonlawyer may built a front of a lawyer, a nonphysician act as a physician, a nonbroker as an honest broker, a non–real estate agent as a bona fide real estate agent. Posing as a legitimate business person, the con artist tries to trap the unsuspecting victim. The typical result of a successful (from the point of view of the con person) con game is the swindling of resources (money, property, land, or rights) from the victim. A lavishly illustrated fictional con game can be seen in the 1973 movie *The Sting*. Maurer's classic work (1940; see also 1974) provides us with further insights and illustrations into this behavior of betrayal.

Conning always involves constructing and presenting a false social reality and deceptive personal identity. The aim of doing this is to build the trust of the victim to such a degree that the he or she develops complete and full confidence in the con artist. Once that is achieved, violating the faked trust and loyalty can be accomplished. In other words, the "sting" takes place, to the miserable disadvantage of the victim. The combination of deception and the violation of unreal trust and loyalty in a criminal arena are the hallmarks of conning. Moreover, although the target of a con game may typically be a specific person, it need not be so. British tycoon Robert Maxwell showed how a con artist can fool and swindle by violating the trust and loyalty of a very large number of innocent people (more than once and in more than one country).

Conning can also be an important aspect of spying. It should not come as a surprise that Seth (1972), for example, feels that Delilah was a spy (agent provocateur in his terms) and actually betrayed Samson. The modern term for that would probably be "honey trap" (or "sex trap").[125] A contemporary example is the exposer of Israeli nuclear secrets—Mordechai Va'anunu. Va'anunu was in the process of providing the London *Sunday Times* crucial information about Israel's nuclear program. In September 1986, only a few days before the story was to be published, Va'anunu disappeared. He was trapped by either sex, or the promise of sex, offered by an attractive woman who called herself "Cindy." Va'anunu stated that on

September 24, 1986, he met "Cindy" for the first time in Leicester Square in London, and they continued to meet several more times. "Cindy" persuaded Va'anunu to leave London and come with her to Rome, supposedly to visit her sister. They left London on September 30, 1986, aboard a British Airways flight to Rome. There they were met by a man who presented himself as the friend of "Cindy's" sister and took them to a private apartment just outside Rome. There Va'anunu was attacked by two men, drugged, taken aboard a ship, and brought back to Israel to stand a trial for treason. In fact, Va'anunu was kidnapped by an Israeli secret service unit. "Cindy" was a Mossad agent, who conned Va'anunu by first building his trust in her and then violated it. She used Va'anunu's attraction to her to lure him into a fateful "honey trap."[126]

Private Investigation

Private eyes have the potential for acting like "traitors." That may happen when they present themselves as not what they actually are, trying to gain the trust and loyalty of their "target," only to violate it later and use it against that "target." In this particular respect, private eyes come very close to con artists.

Professional Betrayal

This category refers to situations where professionals betray the trust and loyalty of other individuals. Examples abound. One simple example involves therapists who take advantage of the vulnerability of their patients and have sex with them. A particularly problematic subcategory of this case involves those professionals who sexually abuse children.[127] Patients who come to therapists for support in resolving their psychological problems surely put their full trust and loyalty in these therapists. Obviously, using that relationship of loyalty and trust to gain access to sexual favors is a severe betrayal of trust. Other cases involve physicians who fail to tell their patients the true nature of their disease, fearing the patients' reactions, or physicians who perform unnecessary surgeries, or lawyers who cheat and take advantage of their clients. These issues are sometimes defined as "ethical problems" and involve a variety of relationships between professionals and their clients.

Likewise, a category of interest to academics is the potential violation of trust and loyalty between researchers and their subjects. The emphasis here is on the one-to-one, personal interactions between the parties. One such spectacular case was exposed in the spring of 1998 by British TV Channel 4. In a fascinating and moving documentary about Soviet cosmonauts Yuri Gagarin and his colleagues, it was revealed that Vladimir

Komarov, one of Gagarin's colleagues, decided to fly a spacecraft that he knew had so many design flaws that it was doomed not to return to Earth in one piece. Komarov volunteered for the mission in order to save Gagarin's life. On April 23, 1967, he went into space and waited there for his death. His last words transmitted to Earth were cursing those who sent him to his death. Following this event, Gagarin organized a campaign for the safety of pilots, which—by the way—was not welcomed by Soviet officials (see Doran and Bizony 1998:196–201).

Another illustration involves scientists who report on observations that have never been made, falsify and fabricate data, plagiarize other works, and persecute scientists with whose views they disagree.[128] Broad and Wade's 1982 book on this topic is appropriately titled *Betrayers of Truth*.

More examples involve bankers and brokers who flagrantly violate the trust given to them by their clients to embezzle money, cheat, and steal, sometimes on a colossal scale. This category is close to con artistry, except that con artists set out deliberately to con their clients and are typically involved in small-scale operations. Also, the type and quality of trust and loyalty between a patient and a professional are different than those involved in a simple criminal "con game." The betrayal of the client's trust here is obvious, and the damage to those clients can be quite devastating.

Brand's Mission.   A most dramatic and tragic case involves a rather diabolical Nazi scheme from World War II.[129] In March 1944 the Nazis invaded Hungary. Adolf Eichmann was assigned the gruesome task of murdering the 800,000 Hungarian Jews.[130] He and his group of Nazis came to Budapest and began their preparations to activate the "final solution" for Hungarian Jews.[131] The Jews in Hungary were divided into a few main groups. They were, however, aware of what the Nazis were doing to European Jews. They tried to organize help and created a "saving committee." On April 25, Eichmann called Yoel Brand, a Hungarian Jew, to his office and told him that the Nazis were willing to spare about one million Jews if the Allies would provide the *Wehrmacht* with 10,000 trucks (to be used, according to Eichmann, only on the Eastern Front), substantial amounts of tea, coffee, cocoa, soap, and an undisclosed amount of money.[132]

On May 19, Brand left Hungary (accompanied by Andor "Bandi" Grosz) with this diabolical "blood for trucks" offer and went to Turkey and from there to Syria. The plan was to present this "deal" to the British. Contrary to British promises, when Brand arrived in Syria, he was arrested by the British authorities on June 7, 1944, and sent to Cairo where he was imprisoned for three and a half months. Bowyer Bell states that the order to arrest Brand was issued by Sir Harold MacMichael, the

British high commissioner for Palestine and Transjordan. In doing this, MacMichael violated his promise to Moshe Shertok, of the Jewish Agency, that Brand would not be arrested. The explanation given by MacMichael for violating his commitment was that "it is war now."[133]

In Cairo, Brand reported that he met with British resident minister to the Middle East, Lord Moyne, to discuss Eichmann's offer and that when Moyne heard about the Nazi "offer" to release about one million Jews, he responded by saying, "How do you imagine it, Mr. Brand? What shall I do with those million Jews? Where shall I send them?"[134] Wasserstein (1982) argues that the "account" given by Brand was a propaganda fabrication and that Moyne and Brand probably never met. In any event, it is obvious that Brand felt bitterly betrayed.

However, one must observe that the role Brand played was very complicated. The debate about whether he was a pawn used by Eichmann to expedite the extermination of Hungary's Jews, or whether there really was a genuine "blood for trucks" deal, has not been entirely resolved. Wyman (1984) points out that the "deal" offered by Eichmann to Brand was probably a feeler from S.S. Reichsfuehrer Heinrich Himmler, whose hidden agenda was to find out whether a separate peace or cease-fire agreement could be worked out between Nazi Germany and the West. Regardless of how truthful Brand's report was,[135] it is obvious from his behavior and testimonies that Yoel Brand felt betrayed, bitter, and extremely angry.[136]

Brand's mission failed. The Americans were willing to enter these negotiations, if only to buy time and save Jewish lives. However, the Soviets (suspicious, as usual, about the West's intentions) and the British (expressing fears that the Nazis might "flood" them with Jewish refugees and thus delay and sabotage the war effort) were not. The result was that the British arrested Brand.[137] Beginning in May 1944, the Nazis deported about 450,000 Jews from Hungary to the death camp complex Auschwitz-Birkenau, where they were systematically gassed and cremated. That happened despite appeals from Jewish leaders to bomb (by air) the railroads leading to Auschwitz, and the camp itself. The appeals were rejected.

Karski's Mission.   The case of the Polish emissary Jan Karski is somewhat similar. Toward the end of 1942, Karski left Poland carrying some alarming messages to the West about the Nazi systematic efforts to exterminate European Jews provided by Jewish leaders in Warsaw. As a representative of the Polish underground, Karski met in July 1943 with President Roosevelt and told him what he had witnessed at Belzec, and in the fall of 1944, his information about the extermination of European Jews was published in the United States.[138] Like Brand's mission, Karski's information failed to elicit a response that was effective in altering the extermination process.

These cases are included as illustrations of professional betrayal because in each case various professionals were presented with alarming information but failed to react in an effective way. The trust and loyalty that were assumed when both Karski and Brand set on their missions were broken. Surely, a greater response could have followed their disclosures than silence and inaction.

The next cell we shall focus on is one where an outside member commits violations of trust and loyalty aimed at the collective. There are two types of betrayal in this cell: surveillance and espionage.

Surveillance

Surveillance is practiced by the military, by police, and by private investigators, and it usually refers to the close supervision of activities of specific citizens.[139] Although violating trust and loyalty are not typically involved in it, some forms of this practice may involve issues of trust, for example, when a spouse asks that his or her partner be put under surveillance without that partner's knowledge or agreement. Thus, although military surveillance does not necessarily involve violating trust or loyalty, other forms may.[140] On the abstract level, one can argue that using surveillance (for example, wiretapping) violates a general sense of trust assumed by citizens. However, when undercover cops and sting operations take place, a much more specific and concrete sense of violation of trust and loyalty is created.

An undercover agent or a sting operation is based on instilling in an unsuspecting target the false feeling that another person is from the same cultural group, is loyal, and can be trusted. Once loyalty and trust are established, they are used to trap the unsuspecting person. Thus, although the undercover agent does not betray the trust of his masters, he is violating the trust and loyalty of the deceived person.

Staples's (1997) provocative suggestion is that Western societies have experienced a shift from focusing surveillance on specific and suspected targets to a culture where everyone is a suspect. In contemporary life, we are all subjected to many types of surveillance on a routine basis. He refers to this phenomenon as the "meticulous ritual of power." Such surveillance includes being taped on video cameras in stores, gas stations, banks, schools, courts, buses, and workplaces; being recorded on audio tapes in elevators and on telephones, and being tested by polygraphs, personality tests, drug tests, genetic screening, and so forth.

Staples's observation calls attention to the fact that in modern, information-processing cultures, much information is gathered about innocent citizens, many times without their knowledge or consent. This information is gathered in formats that offer easy retrieval. Although some of this gathering of information is done for beneficial purposes (for example, personal security), it also can be used against citizens or in ways that are inappropriate and unjustified. When this happens, the issue of violating trust and loyalty is invoked in full force.

Espionage: Spies Versus Traitor-Spies

Espionage does not always involve betrayal. However, it may violate what appears to be trust, but is not. Spies who are part of the collective whose secrets they steal and pass on to others easily qualify as traitors—for example, Jonathan Pollard. Spies who are implanted by one country in another and who pretend to be genuine members of that other country, while passing its secrets to the country that sent them (the same logic would apply to industrial espionage) cannot be considered traitors. Let us look at some illustrations from Israel and elsewhere.

Israel has long been a traditional target for Soviet intelligence efforts, and many of their implanted spies have been caught and have received widespread publicity.[141] Among the more famous are the following.

Ze'ev Avni, one of the most important Soviet spies in Israel, served as an Israeli diplomat in a variety of roles but actually worked for the KGB. He was caught in 1956 and sentenced to fourteen years in prison.[142] Two other spies who were caught in the 1950s were Yitzhak Zilberman and Levi Levi. Zilberman, an engineer who worked for the metal industry in Koor Corporation and for the KGB, was caught and sentenced to nine years in prison in 1959.[143] Levi Levi was implanted as a mole in the Israeli secret service by the Polish secret services. He was caught and sentenced to ten years in prison in 1958.

The head of the KGB station in Israel during the 1980s was Alexander Lumov who was assisted in his job by his wife, Anna Alexei (who worked as a cipher clerk in the KGB station). In 1988 both defected to Israel. That defection helped to expose at least three other spies. One of them was Gregory Londin, who was drafted to the KGB in 1973 and sent as a spy to Israel. He was caught and sentenced to thirteen years in prison in 1988. Another casualty of this defection was Roman Weisfeld, who immigrated to Israel from the Soviet Union in 1980 and was caught and sentenced in 1988 to fifteen years for spying.

Alexander Redlis, who was the coach of the Israeli national ping-pong team, was drafted by the KGB in 1974 and arrived in Israel in 1979. He collected and sent information to his Soviet masters until 1988. For his services, he received thousands of dollars. In December 1996 he was sentenced to four years in prison.

Two other cases illustrate the contrast between a "spy" and a "traitor-spy." Shimeon Levison was an Israeli high-ranking officer in military intelligence who began to provide the Soviets valuable information in 1983. He became a spy out of his own free will. Clearly, Levison qualifies as a bona fide traitor. On the other hand, Anatoly Gendler, an electric engineer, was drafted by the KGB in the 1970s, sent to Israel in 1981, and caught in November 1996. Although he was paid for sending his masters valuable information for a period of fifteen years, he cannot be considered a traitor.

There have been other Soviet implanted spies in Israel, none of whom qualifies for the dubious title "traitor" because they were not bona fide members of the Israeli national collective; they just pretended to be. Two of the most famous Soviet spies in Israel—Markus Klingberg and Shabtai Kalmanovitch—are well worth mentioning.

In 1948 twenty-year-old Markus Klingberg immigrated to Israel. He developed an impressive career, achieving the rank of university professor, and served as the deputy chief of the biological institute in Nes Tziona (a short distance south of Tel Aviv). According to a variety of sources, that institute was the hub of Israeli R&D regarding biological and chemical warfare. In fact, Klingberg was a Soviet spy ("mole"). Klingberg was involved in top secret projects, and the damage caused by him to Israeli national security must have been considerable. He was caught in 1983 and sentenced to life in prison. Despite his ailing health, advanced age, and the fact that the Soviet Union no longer existed, his repeated requests in the 1990s to be allowed to live outside prison for the remaining years of his life were resisted fervently by Israeli officials. However, on September 3, 1998, the Israeli district court of Be'er Sheva finally decided that the ailing eighty-year-old Klingberg could finish his term in a house-arrest environment in Israel under very severe and limiting conditions.[144]

A KGB implanted Soviet spy was twenty-three-year-old Shabtai Kalmanovitch. He immigrated to Israel in 1987 and very quickly established himself as a "flamboyant businessman and socialite" and made successful contacts with various powerful politicians and military officers. He was caught and sentenced in 1989 to nine years in prison.[145]

It was not only the Soviets who operated spies in Israel; there has been at least in one case in which the United States operated an Israeli spy: Major Yoseph Amit.[146] He was arrested in March 1968 (about four months after Jonathan Pollard was arrested in the United States), and the Haifa district court sentenced him to twelve years in prison on charges of espionage. After seven years in prison, he was released with various restrictions.[147]

Two illustrations from the United States of traitor-spies, contrasted with an illustration of a nontraitor-spy, will conclude this section. The most famous case of espionage in recent years in the United States is probably that of the Walkers, or "family of spies," as they are sometimes referred to. Chief Warrant Officer John A. Walker Jr., his son Michael Walker, his brother Lt. Commander Arthur J. Walker, and Navy communications specialist Jerry A. Whitworth passed the Soviets top secret information probably from the 1960s until 1985, when they were caught. The damage to U.S. national security (especially to the U.S. submarine service) caused by this group of spies must have been enormous. Sontag and Drew (1998:249–250) comment that "Studeman . . . testified before a federal judge, saying that the Walkers' ring might have had 'powerful war-winning implications for the Soviet side.' And when Vitaly Yurchenko, a high-ranking KGB officer, defected in July 1985, he told the CIA that the Walker-Whitworth ring was the most important espionage victory in KGB history." John Walker received a sentence of life in prison, his son was given twenty-five years in prison, and Arthur Walker was sentenced to three life terms.[148]

The second case is that of Aldrich Ames, who as a CIA counterintelligence officer spied for nine years (1986–1994) for the Soviets and later for the Russians. His activities cost the lives of American agents and exposed numerous covert operations. Moreover, his activities corrupted the reports of CIA officers as well. Furthermore, Ames passed to his Soviet operators almost all the information that passed his desk, including information about other countries. In this way, he gave the Soviets information about Israeli agents and highly classified information about the Middle East (Yehezkeli 1998). Ames was paid an incredible sum of close to 3 million U.S. dollars for his activities. After his capture, he was sentenced to life in prison.[149]

Clearly, such spies as the Walkers, Pollard, and Ames fully qualify for the term "traitor." They were all Americans who willingly volunteered to pass secret information to another country. They all violated the trust invested in them by, and loyalty they owed to, their country.

Contrasting with these cases is the case of a nontraitor-spy who was implanted by the Soviets in the United States under a false identity. Col. Rudolf Ivanovich Abel (1903–1971) was born in Russia and served in the Red Army's unit of communication (he was fluent in English, Polish, German, Russian, and Yiddish). During World War II, he served in the Red Army's intelligence and is said to have penetrated the German *Abwehr.* During this period, he disguised himself under several different names and jobs. At the end of the war, he was a major in the NKVD (People's Commissariat of Internal Affairs, or secret police). Entering Canada illegally in 1947 under the fake name of Andrew Kayotis, he crossed the border to the United States in 1948. He established himself there, and in the mid-1950s he was working in New York City as a photographer under the name Emil R. Goldfus. In fact, he was in charge of the Soviet spy ring in the New York area and in charge of operations in North and Central America. His contacts with Moscow were made by using radio. Abel made the mistake of giving a newsboy a hollow nickel used to transmit messages, and eventually the FBI got on his trail. On June 21, 1957, the FBI arrested him. In the fall of 1957 he was tried, convicted, and sentenced to thirty years in prison. On February 10, 1962, he was exchanged for Gary Powers, the American U-2 pilot whose plane was shot down over the Soviet Union on May 1, 1960. Abel was transferred to train new intelligence operatives in the Soviet Union and was later immortalized on a Soviet stamp.[150] Abel, one of the most talented spies known, was cleverly implanted in the United States. He most certainly was not a traitor.

Summary

Chapters 2 and 3 form a continuum. In Chapter 2, I presented the main classificatory scheme for the different forms of betrayal, classified by exclusion/inclusion of membership in collectives and the nature of the target. Using these axes yields a table in which one can group different types of violations of trust and loyalty. Chapter 3 discusses each classification in the table and provides empirical illustrations.

The wealth of cases provides empirical substance to the analysis. A major goal of this book is to present a comprehensive conceptual framework in which the many different manifestations of betrayal could be made to fit. This strategy requires that we become aware of their myriad manifestations.

One immediate conclusion from the presentation thus far is that the experience of betrayal is very common. There is nothing sociologically special about betraying or being betrayed. The large number of types of betrayal makes a persuasive argument for the high prevalence of betrayal. Betrayal is characteristic of our culture.

The widespread existence of betrayal, together with its strong denunciation, indicate that a boundary game is being played here. The behavioral patterns that are referred to as "betrayals" are utilized by various cultural agents as boundary markers signifying differences between right and wrong. The social constructions of Judas Iscariot, Benedict Arnold, Nathan Hale, and Mordechai Va'anunu all illustrate this vividly.

The social construction of betrayal is a sociological tale of cultural contrasts and paradoxes. The widespread behavior of infidelity and adultery, together with the strong denunciation of it, provides a good illustration for this. Although trust and loyalty are deeply held values, their common violation indicates that cultures can absorb quite a lot of mistrust and disloyalty and still function. In other words, betrayal is not only tolerated but adds to the colorful mosaic of our cultures. Moreover, many "traitors" are crucial for continued social life—the whistle-blowers, the strikebreakers, the informers, the spies, and others.

Betrayal helps both to mark and to accentuate existing moral boundaries, but it also helps to change them—another cultural paradox. Indeed, many traitors pay a high personal price for their violation of trust and loyalty, but sometimes new social organizations and networks are created along the way.

Part Two

4

Treason

In previous chapters, we examined the different manifestations of betrayal, their constructions, and illustrative cases. One category of betrayal, however, merits special attention—treason. The issues of power, morality, and boundaries in this particular category are critically important and are also very problematic. Indeed, many researchers note that treason, perhaps like pornography, is a matter of geography. This part of the book is thus devoted to examining the nature of treason and some of its empirical manifestations.

There are some questions to consider. Were individuals who have been referred to as "guilty of treason" bona fide "traitors"? If so, in what sense? Did these particular traitors (or their actions) make a difference?

The first thing we need to do is examine the very nature of treason. This chapter is devoted to exactly this purpose. The chapters that follow in this part focus on cases.

If we look at the behavior of the different individuals identified with treason, we find that it displays both secret and nonsecret elements. For example, treason that is committed in secret tends to be identified with espionage. The issues of loyalty and trust play a major part in treason. The traitor, and the collective that is betrayed, negotiate and redefine the direction of loyalty and the meaning of trust. The very nature of treason implies that both loyalty and trust are cast, interpreted, and understood in moral terms. Power determines the end product of these negotiations.

Consequently, moral issues are involved in the construction of the "traitor" (or the "hero"). Even a brief look at such cases as Nathan Hale, Roger Casement, Benedict Arnold, Thomas More, Malinche, and Lord Haw-Haw makes this clear. Moreover, examining treason enables us to go from the personal level of interpretation to the collective level, which is a more difficult exercise in other forms of betrayal.

Characterizations of Treason

Definitions

What is our cultural understanding of the term treason?

The *Oxford English Dictionary* defines treason as "the action of betraying; betrayal of the trust undertaken by or reposed in anyone; breach of faith." The esteemed dictionary calls our attention to an important historical distinction by telling us that

> In old English law, treason was either *high treason*, an offense against the King's majesty or the safety of the commonwealth, or *petit* or *petty treason*, an offense committed against a subject. Petit treason is now punished as murder, and high treason is usually styled simply *treason*. Many acts of high treason are now treated as *treason felony*. High treason—or *treason* proper—is interpreted as the "violation by a subject of his allegiance to his sovereign or to the state (defined in England in 1350–51)."

Petit or petty treason is defined as "treason against a subject; spec. the murder of one to whom the murderer owes allegiance, as of a master by his servant, a husband by his wife, etc. Now only history."[1]

The *Encyclopaedia Hebraica* conceptualizes treason as the violation of trust of the sovereign and states that this is one of the most severe offenses in existence.[2]

The fifth edition (1993) of the *Columbia Encyclopedia* states that treason is an act of disloyalty. It points out that in the twentieth century, treason was mostly a wartime phenomenon.

The *Encyclopaedia Britannica* offers a little definitional twist stating that treason is a general name "for the crime of attacking the safety of a sovereign State or its head." Trust and loyalty are thus built into this definition. It then focuses on the different manifestations of "high treason"—for example, conceptualizing or planning the murder of a ruler; making war against the king; or killing a high official.[3]

A later edition of the *Encyclopaedia Britannica* offers a somewhat more problematic definition. It states that treason refers to "crimes against the State. Treason is the crime of betraying a nation or a sovereign by acts considered dangerous to security." It also makes a distinction between treason and sedition, pointing out that "sedition, though it may have the same ultimate effect as treason, refers generally to the offense of organizing or encouraging opposition to government in a manner (such as speech or writing) that falls short of the more dangerous offenses constituting treason."[4] Making a legal distinction between sedition and treason is significant because it allows two versions of this particular type of betrayal to exist—the harder (treason) and the softer (sedition)—and thus leaves law enforcement with discretion, that is, with potential negotiations regarding the nature of specific behaviors. If the societal definition of treason is based on defining (extending or shrinking) the nature and amount of variance associated with violations of loyalty and trust of particular citizens toward the state, then distinguishing between sedition and treason is an expression of this process. Moreover, this definition is interesting because it assumes that the "state" (or the ruler/s) cannot "betray" its citizens. Furthermore, the definition assumes that it is possible to determine the genuine nature of "security" and what is, or is not, "dangerous" to it.

The *Encyclopaedia of the Social Sciences* states that treason is "essentially a violation of allegiance to the community."[5]

Treason therefore, first and foremost, consists of a behavior that is presumed to have betrayed trust and breached faith and that presents debated loyalties. The issue, of course, is not as simple as it may appear because establishing an act of treason requires an a priori act of establishing a relationship of trust and loyalty. That type of relationship requires in turn some shared consensus regarding the nature of that trust and loyalty.

The issue of a genuine relationship is a crucial one. What if one *pretends* to be in such a relationship but really is not? What if society is so highly differentiated morally that the very concept of a value consensus becomes a problematic issue? What happens when the ruler or the organization violates trust and loyalty? In a society where loyalty is unclear, where trust is problematic, or where moral polarization is strong, treason cannot be easily defined or established. It is reasonable to expect that in such a society, some members may try to mobilize or generate enough power to socially construct and enforce definitions of treason in order to establish new, more appropriate moral boundaries.

The case of a rather famous traitor—Socrates—is illustrative here. Athenian society put Socrates on trial, found him guilty, and sentenced him to death by poisoning in 399 B.C. His crime? Voicing what was interpreted as a challenge to the state. Among other charges, Socrates was accused of corrupting the morals of the younger generation and teaching science in a way that amplified skepticism and disbelief. It was thought by Athenians that anyone involved in such activities was endangering the integrity and the safety of the state. According to Athenian law, Socrates was a criminal. The moral code of Athens did not embrace freedom of expression.

Athenian society, through the moral agents who defined its moral boundaries, condemned and executed Socrates,[6] who rationalized his activity with a very different moral justification. Socrates's prosecutors had more legitimized power, so that when the two opposing systems of morality collided, Socrates lost. In today's Western democratic societies, freedom of expression is hailed as a primary virtue. In regimes that are more totalitarian or theocratic, individuals who speak their mind or challenge the power structure are liable to find themselves imprisoned or committed to insane asylums.[7]

Threat Potential

The threat potential of treason is perceived as very great. It is magnified during periods of armed conflict (from localized clashes to full-scale war). Conflict, as Simmel (1955), Levine (1971), and Coser (1956) have noted, is a time for crystallization of internal conformity in the face of challenges to the state. During such periods, state definitions of trust and loyalty expand and harden, and what otherwise would be considered as normal activity may become defined as treason or sedition. In times of conflict, nation-states tend to increase restrictions, which also increases the temptation to violate them.

Societal Reaction

The *Encyclopaedia Britannica* points out that "the law which punishes treason is a necessary consequence of the idea of a State, and is essential to the existence of the State."[8] Ploscowe adds that treason "is the one natural crime, punishable at all times and in all types of social organization."[9] Judging by the societal reaction to treason, it is indeed one of the most serious offenses imaginable. Both Nettler and Hurst are quick to point out that treason is the only crime defined in the United States Constitution.[10] In Israel the death penalty does not exist, except in a few cases, including treason. The *Encyclopaedia Britannica* points out that punishments for treason were "barbarous in the extreme." For example, "the sentence in the case of a man was that the offender be drawn on a hurdle to the place of execution, that there he be hanged by the neck not until he be dead, and that while yet alive he be disemboweled and that then his body be divided into four quarters, the head and quarters to be at the disposal of the Crown" (women were burnt).[11]

Previous Works on Treason

Quite a few studies of treason have been conducted in the past. These tend to be divided into three categories. One category (the largest, by far) consists of works that take a particular case—for example, William Joyce, Vidkun Quisling, Tyler Kent, the French Admiral Darlan, Aldrich Ames, Benedict Arnold—and discuss it in depth.[12] The second category, and clearly the minority, consists of works that detail a relatively large number of cases, some in an almost encyclopedic manner.[13] These works typically attempt to either give readers the "who's who" in treason or make generalizations based on a relatively large pool of cases. The third category consists of works that focus in more detail on a few chosen cases, typically in specific historical periods or cultures.[14] Unfortunately, no "theory" exists in this area (except, perhaps, Boveri's bold—but unsuccessful—attempt).

Many of the authors have used the criteria of motivation in an attempt to create typologies or explanations,[15] but overall, this approach has not proven very productive in terms of bringing about generalizable conceptualizations regarding treason. Indeed, focusing on motivation must assume that treachery itself is a nonproblematic act and that there is a consensus regarding the nature, and direction, of loyalty and trust. Obviously, these are problematic issues. For example, the line dividing legitimate dissent and disloyalty is not always clear.[16]

In the rest of this section I present some of the major works on treason and their historical contexts.

John Bulloch

Bulloch's 1966 book follows a typical route. Following quite a few short descriptions of cases of treason, his main conclusions are that "there is a design, a continuity of treachery. In general, every traitor has some defect, some mental imbalance which makes him what he is" (p. 178) and that "in the years to come it will be . . . the men who believe, who will outweigh the weak and the greedy who betray their country for gain. Those who commit acts akin to treason will do so consciously and willingly, not weakly and stupidly" (p. 183). Bulloch explains this shift within the context of the cold war.

Like other authors, Bulloch is puzzled about why certain people become traitors, and he resorts to the psychology of personal motivation to explain this. He thus isolates a few reasons for treason: ideological belief, monetary gain, and social isolation. He even cites a case of treason with a homosexual background, where individuals were forced into treacherous acts.[17] His conclusion is very clear: "Traitors are usually sad men; always there is something wrong with them, some defect in their character or some lack in their personal lives, failure in their jobs or in their social adjustments" (p. 151). Bulloch's impression that "traitors are sad people" is shared, very strongly, by West in her 1964 work. Traitors may be sad people (especially those who get caught), but there are *lots* of miserable and sad people all around us and very few of them are traitors in Bulloch's sense of the term.

Moreover, Bulloch's list of motivations raises some doubts about character defects. Is ideological belief a consequence of a character defect? How about greed? To put it differently, there are many people with similar backgrounds and traits who do not become traitors.

Undoubtedly, several different personal motivations play an important part in traitorous behavior: greed, blackmail, sex, ideology, stupidity, vengeance, fear, and sensation seeking, among others. Secret intelligent services have developed quite a body of knowledge on this issue. So-called intelligence officers, whose mission is to recruit traitors, collaborators, and spies, are trained to locate the weak spots of their potential recruits and utilize them to the maximum. True, recruitment of traitors does not always occur in this way, but when it does, knowledge of what motivates individuals to act is important and practical. Individuals who were themselves involved in recruiting traitors (for example, spies) tend to view betrayal through the prism of motivation, because this is their modus operandi.

I have selected examples that illustrate the different types of motivations, in an approach similar to Bulloch's. However, I am primarily interested in the *social nature* of treason and only secondarily interested in the question of personal motivation. Some scholars have pointed out that these two are analytically inextricable. My effort to untangle the two aspects, in the form of prioritization of attention, is done for the purposes of focusing the interpretation.

Because personal motivation may reflect cultural preferences, as C. Wright Mills pointed out, the "sociological imagination" requires that we examine the "personal" within the "social." Another reason for the above prioritization is that charting the different motivations provides us with a finite set of motivations that provides a typology based on motivation.

However, it leaves open the question of why people with similar weaknesses and motivations do *not* become traitors. Thus, focusing exclusively on motivation is, in my view, an inherently flawed approach because it is incapable of providing us with a satisfactory explanation about the very nature of the phenomenon. Furthermore, beyond the specific motivations that may explain the conversion of any particular individual into a traitor, we need to understand the larger cultural and social structures that both produce and enable the very existence of these individual motivations. In other words, we need to expose the *social* basis of treason. If we are to arrive at a better understanding of treason, we must understand that it is a subcategory of the larger phenomenon of betrayal and that it is more important for us to understand the meaning of this larger category in its relevant social context.

Social life is full of conflict and contradiction. Thus the defiant and the deviant are not necessarily undersocialized peripheral misfits or rebels.

Greater emphasis on the structural and cultural dimensions of divided loyalty highlights the sociological dimension of betrayal, providing a dramatic alternative to the view that traitors have defective personalities or are just plain evil. Betrayal, in the perspective presented here, becomes understandable as an everyday cultural event. Its structure is universal, and its specific content becomes culturally and contextually meaningful.

Nigel West

Nigel West published the most recent book on treason (1995), which is almost encyclopedic in size (although his logic in selecting the specific cases is not always entirely clear). Although West is inclined toward personalized, psychological interpretations, he is keenly aware that

> Treachery and betrayal are older than the thirty pieces of silver paid to Judas, but at the end of the twentieth century they are concepts that appear increasingly subjective. Are whistle-blowers to be discouraged as selfish monomaniacs, or are they to be celebrated as protectors of valuable rights? Are defectors nothing more than selfish careerists, or are they brave martyrs defying oppression to stand on principles? In an era which has seen the political pendulum in Europe swing from totalitarianism, to democracy, and then back again to democratic socialism, and during a period when the individual can be seen to have triumphed over the state, the choices are less clear cut. So what was it that compelled the minority to try to change history? (p. 19)

Thus, West does not really offer us a conceptualization of treason, except that it is based on motivation.

Rebecca West

In 1964 Rebecca West drafted one of the classical works in the area of treason, which was republished in 1985. The first edition of her book integrated her previous journalistic reports of the trials of William Joyce and John Amery for *The New Yorker*. These two individuals faced accusations of treason at the end of World War II.[18] As West's interest in disloyalty increased, she attended other treason trials and channeled her intellectual pursuit more and more into espionage. The 1985 Penguin edition of her work has a chapter on William Joyce (Lord Haw-Haw), but the book also delves into cases of espionage after World War II, including some aspects of the cold war.

West discusses such cases as the so-called Cambridge spy ring (mentioned in Chapter 3); Emil Klaus Fuchs (a British nuclear physicist who spied for the Soviets); Julius and Ethel Rosenberg (Americans who passed information on nuclear weapons to the Soviets; both were executed in 1953); the 1961 Portland case involving five convicted British spies who gave the Soviets valuable information about underwater weapons; the 1963 John Profumo affair, which led to the resignation of British prime minister Macmillan;[19] John William Vassal, a British Admiralty clerk who was arrested in 1962 and charged with passing state secrets to the Soviets, and a host of others. Clearly, West focuses on "telling the stories" of some convicted traitors.

Her conclusions are in two areas.[20] First, she points out that the tension between public and private liberties is such that traitors may fulfill an important social function of introducing vital change into our cultures—a kind of positive mutation that helps to change the moral boundaries of society. However, West has a much stronger conclusion regarding the dangerous and socially disintegrative nonideological traitors who cannot resist the appeal of monetary rewards. She calls for a swift and unambiguous public stand against traitors. Whereas West's approach—emphasizing the personal and focusing on the cold war period—has become a sort of standard, my approach is cultural and thus conceptually different than hers.

Margaret Boveri

The next important work is Margaret Boveri's 1956 book, which also surveys a large number of cases of treason. Without explaining why, she begins her work by distinguishing among three forms of treason: (1) treason; (2) propaganda; and (3) collaboration, resistance, and secret service. This framework serves as the backbone structure of her book. Although Boveri is interested in personal motivations of betrayal, she is one of the few who actually makes a genuine attempt to examine treason from a sociological and historical perspective, and thus—theoretically speaking—her work is sounder and more interesting.

Boveri asks several interesting questions:

> Have we here had to do with random individual phenomena or has there been a common element? What is it which brings Ezra Pound and Count Stauffenberg between the covers of the same book? Have they anything in common? . . . The startling fact, however, is that when one examines their aims, their deeds, and their ideas in terms of the society which they faced, there is a remarkable degree of similarity. (p. 389)

She asserts that "treason is a necessary element in the historic development of politically organized societies. All radical political change begins with treason" (p. 13). The question is, why? Boveri's historical and sociological view tries to find out what it is about *society* that brings forth treason.

She is quick to note that treachery is, first of all, a betrayal of trust (p. 13). Her point is that although trust is essential for the functioning of societies, these very same societies become more and more bureaucratized, depersonalized, and characterized by diminishing of trust. These societies produce people who have an "atomized modern consciousness" (p. 391). Clearly, this is an argument similar to Max Weber's pessimistic view about the disenchantment of the world and to Seligman's 1997 treatise on trust. Boveri paints this development with a crude historical brush and states that this "major metamorphosis of European society" is a direct result of a development that began with the French Revolution (pp. 389–391). This logic implies that treason is expected to rise in modernity.

Boveri concludes that at the root of treason lies a revolt against "the prevailing forms of rule developed by the middle class in the nineteenth and twentieth centuries" (p. 391). She relies on one of Rebecca West's fascinating ideas in her study of treason in which West states that in two thousand years of Western civilization and history we have, in fact, done nothing more than completed a theological circle. At the time of Christ, the economic and physical misery of people were explained in theological terms. This explanation was simple, straightforward, and easily grasped by the masses. Two thousand years later, theological issues are treated as if they are economic or social problems. To Boveri's mind, traitors may indicate that people want to free themselves from being enslaved by economic and political categories of thought. Two thousand years of history have not made individuals more reasonable or rational. What traitors may represent is people's rediscovery of, and attempt to return to, their souls.

Although Boveri does not explain treason in preindustrialized cultures, she claims that if we examine what the different traitors surveyed in her book were saying, then one must come to realize that "they did not believe in 'progress' and the absolute sovereignty of reason" (p. 391). It is interesting that many of the spies for the Eastern European countries during the cold war (for example, Blunt and Philby) would probably use the term "progress" to justify their betrayals. Boveri, however, is convinced that "her" traitors "hated the power of money in daily life and the suppression of individuality involved in the average factory or office existence" (pp. 391–392). In other words, these traitors were against revolution and wanted to return to the old conservative moral ideology. She quotes Marshal Pétain, General Back, and others as supporting this idea. These traitors, she claims, presented a similar contempt toward parliamentary democracy: "Quisling wanted to abolish it. Joyce despised it. The Kreisau Circle [a group of anti-Hitler German aristocrats, including von Stauffenberg] was determined to prevent its return, at least in the Weimar form. Stauffenberg rejected the 'egalitarian fallacy.' Laval resigned from the Social Democratic Party" (p. 393).

Boveri concludes her work by stating that "eccentrics like Joyce, Quisling, and Pound were capable of seeing the world only through a blood-shot veil of romanticism" and that the traitor deviants described in her book "may themselves be the heralds of another great historical swing of the pendulum, that they may be in the vanguard of a reaction against the great heresies of the sixteenth and seventeenth centuries" (p. 398). Boveri's work powerfully illustrates the case for the romanticization of deviants and their transformation into cultural heroes.[21] Underlying Boveri's argument is one strong and valid point—the profound moral nature of violating trust.

As interesting and provocative as Boveri's theory is, its credibility is weak. Treason did not begin in the modern era. Not all (or even most) traitors fit her description as counterrevolutionaries (for example, Ozaki Hotsumi, Richard Sorge, La Malinche, the White Rose, the Cambridge Ring, Judas Iscariot, to name only a few). Whether societal trust has decreased or increased in Europe since the French Revolution is difficult to ascertain. However, the one important idea in Boveri's study is its sociological-historical perspective. Fortunately, we have at our disposal a better and more sensitive conceptual framework than the one focusing on disenchantment and bureaucratization.

There can be little doubt that Boveri's work is the most serious attempt to develop a comprehensive theoretical approach to treason. In significant ways, my work follows Boveri; I focus on the macro-sociological level, and I expand the scope of cases beyond Europe. Boveri was indeed correct in assessing that there are common elements among different cases of treason. The similarity, however, does not lie in their personal accountings. It lies with the way we conceptualize treason as deviance.

Chapman Pincher

Pincher's 1987 work excels with illustrations about spies. A large part of his work is devoted to the motivational issue—why do some people become traitors and others do not. This particular focus not only merits analytical attention but has some strong practical aspects as well. Looking at traitorous spies from a motivational point of view may give intelligence officers some tools for dealing with and recruiting such spies. Pincher, of course, is not the only author to examine the motivation of traitors as a possible explanatory principle. Both Akerstrom and Frank Hagan pursue this perspective, too.[22] The main concept Pincher proposes is MICE—that is, that traitors are motivated by Money, Ideology, Compromise, or Ego.

He points out that actual motivations are not discrete and that a complex combination of different motivations may exist. Moreover, other motivations referred to by Pincher as "the flouting of authority and disrespect for the law" may play their part as well.

Pincher provides a rather straightforward definition of treason: "an attempt to overturn the government established by law, including the activities associated with such an attempt, such as the assassination of leaders."[23] This is an interesting but quite problematic approach. On the one hand, a political interpretation given to a criminal activity can very easily, according to this definition, qualify that activity as treason. On the other hand, many cases of traitorous spies, mentioned by Pincher, would be difficult to classify as such with this definition. Such individuals as Pollard, the Walker family of spies, Ames, and Va'anunu would hardly qualify as traitors under his definition. A third problem is his insistence on "government by law." Many dictators, some with horrendous records, would qualify under this definition. Do individuals who go against them qualify as traitors? This leads to another problematic issue. According to Pincher's definition, the activities of an opposition, any opposition, to any government established by any law, can be easily portrayed as being treason.

Pincher frames treason within loyalty but adds that a "traitor's basic role is to betray trust."[24] Distinguishing between major and minor violations of loyalty, he concludes that one major criterion of treason is the damage it causes. Damage he measures by the length of the treason, the time context (during times of war or peace), how many (or whether any) individuals died as a result of the treachery, and the threat to the regime.[25] Although not explicit in his analysis, Pincher does point out that secrecy is an important issue.

Carl J. Friedrich

Friedrich discusses treason within a more general discussion of what he refers to as "the pathology of politics." Examining a variety of such phenomena as violence, corruption, secrecy, propaganda, and betrayal, Friedrich explores the negative and positive functions of the existence of such phenomena. He points out that the legal definitions of treason can be easily expanded to generate an understanding that betrayal "consists of supporting a rival organization, giving aid, whether material or other" and that "treason is basically a violation of trust."[26] Like others before and after him, Friedrich makes the motivational issue a central one and details various motivations to commit betrayal and treason: conflict of loyalties; ideological commitment; homelessness and alienation; and persecution and exploitation of minorities. He does mention that the desire for enrichment can serve as a cause, too (but he omits sex).

However, he is more interested in political forms of treason and, consequently, distinguishes five types of treason: (1) a situation where old values clash with new ones; (2) revolutionary treason; (3) involvement with an external enemy; (4) disregarding orders of a regime; and (5) involuntary treason, when a regime acts in a treasonous way.[27] Friedrich points out that betrayal and treason are not necessarily bad and may actually have a positive function. Like Boveri, he states that these acts may lead the way for crucial and important changes. The July 20, 1944, plot to kill Hitler is one example, and the resistance to the Vietnam War is another. Betrayal, argues Friedrich, like other forms of political pathologies such as violence, corruption, secrecy, and propaganda, facilitates "the adaptation of a system or regime to changing conditions occurring either in the system or in the social substructure, or in the outside environment." These phenomena are "interdependent"; for example, if violence increases, so will treason.[28]

Friedrich seems to limit his characterization of betrayal to cases where secrecy is involved. Inevitably, this particular characterization forces him to delve into cases of espionage. He thus states that the "betrayal of military secrets is the very core of . . . treason"[29] and that "the lure of secrecy consists for the possessor of a secret partly in the possibility of betraying it."[30]

Gwynn Nettler

Nettler's unusual work focuses on treason from the perspective of criminology. Like Friedrich, Nettler directly associates treason with deception and adds that the very idea of treason is based on "the necessity of self-defense" because "loyalty is a necessity of social life."[31] He argues that treason (and related threats to a state's security) is usually a crime of deceit because "perpetrators pretend to be what they are not and they conceal from some associates what they are."[32]

Like Friedrich's work, this approach tends to limit Nettler's analysis to cases of secret betrayal, mostly in the areas of espionage, sabotage, and sedition, but there are several cases it cannot explain, such as Quisling, Pétain, Malinche, and Degrelle, among others. It is no wonder that Nettler feels comfortable with the legal definitions of treason. His discussion takes these definitions as a cornerstone.[33] Overall, although Nettler is one of the few criminologists (or sociologists) who has paid attention to the topic, his work does not really offer us an "explanation" for treason but rather focuses on the legal definition, on which he expands his discussion.

Treason in the United States: Authors and History

There are a few works that focus their attention on treason in the United States. Whereas Bakeless's 1998 work focuses on espionage in the American Revolution, O'Toole's 1991 work targets the history of American intelligence, espionage, and covert action from the days of the American Revolution to 1962. The title of O'Toole's impressive work is *Honorable Treachery*. Rich in historical accounts, O'Toole's work avoids an analytical framework. These two works are representative of most works about treason in the United States; they rely on historical description of various cases to "explain" treason. The meticulous work of Weyl (1950) and the outstanding book by Archer (1971) are also devoted to treason in the United States, and both also use a historical perspective. Archer's work focuses on the distinction between dissent and disloyalty as the major criterion differentiating traitors from others, whereas Weyl is more concerned with a very detailed analysis of particular cases of treason. They both begin their review of American treason in the colonial period, starting with the case of Nathaniel Bacon, who attacked and burned Jamestown in 1676.[34] In surveying some of the important cases of treason in the United States, I have adopted the historical perspective used by these authors.

As the colonies were breaking away from the British yoke and seeking independence, charges of treason were flying in all directions. Such a major conflict required loyalties to be defined and trust to be established. In fact, the Declaration of Independence on July 4, 1776, could be viewed as "the ultimate act of treason."[35] Indeed, within two years, Americans had a national definition for treason, and the the Constitution (ratified on September 13, 1788) included the definition of treason, the only crime defined in the Constitution. As the American War of Independence continued, the list of traitors grew, and a few seem to stand salient in that dishonorable list: Ethan Allen, who after being released from a British jail, negotiated a proposal to make Vermont a Canadian province, which led several congressmen to demand that he be arrested for treason;[36] Benedict Arnold (discussed in Chapter 2) sold valuable military intelligence to the British; and Aaron Burr, an American vice president, negotiated with the British to split Louisiana for a hefty amount of money and conspired to become an emperor of parts of Louisiana and Spanish Mexico (and, perhaps, later have Mississippi join too). Burr was eventually caught in Alabama and brought to Richmond, Virginia, to face charges of treason. The jury found Burr not guilty (and returned a similar verdict on other charges). Later historical work revealed that, indeed, Burr was conspiring against the United States and that he was "without doubt, America's most brilliant traitor."[37]

The breaking away of the colonies from England created difficult questions of loyalty and trust, and conspiracy and treason accompanied the transition to independence. Various individuals and groups had different national visions for the future, not to mention their own personal dreams and expectations.

The War of 1812 brought, again, the issue of treason to the forefront. For example, the connections that remained between Rhode Island and England created new issues of loyalty and trust, and similar questions were raised when President Polk went to war with Mexico over the disputed area between the Nueces river and Rio Grande river. There was so much opposition to this war, that the issue of dissent versus disloyalty was the focus of some rather hot debates.[38]

That conflict was barely finished when the United States faced a new challenge: the Mormon rebellion of the 1850s, which is viewed by both Archer and Weyl as an act of treason. Against charges of being disloyal to the country and practicing polygamy, groups of Mormons rebelled and resisted cooperation and unity with the United States, which showed a great deal of intolerance toward this religious group. Eventually, a political settlement was reached, luckily almost bloodless. Clearly, this conflict concerned differing ideas about acceptable lifestyles and values within the United States.[39]

Another rebellion was headed by John Brown from Kansas, an abolitionist who wanted to create an independent republic of fugitive slaves. In an effort to create a slave uprising, Brown led twenty-one followers (among them were four blacks) in an attack on a federal arsenal on October 16, 1859, at Harper's Ferry, Virginia. The rebels were successful in capturing the arsenal and rounding up sixty citizens as hostages but inadvertently killed the mayor of the town. The rebellion was suppressed quickly, Brown was brought to trial on charges of treason and conspiracy, found guilty, and executed by hanging on December 2, 1859.[40]

Much like the period of the American Revolution and the War of 1812, the period of the Civil War had its share of treason and betrayal. How could it not? The justification for the assassination of President Lincoln was in exactly such a context. Famous traitors, spies, and dissenters on the edge of being considered traitors of the period included Rose Greenhow (who passed secret military information about federal plans to attack the Confederate Army), Belle Boyd (who spied for the Confederacy), Clement L. Vallandigan (who opposed the Civil War and tried to involve the French in an attempt to stop it), and Lambdin P. Milligan (who helped the Confederacy military effort).[41]

Klement's 1984 historical work provides an interesting and sardonic account about secret political societies, conspiracies, and treason trials around the period of the American Civil War. His thoughtful work recreates the out-of-control atmosphere nourished by the military clash, accompanied by political intrigues and some bizarre personalities, all helping to create imaginary conspiracies and rumors, which, in turn, solidify into a social reality where treason trials take place. The author shows how a rumor can be made into an accusation of treason by some rather shabby characters. Let us look at an example.[42]

In 1864, rumors were created that Confederate supporters in southern Canada were involved in a plot to create an uprising in Camp Douglas (a POW camp where more than 8,000 Confederate prisoners were detained), free Confederate prisoners, burn Chicago, and incite an uprising in the Midwest. Quite a fantastic scheme. Nevertheless, some individuals were actually suspected of being involved in this imaginary treacherous plot. As Klement points out: "It was a rather strange turn of events. . . . The 'great conspiracy' was based upon flimsy and questionable evidence that no civil court would have found acceptable. . . . It was a fantasy passed off as fact, a travesty of justice, a political stratagem made respectable by historians."[43]

At the beginning of the twentieth century, labor disputes were the locus of insinuations of treason. Quite a few American industrialists and capitalists defined the various expressions of rising consciousness among laborers as a potential threat to, and betrayal of, free enterprise. On the other hand, laborers who seemed to side with employers, or strikebreakers, were defined as violating trust and loyalty.[44] This period ended when World War I began (1914).

Like other wars, World War I left its legacy in the area of betrayal. Some labor activists were accused of treason. For example, Tom Mooney and Warren Billings were charged with exploding bombs in a crowded street corner on July 22, 1916. Although sentenced to death in a trial that began in 1917, they were not executed; and they continued to insist on their innocence. They were finally released from prison in January and October 1939, respectively. They had spent twenty-two years in prison for a crime they did not commit.[45] Eugene V. Debs never hid his opposition to the war and made no secret of his sympathies for Mooney and Billings. He was arrested and sentenced to ten years in prison and deprived of his citizenship. Debs ran as a socialist candidate for the U.S. presidency in 1920, from his prison cell, and attracted about 1 million votes. President Woodrow Wilson, in reference to Debs's objection to the U.S. involvement in the war, stated, "This man was a traitor to his country."[46]

Other socialist leaders, activists, and pacifists were charged with interfering with the war effort. Anti-British activists were treated in a similar fashion (for example, Jeremiah O'Leary, who was indicted for a "conspiracy to commit treason").[47] It is nevertheless true that German agents were active in the United States in an attempt to mobilize support for Germany and were involved in espionage and sabotage. Weyl estimates that German saboteurs may have been able to damage as much as $200 million worth of war materials, ships, manufacturing plants, and high explosives.[48]

Between the end of World War I and the beginning of World War II, there was intensive pro-Nazi activity in the United States. The goal, at the minimum, was to discourage the United States from joining the war in Europe. A small minority of Americans, some overtly anti-Semitic, thought that fascism and Nazism were the "in thing" and felt obligated to support it, even to the point of creating a Nazi-like political and social movement and organizations. One example is German-born Fritz Kuhn, self-appointed führer of the German-American Bund. His organization managed to attract around 8,000 members to its anti-Semitic and Nazi activities. Kuhn was convicted of embezzlement and forgery in 1940 and sent to prison.

Some other Americans were charged with sedition and with attempts to establish a fascist government in the United States. Some of the more famous propagandists for the Nazi ideology included Mrs. Lois de Lafayette Washburn, who believed that "the Jews" were after her and wanted to sell her into white slavery; Mrs. Elizabeth Dilling, the only American woman who was indicted on three successive occasions for seditious conspiracy against her country and who organized political rallies against the Lend-Lease Act; and Miss Catherine Curtis and Miss Laura Ingalls, who lobbied for the Nazis (Miss Ingalls was actually paid by the German embassy for her services). In her trial, Miss Ingalls, like so many others accused of treason before and after her, told the court: "My motives were born of a burning patriotism and a high idealism. . . . I am a truer patriot than those who convicted me!"[49] Other famous figures were pro-fascist Father Charles Coughlin, who preached endlessly against the Jews and for fascism both on the radio and in his newspaper (*Social Justice*); Gerald L. K. Smith, an ex-pastor who left the pulpit to preach the hatred of fascism and alignment with the Nazi führer, together with Huey Long, William Dudley Pelley (who felt that it was time for the United States to have a Hitler and a pogrom), Francis E. Townsend, and Congressman William Lemke.

While World War II was dragging on in Europe, the United States was getting close to entering the war. In fact, on July 2, 1941, a Washington grand jury convened and for the following fifteen months inquired into the fascist and Nazi activities in the United States. These activities culminated in charges, accusations, trials, and sentences against a number of individuals.[50] A total of 9,405 Axis agents were arrested and brought to trial as a result of these investigations.[51] It is interesting in this context to point out Henry Ford's sympathies with Germany.[52] The chief, and most famous, Nazi agent in the United States prior to its entry into World War II was undoubtedly George Sylvester Viereck. He was instrumental in distributing Nazi propaganda and in promoting an isolationist ideology. Viereck was assisted by another crusader for fascism—Lawrence Dennis (who worked for the state department for seven years) and by Mrs. Leslie Fry, another paid Nazi agent.[53]

One interesting and dramatic Nazi operation that involved violating trust and loyalty, and which resulted in treason trials, took place in June 1942. On June 12, Kapitanleutnant Hans-Heinz Linder, commanding U-202, landed four Nazi agents and four crates of explosives off the eastern end of Long Island near Amagansett using rubber boats. Four days later, on June 16, Kapitanleutnant Joachim Deecke, commanding U-584, used inflatable rubber boats and landed four Nazi agents with explosives at Ponte Vedra Beach, seven miles south of Jacksonville, Florida. In all, eight *Abwehr* Nazi saboteurs, with plenty of explosives, were on American soil. Fortunately for the Americans, this mission of destruction failed. Georg Dasch, who led the group that landed in Long Island and who despised Hitler and Nazism, talked another man into turning himself in, and they betrayed the rest of the group (as well as those who sent him). He contacted the FBI and they surrendered on June 18. Within twenty-four hours his group was in the hands of the FBI, and on June 23 the leader of the other group (Edward Kerling) was captured and the rest were caught on June 27. Some of these eight saboteurs had relatives and friends in the United States, and fourteen such people were arrested, too. One of the saboteurs, Herbert Haupt, was raised in Chicago by a pro-German family. Of the eight saboteurs, six were found guilty of wartime espionage and were executed on August 8, and two received long sentences in jail. Ten of the American relatives and friends who were found guilty of helping the saboteurs, and thus violating their loyalty to the United States as well as the trust of their country, received prison sentences.[54]

However, pro-Nazi individuals and groups were not the only agitators in the United States; agitators for the Left were trying to turn the United States toward communism.[55]

One of the most fascinating cases of treason in that period was that of Robert Jordan, a Harlem self-styled "black führer" who suggested that if black Americans wanted a better future, they had better support, and fight on, the Japanese side.[56]

After the end of World War II, issues of treason were raised in the context of the cold war, the McCarthy persecutions,[57] and again, with much power and forcefulness, during the Vietnam War. Unlike previous wars, this very controversial conflict divided Americans and blurred the boundaries of betrayal and treason.[58]

Archer's main analytic thrust is to contrast disloyalty with dissent. He warns that governments should not equate political opposition with treason, "since today's Government policies may be proved to be wrong tomorrow and changed around completely" (p. 179). "National unity is hardly helped when Government spokesmen attack dissenters as unpatriotic or traitorous" (p. 183). This issue is indeed an important one, but difficult to resolve, because in specific cases the boundary between dissent and disloyalty is often blurred. Appropriately enough, Archer ends his book with a quote from Voltaire: "I disapprove of what you say, but I will defend to the death your right to say it" (p. 185).

Weyl 1950's work raises similar issues. His immense historical review leads him to conclude that major political and military crises tend to be accompanied by a variety of forms of betrayal. He points out that those branded traitors are not always monsters but often true believers. Dissent tends to be, and typically is, regarded as disloyalty and traitorous in dictatorial regimes whose tolerance is nonexistent or very severely limited. Struggling against tyranny is often cast by the tyrants into the language of treason. Democracy, states Weyl, must act differently and allow its citizens the freedom to dissent. However, even democracy must face such issues as aiding its enemies, nationalism, and—Weyl points out—treason against democracy itself, that is, the betrayal of human freedom.

Treason in England: Authors and History

Treason and the history of England almost seem to go hand in hand. Indeed, the topic of treason is very much part of the atmosphere in London. There is the "Traitor's Gate" at the Tower of London, shown to curious visitors. A visit to London's Dungeons, not too far south across the Thames, reveals the stories of other famous traitors, this time in a rather graphic fashion (as does the nearby Clink exhibition). The history of the United Kingdom thus provides us with a large number of cases of treason, some of which are included in Wharam's 1995 work.

A few English cases involving treason (or suspicion of treason) became known worldwide as a result of very famous movies made about them. An outstanding movie about the conflict between King Henry II and Becket is the superbly acted 1964 movie *Becket*, starring Peter O'Toole as King Henry II and Richard Burton as the doomed archbishop of Canterbury, Thomas Becket. Becket, who served under Henry II as archbishop of Canterbury, had a long and bitter dispute with the king, as a result of which he fled England and lived for six years in exile. When Becket returned to England, the old conflict was renewed, and Becket was murdered by four knights in Canterbury Cathedral on December 29, 1170. Becket was canonized in 1173 by Pope Alexander III.

The Thomas More affair was the axis of two very good movies, both named *A Man for All Seasons*. The first was made in 1966 with Paul Scofield playing More. This splendid version won six Oscar awards. A second production was made for television in 1988, starring Charlton Heston as More. More, in a famous conflict with Henry VIII, refused to accept the king as the head of the Church of England. He was charged with treason in what has become one of the most famous treason trials, found guilty, and beheaded in the Tower of London on July 6, 1535. He was canonized in 1935. More, no doubt, was one of the best-known and well-respected statesmen, scholars, and humanists of his time, and perhaps one of the greatest of all times.[59] Another movie involving King Henry VIII (and Cardinal Wolsley) is *Anne of the Thousand Days* (1969), starring Genevieve Bujold as Anne Boleyn and Richard Burton as King Henry VIII.[60] That movie, too, raised issues of loyalty to, and trust in, the monarchy and clergy. Finally, a more recent movie about treason is *Braveheart* (1995), starring Mel Gibson as William Wallace, the legendary fourteenth-century Scottish rebel warrior who led Scots during the first years of their rebellion against British rule. He was captured and was executed (actually, publicly tortured to death) as a traitor on August 23, 1305, in London.[61] The movie won five Oscar awards.

Several books have been written on people defined as traitors in the United Kingdom.[62] Wharam's 1995 work, which is quite legalistic, is one of them. It focuses on eleven famous English treason trials, from the Essex Rebellion (1601) to the trial of William Joyce (1945). Like O'Toole's 1991 work, Wharam's is rich with detail (although not as comprehensive as O'Toole's), and it offers a technical unifying framework—the law—according to which the different trials were carried out.[63]

Weale's 1994 work is focused on British traitors in World War II. He concludes:

> There is a pervasive air of unreality surrounding the story of the British renegades of World War Two. It is difficult to see how even the most intelligent and best educated of them . . . could possibly believe that what they were doing was, as they claimed to believe at the time, in the best interests of Britain. . . .
>
> The common denominator if there is one, which was shared by the renegades and their immediate sponsors, was their utterly unrealistic view of the world, whether out of simple stupidity . . . or for more complex psychological reasons. (pp. 197–198)

And yet Weale's work itself reveals the ideological basis behind some of the more famous renegades (for example, Amery, Joyce, Bailly-Stewart) and a few others. In fact, the Nazis searched for British sympathizers (not to mention anti-Semites) to help their cause. What is so strange, or warped, in the worldview of an ideologist? Perhaps from a Western, democratic contemporary perspective ideological commitment seems "unrealistic," even bizarre, but it only accentuates the strength of that ideological commitment. However, when this explanation falls short, there are always those "complex psychological reasons."

Motivation keeps coming up again and again as an organizing principle. It is indeed an interesting concept. Theoretically, if we were to take all
known cases of treason and classify them according to the motivation of
the traitors involved, we would certainly create an interesting list, perhaps not much different from similar classificatory lists of motivations for
espionage.[64] As important as motivation is, it alone cannot explain treason. To find a more satisfying interpretation, we have to look at social interactions and institutions.

Preceding Weale's 1994 work, Seth's 1973 research focused on the efforts
by the Nazis (aided, to a large degree, by turncoat John Amery) to persuade British and Commonwealth POWs under German control to join
the war effort on the Nazi side and become part of the Nazi *Wehrmacht*.
The name given to this potential force was the British Legion of St. George,
later known simply as the British Free Corps. Although the Nazis controlled several hundred thousand POWs, fewer than a hundred agreed to
participate in the British Free Corps. Thus, this attempt to persuade a mass
of individuals to violate their loyalty to, and the trust invested in them by,
their country simply failed.

There were quite a few famous cases of betrayal in Britain during the
the cold war, especially espionage. As Britain moved from World War II
to the cold war, there occurred a sociological shift from public and open
dissent (on the borderline of betrayal) to secret and deceptive betrayal.

Although English history is full of anecdotes and accounts of betrayal,
other countries have their share, too. Klement's 1984 work, mentioned
earlier, describes how the American Civil War period was characterized
by heightened consciousness of conspiracy and treason. During major
conflicts, issues of loyalty and trust become paramount. Tolerance for dissidence, deviance, and complex moral stands is almost impossible to sus-
tain. Charges of disloyalty and treason can be effective symbolic tools in
the hands of determined leaders in campaigns to redefine moral boundaries and bolster their own agendas. During conflict, the boundaries between patriotism and treason, between loyalty and betrayal, become
clearly delineated; rhetoric creates a social reality where good is pitted
against evil, with no middle ground. Although Klement focuses on the
American Civil War, he cites other cases that support this historical generalization.[65] Similar situations occurred during the McCarthy witch-hunt
against American Communists in the 1950s, the Stalinist purges and persecutions of the 1930s,[66] and the 1490–1650 European witch-hunts.[67]

The generalization we can make here is that in times of crisis and social
change, various moral entrepreneurs will try to take advantage of the
fluid, confused, and uncertain situation to redefine the moral boundaries
of the culture. Their success depends on several factors, chief among
which is their ability to generate, mobilize, and use power.

Focusing on Treason

Although betrayal on the personal level is an interesting topic, one about which numerous novels have been written, our main interest lies with betrayal on the national, state, collective, or organizational level. The main reason is that the two elements so important for our understanding of deviance—morality and power—are very salient there. These elements offer us a way to understand treason.

Treason implies violating one's commitment, trust, and loyalty to a particular symbolic moral universe characterizing a collective. This violation is conceptualized as an almost universal "crime" and is severely punished by most cultures.[68] Treason is thus invoked when an obligation of allegiance (expressed in terms of trust and loyalty) to a particular social (and moral) order exists on the individual level and when an intention to violate that obligation exists, which is duly followed by relevant action.[69] Committing an act of betrayal requires making a moral decision. It means that at least two different behavior options exist and that one of them is defined as immoral and treacherous. This is an important point. In many cases of national or collective treason, the moral choice is not very clear because one may feel loyal to an idea or to a political, social, or moral system different than the one in which that individual lives. Sometimes, these two are mutually antagonistic.

Violating one's trust and loyalty to a national collective, a state, a state organization, or ruler/s will clearly invoke a societal reaction in the form of an accusation in treason. What makes one choice treacherous and another not? The crucial variable here is power—the power of those making the cultural interpretation of a specific behavior to mean that it violates trust and loyalty in the form of "treachery." Thus, the successful definition (that is, the one that is both accepted and serves as a basis for action) of any specific person as a traitor is limited to a particular configuration of power and morality. Change that configuration and a different interpretation will emerge.

Lord Haw-Haw (William Joyce), executed by the British as a traitor, was highly respected and esteemed by Nazi Germany. Likewise, members of the White Rose, executed by Nazi Germany as traitors, were highly respected by the non-Nazi world. Josephus Flavius, respected by the Romans, has been considered an archetypical traitor by many Jews. It is precisely this quality of betrayal that is so interesting and worthy of examining.

This quality of betrayal raises another issue that is relevant to contemporary public discourse. When two or more political or ideological points of view clash, the risk of a particular choice running into cultural interpretations that may define that choice as treacherous is significant. Indeed, when definitions of treason emphasize that it violates "allegiance to the community," the assumption that the nature of this "allegiance" is nonproblematic needs to be challenged.

The Structure and Content of Treason:
A Summary

It is a common observation that treason lies in the eyes of the beholder and that there is no such thing as genuine or authentic treason. Indeed, the specific *content* of treason may not be universal. In this sense, what is defined by some as treason can be defined by others as heroism. The reason for this is that the sociological *structure* of treason is genuine and universal, although it is possible to fill this universal structure with different contents.

Treason is based on a social construction of reality, which is what makes this type of social interaction culturally meaningful. This particular social construction is based on the violation of two specific forms of social relationship, which are typically referred to as trust and loyalty. As pointed out earlier, trust and loyalty characterize the personal and as well as the collective, national, and even international levels.

Violations of trust and loyalty on the personal level are commonly referred to as "betrayal" and on the collective or national level as "treason." Both betrayal and treason often necessitate deceptive behavior and language (for example, concealing, lying) on the part of those involved in these relationships. Moreover, the wide variety of behaviors involved in treason may lead us to conclude that the very category of treason covers qualitatively different behaviors. We shall see that it is not too difficult to deconstruct the different cases of treason to their basic assumptions and facts. Once that is done, the contextual meaning of treason becomes inherently problematic.

Strange as it may perhaps sound, betrayal on the personal level is much less problematic, easier to establish, and clearer to interpret. For example, marriage typically means sexual exclusivity. Violating that is interpreted as betrayal, adultery, cheating, and so forth. It is not difficult to determine who is committing the adultery and who is hurt by this behavior. The violation of trust and loyalty in such cases is obvious. But treason is more difficult to interpret. And yet various manifestations of treason reveal a solid underlying structure.

The structure that defines treason is the violation of trust and loyalty between bona fide members of a national collective. Trust and loyalty and their various violations (including treason) constitute genuine and universal structures. However, the content of what exactly constitutes trust, as well as the direction of loyalty, in specified groups and cultures may vary considerably.

Approaching the Problem

The genuinely important elements of this work are the principles of organization, that is, examining betrayal as a particular form of deviance structured along the violations of the values and norms of trust and loyalty, and classified by the relations of those defined as traitors to the collective or dyad. Once these principles are established, cases can be interpreted within them.

Of course, we cannot discuss treason without context. Some illustrations must be brought in. Good sociology, in my view, involves interesting and instructive puzzles and tales. Although the specific tales of treachery are interesting, I am much more interested in the possible conceptualizations and generalizations that can be drawn from such tales. Rather than focusing on one particular case or building an encyclopedia of treachery, I shall focus in a historical and cross-cultural perspective on several cases and will generate and support exactly those understandings mentioned above.

In producing this work I was faced with the classical problem of historical research, that of selection. Which cases to select? I decided to select the more famous cases, from several cultures, and from specific periods. Clearly, periods of unrest and cultures undergoing profound social and political changes are good places to look for cases of treason. Hence, in the next few chapters I present what I hope are quite a few interesting accounts about specific cases of treason.

In doing this part of the work, I became acutely aware of Anthony Glees's review (in the *Times Literary Supplement*) of Nigel West's 1995 book on treason. Having reviewed West's large encyclopedic volume, Glees notes, exasperatedly, "By the end of the book we are no wiser about the nature of treachery than we were at the beginning."[70] I hope that by the end of this book, the reader will be wiser and will achieve some powerful and practical generalizable insights about the nature of treason, as well as its structure and various manifestations.

Moreover, the study of treason, as one particular manifestation of betrayal, can furnish some very fundamental insights into the character of social order, trust, loyalty, and the assumptions that underpin them all. Faithful to contextual constructionism, examining treason by examining its basic nature, its different empirical manifestations, and the ways in which it is constructed and charged with meaning in a variety of contexts yields valuable insights into the nature of appearances, mirrors, and masks,[71] and how actual behavior contrasts with social constructions.

Violating Trust and Loyalty During World War II: Part 1

The 1939–1945 period of World War II provides a fascinatingly rich time slot within which to examine cases of treason and other forms of betrayal.[1] World War II is particularly interesting, especially the European theater, because at least four different symbolic moral universes clashed there. The first was communism, the second was fascism and Nazism, the third was the older monarchic societies (for example, Yugoslavia), and the fourth was democracies. Each of these politically defined symbolic moral universes represented different cultural worldviews regarding almost every aspect of human life. Moreover, the clash among these symbolic moral universes was fierce, costing the lives of millions of individuals. Power, including the power to annihilate entire ethnic groups, was very prominent.

Thus, this was a period when one master system of governing was supported over another. Such a major change on the cultural level necessarily translates to the individual level in terms of such defining personal characteristics as biographies, worldviews, and identities. This historical conflict provides us with a structure within which cases of betrayal unfold. Such structures may be typical of conflicts like World War II. Retrospectively, and in most people's minds, that was the last war where it was clear who fought who and why—what many have referred to as a "just war," where good and evil were clearly delineated. This perception becomes especially sharp when one examines the conflict between Nazi Germany and the Allies. That is, trust and loyalty were sharply defined. In reality, the picture was sometimes less clear. What better place and time to look for betrayal? In the following pages, we shall examine several different cases of betrayal in World War II.

World War II raised the issues of loyalty, trust, and deceit, on both the personal and national levels, to a magnitude and intensity not frequently found in other historical periods. We will be examining the issue of betrayal in different countries, but it must be remembered that personal betrayal was also an issue, for example, the betrayal of Jews hiding from the Nazis.

One famous case involves what may have been the worst traitor of World War II—Harold (Pole) Cole. When the war began, Cole deserted the British Army and aligned with the Nazis. Although British intelligence thought he was helping to save the lives of Allied pilots who parachuted into occupied Europe, he was actually betraying many of them to the Germans. He was also effective in betraying other Allied agents. As the war progressed, he joined the Americans and helped them hunt down his previous German masters. Cole was shot and killed on January 9, 1946, in a shoot-out with the French police in Paris. Amazingly, among the people he betrayed to the Nazis was his lover—Suzanne Warren—who was also the mother of their child.[2]

One general statement that needs to be made is that clashing armies resort to deception whenever they can; that is, they deliberately mislead their opponents and violate their trust and loyalty. By fooling their enemy through manipulating their trust and loyalty, they can score better and cheaper victories. Military history has several such episodes: the Japanese attack on Pearl Harbor; the surprise attack of Egypt and Syria on Israel in October of 1973; and the surprise Nazi counterattack in the Ardennes (the Battle of the Bulge) in December 1944. However, manipulating the trust and loyalty of opponents is not restricted to the military field. Hitler certainly manipulated both the Allied powers and the Soviets before the beginning of World War II by signing international agreements he had no intention of keeping and by violating them whenever it suited his purposes.

Researchers in recent years have even speculated that Churchill was involved in similar manipulations. First, Rusbridger and Nave (1991) assert that by not telling Roosevelt about the impending attack on Pearl Harbor, Churchill ensured the entry of the United States into World War II. Second, Kilzer (1994) maintains that by deliberately ignoring Rudolf Hess's (Hitler's deputy) mission of peace to England (Hess's strange flight to England occurred on May 10, 1941), Churchill guaranteed that the Soviet Union would be dragged into World War II. Kilzer even implies that Hess's mission was genuine and that it could have prevented both the war and the extermination of European Jews. Third, Dennistone (1997) states that England used secret signal intelligence in an attempt to get Turkey involved in the war on the side of the Allies and to help open a second front against Nazi Germany in the Balkans. With this introduction and the illustrative cases in mind, let us examine the first category of World War II cases.

Fifth Columnism

Origin of Term

One of the more intriguing phenomena to emerge in this period is groups of secret sympathizers and supporters of an enemy who engaged in espionage or sabotage within defense lines or national borders, also known as fifth columnism. The origin of the term is traceable to the Spanish Civil War when the Nationalist general Emilio Mola attacked Madrid in 1936 with four army columns. General Mola coined the term "fifth column" to describe the Nationalist supporters in Madrid who assisted his assault. Later, the British used the term to describe people who sympathized with, or spied for, the Nazis. British accounts blamed a fifth column for the surprising and unexpected rapid collapse of French military forces confronting the successful May 1940 Nazi onslaught. There was also British concern about the possible existence of a fifth column among the many refugees who fled to England from the Continent. Ernest Hemingway's play *Fifth Column* (about the Spanish Civil War) helped to diffuse the term in the United States. Even President Roosevelt believed in fifth columns; he stated in a fireside chat on May 26, 1940, that there was a "Fifth Column that betrays a nation unprepared for treachery."[3]

Fifth Columnism in World War II

During the war, leaders took action to suppress, or encourage, fifth-column efforts. Winston Churchill's order to create the Special Operation Executive, which aimed to kindle the fires of resistance and "set Europe ablaze," must have had the idea of a fifth column behind it.[4] Moreover,

> Churchill had ordered a wholesale round-up of people whom he feared might start a Fifth Column that could be infiltrated by the German Intelligence services. Among these were 150 classed as "prominent." Unity Mitford's sister and brother-in-law, Sir Oswald and Lady Mosley, were among the first to be detained. Others, such as the Duke of Westminster, . . . were warned to keep their mouths shut and not spread defeatist rumors and to sever all links with Germany.[5]

The threat of growing popular support for fascism was very real in the early 1930s.[6] As we shall see in the case of King Edward VIII (later Duke of Windsor), sympathy for fascism touched some prominent figures, who formed various networks of sympathizers.

In the summer of 1940, Major General William Donovan, director of the Office of Strategic Services (OSS) during World War II,[7] helped to draft a document that examined the implications of a fifth column for the United States, which created something of a panic about the penetration of Nazi agents in America.[8] Some of the results of that panic can be seen in an instructive document from the period by Farren (1940). In it, the author calls for workers to assist the war effort and provides them with guidelines on how to identify saboteurs and prevent them from infiltrating important work places.[9] Higham's 1985 work attempts to document the collaboration of some Americans with the Nazis from at least 1933. This collaboration consisted of political support and various conspiratorial plots.[10]

Fifth columnism was not confined to only a European context. A related development took place on February 19, 1942, when President Roosevelt issued an executive directive that culminated in the detention of about 120,000 people of Japanese descent on the West Coast. About two-thirds of these were American citizens with a Japanese cultural heritage (Nisei). It is important to note that many Nisei were eventually drafted into the U.S. Army and Navy and they supported the U.S. war effort in many significant ways. However, the act of detaining such a large number of people clearly had behind it much suspicion, distrust, and a fear of a Japanese fifth column.[11] That fear, one must hastily add, had some empirical grounds in the behavior of the Sudeten Germans (discussed later) and some populations in the Ukraine, Yugoslavia, and a few other countries, who provided support for Nazi ideological and territorial expansionist claims. One of the major retrospective counterarguments is that these Nisei were U.S. citizens and hence owed their allegiance to the United States, which they trusted. However, this argument did not hold much sway in 1942.

As late as 1946, a Canadian royal commission that had studied Igor Gouzenko's defection (discussed in Chapter 3) stated in its report that the Soviets had been involved in creating a fifth-column organization in Canada. In reality, the Soviets in Canada were involved in operating a rather mundane intelligence organization whose goal it was to collect information about atomic weapons.

Basically, fifth columnism means that a country (say, country X) controls a large number of people who live in another country (say, country Y). These people are organized secretly and pretend to be loyal and trustworthy citizens of country Y, while in fact their loyalty and trust belong to country X. Thus, they conceal their true loyalty and engage in continuously deceitful behavior. Once hostilities erupt between country X and country Y, a fifth column becomes a resource for espionage, subversion, and sabotage, creating unrest and chaos.

Fifth columnism has been generalized to also include political influence and subversion. Although country X may utilize a fifth column to create chaotic conditions, enabling the invasion of country Y, country X may alternatively use a fifth column to better control events within country Y. It was in this context that the Nazis used political espionage during the war to influence political decisionmaking processes in their favor, and even created such processes.[12] For example, up to September 1939, it was a Nazi-stated goal to keep England out of a continental war. Until the Japanese attack on Pearl Harbor, it was a stated Nazi political goal to keep the United States "neutral" and out of the war (Britain, of course, had a diametrically opposed goal). To help achieve this goal, the Nazis supported sympathizers in these countries. Thus, both political and military efforts are included in fifth columnism. Metaphorically speaking, it is not too difficult to imagine that, like termites, a fifth column can erode the determination, strength, and capabilities of country Y to such an extent that country X could conquer it with ease and swiftness. The issues of moral boundaries and the betrayal of loyalty, trust, and deception are all very neatly focused in fifth columnism. In many aspects, a fifth column is perhaps the ultimate example of treason.

Research on Fifth Columns

Ripka focused his 1945 work on the Henleinist pro-Nazi movement in Czechoslovakia. He showed how Henleinists were involved in sabotage, espionage, the accumulation of explosives and weapons, and deceptive operations. He describes the activities of these pro-Nazis in Czechoslovakia in terms of a fifth column.

Another document, titled *The German Fifth Column in Poland*, published by the Polish Ministry of Information in 1940, examines the issue of the German minority in Poland and in other European countries, such as Belgium, Holland, Luxembourg, France, and Norway. It concludes that "subversive activities and conspiracy against the State were the program and political conception dominating the German minorities during the period preceding the war" (pp. 11–12). These minorities became one of the standard excuses that the Nazis used to justify their brutal and unprovoked invasions of these countries.

It is interesting that both this document and Ripka's (1945) examine, in detail, the claim that German minorities were ill-treated and severely discriminated against by their host countries. Ripka, for example, notes that during 1937–1938, Germans made up 22.3 percent of the population of Czechoslovakia and they held 24 percent of the seats in parliament and 23.1 percent of the civil service posts. Likewise, no claims of discrimination against Germans in Poland (or the existence of a fifth column there) could be empirically proven.

Although this attempt to expose the hypocrisy of the Nazis' claims is interesting and instructive, it would not have made any difference to the

Nazis. The "German minority" issue was just an excuse used for public consumption. The real motivation was one of racial German hegemony and expansionism, as indeed stated quite bluntly in Hitler's *Mein Kampf.* Regardless of this, German minorities were called upon (and expected) by the Nazis to aid them in their political and territorial claims before and after the Nazis seized power. The nature of this help ranged from political support to espionage, conspiracy, smuggling weapons and explosives, and sabotage.

The most comprehensive work about fifth columns is that by Louise De Jong.[13] De Jong examined meticulously the existence of a possible German fifth column, country by country, in Spain, Austria, Czechoslovakia, Poland, Norway, Balkans, Switzerland, and in more general terms, in Western and Eastern Europe and the United States. The answer she provides to questions of the existence and effectiveness of Nazi fifth columns is complex. On the one hand, there can hardly be a doubt that elements of a fifth column existed. That is, there were indeed German minorities (and their respective organizations) whose goal it was to destabilize the regime of their host countries and cause its downfall. Although the most prevalent activity of these organizations was espionage, they were also involved in sabotage and tried to disrupt daily life. However, the frequency, size, and type of activities of these organizations ranged widely among different countries. For example, whereas fifth-column activity was rather strong in Czechoslovakia, it was virtually nonexistent in Poland. De Jong notes that the activities of these Nazi sympathizers resulted partially from instructions that came directly from Nazi Germany (for example, pre-*Anschluss* Austria) and partially from these individuals' own interpretation of their identification with Nazism. Were they effective? Again, the answer is complex and is case specific.

They were quite effective in Czechoslovakia. Konrad Henlein had already established a Nazi-like party in October 1933. During the 1935 elections, this party won about 60 percent of German-speaking voters. The activities of the pro-Nazi Henleinist movement were very helpful to Hitler. Their continuous provocative agitation in the Sudetenland (which increased after the Austrian-German *Anschluss* in March 1938) apparently helped to persuade the British that the Nazi claim to parts of Czechoslovakia had "something to it" and that Czechoslovakian integrity could no longer be maintained. That the Czech government was very effective in quickly and swiftly squelching the specific September 1938 agitation was of no use to Czechoslovakian national integrity. The weak state of the British armed forces at that time, coupled with what appeared to be a disbelief that Czechoslovakian unity could be maintained, contributed to the signing the Munich Pact. Indeed, following that September 1938 agreement, the Sudetenland was given to Nazi Germany, and Konrad Henlein was amply rewarded by the Nazis with the appointment as head of the Sudetenland. In May 1939 he was promoted to the position of Gauleiter, heading the civilian administration, in Czechoslovakia.[14]

However, De Jong points out that in most of the countries she surveyed, the German minority was not strong or organized as an effective political force. What most Nazi sympathizers in most countries did was simply to talk loudly about their new belief and used German Nazi insignia and figures in public as points of identification. It needs to be added that in such countries as Holland, Switzerland, and Britain, the German groups, as such, simply did not have legitimate grievances. Consequently, Nazi organizations in these countries never acquired extensive popular support. One example is South Africa, where the government exposed and broke a Nazi organization.

Obviously, the Nazis were always interested in increasing tensions and unrest in societies that objected to them, and so they always encouraged subversive activities aimed at promoting such disintegrative processes. The best case of this is Austria. It is quite clear that Kurt von Schuschnigg's Austrian government fell because of the systematic activity of a group of Nazis, headed and supported by Berlin and Munich.

Thus, fifth columnism had a rather problematic empirical existence in World War II. As a conceptual propaganda tool, it was priceless. At a time of great anxiety and uncertainty, the idea that some sort of widespread powerful secret conspiracy existed, whose purpose was to disintegrate countries from within, fed hidden fears and was used to explain some otherwise puzzling phenomena (for example, the rapid collapse of France). However, a careful examination, country by country, for the existence of a fifth column reveals a complex reality that is not very supportive of the concept. As could be expected, following World War II, the term slowly vanished from use. The main reason for this was probably that with very few exceptions (for example, Austria), no genuine widespread Nazi fifth columns actually existed, a realization that became quite clear during the postwar years.

It needs to be added that the above conclusion is valid only if we take the term "fifth column" to mean a well-organized conspiratorial body, as the term originally meant. If we reinterpret the concept to denote a body of sympathizers, then the term could be used to mean the facilitation of change from one political/cultural form to another. However, such a reinterpretation of the term, eliminating its original conspiratorial nature, raises other difficulties. For example, what if a large part of the population of a country—openly and publicly—believes that the country should follow a path that others object to? What if others view this part of the population as treacherous or as composing a fifth column? Clearly, in a situation where a population is so badly split between different worldviews, and one part decides to use the rhetoric of treason to describe its disagree-ment with dissenters (that is, to delegitimize opponents as disloyal and untrustworthy), the concept of fifth columnism becomes completely in-valid and useless. An example that comes to mind is the accusation made by so many in the Jewish Israeli political right (and religious right) that the Israeli left is "treacherous" (some have even used the term "fifth column"). As recently as November 1999, accusations were made in Israel by some ultra-Orthodox Jews that immigrants from Russia to Israel constituted a fifth column because they were set on corrupting the country.

Collaboration

The definition of the term "collaboration" is context dependent. In the neutral sense of the term, it means cooperation, or harmonious work and effort. Many professional, academic, political, and economic teams "col-laborate." However, within the non-neutral context of a conflict, or war, the term typically denotes something like "working with the other (en-emy) side" or helping occupying forces. Thus, the meaning of the term depends on one's point of view, that is, on morality and on one's power to enforce particular moral interpretations.

For example, in the Israeli-Palestinian conflict, what Israelis have de-fined as "Palestinian assistants," in what may appear as a positively charged jargon (*say'an* in Hebrew), were referred to as despised "collabo-rators" by other Palestinians. It is significant that even in Israeli Hebrew slang, such Palestinian collaborators have been referred to as *shtinkers*, meaning "those who stink"—clearly a negative reference. Overall, around 5,000 Palestinian collaborators (mostly undercover) have helped Israel in its occupation of the West Bank and Gaza Strip, of whom around 1,200 have been murdered by other Palestinians.[15]

Intelligence (police and military) collaborators have a limited length of operational life. After that, the organization that used them must shelter them, sometimes for very long periods of time. The question of betrayal arises at two points in the career of such collaborators: the decision to col-laborate and life after the operational period ends.

Collaboration forces into sharp focus the issues of morality and power, as well as those of trust and loyalty—their direction and violation. Al-though there are different types of collaboration, I shall continue by fo-cusing on one of those types—collaboration within the context of a na-tional conflict, which is an integral part of treason.

Background

The general background in Europe after World War I was one of major economic crisis and shadows of both communism and fascism looming over the land. This was a period of unrest, uncertainty, confusion, and opportunity regarding changes to boundaries of morality. The ascent of Hitler's National Socialism must be viewed within this context. The Europe that Hitler was facing had quite a few fascist movements, most of which were rather sympathetic to him. Mussolini's Italy and Franco's Spain moved directly into fascist totalitarian social orders. Other countries had fascist movements, but not as strong. Thus, for quite a few people, the "choice" appeared to be between communism and fascism (or its Nazi variant).

Let's briefly review some of the key dates and events during the period. Hitler was appointed chancellor on January 30, 1933. Following the Reichstag fire on March 5, 1933, Germany went to Reichstag elections. The Nazis won 288 out of 647 deputies (44.5 percent). After consolidation of Hitler's power, new elections in November gave the Nazis 93 percent of the votes. In March of 1936, Germany denounced the Locarno Pact, and German troops were sent to the Rhineland. In March of 1938, German troops crossed the border into Austria. September 29–30 witnessed the pitiful and wretched appeasement attempt at Munich by French premier Daladier and British prime minister Chamberlain to Hitler and Mussolini.[16] The spring and summer of 1939 witnessed quite a few public calls to Hitler to avoid war, to no avail.

Germany attacked Poland on September 1, 1939, and World War II began. Within a short period of time, Nazi Germany occupied and controlled much of Europe: Belgium surrendered in May 1940, France yielded in June 1940, and Romania in October 1940. In 1941 German troops marched into Bulgaria (March), launched major offensives in North Africa, Yugoslavia, and Greece (April), and on June 22, the victorious Nazi *Wehrmacht* attacked the Soviet Union. German U-boats experienced major victories in the Atlantic, and Britain was heavily bombed from the air. Until the summer of 1941, and following the initial Nazi victories on the Russian front, Europe seemed to yield to Hitler. But in 1943 it began to be clear, as the U-boats were losing the Battle of the Atlantic, Stalingrad was retaken by Soviet troops, and the Nazi North African campaign was collapsing, that Nazi Germany was probably going to lose the war. In June 1944, following the landings of Allied forces in Normandy, it became obvious that Nazi Germany was losing the war. The question was, how long before it would collapse completely. That happened in May 1945.

The Meaning of Collaboration

Millions of people were under Nazi occupation between 1939 and 1945, and until 1943 it seemed that the Nazis had a very strong grip over Europe. The Japanese initial expansion in the Far East created a somewhat similar situation. Both Germany and Japan controlled large areas and populations using relatively small military forces. How was that possible? Warmbruun (1963) suggests two major a causes for the success of that control: (1) swift and decisive military defeats; and (2) threats to use violence and actual use of it. What was one supposed to do? How was one supposed to behave under one of the most ruthless and racist regimes to have ever existed on this planet?

> Collaboration and resistance . . . are vague [terms] and defy precise definition; collaboration could mean anything from volunteering for the Waffen S.S. to buying a picture postcard of Marshal Pétain, likewise "resistance" could be derailing an enemy troop-train or singing an obscene parody of "Lili Marlene"! (Littlejohn 1972:336)

Littlejohn's work is focused on those he termed "patriotic traitors" and describes, in detail, collaborators with Nazi Germany in different European countries. However, it is important to note that the very same term can easily be applied to such individuals as Willy Brandt, Marlene Dietrich, or Claus von Stauffenberg (discussed in later chapters). It is also important to note that Nazi Germany was not the only occupying force. Imperial Japan occupied large parts of Southeast Asia and China, and Italy controlled other parts in southern Europe and North Africa. During the war, and afterward, countries fell under the occupation of different Allied countries, but more pronounced was the occupation of many countries by Soviet troops.

Warmbruun points out that collaboration with the Nazi occupation in Europe assumed one of three forms.[17] First was "voluntary collaboration," which meant embracing Nazi interests, for whatever reason, ranging from such motivation as personal gain to political identification with National Socialism. This position typically meant that many parts of the original culture of the preoccupied state were washed away in favor of the Nazi culture as dictated by the Nazi masters. Warmbruun has no doubt that this particular form of collaboration is akin to treason. Second was "submission to German demands on the grounds of 'superior force.'" Warmbruun finds this particular behavior to be unavoidable "accommodation," because not complying could mean death. Collaboration here meant the minimum necessary. Obviously, "superior force" was not always deadly, and "accommodation" could provide a cover for those who were not willing to take even moderate risks. Third was "reasonable collaboration," a position typically taken by administrators and justified on the grounds of having to protect and shield the population, or parts of it, from the horrors of a brutal occupation. Warmbruun is obviously weary of this "wise guy" approach. He points out that "any collaboration with the absolute evil represented by National Socialist principles, policies, and institutions, backed up by the police power of the totalitarian state, was bound to corrode the good intentions of all collaborating individuals or groups" (Warmbruun 1963:274).

As he so wisely points out, the policy of "reasonable collaboration" was taken by the Jewish Councils under Nazi occupation,[18] and it led to self-defeat and self-destruction. The Jews who operated those councils thought they were doing some good, perhaps even deluding themselves that they could save some Jews. But that hope, given the Nazi Final Solution plan, was a vain one. While perhaps not always fully aware of it, many of these Jews simply played a role for the Nazis by counseling other Jews to submit.

> In each occupied country the great majority of the population came to terms with the reality of the occupation. . . . Most people, against their will, were caught in a social system which of necessity continued to function under the occupation, to some extent to the advantage of the German war economy, . . . Unwilling adjustment was the rule—intentional resistance the exception.[19]

The patterns of collaboration during World War II occurred in several areas: political, military, administrative, and economic. In each of these areas, helping the enemy assumed different depths and forms.[20]

Collaboration could mean the crossing of moral boundaries by violating precollaboration trust and loyalty. And yet the content and direction of trust and loyalty are the main issues here. Without determining their nature, the meaning of collaboration (and it is primarily a moral meaning) simply dissipates. Indeed, some of the most spectacular cases of treason date to this period. Let us look at some.

Collaboration in Europe, 1939–1945

Adolf Hitler was appointed chancellor on January 30, 1933. From that point in time, Nazi expansionism was only a matter of time and expediency. As the Nazis conquered more territories, more people fell under Nazi political, economic, military, and cultural hegemony and control. The choices these people faced were few. Collaboration and resistance were two general options, divided into numerous subcategories. Questions of resistance[21] and collaboration,[22] and the way in which these options directly related to issues of trust, loyalty, and their violation, were an almost daily reality for people under occupation. Who or what was one supposed to trust? To whom or to what did one give loyalty? Let's examine some of the possibilities.

Austria and Seyss-Inquart

The first country into which the Nazi *Wehrmacht* marched was Austria (March 12, 1938) in the process of the *Anschluss* ("union") between Nazi Germany and Austria. That step followed a long history of Nazi aggression. First, on July 25, 1934, Austrian chancellor Engelbert Dolfuss was murdered in the Chancellery in Vienna by Austrian Nazis who wanted Austria to become a Nazi state. When this did not work, Hitler threatened the new chancellor—Kurt von Schuschnigg—on March 11, 1938, and demanded his resignation. The reason for this specific threat was that Schuschnigg was planning a plebiscite on Austrian independence. Hitler demanded that Schuschnigg be replaced by an Austrian Nazi—Arthur Seyss-Inquart. This took place on March 11. However, the plot became even more interesting when Nazi Hermann Goering told Seyss-Inquart to send a cable to Germany demanding the entry of the Nazi army into Austria to restore order. Indeed, Seyss-Inquart obeyed the suggested guidelines, and consequently, units of the *Wehrmacht* marched into Austria. Seyss-Inquart, an enthusiastic supporter of the *Anschluss* and a longtime devoted Nazi, became the Reich governor of Austria.

Seyss-Inquart did not hide his Nazi sympathies or his political views. His actions helped to terminate Austrian independence, which led to the integration of Austria with Nazi Germany. Seyss-Inquart remained in office until April 1939. Seyss-Inquart's career continued, and from May 1940 until 1945 he was Reich commissioner in the occupied Netherlands. Among other actions, he was directly responsible for making the Netherlands' economy serve Germany, recruited forced labor on the magnitude of 5 million people who were sent to Germany, and was effective in the rounding up of about 117,000 Jews who were sent to their deaths in Poland. He was arrested in May 1945, tried at Nuremberg, found guilty of war crimes, and hanged on October 16, 1946.[23]

Was Seyss-Inquart an Austrian traitor? To answer this question one must answer some other difficult questions. For example, how may Austrians actually supported the *Anschluss* in 1938? If very many did, then Seyss-Inquart did not betray the trust and loyalty of many, or even possibly the majority of, Austrians. On the contrary. Also, if the aspiration to unite Austria with Nazi Germany was viewed as a positive and necessary process, for the benefit of both countries, then the invocation of the label "treason" in this case becomes very problematic. Was he loyal to Austria? Again, answering this question depends on whether Austrians viewed the *Anschluss* with Nazi Germany in 1938 as a positive or a negative step and whether the *Anschluss* can be perceived, ideologically, as a positive process. The main reason Seyss-Inquart was tried (and convicted) as a traitor was that his morality and politics were such that he gave up Austria's independence as a cultural, political, and social entity. However, it is not too difficult to argue that Seyss-Inquart was loyal to the idea of an expanded, integrated Nazi Reich, and so his behavior may have presented a consistent patriotic motivation.

Czechoslovakia

The Munich Pact (September 29–30, 1938), in which England and France agreed that Nazi Germany could acquire the Sudetenland, actually meant the end of Czechoslovakia as an independent state. It did not take long. Within a few months Nazi Germany took over the Sudetenland, Poland seized a small border district, Slovakia became a vassal German state, and the leftovers of Bohemia and Moravia were occupied by the Nazi military in March 1939. If citizens of Czechoslovakia, and the Czech president, Eduard Beneå, viewed Western countries with scorn and suspicion and felt betrayed by both England and French, who can blame them? In a hopeless policy of appeasement, French and English politicians sacrificed the integrity of Czechoslovakia, exposed its citizens to Nazi rule, and certainly did not achieve the goal they wanted—the prevention of another world war. The Nazi occupation of Czechoslovakia was relatively benign; the Nazis felt that they could maximize economic exploitation and squeeze more out of Czechoslovakia by using benign means rather than by using harsh repression. Correspondingly, resistance to Nazi occupation was not very strong, at least not until the 1940s. The most notable act of resistance was the assassination of Reinhard Heydrich (May 27, 1942) by Free Czech agents (trained in England and parachuted into Czechoslovakia for the task). His death, a week later, resulted in the Nazi massacres and destruction of the villages of Lidice (June 9, 1942) and Lezaky.

Following the November 1938 Munich Pact, Eduard Beneå resigned his post as president.[24] His successor was Emil Hacha. Put under brutal pressure in Berlin, sixty-seven years old, and in poor health, Hacha signed a surrender document in March 1939. Although he continued to serve as the nominal head of state of what was left of Czechoslovakia, the state was actually managed by its Nazi rulers.[25] Mastny points out that Czechoslovakia was Nazi Germany's first conquest and remained under Nazi rule the longest time. Under pleas from Emil Hacha's government, Czechs were asked to refrain from acts of resistance. However, the assassination of Heydrich (ordered by the London-based Beneå) unleashed a campaign of terror by the Nazis. Mastny claims that by 1942 the Nazis had simply crushed the Czechs popular will to resist, a situation that remained in effect until the end of the war, and that "at no time did the Czechs challenge the Nazis with a significant resistance movement."[26]

It is difficult not to ask whether Hacha was a traitor and thus examine what some view as his tragic role. He was sympathetic to Nazi Germany before the Nazi occupation of Czechoslovakia, urged his people to support the Third Reich, and expressed satisfaction and joy at Germany's victory over France.[27] Although he was arrested after the war and died in prison waiting for his trial on charges of collaboration and treason (June 27, 1945), it is clear that he tried his best to keep as much of what was left of his country intact and independent. However, that task was hopeless under Nazi rule. Though not as powerful and strong as Vichy's Pétain, Hacha was cast into a somewhat similar position.[28] It is noteworthy that the collaboration of the Czechs was very useful for the Nazis. In 1941, for example, Czech industry provided about 30 percent of German armor, 40 percent of its automatic weapons, and close to one-third of its trucks. Obviously, there were some good reasons for the relatively benign treatment of Czechoslovakia by the Nazis. Nevertheless, close to 70,000 Czech Jews were sent to their deaths,[29] and close to 350,000 Czechs perished as a result of Nazi occupation.[30]

MacDonald and Kaplan provide an illustrative description of life under Nazi occupation in Czechoslovakia. For example, in January 1941 the BBC called people under Nazi occupation to mark the letter "V" on walls as a sign for "victory." Compliance of people in Prague was enthusiastic because this behavior offered a form of resistance and a marking of moral boundaries in a way that did not provoke bloody reprisals. Moreover, the campaign was very successful throughout Europe until the Germans themselves adopted this sign. In the summer of 1941 Prague was flooded with huge "V" signs—on walls, locomotives, and bulletin boards. Germans used the sign to proclaim faith in German victory.[31]

Two possible cases of betrayal may be examined in the Czech context. One was during the Sudetenland crisis. During that crisis, which began to heat up during April 1938, Konrad Henlein—head of the German Sudeten party, in reality a Nazi party—called for autonomy for his people. Henlein's political agitation was very useful for Nazi Germany and played directly into Hitler's expansionist intentions. Although by September 15, 1938, the Czech government had the agitation under control, and Henlein fled to Germany, the Munich Pact voided that control. Following the Munich Pact, Henlein was appointed the Gauleiter of the Sudetenland in October 1938. The fact is that he exercised little power, and many of his supporters were killed by the Nazis. In 1945 Henlein committed suicide while in an Allied internment camp.

The other case occurred following the Nazi occupation of Czechoslovakia when a local Czech political organization was allowed to exist—the National Cooperation—headed by the Czech fascist General Rudolf Gajda. Could Gajda and Henlein be considered traitors? Indeed, they assisted in the disintegration of their country and participated in a process that meant the end of Czech independence and subjugation to Nazi Germany. From this point of view, they indeed violated the basic trust and loyalty between citizens and their country. However, both were also committed fascist Nazis and thought that their country's genuine good future was with Nazi Germany, and their actions were based on that belief. They trusted, and were loyal to, Nazi Germany, and they displayed their preference in public. It is interesting to note that at the end of World War II, Czechoslovakia regained the Sudetenland, and under the terms of the Potsdam Allied Agreements (July–August 1945), the Sudetenland German population was expelled.

Poland

Hitler invaded Poland on September 1, 1939. Nazi rule of Poland was ruthless. Overall, no major ideological collaboration by Poles is documented (although the invading Nazi *Wehrmacht* was assisted by different individuals). Indeed, no political or ideological supporting Polish group existed for the Nazis. However, as the Nazis' brutal occupation developed, some forced forms of limited collaboration took place, especially in concentration camps and Jewish ghettos. In return for more control, even if sometimes for a limited period of time, there were those willing to serve as *Kapos* ("trustees") or *Sonderkommando* (participants in the extermination process in Nazi concentration camps). The *Judenrat* was the council of Jews set up as the self-governing body of the various ghettos constructed by the Nazis in occupied Eastern Europe.[32] Jewish members in *Judenrats* had complex motives to collaborate with their torturers and executioners. Some thought they could save themselves and their families; others thought that they could serve the community and help it survive. Retrospectively, it is obvious that the Nazis used the *Judenrats* to achieve better control and exploitation of the local Jewish population; hence, serving in a *Judenrat* was a blocked exit that, in most cases, led nowhere.

It is worth noting that many Poles were mobilized by the Soviets to either fight the Nazis under Soviet command or join cadres of communists in preparation for a Polish communist regime. Many other Poles, defining themselves as patriotic, viewed these steps as collaborative and treasonable because they were putting what they viewed as genuine Polish national interests in second or third place. One needs to be reminded at this point that Stalin managed to lure most members of the Polish Communist Party into the Soviet Union in 1938, where they were all murdered. Moreover, carried out by direct orders of Stalin and the Soviet Politburo, Soviet NKVD personnel massacred more than 4,000 Polish officers in the Katyn forest near Smolensk. These vile mass murders took place probably in

April and early May of 1940.[33] Those Polish officers were among 180,000 other Polish prisoners of war who fell into the hands of the Red Army during the Nazi-Soviet partition of Poland in 1939.[34] These murders, obviously, raise some interesting questions of trust and loyalty between Poland and the Soviet Union under Stalin.

Nazi Germany's *Wehrmacht* developed a successful military attack westward in the spring of 1940, conquering first Denmark and Norway (April), and then continuing going through the Ardennes invading and conquering Belgium, the Netherlands, and Luxembourg (May), and France (June). The defeat of France in the summer was followed by a Nazi invasion and occupation of the Channel Islands. This swift military move put several Western European countries under full Nazi control. Suddenly, issues of collaboration and resistance became an everyday reality for millions of Western Europeans. The experiences of the Poles and the Czechs provide some clues to what was about to transpire.

Denmark

Two Nazi German divisions invaded Denmark on April 9, 1940. Copenhagen was taken within twelve hours, and Denmark accepted the Nazi occupation. Denmark was not the target of the German military move, but controlling Denmark was crucial for the German military campaign against Norway.

The Danish government was allowed to maintain parts of its powers, and such organizations as the police, courts, and even the laws were retained. Even a downsized Danish army was allowed to exist. Clearly, the Danes wanted to keep as much of the country's administration as possible in Danish hands, and a national coalition was formed for that purpose. For such a policy to succeed, the Germans had to be persuaded that a genuine cooperation existed. It did, for a long time (1940–1943). On the other hand, it was expected by the Danes that the German interference in Denmark's internal affairs would be minimal. It was not. The Germans kept demanding military equipment, removal of ministers, and so on. To prevent a compulsory conscription to the army, about 100,000 Danish workers were required to go to Germany. Following the Nazi invasion of the Soviet Union, the Danish Communist Party was banned, and the Danes had to agree to the recruitment of the so-called Danish Free Corps to participate in the war effort. Until 1943, most of the Danish population seemed to have supported a policy of collaboration in return for limited independence.

Although a small Danish Nazi party existed in Denmark even before the German invasion and occupation of the country, it must be noted that many Danish diplomats outside Denmark supported the Allies. Such Danish territories as Greenland, Iceland, and the Faeroe Islands became available to Allied forces, and the Danish merchant fleet sailed to Allied ports and helped the Allied war effort. The Danish collaboration with the Nazis was strained.

As the German demands on the Danish economy grew and military losses for the Nazis increased, Danes became more defiant. In 1943 strikes occurred, an underground Freedom Council was created, and when anti-Semitic laws were introduced (October 1943), most of the country's 8,000 Jews had already been moved to neutral Sweden. In response, the Nazis tightened their totalitarian grip on Denmark. By 1944 the Nazi occupation of Denmark resembled the occupation in other areas, and much of the Danish independence was withdrawn. Danish resistance grew day by day, thriving on the lack of inner factions, and was ready for a full-scale rebellion. That became unnecessary when the German military surrendered on May 5, 1945.[35]

The nature of the Danish collaboration with the Nazis is interesting. The theoretical trade-off was "collaboration" for "limited independence." For a while, this policy worked as expected and apparently enjoyed popular support. Thus, the use of the term "treason" in this particular context may be inappropriate because violation of the trust and loyalty of most of the Danish population cannot be established.

After the war, 14,000 prison sentences were given to Danes accused of collaborating with the Nazis (that is, about 374 Danes out of every 100,000 were jailed for this offense). Denmark also carried out twenty-three out of forty-six death sentences it passed against collaborators.[36]

Norway and Quisling

Immediately following the Nazi incursion into Denmark, Germany attacked Norway (on the same date, April 9, 1940), which was the principal goal of their military move (operation "Weser Exercise"). The major reasons were the need for Swedish iron ore, raw materials from Scandinavia, and strategically located bases for both Nazi submarines and aircraft, which were used against Allied convoys and naval shipping. Moreover, Nazi ideology viewed Norwegians as a related but wayward Nordic tribe that needed Nazi-guided persuasion to return to its proper place—the Nazi Third Reich.

Following a military effort that took the Germans two months to complete, they occupied the whole country. The Norwegians, aided by British and other forces, fought valiantly, causing the *Wehrmacht* very serious casualties and losses (especially to the German *Kriegsmarine*). King Haakon VII and the Norwegian royal family, the cabinet, and many members of parliament were able to escape to the United Kingdom (June 7). There they established a government in exile, but not before rejecting the Nazi demand for the establishment of a Norwegian Nazi government headed by Norway's Nazi—Vidkun Quisling.

Norwegians did not follow the Danish case, and Nazi rule was never accepted. Resistance to the Nazis began to be organized after the invasion. However, the realization that freedom from the Nazi yoke could only be achieved once the Germans lost the war and surrendered dictated a restrained struggle. That struggle was difficult because, among other things, Nazi agents had penetrated underground groups.

One of the more spectacular series of sabotage acts of the Norwegian resistance was the continuous action against a heavy water plant.[37] First action was supposed to be carried out by parachuted British engineers and aided by Norwegian Special Operations Executive (S.O.E.) agents in October–November 1942 (the failed "Vemork raid").[38] Second was the February 28, 1943, sabotage of the plant by Norwegian S.O.E. agents, which was successful only in slowing production, not stopping it completely. An unsuccessful air raid on the plant took place on November 16, 1943, by 140 bombers of the Bomber Command (U.S. Air Force 8th Division in Britain). This raid prompted the Germans to transfer the large stockpile of about fourteen tons of heavy water manufactured by the Norsk Hydro Hydrogen Electrolysis plant at Vemork to Germany. On Sunday, February 20, 1944, the Norwegian ferry *Hydro*, carrying the entire heavy water stockpile, was sabotaged (with explosive charges) by S.O.E. agents and sunk to the bottom of Lake Tinnsjoe, one of Europe's deepest lakes.[39]

Norway was liberated on May 8, 1945. Its prewar government returned on May 31, and King Haakon returned on June 7.[40]

The Nazi occupation of Norway was the context for one of the most notorious of traitors: Vidkun Quisling. Quisling was born in 1887 in Fyresdal (located in the west-central part of the province of Telemark), Norway. His father, Jon Laurits, served as both a pastor and a state bureaucrat. His mother, Anna Caroline, was fifteen years younger than his father. The couple had four children and placed a strong emphasis on education. Consequently, all four children received the equivalent of a university education.

Quisling showed an early interest in history, abstract ideas, and some mysticism, as well as a national zeal. He entered the War College in September 1905 and graduated from that college in 1908 as a lieutenant in field artillery, first in his class. Following a short break in his military career to earn some money as a teacher, he returned to it in 1909 and enrolled in the Military Academy. He graduated from that academy in 1911, again first in his class (in fact, he earned the highest grade ever granted by the academy). Following this splendid career, Quisling became a junior member within the Norwegian General Staff. He not only served in head-quarters but experienced some field commands as well. During a tour of duty as an artillery officer, he was promoted to captain, and in 1918 he was promoted to adjutant. Quisling's path up to this point indicated that he was settling into the long and monotonous career of a military officer. Indications are that his style of command was kind, and he was highly respected.

The Norwegian military assigned Quisling to study Imperial Russia and to determine its military capabilities. He was able to fulfill this task with a deep immersion into Russian culture, and so vast was his knowl-edge that when the post of military attaché became available in Russia in 1918, he was appointed to it. However, the political instability in Russia was such that he served there from only April to December 1918; when he returned to Norway he was appointed to a two-year tour of duty in Fin-land. Having completed this mission, he returned to Norway and then went again to Russia, this time as part of Fridtjof Nansen's mission of re-lief (bringing food) to Russia. In Russia he met and married his first wife (Alexandra, in August 1922). Because he overstayed in Russia, his mili-tary career was interrupted, and he was dismissed from the General Staff in August 1923. Then he met and secretly married his second wife (Maria, September 10, 1923) before divorcing his first wife (no record of the di-vorce exists). After a period of travel, Quisling returned to Russia, where he apparently learned to despise communism. In 1929 he returned to Norway. Having been away for so many years, he had to carve himself a new niche in Norway.

Quisling chose to begin a political career within the sphere of radical conservatism of the early 1930s. That alliance would gradually take him into political networks that would present and promote the Norwegian version of fascism and, later, Nazism. He started by assuming some cen-tral positions in the Norwegian Nordic Folk-Rising Party.

In 1931, a political crisis engulfed Norway, the government resigned, and a new minority government was created, headed by Pedar Kolstad. Kolstad, who was leading the Agrarian Party into assuming power, lacked good candidates for various positions in the new government. It was suggested that Vidkun Quisling was a dependable and worthy can-didate for the position of minister of defense. Kolstad accepted the recom-mendation. Thus, on May 12, 1931, Quisling became Norway's minister of defense. With this appointment, he left his previous party and joined the conservative Agrarian Party. Although Quisling's tenure as the minis-ter of defense showed his competency as a capable day-to-day administrator, it was also dotted with various political controversies and conflicts. Quisling did not hide his moral, political, or ideological views, and he tried to expand the power of his position. Eventually, on March 3, 1933, Quisling was forced to resign. His main achievements were the creation of a state militia *(Leidengen)* and his rise from relative anonymity to one of Norway's recognized (and controversial) figures.

After resigning as minister of defense, Quisling formed in 1933 the Nasjonal Samling (N.S.—National Union Party), over which he had complete control. The N.S. emphasis on nationalism was attractive to some young people, and its antilabor stands attracted some support from business people. Moreover, Quisling and the N.S. never hid their affinity and admiration for Nazi Germany (and fascist Italy). Most N.S. supporters were young and joined for ideological reasons; others simply believed and admired Quisling personally. However, the party did not attract many supporters and did very poorly in the 1933 election. Nationally, the Nasjonal Samling

gained 27,850 votes out of a total of 1,248,686 cast, amounting to 2.23 percent of the electorate. Of the N.S. votes, 14,942 came from the rural districts and 12,908 from the towns, which respectively was 1.76 percent and 3.21 percent of the total in the rural and urban divisions of the electorate.[41]

Following the 1933 election, the N.S. made some changes to its platform, the most significant of which was a gradual transition between 1934 and 1936 to fascism, both in ideology and in adopting typical Nazi-like external signs (using the Nazi salute from 1934, and referring to Quisling as the *partifører*, or simply as the *Fører*, meaning the leader).[42]

The 1936 election put the N.S. to a real test of power, the test of a basically nondemocratic party competing for power within a democratic framework. Quisling gradually focused his antagonism on the democratic system itself, and by doing that doomed the N.S. and himself to a marginal role in a population that embraced democracy. Among other things, some N.S. meetings were the scenes of violent clashes.[43]

The general election took place on October 19, 1936, and the N.S. won only 26,577 votes (that is, less than in the 1933 election in absolute terms). The N.S. vote declined from 2.23 percent of the total vote in the 1933 election to 1.83 percent in 1936. The decline in rural areas was from 1.76 percent in 1933 to 1.4 percent in 1936 (a drop from 14,942 to 14,151 votes) and in urban areas from 3.21 percent to 2.74 percent (a drop from 12,908 to 12,426 votes). The N.S. was clearly losing support.[44] The drop in support and popularity had its impact on the N.S., and in 1936–1937 it experienced disintegration and gradually turned into what Hoidal refers to as a marginal sect.[45] Consequently, during 1937–1939, Quisling began to turn more of his attention to Nazi Germany.

Quisling's first contacts with the German Nazi Party had been made in the early 1930s. In 1934 the head of the Scandinavian desk of the Nazi Party's office for foreign affairs (headed by Alfred Rosenberg)—Thilo von Trotha—visited Norway and attended the annual meeting of the N.S. in Stiklested.[46] The Nazis, however, were fully knowledgeable about the disintegration and insignificance of the N.S., and they were not too enthusiastic about either Quisling or the N.S. In 1939 Quisling sent congratulatory cables to both Franco in Spain (February 28, 1939) and Hitler (April 20, 1939). Hitler was referred to as a "hero." A lower clerk for Franco acknowledged receipt of the message, but Hitler never responded.[47] The Nazi attitude toward Quisling and the N.S. was clearly informed and ambivalent. However, this ambivalence did not prevent the Nazis from supporting Quisling, or Hitler from meeting him.[48]

The main reason for these contradictions and zigzags was that although the Nazi foreign office had a realistic evaluation of Quisling's marginal position, Hitler either liked him or thought that something could be gained from Quisling. In fact, during their first meetings, one of the topics they discussed was Germany-Norway cooperation. It is clear that in that meeting Quisling presented to Hitler his plans for a pro-Nazi coup in Norway. Quisling was interested in political cooperation and in Norway becoming an independent pro-Nazi state within a Nazi German federation. Although Hitler delayed his response to Quisling's initiative, the Nazis were quick to translate Quisling's political aspirations into practical military terms. They were in the process of planning their offensive to invade and conquer Norway, and they recognized that Quisling could be useful.

When the legitimate Norwegian government left Norway following the Nazi invasion of April 9, 1940, Quisling announced on the radio that he had become both the prime minister and foreign minister and was heading a national government. That government was headed by a man who had failed in two elections and was certainly pro-Nazi. However, the Nazis remained ambivalent. On April 15, 1940, within a week of the invasion, they dismissed him because—among other things—he could not maintain a stable government and he attracted too much hostility. Instead of Quisling's national government, an Administrative Council was created, and Nazi Germany appointed a *Reichkommissar* to rule the conquered country—Josef Terboven.

Terboven, a bank clerk by profession and a party official in the Rhine province, was summoned to Hitler's office on April 19 and told that he was to become the chief Nazi administrator in Norway, effective April 24, 1940. Terboven was to administer Norway brutally, cruelly, and ruthlessly, as ordered by Hitler, until the end of World War II. On May 8, 1945, Terboven committed suicide in Norway.[49]

Of course, Quisling was such a true believer that he never gave up. His political aspirations created a chronic tension between him and Terboven.

Quisling in uniform at his desk, November 1940.
SOURCE: *Reprinted from Oddvar K. Hoidal,* Quisling: A Study in Treason
(Oslo: Norwegian University Press, 1989). Photograph by the Norwegian News Agency.

Moreover, Quisling wanted to expand the membership of the N.S., negotiate more independence for Norway, and shape Norwegian society to fit his fascist, racist, and anti-Semitic ideas. Following the Nazi conquest of Norway and the banning of all other political parties, the N.S. enjoyed economic prosperity (due largely to the confiscation of the property of other parties). The new funds it acquired were used to rebuild the party. Numbers were important for Quisling because the Nazis responded to his demands for more power by pointing out that support for him was meager. However, membership in the N.S. grew steadily, and the party membership reached its peak in the fall of 1943 with more than 43,000 members. Hoidal estimates that membership in the N.S., including its youth movement, approximated 60,000.[50] However, in 1941 it was obvious that despite all efforts, the gap between the N.S. and the majority of Norwegians was too great to bridge. Hoidal, puzzled by the poor support Quisling won, suggests that

> Quisling's failure to attract a mass membership was largely due, in the final analysis, to the obvious fact that he was perceived as a collaborator. He was directly associated with the power that had deprived Norway of its sover-

eignty. His insistence that he was carrying out a campaign to win back independence within a greater Germanic federation was disregarded as inconsequential propaganda by the overwhelming majority.

The public's view of him as a traitorous conspirator became even stronger as the occupation progressed because of his acts. To prove to the Germans that he deserved to be trusted as the head of government, he assisted their war effort by taking part in the formation of Norwegian military units, recruited to fight on Germany's behalf.[51]

. . . The overwhelming majority of the people regarded their opposition to N.S. as a fight against evil. . . . N.S. was further weakened by its inability to attract influential people into its ranks.[52]

In February 1942, Quisling was appointed minister president of Norway. This move gave the false impression that Norway had gained some independence, with Quisling heading a new government. However, Quisling and his government were totally under the command of Terboven. Quisling's attempts to expand his sphere of influence over Norway were unsuccessful. Consequently, during late 1942 and throughout 1943, he tried to achieve greater control through tighter collaboration with Nazi Germany, helping its war effort.[53] However, his mobilization efforts failed. Complete failure and collapse developed in 1945.

Quisling surrendered himself to the police on May 9, 1945. He was charged with treason because of his activities, which included the usurpation of governmental power, attempts to mobilize Norwegians, orders to cease resistance to the Nazis, and attempts to bring Norway under foreign rule. Negotiations took place, and a trial followed. Quisling responded to the charges by stating that he was not guilty, and he denied some of the obvious charges. Those denials were contrary to the facts that were presented to the court (for example, conspiring with Hitler and Raeder to place Norway under Nazi rule; getting funds from the Nazis; helping the Nazis during the occupation). The court decided that Quisling was guilty on charges of betraying his country (September 10, 1945), and he was sentenced to death. An appeal to the Supreme Court was rejected, and a mercy plea (by his wife, Maria) was rejected. He was executed on October 24, 1945, 2:40 A.M., in Akershus Castle by a firing squad of ten men. Quisling maintained, even minutes before his execution, that he was innocent.[54] In fact, in his defense testimony he stated, "If my activity has been treason . . . then I wish to God for Norway's sake that a good many of Norway's sons would become traitors like me, only that they be not thrown into jail."[55] Clearly, although the large majority of Norwegians viewed him as a traitor, he most certainly viewed himself as a genuine patriot with an inspired vision for the future of Norway.

Charges of collaboration and treason did not end with the execution of Quisling. Almost 93,000 individuals suspected of being connected to the N.S. were investigated. They included not just N.S. members but non-N.S. collaborators as well. About half were either found not guilty or not brought to trial. Although 46,085 Norwegians were found guilty, most were passive N.S. members who received penalties ranging from fines to deprivation of civil rights for limited periods. About 18,000 people were imprisoned. By 1948 only 3,200 remained in prison.[56] Of every 100,000 Norwegians, 633 were in prison for charges of collaboration,[57] and of the thirty Norwegians who were sentenced to death, twenty-five were actually executed.[58]

Although Quisling is constructed as a genuine traitor, his treason has problematic aspects. He identified with Nazi Germany and believed that Norway should be an independent state within a German-dominated federation. He did everything in his power to realize this end by collaborating with the Nazis. Unfortunately for him, very few Norwegians were willing to embrace his "vision," which so many of them, apparently, considered a frightful nightmare. It was thus inconsistent and deceptive for Quisling to deny at his trial the obvious facts disclosing his intimate relations, conspiracies, and collaboration with the Nazis.[59]

Nazi Germany began its offensive in Western Europe (code-named "Fall Gelb")[60] on May 10, 1940. Driving an awesome military war machine consisting of 119 divisions (plus another twenty-three later in the operation) through the Ardennes, it managed to bring about the collapse of the French military within a month. Along the way, the Nazi *Wehrmacht* invaded three neutral countries: Luxembourg, Belgium, and the Netherlands. Issues of occupation, collaboration, and resistance became an immediate and day-to-day reality in these countries.

Luxembourg

The tiny country of Luxembourg, with a population of close to 300,000 people, was occupied by the Nazis on May 10. The ruling family and government escaped to England where they formed a government in exile. Although most Luxembourgians did not welcome the Nazis, about 2,000 joined the German military. After the war, about 10,000 Luxembourgians faced charges of collaboration with the Nazis.[61]

Belgium

In terms of collaboration, the picture in Belgium was different. Despite initial military resistance, Belgium surrendered on May 28. King Léopold negotiated the surrender, after which he retired to his palace until June 1944. It is clear that the Belgian king negotiated with the Nazis (including a November 19 meeting with Hitler) in the hope of gaining some sort of a political settlement for his country. Léopold viewed the Belgian government in exile (in London) with scorn and regarded them as "traitors." Germany annexed two Belgian cantons, and the rest of Belgium was controlled by the Nazi military machine, headed by General Alexander von Falkenhausen, until June 1944. In fact, von Falkenhausen left the actual decisionmaking and rule of Belgium to Eggart Reeder, who was the president of the military administration.

During the German occupation of Belgium, there emerged pro-German groups that identified with Nazi goals and ideology and sought integration into Hitler's Third Reich. Two of these groups, and their leaders, are well worth noting. One group developed in Flanders, the Vlaams Nationaal Verbond, or National Flemish Front (V.N.V.), headed by Staf de Clercq, and later by Hendrik Elias. By 1940 this group was already a close ally of the Nazis. Consequently, quite a few members of the V.N.V. were given important positions in both local and central government. Moreover, V.N.V. members served in the Nazi war machine in Belgium and on the eastern front. A second group, the Nazi-sympathizing Rexist movement headed by Léon Degrelle, developed in Francophone Belgium. At first the Nazi *Wehrmacht* neglected Degrelle; however, after Degrelle created the Légion Wallonie, and that legion fought on the eastern front with some distinction, the group quickly became close to the S.S. within Belgium.[62]

Degrelle was born in 1906 in Bouillon, Belgium. At a very early stage in his life, he was influenced by Charles Maurras, a French nationalist. Degrelle became convinced that law, order, and monarchy were the most crucial factors for a nation. However, he did not stop there; his beliefs were also aligned with Nazi ideas of racial "purity" and anti-Semitism. In 1930 he established the Rexist movement, which was a Belgian fascist group modeled after Mussolini's Italian movement and which imitated Nazi tactics. Hitler, flattered by the imitation, is quoted as having said, "If I had a son, I would want him to be like Degrelle."[63] Much like the Norwegian case of Quisling, Belgians were not very impressed with Degrelle or with the Nazi führer's compliments on his behalf. Degrelle lost the crucial election of February 1937. The Nazi occupation of Belgium in 1940 breathed new life into Degrelle. He was revived politically and culturally. When he joined the forces of the Walloon legion to fight on the eastern front, Degrelle gained considerable respect in the eyes of the Nazis. Out of an original force of about 850 men, only three survived three years of fighting. In 1943 Degrelle negotiated the transfer of the legion to the Nazi Waffen S.S., and he was awarded several military decorations, including the Iron Cross with Oak Leaves.[64]

In 1945 Degrelle escaped to Spain. A Belgian high court sentenced him to death (in absentia) on charges of treason. Degrelle went to Argentina in 1946 but later returned to Madrid. A television interview he granted in April 1973 to a Dutch channel revealed that he regretted nothing. Among other things, he is reputed to have stated, "I am only sorry I didn't succeed, but if I had the chance, I would do it all again, but much more forcefully."[65] Degrelle died in Spain in 1994.

Much like Quisling, Degrelle was attracted to a fascist, pro-Nazi ideology early in his life. He never concealed his political and ideological sympathies, and when the Nazis conquered Belgium he felt that there was a golden opportunity to actualize some fascist and racist dreams he had been harboring for a long time. Like Quisling, he failed the free democratic test of elections by the people of his country. Whereas Quisling served as his country's minister of defense prior to the Nazi conquest, Degrelle never reached such a high position. However, judging by the decorations he received, Degrelle must have been a courageous individual.

It must be added that the fascist movement had contempt for conventional elections. Elections were viewed as a barrier to the authority of the fascist movement itself. Thus, those who were not too enthusiastic about fascist movements in regular elections were seen as needing correction or cleansing from the influence of what was referred to "bad and hostile elements." From the fascist point of view, a lack of support in conventional elections, while unfortunate, was not taken as a major ideological obstacle.

After the war, Belgians arrested between 50,000 and 60,000 of their own people on charges of treason; 596 of every 100,000 Belgians were in prison on charges of collaboration, and "Belgium pronounced the death penalty on 4,170 people, of whom 230 were executed."[66]

The Netherlands

The Nazi *Wehrmacht* invaded the Netherlands on May 10, 1940. Following the heavy bombardment of Amsterdam on May 14, the Dutch surrendered the same day. Queen Wilhelmina fled to England, and a government in exile was formed in London. The Nazis viewed the Dutch as descendants of an Aryan race, in need of reintegration with the Third Reich. Hitler appointed Arthur Seyss-Inquart in charge of the Netherlands, aided by German S.S. and Police Chief Hanns Albin Rauter. Between these two Austrians, they managed to get out of the Netherlands all that it was possible to take out in terms of food and merchandise and ship it to Germany. These Nazi masters ran a harsh and brutal conquest administration.

Although there was a Dutch resistance movement,[67] there were also some cases of possible betrayal. Before the Nazi invasion, there actually was a Dutch Nazi Party. In the 1937 general election, that party won about

4 percent of the electorate.[68] The size of the party grew from around 30,000 members before the Nazi invasion to about 50,000 after the invasion.

Although Anton Adriaan Mussert, the leader of the Dutch Nazi Party, kept funneling suggestions to Hitler about Aryanizing the Dutch people, he never received any serious answer from Berlin.[69] He was appointed by the Nazis in 1942 as the leader of the Dutch people, but his leadership was on paper only. On May 7, 1945, Mussert was arrested by the Dutch as a traitor and collaborator, and he was executed by hanging at The Hague on May 7, 1946.[70]

Another interesting case is that of General Hendrik Alexander Seyffardt, who was the chief of staff of the Dutch army between 1929 and 1934, when he retired as a lieutenant general. Following the German occupation of the Netherlands, Seyffardt came out of retirement, changed sides, and became a major collaborator with Nazi Germany. He willingly lent his past reputation to the Nazi cause and formed a volunteer unit called the "Vrijkorps," which fought with the Nazi *Wehrmacht* in the Soviet Union. He was assassinated in The Hague on February 5, 1943.[71]

Foot estimates that out of a population close to 9 million, "over 5,000 Dutchmen joined the Waffen-S.S., and another 54,000 belonged of their own free will to various other Nazi organizations."[72]

Clearly there were many Dutch who were Nazi sympathizers and who assisted the Nazis in hunting down Jews. About 80 percent of the estimated 150,000 Dutch Jews were exterminated, and only about 4 percent of the 110,000 who were deported to camps returned.[73]

After the war, the Netherlands had 130,000 of its own people arrested on charges of treason, and 40,000 served prison sentences (about "419 out of every 100,000 Dutchmen"). Overall, "as many as 60,000 Dutch collaborators were deprived of their civil rights, and the Netherlands carried out thirty-six out of 130 death sentences."[74]

The cases of Quisling, Degrelle, and Mussert share similarities. In each case, a preoccupation Nazi sympathizer failed politically within his own country. None of them hid their sympathies, and they all seized the first opportunity they had to try and push their pro-Nazi ideas. Yet none of them were successful.

France

On June 22, 1940, within about six weeks of the successful Nazi invasion, France's military machine was incapacitated by the superior military war juggernaut of Nazi Germany, and France was forced to sign an armistice agreement with the Nazis. Dank[75] implies that when the French army retreated, French citizens, fearing German reprisals, prevented the French Army from sabotaging bridges or even fighting sometimes. French losses were astounding: about 90,000 dead and 200,000 wounded plus about 1.9 million prisoners or missing. France was divided into several administrative areas. From that point in time, the issue of French collaboration with the Nazis became a painful and complicated reality for the French. Of the areas into which France was divided, the southern zone is of most interest to us.

Marshal Philippe Pétain.   The man who replaced Paul Reynaud as French prime minister on June 16, 1940, was Marshal Philippe Pétain. Born in 1856, Pétain was the victor of the World War I battle of Verdun and had gained the position of a military hero. He was the one who had negotiated the armistice agreement with the Nazis and the one who signed it. In fact, on June 17, 1940, at 12:30,

> the quavering broken voice of a Marshal of France, the eighty-four-year-old Philippe Pétain, announced over the radio that France had lost not just a battle but the war as well. . . .
>
> "Françaises! At the Request of the President of the Republic, I assume as of today the direction of the government of France. . . .
>
> I give to France the gift of my person to alleviate her misfortunes. . . . It is with a sad heart that I say to you today that the fighting must stop."[76]

Pétain headed the French collaborationist regime, whose headquarters were in the resort town of Vichy. Between July 1940 and August 1944, Pétain's regime developed a genuine collaboration with the Nazis: military, political, economic, cultural, and personal. Some authors even claim that the very meaning of World War II collaboration can, and should, be traced to Vichy's France. Hirschfeld and Marsh's 1989 collection is reflective of the great number of books written on this subject, revealing the depth and scope of French collaboration in ideology, fine arts, filmmaking, theater, and in political and economic areas. Indeed, an orchestrated attempt was made to convert France as much as possible to German National Socialism.[77] Moreover, the collaborationist direction taken by the Vichy government was presented as a new, positive, and bold political order for France. Viewing itself as the rightful government of France, this collaborationist regime had no difficulty deciding that others were traitors. The events involving Charles de Gaulle, who later became president of France, are instructive.

Charles de Gaulle (1890–1970), a veteran of World War I, was promoted to brigadier general on June 1, 1940, fought the Nazi invasion, and was appointed undersecretary for national defense by French prime minister Reynaud on June 6. De Gaulle's tenure in his new post lasted only ten days. On June 16, Reynaud resigned and Pétain, who replaced him, negotiated the armistice with Hitler. This meant the end of de Gaulle's short

Pétain with his enlarged government, 1940. Pierre Laval is to the left of Pétain, and General Weygand is on the right.

SOURCE: *Reprinted from Werner Rings,* Life with the Enemy: Collaboration and Resistance in Hitler's Europe, 1939–1945, *translated by J. Maxwell Brownjohn (London: Weidenfeld and Nicolson, 1982). Photograph from Suddeutscher Verlag, Munich.*

career in Reynaud's government. On June 17, 1940, a Royal Air Force airplane transported de Gaulle to London. From there, on June 18, 1940, he made his famous speech on the BBC urging Frenchmen to continue fighting the Nazis because France, in his words, had lost a battle but not the war. The rest is history. De Gaulle eventually became the undisputed leader of the Free France movement.

Pétain's regime had no difficulty deciding what to do with the recalcitrant de Gaulle. Pétain ordered him to return to France, but de Gaulle refused. Consequently, on July 4, 1940, he was sentenced, in absentia, by a court-martial appointed by Pétain, to four years in prison. This obviously was ineffective and was thus perceived as insufficient. The Vichy regime then declared de Gaulle a traitor to France.

> The Vichy minister of war, General Colson, on July 12 ordered him tried for treason and desertion in time of war. This time (August 12) the verdict was . . . death in absentia and confiscation of all property.

Pétain later wrote: "This verdict was required by the need for discipline, to set an example, in order to stop the exodus of French officers out of the country, but it is clear that this verdict in absentia can only be in principle. It has never been my thought that it would be imposed."[78]

It is important to note that the above memo written by Pétain was drafted in August 1944 when it was clear that de Gaulle won.

After the war, Pétain was put on trial, which began on July 23, 1945. Although technically he was charged with a few specific crimes, the gist of the trial was that he betrayed his country by collaborating with the Nazis and working with them against the interests of France. During Pétain's trial, French premier Edouard Daladier was put on the stand to testify.[79]

Before delving into Daladier's testimony, some background facts about Daladier must be mentioned. Daladier had to resign his third premiership (on March 20, 1940) because of doubts about his prewar leadership (he was replaced with his political rival Paul Reynaud). He was arrested by the Vichy collaborationist government in September 1940 and tried at Riom (1942) on charges that he had direct responsibility for the French defeat. His trial was only one among many that the collaborationist Vichy government initiated. The purpose of the trials was to construct the image that prominent French politicians were directly responsible for the beginning of World War II as well as for what was referred to as "political corruption," which was blamed for France's military defeat. Because the defenders were allowed to speak freely, the trials became embarrassing for Pétain, and thus they were suspended.[80] Daladier was handed over to the Germans after the trial (in which he defended himself admirably) but was freed in 1945.

This is what Daladier had to say when he was asked by the prosecution whether Pétain betrayed his country: "In all conscience, I will answer that in my opinion Marshal Pétain betrayed the duties of his office." When required to elaborate he added: "The word treason has many different meanings. There are men who betray their country for money; there are men who betray it sometimes out of pure incompetence. . . . As for Marshal Pétain I will state frankly—even though it pains me—that he betrayed his duties as a Frenchman."[81] It is interesting to note that Daladier seemed to have used the criterion of motivation in deciding whether Pétain was a traitor, as well as the character of his treason.

Pétain denied the charges against him and stated that he tried to help as much as he could and was able to maintain France's unity for four difficult years. On August 15, 1945, Pétain was found guilty and sentenced to death. The sentence was never carried out, and he died in prison in 1951.

Was Pétain a traitor or a hero? Lottman (1985) finds it difficult to answer this question. Pétain himself most certainly did not think he committed treason, and he was not the only one.[82] The way in which he conducted himself while heading the Vichy government was obviously aimed at maintaining, as best as he could, French nationalism under very difficult conditions. However, the price he paid for that unity was much too high in terms of the depth of his collaboration with the Nazis, and it is very doubtful that what Pétain wanted was achievable at all. Moreover, his goals were not always clear.

Pierre Laval.   Pierre Laval provides us with another case of a traitor-collaborator. He was Pétain's vice premier until December 1940, when Pétain dismissed him. Attempts to replace Laval with others did not work well, and under Nazi pressure, Laval was reinstituted in April 1942.

Born in 1883, he later became a lawyer, and his initial career was affiliated with French socialism. However, he drifted to the right. On June 25, 1940, he joined Pétain's collaborationist government and was very effective in promoting French-German collaboration, in which he was a genuine believer. Laval was certainly favored by the Germans. After his return to power in April 1942, he broadcast an appeal to the French people to work hand in hand with the Nazis (June 1942) and added that he supported a German victory in order to prevent communism from prevailing. Laval tried to get some concessions from the Germans in return for collaboration, but that did not work out very well. He was effective in providing French workers for Germany and gave the Germans foreign Jews who lived in France. These steps were rationalized as sacrificing the few in order to save the many. However, Nazi demands were growing, and Laval's policy simply collapsed. After the war, Laval tried to find asylum outside France but did not succeed. He was extradited to France where he was sentenced to death (in a rather controversial trial). Although he tried to commit suicide by taking poison, his life was saved only so that he could be executed on October 9, 1945.[83]

Although "the collaborationist movements represented a very small if vocal proportion of the French population during the German occupation,"[84] the Vichy government, headed by Laval and Pétain, certainly marked a direction of voluntary and willing collaboration. Thus, Laval and Pétain are probably the most prominent names associated with French collaboration during World War II.[85]

The collaboration of the French with the Nazis produced many individual cases of betrayal.[86] After the war, the issue of dealing with collaborators came up. The widespread collaboration was such that it was not possible to prosecute every collaborator. However, tens of thousands of collaborators were prosecuted. Following the liberation of Paris by the Allies, hundreds of French women with shaved heads were forced into the streets carrying big signs stating that they had had intimate relations with Germans.[87] According to official figures, the resistance executed more than 10,800 persons suspected of collaborating with the Nazis. This is Selwyn's description of one such case:

> Robert Brassillach, the young editor of the pro-Vichy Je Suis Partout, insisted
> . . . that he acted in the best interests of his country. He had undoubtedly
> been consistent. His views as a journalist had been fascist before the war.
> Brassillach had simply not changed them. He died before a firing squad on 6
> February 1945 at the fortress of Montrouge with a cry of "Courage! Vive la
> France!"[88]

Although after the war many of the collaborators were prosecuted and punished, the scope of these prosecutions is difficult to assess. "In France, more than 6,000 men and women were condemned to death for collaboration with the Germans, let alone those who met a summary fate immediately after the liberation."[89] A different set of numbers is provided by Dank who notes that French courts had to deal with 125,000 cases of women and men who were charged with collaboration with the Nazis and betraying France. Of those, 2,853 were sentenced to death, and of those, 767 were actually executed. According to Dank, post–World War II France sent to firing squads more people than any other occupied country in Europe.[90] Archer provides still a different number: "In 1946, the French, purging citizens who had turned collaborationist during the Nazi occupation, arrested half a million men and women on charges of treason."[91]

Novick's work also tried to assess this issue and is probably the better one. He maintains that from the known cases in the Cours de justice, 45,017 were not prosecuted and 50,095 were heard; around 39,000 were sent to prison. Novick notes that "presidential commutations spared all but 3 of the 8 men sentenced to death by the High Court, and all but 767 of the 2,853 sentenced to death by the cours de justice."[92] In the Chambres civique, 67,965 cases were processed.[93] Novick also tried to assess some summary executions statistics. His research indicates that there are two sets of data. One set indicates that 5,234 cases occurred before liberation and 4,439 after it (totaling 9,673 cases). The second set considers cases where the motive could not be established satisfactorily (1,955 cases) and adds pre- and post-liberation cases (8,867) for a total of 10,822 cases.[94] Having painstakingly examined the issue of the magnitude of summary executions of suspected collaborators, Novick comes to the conclusion that the "official numbers" (ranging between 9,200 and 11,100 cases) must be taken as a minimum. The methodological problems involved in assessing the numbers, and hence the magnitude of the French reaction to collaboration in this regard, are simply too complex to be solved. However, even these minimal numbers are high, and Novick indeed adds that "94 out of every 100,000 Frenchmen were imprisoned for collaboration."[95]

Clemency, however, began in 1947, and in March 1954 all punishments given in absentia were canceled. By 1964, not even one collaborator remained in any French prison.[96]

Visiting Vichy.   Between June 24 and June 27, 1998, I visited Vichy, a small, quiet, and very pleasant French town about three hours by train from Paris. The amazing thing is that there is absolutely nothing in Vichy that presents any connection to the World War II period. I had to ask a French colleague to show me the building where the Vichy government was. There were no markings, no signs, nothing. The "Vichy Guide" pamphlet distributed to tourists (as well as the interpretations given in local organized tours) state the following:

THE END OF THE THIRD REPUBLIC, THE WAR, AND THE OCCUPATION

After the 1940 French defeat, Maréchal Pétain was in charge of forming a new government. Général de Gaulle broadcasted his famous call from London on June 18.

The French government, unable to stay in Paris, moved to Bordeaux.

After the 1940 Armistice, the government had to leave Bordeaux, occupied by the German Army, and moved to Vichy. The reasons for this choice were the hotel facilities of the "queen of spa towns" and a modern telephone switchboard.

On July 1, the government took possession of the hotels. Six hundred members of parliament voted in favor of the Fourth Republic. The republican regime was abolished. The French State replaced it, with Philippe Pétain as head of state (only eighty members of parliament out of six hundred opposed the bill).

From that date onward, Vichy became the capital of the French State for four years.[97]

There was not a word about the nature of the defeat, about a death sentence for de Gaulle, or the nature of the collaborationist "French State" ruled from Vichy.[98] Thus, the question of the necessity and legitimacy of the Vichy regime is still not settled in France.

Resistance.   Collaboration requires discussing French resistance as well. There were forms of French cultural resistance and contempt for the Germans. However, the most famous French resistance was the Maquis.[99]

French resistance began with sporadic individual acts, and armed action was rare at that stage. As the war continued, and Nazi Germany invaded the Soviet Union, resistance grew as different groups began to organize and act. After much effort and sacrifice (including that of Jean

Moulin who was captured on June 21, 1943, tortured, and killed), the Maquis was created in 1943. Struggling with objective difficulties, the Maquis eventually mastered armed resistance. The cost was high. About 90,000 resisters were killed, tortured, or deported, and thousands of others suffered Nazi reprisals.

Admiral Jean François Darlan.   We shall end the section on French collaboration with the case of Jean François Darlan. When World War II began, Fleet Admiral Darlan was the commander in chief of the French Navy. The navy was a modern and powerful force concentrated in the Mediterranean Sea. It had seven battleships (two of which were battle cruisers), seven heavy cruisers, twelve light cruisers, seventy-one destroyers, and seventy-six submarines plus a large number of smaller and auxiliary craft. After the defeat of France (June 1940), Darlan assured British prime minister Winston Churchill that the French fleet would never fall into German hands. However, following the surrender of France, Admiral Darlan did not order the French fleet to sail to British or neutral ports. Instead he ordered his fleet to sail to French colonial bases in North Africa. The British were obviously suspicious of the intentions of the French fleet, and fearing it might act against them, they sent strong British naval forces to engage and neutralize the French naval forces in Mers el Kébir (a naval base near the Algerian port of Oran) and Alexandria (July 3–6, 1940).[100] A few days after the defeat of France, Darlan gave his allegiance to Marshal Philippe Pétain and accepted a position as minister of the navy and later as vice premier (February 1941) in the Vichy regime.[101]

As vice premier in the Vichy government, Admiral Darlan pursued a policy of limited cooperation with the Axis powers. He most certainly presented a slick and evasive front. Darlan confided to the U.S. ambassador, William D. Leahy, that he would dissociate himself from collaboration and would welcome strong Allied intervention if supported with adequate strength (Boveri states that Darlan mentioned a force of 500,000 men).[102] Darlan's zigzagging created a situation where neither the Germans nor the Allies really knew where his loyalties lay or whether Darlan could be trusted.

Early in 1942 Darlan lost his ministerial posts when Laval returned to power, but he was given command of all French armed forces and named high commissioner of French North Africa.

The Anglo-American invasion of French North Africa was launched on November 8, 1942.[103] Despite attempts to secure French nonresistance, the invading Allies did encounter resistance by French forces, especially at the naval base of Oran. That port was assaulted on November 8, 1942. Despite its formidable defenses, opposition was overcome within two days of the landings.[104] It so happens that at that particular time, Darlan was visiting his sick son in Algiers (his visit began November 6). The French resistance to the Allies and Darlan's presence in Algiers provoked negotiations between Eisenhower's deputy, Mark Clark, and Darlan (November 9). The Nazis began applying pressure on Pétain to accept German "support" in Tunisia. Pétain was trying to gain time and prevent German occupation of southern France and thus kept sending Admiral Darlan contradictory and vague messages. Darlan was able to delay a cease-fire agreement to November 11, when German forces entered Vichy-controlled France.

Darlan's success in securing the active support of French officers in Tunisia was only partially successful, and the situation remained confused. The remains of the French fleet in Toulon delayed sailing to North Africa and scuttled more than seventy fleet units on November 27. Since Darlan's authority was accepted by at least part of the French forces in North Africa, General Eisenhower designated him commander and political head of French North Africa. Eisenhower's move was severely criticized in Britain and the United States, causing much embarrassment.[105] And yet Stalin had a favorable view: "I consider it a remarkable feat on your part that you have succeeded in drawing Darlan and the others to the side of the Allies."[106] How does one describe someone who collaborated with the Nazis who then helps the Allies? The solution was the designation of Darlan as a "temporary expedient."[107]

Verrier's 1990 work implies that Admiral Darlan was a key player in a pivotal episode of World War II. Behind Darlan's presence in Algiers in 1942, says Verrier, lay a conflict between Roosevelt and Churchill, on which hung the fate of France. He claims that the "choice" both Churchill and Roosevelt faced was between Darlan and de Gaulle. Verrier is quick to point out that Darlan was Pétain's former deputy and Roosevelt's collaborator in maintaining the Vichy administration of North Africa as a full and repressive force.[108] Roosevelt was apparently not a great admirer of de Gaulle and preferred Darlan. According to Verrier's interpretation, the reason for this preference was Roosevelt's interest in reducing the size, influence, and power of the French empire. To accomplish that, a complaisant Frenchman had to be found. Darlan seemed like the ideal choice for that purpose.

On Christmas Eve, 1942, Fernand de la Chapelle Bonnier (1922–1942), a twenty-year-old member of the French resistance entered the office of Admiral Darlan and fired at him two deadly shots from a 7.65-caliber pistol. Bonnier was a member of a group of five young anti-Nazi Frenchmen who plotted the assassination because they thought Darlan was a traitor. Although he viewed himself as a national hero, others did not. A court-martial ordered by General Henri Giraud (see below) condemned him to death. He was executed on the morning of December 26, 1942.[109] Clearly,

Darlan's assassination removed a possible obstacle to de Gaulle's march to become the leader of France. Moreover, it allowed a morally nonproblematic person to take the helm. It is probable that Darlan's wartime zigzags would have encumbered a postwar French political career.

In view of Verrier's 1990 work, it is possible that the assassination of Darlan was a major crossroad in the modern history of France. It eased de Gaulle's rise to leadership. However, one must remember that even if Verrier's work is valid, elevating Darlan could not have been an easy task in view of his public image and collaboration with the Nazis. Indeed Wheal, Pope, and Taylor note that the assassination of Darlan spared "the Allies further embarrassment" and eased "the relations with French Colonial forces."[110] Thus, any such plan to undermine the influence of France, as suggested by Verrier, had to consider the shaky public position of Darlan.

After the assassination, General Henri Giraud (1879–1949) assumed the position of high commissioner for French North and West Africa. Giraud, clearly and publicly anti-Nazi, had been taken prisoner during the Nazi attack on France in the summer of 1940 but escaped in April 1942. In November he was taken to Algiers in a British submarine to help in operation Torch. The Allies (especially the United States) considered Giraud a more suitable person for their purposes than de Gaulle. However, de Gaulle—notorious for his stubborn independence—managed to politically neutralize him, and de Gaulle's maneuvers cost Giraud his American support as well. In April 1943 he quit his position as high commissioner for French Africa. Continued confrontations with de Gaulle led to his resignation from his second position as commander in chief of the Free French Army in April 1944.[111]

In retrospect, it seems obvious that Darlan had become a problematic figure. Verrier (1990) states that Darlan was Churchill's "odious Quisling," George Patton's "little red-faced pig," and Robert Aron's "great enigma of the war." Indeed, Boveri's work on treason in the twentieth century devotes a whole chapter to Darlan.[112] Attacked in the press, distrusted by both countrymen and foreigners, how could he have justified his actions?

According to Boveri (1956), Darlan justified the decision to leave the French fleet in French ports by stating that "if he had ordered it to set sail and put in at a British or Canadian harbor the German reprisals in Metropolitan France would have been terrible" (p. 126), adding that "he had obtained a promise from the Germans that the fleet would not be touched, and had in turn promised Churchill at their last meeting that the fleet would never fall into German hands. This engagement was respected by Darlan and his subordinates to the last minute detail" (p. 127). Boveri (p. 128) states that Darlan's son was ill with polio and that Roosevelt's kind treatment of Darlan should be understood in that humane context (Roosevelt himself was crippled by that same disease).

Boveri, as well as others, points out that the cooperation of some Allied figures with Darlan was made with much uneasiness. But the realization that North African French troops were committed and loyal to Vichy necessitated that cooperation. Indeed, that is why Robert Murphy, President Roosevelt's special envoy, began negotiating with Darlan. In an apologetic letter to Roosevelt, Churchill shows full awareness of the moral implications of using Darlan:

> The more I reflect upon it, the more convinced I become that it can only be a temporary expedient justified notably by the stress of battle. We must meet the serious political injury which may be done to our cause, not only in France but throughout Europe, by the feeling that we are ready to make terms with the local Quislings. Darlan has an odious record. It is he who has inculcated in the French Navy its malignant disposition by promoting his creatures to command.[113]

Roosevelt's withdrawal of support from Darlan decreased French readiness to cooperate in North Africa.

Shortly before his assassination, Darlan wrote letters to Churchill, Eisenhower, and Leahy.[114] Perhaps his best defense can be found in his letter to Churchill dated December 4, 1942, in which he stated:

> From January, 1941, until April, 1942, by order of my chief, Marshal Pétain, I carried out policies without the implementation of which France and her colonies would have been crushed. These policies were unfortunately diametrically opposed to yours. What else could I have done? You were in no position to offer the slightest help, and any gesture in your direction would have brought disaster to my country.

His letter to Eisenhower also indicates his realization of declining American support and his bitterness about it.

Although Churchill bitterly opposed Darlan's handling of the fleet, he nevertheless paid careful tribute to Darlan and noted that, as he had promised, the French fleet never fell into German hands.[115]

How are we to view Darlan's actions? Was he a collaborator and traitor? The Nazi defeat of France placed him in a very complex situation. He was the commander in chief of a powerful navy. What was he to do? Collaborate with Pétain's Vichy government? Order the fleet to sail to British ports? That very same navy, one must remember, had been an ally of Britain and, in fact, assisted in the evacuation from Dunkirk. What were his interests? Among other things, he wanted to preserve the French empire and colonies, maintain the integrity of the French fleet, and minimize the effects of the occupation of France—all in the face of determined and ruthless Nazi rule. It was an overwhelming task.

Moreover, it was probably not a realistic goal. For example, to what extent was it realistic to expect to maintain a peripheral colonial independence while the empire's center was occupied by enemy forces? The real test for Darlan, and individuals like him, was whether to grind one's teeth, collaborate with the Nazis, and try to minimize damage to France, or to face Nazism for what it really was and defy it in the strongest possible way—that is, join the British. Once we accept that Darlan saw the reality of the occupation, decided to play along, and tried to minimize damage, then his zigzagging actions become understandable. Not morally justified but understandable.

Darlan, perhaps well-intentioned, failed to see the evil of the Nazi regime and preferred to collaborate with it. One needs to be reminded that Darlan could have taken the risk and joined the Allies. However, this is only part of the story. The other part is that Churchill and Roosevelt were concerned with the postwar world order, and so was de Gaulle. The potential and actual inner political conflicts among members of the Allied forces also played a part. At the very least, Darlan did collaborate with the Nazis, causing at some points more trouble to the Allies. To answer the question, was Darlan a French Quisling (in the jargon used in Churchill's letter), we need to ask, from whose point of view?

The Channel Islands

The Channel Islands comprise nine islands, the largest of which are the islands of Jersey and Guernsey, positioned about forty miles west of Cherbourg and about eighty miles south of England. Following the German victory over France, Germans began bombardment of the islands on June 28, 1940. Invasion and occupation began on June 30. This military move cost the lives of forty-four islanders and the evacuation of about 30,000 civilians. About 60,000 remained in the islands. The occupation ended on May 9, 1945, when the German garrison there surrendered. The conquest and occupation of this British territory was the closest the Germans ever got to the mainland of Britain.

The issue of collaboration with the Nazis in these islands was a complicated one. It appears that previous claims that the occupation was moderate reflected the experience of the islands' collaborative administrators, who were treated well by the Nazis. Life for the ordinary islander was harsh, as starvation, imprisonment, and harsh fines were commonplace. In September 1942, 2,000 British-born citizens were deported to internment camps in Germany, and in January 1943, another 200 were deported as revenge for a British commando raid. Collaboration was also common, not only by local administrators (who helped the Nazis control the islands and cooperated in the deportation of Jews to concentration camps), but also by black marketeers, informers, and a host of British women, referred to as "Jerry bags," who dated soldiers from the German garrison.[116]

Concluding Discussion

Chapters 5 and 6 provide us with a broad view of some of the issues of treason during World War II. In these chapters, we examine the empirical meaning of treason in a situation of extreme conflict where moral boundaries are continuously challenged and when loyalty and trust become debatable issues. In a series of cases, we have seen how simple appearances contrast with complex realities and how, in each case, treason is defined within a specific context.

Fifth columnism is a conspiracy aimed at disintegrating a government from within a country. Close examination of the reality behind this concept reveals a complex factual level, where fifth columnism may be less prevalent than commonly believed. The term "fifth column" has also come to refer to political influence and subversion.

Collaboration also provides us with a complex reality. The popular image of World War II collaborators is a negative one; it implies that collaborators were willing to close their eyes to the evil of Nazism and help it to achieve its goal of European domination. In many cases, this evaluation is valid. However, once we accept that the moral judgment of "collaboration" is not clear-cut, then we can examine the complex reality.

There are different types and levels of collaboration, and one needs to ask, what real choices did people have under Nazi occupation? Could they choose the least damaging one, or even one of the many forms of resistance (active or passive)? The reality behind "collaboration" was much more complex than the simple black-and-white dichotomy. There were many forms of collaboration and resistance, each with a somewhat different moral charge.

Moreover, some of those referred to as "collaborators" believed in the Nazi ideology and were committed to it prior to the Nazi occupation (for example, Degrelle, Quisling, and Seyss-Inquart). Although evaluating their activities as treacherous may seem to be a complex issue, the violation of trust and loyalty can be established in each of their cases. Obviously, it requires that we define whose loyalty and what trust they breached. Doing that may necessitate taking a stand, which brings us back to Chapter 1, where it was pointed out that this study requires making judgments. The issues of loyalty and trust in collaboration are sharp and painful. Overall, one can examine—in detail—the realities in which potential traitors were immersed, their possible options in terms of action, as well as their actual choices. And in each of the cases presented in this chapter, choices are assessed in terms of realities and options. From this perspective, the important point is that regardless of the specific direction of the violations of trust and loyalty, in each of these cases, it is possible to establish that such violations in fact took place.

The issue of collaboration in World War II surfaced again during the 1990s. It is now clear that Swiss banks and European insurance companies collaborated with the Nazis in their confiscation of economic assets from Holocaust victims. Holocaust survivors demanded compensation for the profits made by these institutions from their confiscated assets. During 1998 the claim was expanded to include the collaboration of various industries with the Nazi war machine and the Nazis' use of slave labor during the war.[117] The same issues we faced in examining treason and collaboration during World War II in this chapter also surfaced in these recent discussions about collaboration.

We shall continue our examination of cases of betrayal during World War II in Chapter 6.

6

Violating Trust and Loyalty During World War II: Part 2

In the previous chapter we examined a few cases of betrayal in Western Europe, as well as cases of collaboration and fifth columnism. In this chapter we shall continue this examination by looking at some cases in Eastern Europe, Germany, the Far East, and the Middle East.

Yugoslavia: The Chetniks and General Draža Mihajlović

Here is another illustration for the complicated meaning of trust, loyalty, and treason. This case concerns the background of the Nazi invasion into the Balkans. The German attack on the Balkans on April 6, 1941, exacerbated the inner tensions in the Royal Yugoslavian Army, which reflected the deep cleavages characteristic of Yugoslav society. During the attack, Croat units mutinied, and many welcomed the Nazi invasion. By April 16, the Yugoslav army simply disintegrated. Once King Peter II (1923–1970) and his government fled to England in 1941, resistance based on Serbian nationalism began. In late 1941 royalist Serbian Yugoslav commander General Draža Mihajlović, born 1893, organized and led the resistance to the Axis army. His guerrilla forces called themselves Chetniks and operated only in Serbia.

At the time of its formation in 1941, the Chetnik resistance was hailed in the West as the first guerrilla movement in Europe to fight the Nazis. General Draža Mihajlović's reputation as a nationalist leader was both local and international. In fact, he was appointed minister of defense by the Yugoslav government in exile in London. However, it did not take long for General Mihajlović to find himself in conflict with a different new force. That force was the Communist-led guerrilla movement, commanded by

Croatian Josip Broz, also known as Marshal Tito (who was the general secretary of the Yugoslav Communist Party prior to World War II). Tito's organized forces were called "Partisans," after the irregular forces who fought against Napoleon in Spain in 1808 and in Russia in 1812.

General Mihajlović made repeated truces with the Germans in an attempt to minimize casualties. Marshal Tito was much more aggressive and ruthless in his tactics and consequently more effective. This difference did not escape Churchill's attention. At a conference in Teheran (November 28–December 1, 1943), the first meeting of Winston S. Churchill, Joseph Stalin, and Franklin D. Roosevelt (the Big Three), the Allies decided to support Tito's forces. It is worth noting Lees's (1990) somewhat different version. He suggests that British Communists fed Churchill misleading information regarding General Mihajlović's activities and that this information led him to prefer Tito. Lees implies that Mihajlović was actually betrayed.

As clashes continued with the Partisans, the Chetniks, lacking real support from the Allies, were drawn into the sphere of Nazi Germany through continued negotiations, and their collaboration with Axis forces increased. They first collaborated with the Italians, and later with the Nazis, to combat the Partisans, whom they viewed as the primary enemy. During this phase, the Chetniks collaborated quite openly with the Nazis in Yugoslavia. At the very least, it is clear that although General Mihajlović opposed the Nazi occupation, he most definitely collaborated with them on more than one occasion.

The Chetniks were destroyed in May 1945, after their attempts to gain support from the Allies and the local population failed. General Mihajlović went into hiding but was caught on March 12, 1946, and taken to Belgrade the next day. On June 10, 1946, his trial on charges of collaboration with the Nazis and for high treason and war crimes began. The well-publicized trial lasted until July 15. He was found guilty and sentenced to death. On July 17, 1946, a firing squad executed him. Twenty-three other collaborators were also tried with him. In 1992 Serbia erected a monument memorializing Mihajlović at Ravna Gora, rehabilitating him (and several other World War II collaborators).

Chetniks used mass terror against their enemies. Some of the most outrageous acts took place between October 1942 and February 1943. Among other acts, the Chetniks were involved in "cleansing" actions against Muslims and Croatians in counterterror activities. It is important to note that the Chetniks were not the only collaborators with Axis forces. There were other Serbian and Slovenian forces who collaborated with Nazi Germany.[1]

As in other European countries, the Nazi occupation made the issue of the content of betrayal a complex one in Yugoslavia. The personal decisions of Mihajlović and individual Chetniks were directly related to the existing political and military reality; that is, decisionmaking was related to power, as well as the complex (and sometimes conflicting) interests and moralities in which loyalty and trust were contextualized.

It is, perhaps, unfair not to mention in this context the secret fascist organization that was founded around 1929 by extreme Croatian nationalist Ante Pavelić—the Ustachi. Following the fall of Yugoslavia in 1941, Pavelić and the Ustachi declared (on April 10) the establishment of an "independent" Croatia, and under a Nazi umbrella they ruled it ruthlessly, violently, and mercilessly until 1945. This regime committed numerous barbarous and brutal purges and massacres against those they viewed as their "opponents"—Jews, Muslims, Orthodox Serbs, and others. After the end of World War II Pavelić escaped to Argentina.

The issue of whether Pavelić and the Ustachi were traitors is an interesting one. They collaborated with the Nazis and were involved in some extremely brutal activities, but from the late 1920s on, these individuals had never hidden their desire for an independent fascist Croatia, minus ethnic groups they did not want in their nightmarish "state." Although it is possible, and even imperative, to accuse the Ustachi and Pavelić with war crimes and atrocities, betrayal may be a more difficult charge to support because one needs to establish exactly who they betrayed. Although it is possible to argue that these terrorists violated the trust and loyalty of other Yugoslav citizens, it may be equally argued that many of their victims never trusted or were loyal to the Ustachi, and thus the term "betrayal" here is on a higher level of citizens (with power) against citizens (without power), like Stalin's purges, Hitler's genocide—or state-sponsored terrorism. Moreover, like the many Germans who welcomed Hitler, many Croatians welcomed the Ustachi. For those, no betrayal was involved.[2]

Romania: The Iron Guard and Antonescu

In March 1939 Romania and Germany signed an agreement that established the priority of Germany in the Romanian economy. Basically, Germany helped to develop the Romanian economy, and the majority of Romanian products were purchased by Germany. This 1939 agreement continued a trend of increased mutual dependence and cooperation between the two countries that had begun after the 1938 Munich agreement. This trend was reinforced in May 1940 when the Romanian government decided to align with Germany. Following a series of agreements, almost one-third of Romania was given to other countries, and in return, other parts of it remained under Romanian control. Following these forced concessions, King Carol II was forced to step down, and his son Michael took over (September 6, 1940). Prior to his abdication, Carol had appointed

General Ion Antonescu as the powerful premier (September 4). In October 1940, the Germans were already in the process of creating a Romanian army, and more of the Romanian economy was shifted to fit the needs of the German war machine.

At first, the infamous Iron Guard—a military organization of the Romanian fascist movement—was a partner to Antonescu. A ruthless and violent group that practiced violence against both its opponents and Jews, the Iron Guard and its terrorist tactics eventually interfered with Antonescu's regime. He thus began to disarm them (and strengthened the army). This caused the Iron Guard to rebel against Antonescu and Germany (January 21, 1941). That rebellion was crushed, and by January 27, 1941, Antonescu had formed a new government (composed mostly of military officers).

So far it was clear that Romania, as a country, was shrinking and that it was being drawn more and more into the clutches of Nazi Germany. Did King Carol betray his country's interests, integrity, trust, and loyalty by giving up so much territory and compromising Romania's sovereignty? Did he have any other options? Was the Iron Guard betraying Romania? It certainly violated, brutally, the trust and loyalty of other Romanian citizens by using violence against them (like the Ustachi).

There is little doubt that Antonescu collaborated with the Nazis. His suppression of the Iron Guard was made on purely pragmatic grounds (they were interfering with the preparations for the Nazi invasion of the Soviet Union). However, Hitler's respect for Antonescu helped the latter keep a semblance of an independent Romania. The price for that was Romanian support (economic and military) for the Nazi war effort. When Germany invaded the Soviet Union on June 22, 1941 (Operation Barbarosa), Antonescu ordered Romanian army divisions to join the invasion. He also managed to secure the support of the Romanian people for that war effort. The short-term gains of that military cooperation were such that Romania recaptured some of the territories it had previously lost.[3] However, as the war with the Soviet Union continued, Romanian troops suffered increasing casualties. Consequently, Antonescu's popularity decreased.

Was Ion Antonescu a traitor? Born in 1886, Antonescu developed a military career and by 1932 had been appointed minister of war. Following his appointment as premier in September of 1940, Antonescu established a pro-German military fascist dictatorship known as the National Legionary State. Within a month of his appointment, Antonescu had signed a pact with the Axis powers and won Hitler's trust.

At the beginning Antonescu enjoyed popularity, and with the success of the early war effort in the Soviet Union, he promoted himself to the rank of marshall. However, the military losses involved in the continued

Romanian involvement in Nazi Germany's war in the Soviet Union prompted Antonescu to search for ways to pull Romania out of the German alliance, and he began to explore the possibilities for negotiation of a peace settlement. These efforts increased after the Nazi defeat at Stalingrad (January 1943), but they failed when Antonescu refused the Allies' demand for an unconditional surrender. Eventually, with the Russian invasion of Romania imminent, King Michael signed an armistice agreement and had Antonescu arrested on August 23, 1944. In 1946 Antonescu was charged with treason and war crimes. A Romanian communist "People's Court" found him guilty and sentenced him to death. He was executed on June 1, 1946.[4]

Romania is an interesting case that gives us a different perspective on betrayal. Basically, Romania acted as an ally of Nazi Germany. And yet when the fascist Iron Guard seemed to pose a threat, it was crushed. As the tide of the war turned against the Nazis, pressure grew within Romania to change course. Thus, before 1943, in Nazi-friendly Romania, the Iron Guard was regarded as extreme and traitorous. After 1943, Antonescu's search for ways to break away from the Nazi alliance was seen by the suspicious Nazis as an indication that Romania was potentially a traitorous state.

The Soviet Union and
Lieutenant General Andrey A. Vlasov

Andrey Andreyevich Vlasov's (born 1900) first significant military assignment in the Soviet Red Army was his appointment as advisor to Chiang Kai-shek from 1938 to 1939. In January 1941 he was appointed commander of the 4th Armored Corps in Lvov. In February he was awarded the Order of Lenin. The Nazis invaded the Soviet Union in June of 1941 (Operation Barbarosa). Vlasov proved his courage and ability in the defense of Kiev in August–September 1941. Although the Red Army lost Kiev, the holdup of the German forces there delayed the Battle of Moscow to the winter. In October 1941 the Nazis were about sixty miles west of Moscow. During the Battle of Moscow (mostly, October–December) Stalin appointed Vlasov as commander of the newly formed 20th Army. That army played a significant role in resisting and repelling the German attack. His promotion to lieutenant general came in January of 1942. On that occasion he was awarded the Order of the Red Banner. He was given a new command, the Second Shock Army, and assigned to the Volkhov front.

Since October 1941, German and Romanian forces, headed by *Wehrmacht* Field Marshall von Manstein, had been engaged in what has become known as the Battle of Sevastopol. Although Manstein's 11th Army was not very successful in its first assault, Manstein devised a different strategy. He focused on first isolating and then purging Soviet military presence from the Kerch Peninsula (at the easternmost tip of the Crimea). By mid-May 1942 his strategy had yielded some spectacular successes. His forces had wiped out two Red Army divisions and captured almost 170,000 prisoners. Following this success, the fate of Sevastopol was sealed. During June 17–30, Sevastopol fell to the Nazis, who captured an additional 90,000 prisoners.

During these fierce and fateful battles, Vlasov's command was surrounded by German forces in May 1942. Refusing to surrender, he was captured by the Germans.[5] Whereas official Soviet versions state that Vlasov had been in contact with the Germans since the Battle of Kiev and thus gave himself up immediately after the Soviet defeat in Sevastopol, Andreyev asserts that following the collapse and dispersion of his 2nd Shock Army troops, Vlasov wandered in the forest for more than two weeks before being captured (June 24 to July 12), probably reflecting on what had happened.[6] Andreyev feels that these two weeks are crucial for understanding Vlasov's later behavior. During that time, Vlasov's mind changed from "that of a prominent Soviet commander to that of a collaborator with the enemy, and prepared the ground for his subsequent decision to try and form an anti-Stalin Russian Liberation Army".[7] That transformation was neither simple nor easy.

Overall, it is important to understand the context of these events. Thousands of prisoners were taken by the *Wehrmacht* on its eastern front. Stalin's totalitarian rule was very unpopular, and the Red Army itself experienced intensive Stalinist purges. Few Soviet POWs, at least initially, had the stamina to fight for the Soviet Union. That changed as the war continued and the brutal nature of the Nazi conquest became clear. Foot points out that the Germans captured nearly 5 million members of the Red Army, noting that

> the Germans treated captured Soviet personnel abominably: about five-sixths of the soldiers of the Red Army who were taken prisoner did not survive the war. . . . These men were hardly given food or shelter at all; their officers were, with few exceptions, shot after interrogation, and the rest were left prey to lice and typhus. Those who got the chance volunteered to join General Vlasov's renegade army—anything to escape from the pit they were in. German policy in this respect was dictated by Nazi racial myth, which held that . . . Slavs were only a superior form of cattle.[8]

Persuaded to side with the Germans, Vlasov first made propaganda broadcasts in which he voiced the distrust of Stalin felt by the Red Army.

Vlasov inspects the troops of his Russian Liberation Army.

SOURCE: *Reprinted from Werner Rings,* Life with the Enemy: Collaboration and Resistance in Hitler's Europe, 1939–1945, *translated by J. Maxwell Brownjohn (London: Weidenfeld and Nicolson, 1982). Photograph from Ullstein Bilderdienst, Berlin.*

Initially, Vlasov (as well as other Soviet POWs) was distrusted by Hitler, who viewed them as inferior people. Thus, Vlasov's activities were confined to making propaganda, and he was not given the means or authority to form an army, which is what he really wanted. But as the war turned against Nazi Germany, Nazi taboos were somewhat relaxed. In November 1944, Reichsführer Heinrich Himmler, head of the Schutzstaffel (the S.S.), allowed Vlasov to form the Anti-Stalinist Committee for the Liberation of the Peoples of Russia. Vlasov recruited soldiers from POW camps and those who had been brought back from Russian territories as forced labor. Vlasov then set up three divisions of Russian soldiers. This military force became known as the Russkaya Osvoboditelnaya Armiya or Russian Liberation Army (R.O.A.). The idea was to create a free Russian army that was not under the authority of a communist regime. On November 14, Vlasov and the R.O.A. published a manifesto in Prague. In it, Stalin's annexation of foreign territory and his policy of repression of indigenous Russian nationalities were attacked (Andreyev 1987:124–133).

At the end of the war, one R.O.A. division was involved in fighting the Red Army at Frankfurt-on-the-Oder.[9] Another division was involved in the 1945 Partisans' uprising in Prague (May 1–2). Requests for support from Patton's 3rd army before the arrival of the Soviet Ukrainian Front were ignored. Lacking the support of other forces and fearing that the Nazi forces commanded by General Toussaint would destroy Prague, the rebels appealed to Vlasov. At that point, Vlasov had about 20,000 troops stationed to the west of Prague. The R.O.A. arrived in Prague on May 8, 1945, and although they were poorly equipped, they managed to defeat German reinforcements before withdrawing. However, when Konev's Red Army arrived the next day in Prague, the city was cleared of Germans.[10]

R.O.A. troops surrendered to the U.S. 7th army. However, in accordance with one of the agreements reached during the Yalta Conference,[11] Vlasov, his troops, and six other generals were handed over to the Soviet army. Many of the troops committed suicide. General Vlasov was arrested by Soviet authorities on Czech soil in May 1945, and on August 1, 1946, he and the other generals were hanged in Moscow on charges of treason and espionage.[12]

Vlasov's defection to the Nazis needs to be viewed in context. To begin with, Stalin's rule was very unpopular. Vlasov's anti-Soviet and anti-Stalin feelings had deep roots. The horrors of Stalin's regime, his brutal collectivization of farming, and his bloody and ruthless purges of the 1930s were not easily forgotten. Moreover, several historians have noted the enthusiasm with which the Nazi *Wehrmacht* and S.S. units were welcomed by local Soviets when Operation Barbarosa commenced. Many believed that the Germans were coming to liberate them. Indeed, Andreyev argues that "defeatism, the doctrine that urges soldiers to weaken their own side so that the regime might be more easily overthrown, was exhibited on a much larger scale in 1941 than could even be considered normal."[13]

Burton (1963) refers to Vlasov and his followers as the "Vlasov defeatist movement." He points out that the number of Soviet citizens who participated in the war effort on the side of the Nazis "was not of primary importance" and that these individuals were effective only in freeing "German military strength for combat, taking over . . . such service functions as anti-partisan warfare, anti-aircraft duties, and services of supply." In terms of frontline fighting, they rendered service against the "Allied invasion of Italy and of France . . . where [they] gave good accounts of themselves in action."[14] Clearly, Burton downplays the role of these turncoats, unaware of the contradiction in his own description. The Soviet forced labor that was sent to Germany helped in the war effort as well, and many of these forced laborers later joined the R.O.A.

Burton interprets the Vlasov movement as a reflection of Soviet citizens' attitudes toward their own regime. He notes the many defections in the Red Army, especially in the first six months of the Nazi invasion.[15] The events of the summer of 1941 clearly indicated the widespread discontent of the Soviet citizenry. During the first phase of the Nazi invasion into the Soviet union, Soviet citizens welcomed the *Wehrmacht* as a liberating army.[16] If Hitler had taken advantage the Soviets' hatred for Stalin, his invasion of the Soviet Union might have ended differently. However, his racist ideology, which led him to view and treat the Slavs with scorn and contempt, effectively prevented such an occurrence.

Andreyev point outs that many Soviet citizens in German hands, particularly prisoners of war and forced laborers, made clear their opposition to Stalin between 1941 and 1945. This raises the question of whether these individuals should be viewed as traitors and collaborators. For some, the answer seems clear because they joined the Nazis in actively fighting the Red Army. The nature of this violation of trust and loyalty appears obvious. For others, it is not so clear.

Should resistance to Stalin's regime, while professing loyalty to Russia, be considered treason? Whose trust and what loyalty were violated? And what exactly was its nature? Andreyev prefers to call those Soviet citizens who expressed their opposition to Stalin through military, civil, and political means the "Russian Liberation Movement."[17] The most crystallized form of this opposition, in the shape of a military organization, was the military unit headed by Lieutenant General Andrey Andreyevich Vlasov.

This discussion shows how difficult it is to adhere to technical definitions of treason—and how futile it is. The political, social, and military reality in which the Russian Liberation Movement operated requires us to make moral judgments about who betrayed whom.

Other Soviet military resistance units had been created before Vlasov's R.O.A., but Vlasov gave these groups the power, respectability, and impetus they had lacked. However, during most of the war, even Vlasov's strongest war effort was in the propaganda front. Not until January 1945, was he actually allowed to create a military unit. Thus, in reality, Vlasov's "army" was little more than words.

In the context of World War II, resistance to Stalin took the form of defeatism. Andreyev (1987) examines the debate regarding Soviet defeatism very critically and argues that in reality the situation was quite complex. For example, the Soviets did not sign the Geneva Convention, and so it is not clear to what extent their POWs were protected. West (1985) argues that treason involves betraying the state's protection, but what kind of protection did Stalin's regime offer? To the extent that it did offer any protection, what was the nature of this protection? Vlasov, asserts Andreyev, was basically a propaganda tool until about November 1944.[18] It is also clear that by deciding to openly join the Nazis, Vlasov was entering an immensely complicated political arena for which he lacked any training or experience.[19] As Keegan points out, "Vlasov was . . . an idealistic man who hated the tyranny of Stalin and made the mistake of seeing the Germans as potential liberators."[20]

Unfortunately, many documents relating to the R.O.A. were deliberately destroyed out of fear that they would fall into Soviet hands and be used as evidence. However, as time has passed, the threat has diminished, and more individuals have been willing to provide information. However, as the context of Vlasov's actions becomes clearer, the nature of his betrayal becomes more problematic.

The Nazi *Wehrmacht* and the Red Army were locked in a titanic clash. The defection of a resourceful, high-ranking, and decorated officer is—simply put—a violation of both the trust and loyalty invested in that officer by his country. Thus, many Soviets viewed Vlasov as a traitor and an opportunist. However, unfolding the context of that famous defection creates uncertainties about the nature of that loyalty and trust.

The issue of Vlasov's betrayal must be juxtaposed against the reality in which he functioned. His actions were certainly influenced by the cataclysmic events in which he took part. Thus, determining whether Vlasov was a traitor or a hero depends—almost completely—on how one views Stalin's rule of the Soviet Union. Technically, Vlasov betrayed the trust and loyalty invested in him. However, one must consider what it was that he betrayed and his aspirations to help create a different Russia. Viewed in this way, that is, comparing the reality with the image, the issue of portraying Vlasov as a traitor becomes problematic.

Treason Within the Third Reich

Although the heading of this particular section may seem a bit strange, Nazi Germany was a state, and it enacted laws and had a judicial system.[21] What happened to people who were perceived to violate their trust and loyalty to Nazi Germany and the führer? Generally speaking, like those defined as traitors elsewhere, they were severely punished. The brutality and ruthless nature of the Nazi regime only made that more pronounced. As Zentner and Bedurftig (1997) point out,

Volksverrat was a generic term for . . . high treason, state treason, and territorial treason, among other such crimes. Any attack on the authority of the state
or on the "idea of the *Volk* Community" that underlay National Socialism
constituted treason against the *Volk*. . . . High treason and state treason were
by nature the same crime. . . . National Socialist criminal law . . . accorded
the highest priority to the persecution of *Volk* treason." (p. 1006)

Of course, in the totalitarian nature of Nazi Germany, opposition to
Hitler, to Nazi ideology, or to the Nazi state was perceived as treason. It is
thus well worth our while to look into some of the cases.

Hitler Charged with and Convicted of Treason

It is, perhaps, appropriate to begin this section by noting the fact that
Adolf Hitler himself was charged with and convicted of the crime of high
treason. In brief, here is the tale.

By 1923 Hitler was convinced that the end of the German Weimar Republic was in sight. He thought this was an opportunity to enlist the support of the army and create a new nationalistic order for Germany. He recruited World War I general Erich Ludendorff to support this plot, and on
November 8, 1923, they launched the now famous Beer-Hall *Putch* in Munich. When the Nazis marched on November 9 in the Munich streets in
the direction of the war ministry, police opened fire on them, causing the
group of marchers to disperse. That was the end of that failed and amateurish *Putch*.

Hitler was caught and on February 26, 1924, only about three months after the failed *Putch*, was brought to trial (before a very sympathetic judge)
on a charge of high treason. Hitler would not have given up such an opportunity and used the legal proceedings to launch a personalized propaganda campaign. His speeches in the court were among his very best, and
they obviously left a strong impression. This, however, did not help much.
He was found guilty as charged and sentenced to five years in prison.

Hitler served only nine months of the sentence. His imprisonment at
Landsberg am Lech was far from difficult, and his life in prison was more
like life in a sanatorium.[22] It was there that Hitler began to draft (by dic-
tating to Rudolf Hess) his book *Mein Kampf*, which summarized his political and ideological philosophy and his prescribed direction of action.

It must be remembered that Hitler was found guilty of treason by the
legal organs of a democratically elected German government. However,
when Hitler came to power, he would not allow his political rivals to enjoy a similar tolerant and forgiving criminal justice system.[23] A conviction
on charges of treason in Hitler's brutal and cruel Third Reich typically
meant the death penalty.

The case of Adolf Hitler as a traitor illustrates the main problem involved in treason. It was the Weimar Republic that viewed him as a traitor. Most certainly, Hitler and his supporters did not view it in that way. From their point of view, the very establishment of the Weimar Republic was the result of a betrayal. The trial of Hitler illustrates the clash of two very different symbolic moral universes, one succeeding the other in a rather quick fashion. Indeed, a more generalized observation can be made here: Leaders of an incoming regime can be viewed as "traitors" to the old, and vice versa.

Some of the statements Hitler made in public during his trial are worth quoting. Having taken full responsibility for planning the *Putch*, he said that he was such a nationalistic German that he "would rather be hanged in a Bolshevik Germany than perish under the rule of French swords." He then added, "Even if you judge us guilty a thousand times, the goddess of the eternal court of history will laugh and tear up the verdict of this court, but she pronounces us not guilty."[24] Furthermore, as stated in *Mein Kampf*, Hitler did not even accept the democratic rules of the game. His political agenda was that for Germany to become powerful and thrive, a people-supported dictatorship was required. He despised the constitution of the Weimar Republic (August 14, 1919).

In 1924 the Weimar Republic had the authority and power to prosecute and punish Hitler. Within thirteen years or so, the situation would be completely reversed. Hitler had the opportunity to actualize what he envisioned and preached as his political dream. It was, in fact, a genuine nightmare to free people in the rest of the world and—in the final analysis—to Germans as well.

Aside from Hitler's past record as a democratic state-convicted traitor, it is worth our while to examine at least some of the more famous cases that his regime persecuted as treason.

Resistance to Hitler

No act of any anti-Hitler person or group within Germany marked the end of Nazi Germany. One can safely state that Hitler's regime was never seriously challenged or threatened from within. It was the combined military effort of the Allies that ended the existence of that vile regime. However, there was opposition to Hitler. That opposition was disorganized, antagonistic, hesitant, and unable to unite for a meaningful coordinated action aimed to eliminate Nazism. In fact, although there were quite a few attempts to assassinate Hitler (Benz and Pehle 1997:120–122), there was only one time when Hitler came close to be actually killed, and that was the July 1944 failed attempt to assassinate him with a bomb. Any opposition within Nazi Germany faced a ruthless and relatively efficient security police.

Looking at the different resistant groups within Nazi Germany, Zimmermann points out:

> There is no doubt that the contrasts among the different resisting groups, and the weaknesses of their political and social perceptions, are of secondary importance. The crucial factor was their willingness to defend the honor of the human race against a total disintegration of Christian and human values resulting from the unlimited rule of a political regime which was based on an exaggerated use of force, ruthless brutality, personality cult, ideological zealotry, cynicism, loathe for human values, corruption, and arrogance.[25]

It is important to note the moral and political aspects of discussing the opposition to Hitler. As Zimmermann points out, examining the "resistance" to Hitler can be used to ease guilty consciences, indicating that not everyone was part of one of the darkest regimes in human history.[26] The more resistance one can find, the better. Overall, about 10,000 people were executed on charges of disloyalty to Hitler's regime.

Another relevant question is, what *is* the nature of resistance? On the one hand, we have either individuals or groups who speak against the regime or organize actions against it. On the other hand, we may have such passive forms of resistance as expressing disgust, objections, evading different tasks, and the like. Discussion of resistance in the Third Reich typically focuses on the first type and not on passive forms.

There is a fair amount of research on resistance in Nazi Germany.[27] As it is virtually impossible to review even most of it, I will focus, briefly, on several famous cases: the White Rose, the July 20, 1944, assassination attempt on Hitler's life, Dietrich Bonhoeffer, Carl Friedrich Goerdeler, Admiral Wilhelm Canaris, and Marlene Dietrich.

The White Rose. During the late 1960s, the West was rocked by a series of student revolts that threatened to destabilize regimes and alter social orders. Those revolts were researched quite intensively. However, during all that time, not many (if any one) cared to remember that a small group of students at the University of Munich, supported by one faculty member, chose to express their sense of horror at the Nazi regime. These rebels organized a group of resistance within the university at the height of the Nazi regime in 1942. The scope and magnitude of this "revolt" (actually, a very moderate expression of dissent) were minuscule compared to the revolts of the late 1960s. However, to do this as early as 1942, against such a ruthless regime, definitely took much integrity and courage. They all took a tremendous risk and paid with their lives for their defiance. Their "actions" were mostly verbal criticisms and dispersion of pamphlets, far less than what so many students did in 1968. Their story can be found in quite a few studies,[28] as well as in the fact-based 1983 German movie *The White Rose*. The essence of that group's story is as follows.

The name "the White Rose" refers to a group of students at Munich University that formed in 1942 and lasted into 1943. The students whose names are most frequently mentioned are Sophie (born 1921) and her brother Hans (born 1918) Scholl, Willie Graf, Christoph Probst, Alexander Schmorell, and one faculty member—Professor Kurt Huber.

Hans was a medical student, and Sophie specialized in biology. Professor Huber taught philosophy and encouraged the students to take the rebellious stand. Students in the White Rose were in touch with students from other universities. Although in mid-February Hans and Sophie participated in a demonstration in Munich, quite an occasion in Nazi Germany, their most overt action was dispersing (anonymously) pamphlets against the Nazi regime in which they called citizens to topple the Nazi regime of fear and terror. The students began dispersing the leaflets in mid-June 1942, and altogether, they produced six of them. Following the surrender of Field Marshall Paulus's 6th Army in Stalingrad (February 2, 1943), the White Rose published its sixth and final pamphlet. In it, it was stated: "Three hundred and thirty thousand German men were senselessly and irresponsibly driven to their deaths by the brilliant strategy of that World War I corporal. Führer, we thank you. . . . We grew up in a state where all free expression of opinion has been suppressed."

The building superintendent, who witnessed the Scholls dispersing their latest batch of leaflets from an upper floor, reported them to the Gestapo on February 18, 1943. Munich University, headed at that time by an S.S. officer, denounced their activity. Together with four others, they were arrested and brought before the Nazi People's Court ruled by the infamous and dreaded "hanging judge" Roland Freisler on February 22, 1943.[29] Freisler found the Scholls and Probst guilty of treason and sentenced them to death. Supposedly, Reichsführer Himmler was not interested in creating martyrs and demanded that the execution be delayed. However, his telegram arrived too late and the condemned were beheaded. Professor Huber, Alexander Schmorell, and Willie Graf were arrested later. Their trial took place in Munich in Freisler's courtroom on April 19, 1943. They were found guilty of treason and sentenced to death. Others were sentenced to prison and fines.

Born in 1893 in Switzerland, Professor Huber taught philosophy and psychology at Munich University from 1925, where he was appointed professor in 1926. Huber opposed Nazism and was the one who helped the Scholls draft their leaflets. He was beheaded on July 13, 1943. Alexander Schmorell was also beheaded on that day. Willie Graf was beheaded on October 12, 1943.

It is interesting to note that on February 3, 1945, Freisler was killed during an Allied air attack from a bomb dropped by an American plane. This happened in the midst of another treason case. The trial was of Frau Solf and her daughter Grafin Ballestrem, who were associated marginally with the July 20, 1944, plot to kill Hitler, which brings me to our next topic.

The July 20, 1944, Assassination Attempt Against Hitler.   Aside from an attempt to plant a defective bomb in his airplane (March 13, 1943), and von Gersdorff's failed attempt to personally bomb him (March 1943), the only time Hitler really came close to being killed was the assassination attempt on July 20, 1944. The person behind this failed assassination attempt was Colonel Count Claus von Stauffenberg (born 1907). That Stauffenberg was a military man was no coincidence; the relationship between Hitler and the German military was complicated.[30] There had always been a group of military officers who were unhappy with Hitler's regime. However, for the most part, officers were unable and unwilling to coordinate an effective opposition to Hitler. Von Stauffenberg finally managed not only to organize such a group but also took upon himself the risk of smuggling a suitcase with a time bomb into Hitler's headquarters at Rastenburg, East Prussia (known as the "Wolf's Lair"). The bomb exploded, as planned, on July 20, 1944, at 12:42 P.M., causing much damage to property and wounding and killing several officers, but somehow Hitler sustained only minor injuries, although he was only twelve feet away from the explosion.

Hitler's rage culminated in the identification and capture of all the conspirators, even those who were only remotely associated with it (for example, Field Marshal Erwin Rommel), and the execution of most of them, sometimes in a vicious manner. Overall, almost 5,000 individuals were executed, as Hitler utilized the opportunity to eliminate many of his opponents. Clarifying the Nazi moral and political boundaries in this lethal manner brought the Nazi Party to new peaks of power; the failed assassination plot was used to redefine the Reich's moral boundaries and to reaffirm trust in and loyalty to Adolf Hitler.[31] This was accomplished by successfully constructing the conspirators as traitors. Moreover, loyalty to the Nazi führer was constructed as the equivalent of honor. "Our Honor is Loyalty" was the motto of the S.S. and an oath by which they swore. From the Nazi Party point of view, this failed coup was an effective tool for generating more social integration and cohesion around Hitler at a very difficult time.[32]

Dietrich Bonhoeffer.   Born in 1907, Dietrich Bonhoeffer was a remarkable German Protestant theologian who opposed Nazi Germany. He was arrested on April 5, 1943, and sent to Buchenwald. During this time, he wrote some of the most moving documents against Nazi Germany and detailed his ideas for a new form of religiosity. He was later tried by a summary court-martial and executed at Flossenburg concentration camp on April 5, 1945. There were other Germans who shared Bonhoeffer's point of view. One of them was the popular World War I U-boat commander Martin Niemoller, winner of the Iron Cross, who left the navy to become a pastor. Although at first he supported Hitler's regime, he was later convinced that Hitler posed a genuine danger to Germany and sided with Bonhoeffer in opposing the regime. His activities led to charges of treason, and he was sent to a concentration camp, where he spent eight years.[33]

Carl Friedrich Goerdeler.   Carl Friedrich Goerdeler (born 1884) was a jurist, lord mayor of Leipzig, and a major civilian figure in anti-Hitler conspiracy. Although in the early phases of Hitler's regime he was part of the administration, in 1936–1937 he became disillusioned with Nazism and began to distance himself from the Nazis and to openly oppose them. A personally powerful, persuasive, and impressive man, he became one of the main figures in the July 20 assassination plot, lending it civilian support and moral integrity. Following the failure of the plot, he was identified as one of the main conspirators, arrested, and sentenced to death. He was hanged on February 2, 1945.[34]

Admiral Wilhelm Canaris.   Admiral Wilhelm Canaris was one of the more devious, enigmatic, yet interesting figures of German opposition. Born in 1887, he began a naval career in 1905 and served in naval intelligence during World War I and participated in several daring operations. After the war, he remained in the German navy. In 1935 Captain Canaris became head of the *Abwehr* and was later promoted to the rank of admiral.[35]

Though small at first, the *Abwehr* grew to become a large and important organization by the beginning of World War II. It seems quite clear that Canaris was never too thrilled about Hitler, and both he and the *Abwehr* were a locus of resistance to Hitler. Unwilling to openly express opposition to Hitler, Canaris conspired against Hitler under the cover of his job. He thus exhibited behaviors that involved plots, subplots, ambivalence, uncertainty, and the like. The "mystery" around him is due—at least in part—to this ambivalence. Thus, Canaris pretended trust in and loyalty to Hitler, but in fact had probably none.

The Nazi security service was not ignorant of Canaris's ambivalence. Eventually, the suspicions against him accumulated to such a degree that in February 1944 Hitler ordered Canaris to stay out of Berlin, and the *Ab-*

wehr was put under the directorship of S.S. Reichsführer Heinrich Himmler. Although Canaris was not involved in the July 20 attempt to assassinate Hitler, he was arrested following the confession of one of the conspirators. There was plenty of information leading to the conclusion that
he was definitely not loyal to the Third Reich. He was hanged in April
1945 at Flossenburg.

Assor's conclusion—clearly reflecting a moralizing point of view—is
that Canaris was a "genuine German patriot" who opposed Hitler and
tried to both be effective as an intelligence officer and reduce the damage
caused by Nazism. Unfortunately for Canaris, the journey down this double road could not last for very long.[36] Manvell and Fraenkel's analysis
(1969) asserts that the nobility and religious idealism of conspirators like
Canaris made them less effective as conspirators because they were inhib-
ited morally as well as physically. Resisting Hitler required some serious
soul-searching, determination, stubborn resolution, and a strong sense of
both purpose and righteousness. However, Canaris—despite his proven
courage—was ambivalent. He hated violence; as an intelligence person,
he preferred to outmaneuver his opponent than confront him, and he
seemed to enjoy intrigue for its own sake. He must have loved his country from a traditional, right-wing point of view, in which Hitler was perceived as a destroyer.

Marlene Dietrich.   Marlene Dietrich, one of the world's most famous
entertainers, was also involved in some interesting moral issues. Born on
December 27, 1901, in Berlin, she developed an extraordinary career as an
actress. Her career took off following her unforgettable role as the seduc-
tive cabaret singer Lola, in the 1930 German movie *The Blue Angel* (directed by Josef von Sternberg). An anti-fascist, Dietrich left Germany in
1933 and refused to return until 1945 because of the Nazi regime. When
Hitler requested that she return to Germany (and make films there for
Nazi Germany), she flatly refused. From 1937 on she lived mostly in the
United States and acted in a number of movies. Dietrich became an
American citizen (in 1937), and during World War II she entertained
American soldiers, wearing a U.S. Army uniform. Many Germans never
forgave Dietrich for choosing not to align herself with Nazi Germany
during World War II.

In 1960 she appeared in Germany, but her series of performances were
disturbed and threatened by demonstrations and bomb threats. Some ed-
itorials characterized her as a traitor. Dietrich reacted by refusing to return to Germany. After her death on May 6, 1992 (in Paris), she was
buried, according to her wishes, in Berlin, next to her mother. In 1993, her
marble tombstone was vandalized. However, no desecration of her grave
has occurred since then.

In November 1996 the municipality of Berlin considered naming a city street after her. Reports in the international press testify that following the announcement, representatives of the neighborhood involved (Shonenberg) received letters and phone calls from individuals who characterized Dietrich as "non-German" and as a "traitor." Dietrich's choice to not trust, to not be loyal to, and to not align herself with Nazi Germany has been interpreted as treason by those who chose to embrace Nazism. This case illustrates how problematic the characterization of treason can be for those involved in a moral struggle, even in what otherwise seems to be a clear-cut case.

The Far East

Wasserstein (1998) examines some specific forms of collaboration by different individuals, some of them in key political and economic positions, especially in Shanghai during the Japanese occupation. Foot points out that the context of collaboration in the Far East was very different than in Western Europe.[37] To begin with, many Far Eastern countries were under colonial occupation prior to the Japanese invasion. Initially, many of these countries welcomed the Japanese because they felt that the Japanese were liberators who were about to grant these countries independence. As time passed, that tragic misperception was exposed, forcefully and brutally. Even when the Japanese did grant some form of independence (for example, Burma and the Philippines), it was a charade; in Burma, some of the leaders collaborated with the pre-Japanese colonial power. It became obvious that the last thing the Japanese conquerors were interested in was the political, economic, or social well-being of the newly conquered nations. The main goal of the occupation was to enrich the conquerors. The conquerors demonstrated their contempt for non-Japanese people through the humiliation and degradation of the vanquished.

This is the background for such phenomena as the "comfort women";[38] the Rape of Nanking, where a quarter of a million people were slaughtered within six weeks;[39] the Japanese Imperial Forces' special unit, which was involved in a human experimentation program;[40] and the Bataan Death March,[41] during which Japanese troops forced about 78,000 starving Allied prisoners of war to march 105 kilometers from Mariveles to prison camps in San Fernando and along that way the POWs were "beaten, clubbed, and bayoneted."[42] It is estimated that up to 14,000 died along the way.[43]

Thus, while local people may have hoped that the Japanese conquest might free them, the reality was that it replaced one colonial occupation with another, which was, in most respects, much worse and more ruthless. This situation was similar to the situation in Eastern Europe during the Nazi occupation that drove away Stalin's dictatorial regime.

Collaboration with the Japanese under these conditions was not very appealing. However, local people seemed to collaborate in one specific area, and that was in the deliberate campaign by the Japanese to erase all traces—cultural, political, and economic—of the occupation of the American, Dutch, French, and British colonial powers in Southeast Asia. In the long run, that particular aspect of the otherwise brutal and ruthless Japanese occupation may have been useful in cultivating local people's striving for independence, by providing them with an opportunity to formulate their own aspirations in the political, cultural, and economic areas. China provides a good illustration for both the brutal Japanese occupation and later independence.

It is well worth noting that some of the Japanese military commanders did try to set up collaborationist puppet Chinese governments, for example, in Manchuria and Inner Mongolia by the Kwantung Army, the North China Area Army, and the Central China Expeditionary Army. Although none of these Japanese attempts was very successful (they were discredited from the beginning), some of them did control various resources and had coercive powers. Perhaps one of the more famous of these was the Kwantung Army's conquest of Manchuria and the creation of the puppet state of Manchukuo headed by the emperor Pu-Yi. In fact, the Japanese commander of the Kwantung Army—General Minami Jiro—was "appointed" Japanese ambassador to Manchukuo. General Jiro, simply put, governed Manchukuo (with very little—if any—guidance or control from Tokyo). Pu-Yi, the puppet Chinese ruler of Manchukuo from 1932 (and "the last emperor of China"), was imprisoned in Siberia by the Soviets after their invasion of China in 1945. He was returned to China in 1950, where he was imprisoned again. Having converted to communism, he was released from prison in 1959, and until his death in 1967 he worked as a gardener in Peking's botanical gardens and in the Chinese department of historical archives.

The Japanese were also able to create puppet Chinese armies, the sizes of which are still under debate. However, these were not effective fighting forces and were not trusted by the Japanese themselves. As in other places (for example, Norway and France), they became associated with betrayal.[44]

By most Western criteria used after World War II, Pu-Yi was a traitor. He collaborated with the occupying Japanese forces. Dear and Foot point out that he accepted the Japanese offer to become the new state's chief administrator with "eagerness."[45] True, he had been enthroned at the age of three as Emperor Hsuan T'ung, but he was deposed in the 1911 Chinese revolution. Thus, his personal motivation to rule the Chinese may have overcome his political and cultural sensibilities, and he agreed to become a puppet emperor "ruling" part of China. He may have also hoped, like Quisling, Pétain, Vlasov, and a host of other European politicians, to gain some independence for his country. Regardless of how one looks at it, Pu-Yi did collaborate with the Japanese occupation, certainly to their benefit. It is interesting to note that despite this fact, he was allowed to live his natural life (he died in 1967 at the age of sixty-one) and was not executed like European collaborators. Although one should not make sweeping generalizations from this single special case, the way Pu-Yi was treated might prompt some thoughts about possible differences between European and Chinese forms of justice.[46]

Japan

It is not too easy to find Japanese forms of betrayal. However, two rather famous ones, from very different perspectives, involve Ozaki Hotsumi and what has become known as Tokyo Rose. I discuss Tokyo Rose in detail in Chapter 7; here I discuss, briefly, the case of Ozaki Hotsumi. To understand the context, one needs first to review the case of another famous World War II spy—Richard Sorge.

Richard Sorge

Richard Sorge is often described as one of the most successful known spies. He was born in 1895 in Baku, Russia to a Russian mother and a German father (a mining engineer who worked for the Imperial Russian Oil Company). At the age of three he was brought to Germany, where he grew up. In October 1914 he volunteered to serve in the German Army in World War I on the western front, where he was wounded three times. During the last two years of the war, he studied at the universities of Berlin, Kiel, and Hamburg. After the war he obtained a Ph.D. in political science from Hamburg University.

Disillusioned by the devastation created by World War I, Sorge gravitated slowly toward communism. His commitment to communism became much firmer after the October 1917 Russian Revolution (he later became an admirer of Stalin). Sorge's full conversion to communism occurred probably in the early 1920s. He joined the Communist Party and began to recruit people to communism. Sorge worked as a history teacher in Hamburg, Germany, but his attempts to recruit members to communism during school hours caused the schoolmaster to dismiss him. His commitment to communism then led him to Moscow.

In 1924 Sorge moved to Moscow and even acquired Soviet citizenship. There he began to work for the International Liaison Department of the Communist International. Following the end of the war, he also operated as an agent for the Comintern.[47] He developed the cosmopolitan existence of a Comintern agent on different assignments in Europe and Asia. There he was recruited to become a spy by Dimitry Manuilsky, head of the foreign intelligence division of the Comintern. His training in Moscow (1924–1927) resulted in missions to Scandinavia (1927), the United States (1928—Los Angeles, to collect information on the film industry), and Britain (1929—an unclear mission in London). Sometime during 1929–1930 General Yan Karlovich Berzin, head of the intelligence unit of the Red Army, managed to recruit Sorge to work for his department. From that time on, Sorge was actually working for the Soviet military intelligence organization—the G.R.U.[48]

Berzin sent Sorge to Shanghai (1930). His mission was to solidify Soviet espionage activities there and provide the Soviets with information about the situation in China and about Chiang Kai-shek. As Japan was emerging as a central force in the Far East, Sorge was recalled to Moscow, where he was involved in lengthy discussions about the future direction of Soviet intelligence efforts in the region. These discussions ended with his assignment to Japan.

However, before going to Japan, Sorge went to Germany. There he became a correspondent for several newspapers and a member of the Nazi Party; eventually he developed a close relationship with the Nazi leadership. These activities were part of a plan of purposeful deception. Sorge was playing the role of a dedicated, trusted, and devoted Nazi but was, in fact, using this guise as a cover for spying in Japan for Stalin.

The plan worked almost perfectly. Sorge, a Soviet spy, was perceived by the Nazis as one of them. As a trusted correspondent for the *Frankfurter Zeitung*, he traveled to Tokyo, where he also became the press attaché in the German Embassy (October 1933). His position in the German Embassy gave him access to the information available there (including files, messages, and covert discussions). Thus, Stalin had in Tokyo a spy who had access not only to Japanese sources but to German secrets as well. Sorge passed all the information at his disposal to his operators in the Red Army intelligence from 1933 to 1941. Sorge, however, did not work alone. From Tokyo he operated a spy network.

The Japanese secret service—Kempai Tai—very slowly closed in on Sorge and his ring of spies. Japanese electronic engineers were monitoring the radio transmissions sent by one of Sorge's men, Max Clausen, but experienced difficulties pinpointing its origin.[49] Both Seth and Bower note that Sorge's Japanese lover—Kiyomi—was working for the Kempai Tai, and so he was very closely watched.[50] On October 15, 1941, to the complete shock of the Germans, he was arrested in his home in Meguro. Following Sorge's arrest, his ring of spies (about thirty-five members altogether) was exposed and its members arrested. The Japanese were very successful in eliminating Sorge's spy network completely.

Again, Seth and Bower note that Sorge spent the evening and night before his arrest with the woman who made his arrest possible—Kiyomi—and that she was in the house at the time he was arrested.[51] From Sorge's point of view, Kiyomi violated his trust and loyalty and hence betrayed him. However, much like Biblical Delilah, Kiyomi never had a genuine loyalty to Sorge, and his trust in her was thus misplaced and founded on deceit. Sorge's trial took place on September 29, 1943. He was sentenced to death, but his execution was delayed until November 7, 1944, when he was hanged in Sugamo Prison in Tokyo. In 1947 Kiyomi was shot to death outside a club where she used to perform, "probably by agents of Smersh attempting to avenge the death of their brilliant spy."[52] The Soviets awarded—posthumously—Sorge the "Hero of the Soviet Union" and honored his memory by creating a stamp carrying his picture.[53]

Because of the nature of Stalin's regime, it is not entirely clear to what extent Stalin trusted the information passed on to him by Sorge.[54] However, there is little doubt regarding the value of the intelligence passed on by Sorge. Two very important pieces of information were passed on to Stalin. First, Stalin was given a three-week advance notice about Hitler's plans to invade the Soviet Union. Sorge informed Stalin in May 1941 of the planned German attack on the Soviet Union and specified June 20 as the date of attack. The actual attack took place on June 21. Stalin, however, discounted the information. Second, Sorge informed Stalin that Japan had no intentions of initiating hostilities against the Soviet Union. Sorge estimated, based on his German and Japanese sources, that Japan's strategic interests were in southern Asia and the Pacific and not in Siberia. This enabled Stalin, perhaps not too enthusiastically or trustingly, to pull army units out of eastern Siberia in the fall of 1941 and reposition them to defend Moscow. This, most certainly, was very crucial in the Battle of Moscow. If Stalin had more fully trusted his man in Tokyo, the combination of these two items of information would have enabled him to move military units from the borders with Japan to face the Nazi invasion much earlier and more forcefully. Other important pieces of information provided by Sorge's espionage ring were the forecasting of "the Japanese military mutiny of February 1936 and the Japanese invasion of China in July 1937."[55]

Ozaki Hotsumi

Although Richard Sorge is a very prominent figure in the literature of World War II espionage, Sorge's primary Japanese collaborator, Ozaki

Hotsumi, is often omitted. However, without Ozaki, much of Sorge's valuable intelligence work could not have been accomplished. Sorge even admitted that when he wrote in 1941 that Ozaki "was my first and most important real confederate. . . . Our relationship, both business and personal, was perfect. The information he collected was the most accurate and the best that I ever obtained from any Japanese source, and I formed a close personal friendship with him at once."[56] For many Japanese, Ozaki is considered *the* traitor. The letters that Ozaki wrote his wife, Eiko, from prison were published as a book in 1946, and it became a best-seller, selling more than 100,000 copies in Japan between 1946 and 1962.[57]

Johnson's 1990 book, *An Instance of Treason: Ozaki Hotsumi and the Sorge Spy Ring*, provides a very detailed account of Ozaki's treachery for the English-speaking audience. I shall, therefore, describe the case in brief. Ozaki Hotsumi was born in 1901 in Tokyo but raised in Taiwan (then Formosa), where his father worked as an editor. He attended Tokyo Imperial University (1919–1925), from which he graduated in 1925. Following his father's footsteps, he joined the Japanese newspaper *Asahi Shimbun* in May 1926 as a reporter. He was not very successful at a city desk job, and in October 1927 (at his own request), he was transferred to the Chinese section of the *Osaka Asahi*. While he was studying, specializing in the "Chinese problem," he also used his time to study Marxism and communism.

A month after his move to Osaka, Ozaki married his sister-in-law. Although such a marriage would have received little notice in any Western culture, it was extraordinary in Japan.[58] However, contrary to a naive assumption, Ozaki did not "steal" his brother's (Honami) wife (Eiko). Eiko and Honami's marriage was going nowhere, and they had separated in 1927. The Ozaki-Eiko romance developed during the spring and summer of 1927. During the summer, Honami married another woman, and Eiko was free to remarry. Ozaki's move to Osaka in October 1927 was followed by Eiko moving there in November, and the two were married.[59] However, it seems that Ozaki was not very faithful to his wife. He apparently violated both her trust in him and his loyalty to her, as he had several mistresses.[60]

In 1928 he was assigned a correspondent post in Shanghai, where he remained until 1932. Ozaki and Eiko's only daughter, Yoko, was born there on November 17, 1929. Ozaki's fateful meeting with Sorge took place in 1930, probably in October or November.

It is interesting to note that the woman who introduced Ozaki to Sorge was Ms. Agnes Smedley, a traitor in her own right. Agnes was born in Missouri and committed herself to anticolonialism in 1917.[61] She was an active member of the Socialist Party. In 1918 Agnes was indicted on charges of espionage. She was part of an Indian nationalist spy ring, who contacted the Germans in order to smuggle weapons and propaganda, and she was involved in schemes aimed at undermining British colonial rule. After her arrest, she moved to Berlin, continuing to support the Indian nationalist cause. In November 1928, Agnes traveled to China as a correspondent for a German newspaper and involved herself in the Chinese revolutionary movement. Later that year, she moved to Shanghai and became Sorge's assistant in recruiting members for his spy ring and probably became his mistress as well (for a while at least).[62]

As Johnson points out, Sorge and Ozaki liked each other from the first moment they met. They discovered that they both despised the foreign imperialist intervention in China. At that time, Ozaki thought that Sorge (he actually met him when Sorge called himself "Johnson") somehow represented the Communist International, and he thus believed that he was assisting the Chinese revolution by providing the Comintern with aid. Only after his arrest in 1941, did he learn that Sorge was working for Soviet military intelligence.

Ozaki never joined the Communist Party, but he was what Johnson refers to as a "proto-communist," believing that Japan's better future lay with some form of communist social order. By today's standards, Ozaki was probably a liberal who abhorred fascism and had a strong Marxist tendency. The link between Ozaki and Sorge was not only personal but expressed a deep ideological commitment to a Marxist, communist worldview as well. However, it is fair to quote from one of Ozaki's letters to his wife, Eiko: "I am not first and foremost a Communist."[63] Johnson adds: "The most significant tribute to his independence was paid him by his judge, Takada Tadashi. After the trial, Takada privately said that Ozaki was a man of virtue, devoted to his ideals, and the very model of a patriot."[64]

When Ozaki left Shanghai in 1932 and returned to Osaka, he broke all contacts with Sorge until 1934. During this interval some critical events took place: the May 15, 1932, assassination of the Japanese premier by naval academy cadets; the February 20, 1933, arrest and murder of the famous Japanese novelist Kobayashi Takiji at the Tsukiji police station in Tokyo; and the February 27, 1933, burning of the German Reichstag. When Sorge met Ozaki in May and asked him to help the Comintern, Ozaki agreed.[65] Sorge had deceived Ozaki about the true nature of his masters; they were a professional espionage organization, not a bona fide ideological group.

Ozaki established himself as one of the main Japanese commentators on China. He was intelligent and shrewd and had a sharp eye and a clear mind. His analyses were read by many people and influenced decision-makers. Although he left China in 1932, his analyses were accurate and to the point. He kept warning the Japanese government about the rise of Chinese nationalism as a result of the provocations committed by the Japanese Army, and he noted that this nationalism served well the interests of the Chinese Communist Party. Between 1937 and 1940, he published six books. Ozaki's expertise on China affairs was not a "cover." He was indeed a genuine expert on China. During the Sino-Japanese War, Ozaki provided continuous evaluations of the situation. Moreover, he was appointed as a consultant to Japanese premier Konyoe's first cabinet and was involved in official research. Thus, Ozaki had direct access to the highest echelons of the Japanese ruling network. Since Sorge was attached to the German Embassy in Tokyo, he had access to the highest-level German reports. It is no wonder then that between the two of them, such high-level intelligence was secured for Stalin.

After Sorge was arrested, Ozaki's turn came. He was arrested on the same day that Sorge was, that is, October 15, 1941. This was the last time Eiko saw him until 1943. However, while in prison, Ozaki wrote Eiko more than 200 letters (between November 1941 and November 1944). These letters were published in 1946, and they provide insight into a complex man. As Johnson points out, much of what we know about Ozaki is from these letters.

Ozaki's trial opened on May 31, 1943, and on September 29, 1943, Judge Takada sentenced him to death. An appeal was presented in February 29, 1944, and reached the supreme court on March 5. On April 5, the supreme court rejected the appeal (because, among other things, Ozaki was still considered a Marxist). Other appeals were unsuccessful, and on the morning of November 7, 1944, Ozaki was hanged (with Richard Sorge) at Sugamo prison. Thus ended the lives of two extremely remarkable men committed to a similar ideology.

Although Johnson asserts that Ozaki is considered the greatest traitor in Japanese history, one needs to understand the context of his acts of treason. To begin with, Ozaki was Japanese, that is, part of the Japanese collective. He most certainly violated both the trust invested in him by the Japanese and their loyalty at a most difficult period in Japan's history. He pretended to be trustful and loyal but in fact passed his country's most secret intentions to a hostile nation. By all criteria, Ozaki fits very well the characterization of a traitor. His agreement to help Sorge resulted from his belief in some interpretative form of Marxism. Thus, both Sorge and Ozaki were motivated by ideological reasons. Both were very keen political commentators and journalists. Johnson points out that while Sorge was feeding his Soviet operatives with classified intelligence, he provided the Nazis with regular political analyses, which they valued quite highly.[66] Ozaki established himself as quite an authority on China, and Sorge established himself as quite an expert on Japan.

In some respects, Ozaki was a true believer in a Marxist ideology. His vision for Japan was a socialist-communist future, and he felt that such a future was a much better alternative to the type of fanatical Japanese nationalism he was witnessing. In his own mind, he was certainly convinced that he was helping to prevent the ascendancy of fascism. However, rather than come out in the open and fight for his views, he pretended to be loyal to the prevailing nationalistic views, while he secretly tried to help Japan's enemy. The type of "patriotism" Ozaki displayed remains a subject for debate. Indeed, Johnson documents the attempts of some Japanese groups to rehabilitate and construct Ozaki as a hero.[67] However, "undoing" Ozaki's treason may be difficult or even impossible. Thus, working in stealth and disguising one's true ideological identity may have a lasting negative social price.

Japanese Americans

Following the Japanese surprise attack on Pearl Harbor (December 7, 1941), American authorities felt so threatened that they decided to intern around 120,000 American residents with Japanese origins (most of whom were American citizens). Despite the fact that President Roosevelt had no reliable information suggesting that these American citizens were involved in subversive activities, and that such measures were not suggested or taken against Italian or German Americans, the president signed executive order 9066 on February 19, 1942, which gave the military the authority to intern Japanese Americans. On March 2, 1942, Lieutenant General DeWitt, head of Western Defense Command, declared California, Oregon, and Washington to be areas from which all residents of Japanese descent should be excluded. Consequently, around 110,000 Japanese Americans (of whom about 64 percent were American citizens) were forced to leave their homes and businesses and sent to one of ten relocation centers.

These Japanese Americans were forced to abandon their homes, property, status, friends, and interests in their communities and pressed into hard labor. The unsubstantiated suspicion was that they constituted a fifth column, potential (or actual) traitors, and that their supposed loyalty to their country of origin—Japan—was such that they would necessarily violate their loyalty to the United States and its trust in them. That is, they would betray their American citizenship. The U.S. Supreme Court initially upheld the relocation policy, but in 1944 declared that the detention of persons whose loyalty was not compromised was unconstitutional. The internment camps were thus closed in 1944, but Japanese Americans continued to experience discrimination. However, one development helped to counter this discrimination: the heroic battle performance of the Nisei.

The Nisei, or Japanese American troops, fought valiantly and proved their loyalty numerous times. Units involving Nisei, as well as individual

soldiers, were repeatedly awarded military citations. Certainly, the courageous performance of Japanese American units during the war helped
neutralize the feelings involved in the incarceration of other Japanese
Americans.[68] The memorable 1951 motion picture *Go for Broke* focuses on
the 442nd Regimental Combat Team, which was composed of Nisei, sustained heavy casualties in 1944–1945, and won many commendations for
valor, including a Congressional Medal of Honor.[69]

Egypt

During World War II, Egypt was ruled by King Farouk (1920–1965).
British rule of Egypt was resented by Egyptian nationalists, and many
Egyptians were striving for national independence.[70] Farouk displayed a
reluctant pro-British stand (to which he was bound by a treaty he signed
with Great Britain) but retained a pro-Axis government. Thus, he appointed a pro-Nazi prime minister, and he and some nationalist officers
such as Gamal Abdel Nasser and Anwar Sadat (both later became Egyptian
presidents) cultivated hopes for a German victory because they believed
that such a victory would get them closer to national independence. As
Weinberg's monumental work points out, given the political and social
nature of Nazi Germany, such a belief could only be characterized as "too
ridiculous to be worthy of serious discussion."[71] That belief translated itself into actions as they maintained contacts with the Germans. What
these Egyptians did not comprehend was that German rule would be significantly more oppressive than the British.[72]

When the Axis victories, led by Rommel's Afrika Korps, in the North
African desert threatened Cairo in 1942, Farouk was forced by the British
to dismiss his pro-Nazi prime minister, and his pro-Nazi officers were arrested. "When the Axis powers were on the brink of defeat, Egypt declared war on Germany and Italy in February 1945 so that she could join
the United Nations."[73]

The British Imperial War Museum keeps in its archive a document concerning "Farouk I, King of Egypt."[74] According to this document, on July
28, 1942, "two Egyptian military planes ... [flew] ... to Field Marshal
Rommel's headquarters ... [with] ... important maps and plans intended for the German military authorities." The document accuses King
Farouk of maintaining a two-year negotiation process with the Nazis, including an exchange of letters with Hitler. Among other things, Farouk
yearned for a Nazi victory, supported the pro-Nazi rebellion in Iraq
(April 1941), and called for the bombardment of Jerusalem and Tel Aviv.
From a British point of view, Farouk's actions certainly placed him very
close to being a bona fide traitor. However, that could not have been the
judgment from an Egyptian nationalistic point of view.

Concluding Discussion

This chapter extends the discussion of cases of treason in World War II. We have examined the context in which the different traitors operated, the options they had, and the choices they made. Mihailović, Antonescu, Vlasov, von Stauffenberg, Pu-Yi, Ozaki Hotsumi, King Farouk, the Chetniks, the Iron Guard, and the White Rose were defined by contemporaries as traitors because they were perceived to have crossed the boundaries of trust and loyalty. Thus, structurally, the characterization of traitor fits because in these cases a violation of trust and loyalty existed.

The threat presented by these individuals to their respective states was grave. However, when these cases are closely examined in terms of historical context, the issues of violating both trust and loyalty in terms of content and morality (that is, their construction) become complex. With the exception of the case of Japanese Americans, it is not sufficient to state that the different individuals violated trust and loyalty. From a moralistic point of view, one must consider the question of trust and loyalty to whom? In the case of Japanese Americans, the question can be reversed; that is, many of them felt that their country (the United States) betrayed *their* trust and loyalty.

Weimar Germany prosecuting Hitler for treason (and he most certainly presented the gravest threat for that unstable democracy) and the Third Reich prosecuting those who were perceived as untrustworthy, disloyal, and threatening to Hitler provide us with a similar illustration. As the moral boundaries of Germany shifted, the very meaning of trust and loyalty changed radically. In both cases, those who were perceived to have violated trust and loyalty were labeled traitors and treated accordingly. The threat potential in each case was indeed large. However, morally, it is problematic to equate Weimar Germany and the Third Reich. In moral terms, they were radically different. Thus, although the structural meaning of treason in both societies was similar and based on analogous violations, the content of these different cultural contexts, and consequently the moral meaning and significance of these violations, was very different.

In Chapters 5 and 6, we focused on individual cases of treason in a very turbulent period. In each case, a better understanding emerged when the image was contrasted with the reality. Moreover, we could see how in each case, the same universal structure of violations materialized. But we did not stop there; we took one more step by viewing not only the *structure* of the violations, but their *content* as well, which necessitated the use of morality as a criterion for evaluating the cases.

The next three chapters delve in detail into three cases of betrayal in World War II. Chapter 7 examines the "radio traitors," those who used the relatively new radio technology to disperse to their enemies messages of despair, propaganda, and misinformation in order to weaken their will to fight. There were quite a few such individuals, but we shall focus on two: Lord Haw-Haw and Tokyo Rose. Chapter 8 focuses on individual cases of intellectual betrayal. There, we look at a curious phenomenon— intellectuals who are gifted with humanity, sensitivity, and empathy lending support to the cruel, the crude, and the oppressive. Finally, we shall examine, in great depth, the case of a traitor king—Edward VIII.

7

Radio Traitors:
Lord Haw-Haw and Tokyo Rose

The term "radio traitors" was used by both Weyl and Edwards to describe a special situation during World War II.[1] During the war, both
Japan and Nazi Germany recruited individuals to transmit, via radio,
propaganda to their opponents (and supporters). It is important to emphasize that the Allies used such transmissions as well. The new radio
technology thus gave rise to a new form of betrayal, using radio waves to
commit treason.[2] Indeed, there were quite a few such traitors.[3] The methods of recruiting radio traitors varied. Some did it willingly because they
were committed ideologically. Others were offered money or other inducements. Still others were recruited from prisoner-of-war camps under
threats or for promises for better living conditions. As both Weyl and
Archer note,[4] such traitors included the following: Robert H. Best, who
transmitted for the Nazis;[5] British comic author P. G. Wodehouse (creator
of Bertie Wooster and Jeeves), who made a series of radio transmissions
from Berlin to England and the United States in 1941, for which he was
paid by the Nazis;[6] Mildred Gillars—also known as "Axis Sally"—who
broadcast for the Nazis and was sentenced in 1949 to ten to thirty years in
prison in the United States;[7] and Jane Anderson—also known as "Lady
Haw-Haw" and "the Georgia Peach"—who transmitted for the Nazis to
the United States four times a week.[8] However, two radio traitors won
particular fame: Lord Haw-Haw and Tokyo Rose. In this chapter, we shall
explore these two cases in detail.

The Case of William Joyce—Lord Haw-Haw

Lord Haw-Haw is a case that is framed in Europe during World War II.
William Joyce, after having lived in England for thirty years, left London
in the summer of 1939 for Berlin just as World War II was beginning. He
joined the Nazi cause out of his own free will and informed choice, enthu-

siastically and without any coercion. Joyce gained worldwide fame for being the person who broadcast Nazi propaganda to Britain and other countries. He was arrested after the war, charged with treason, found guilty, and hanged in January 1946.[9]

Background

William Joyce, also known as Lord Haw-Haw, was born on April 24, 1906. His place of birth is not insignificant: Brooklyn, New York. His father, Michael, was born in County Mayo, Ireland, in 1868, and emigrated from Ireland to the United States in 1888, when he was twenty years old. In 1894 Michael became a U.S. citizen, following his declaration of intent to do so in 1892. In 1904, with a U.S. passport, Michael went to England for a visit. That visit was momentous for Michael. It was then that he met his future wife—Gertrude Emily Brooke ("Queenie"), of Shaw, in Lancashire. Gertrude was a physician's daughter and about ten years younger than Michael. The two married in New York on May 2, 1905. William was their first child (they had two more sons).

Having made some money in the United States, Michael apparently felt that it was time to return to his home country. The Joyces left the United States in 1909 to settle in County Mayo. William was then three years old. They returned as U.S. citizens with U.S. passports. Michael's heart was with Ireland, and he apparently regretted becoming a U.S. citizen, to the point of "denying on occasion that he had ever become a naturalized American."[10] He insisted that he and his family were all British. In fact, Selwyn points out that Michael was seen by his younger son Quentin burning his American citizenship documents in 1935. Young William was thus educated in Ireland, with strong English inclinations, and he was raised in an atmosphere of extreme conservatism with strong imperialistic ideas.[11]

William Joyce–Lord Haw-Haw

William had his nose was broken in a schoolyard fist fight, but he did not report his injury. Consequently, it was not treated properly, and his voice acquired a nasal tone.[12]

In those years of William's childhood, Ireland was in the clutches of political turmoil. Michael sided with the British Crown. In 1920, at age fourteen, William also joined the struggle against the Irish nationalists by collecting intelligence for the infamous "Black and Tans," the irregular Crown forces.[13] Thus, William associated himself with brute force at an early age. He most certainly saw what effects clandestine operations

could achieve. Testimony from the period indicates that William was fa-
natically devoted to England and opposed to what he saw as the Irish in-
surgency. William's service came to an end when a truce was announced
on July 11, 1921, and the paramilitary units of the Black and Tans began to
retreat in October. Extremists on both sides felt that they had been betrayed.[14]

The establishment of an Irish Free State left the Joyces little choice.
Fearing the revenge of Irish nationalists, they moved to England (December 8, 1921). William lied about his age and enlisted in the British Army.
When his true age was disclosed, he was released from the army after
only four months of service.[15]

It is clear that from his very early years, Joyce preferred physical action,
combat, intrigue, manipulation, military discipline, and self-improvement.[16]
Joining the Black and Tans, and his attempt to join the army, so very early
in his life, most certainly reveals an opinionated, determined person with
a clear affinity for conservatism and a fascination with force. These actions
also involved lies, disguise, and pretense at a very early age.

In August 1922, William Joyce wrote a letter to London University,
which is frequently quoted. In it, he states that he was born in the United
States to British parents and that "in no way" was he connected with the
United States. It expresses extreme, perhaps even juvenile, loyalty to the
Crown. This letter was reinforced by a letter from his father, Michael, who
added that "we are all British and not American subjects." It is clear that
although the Joyces' presentation of themselves as exclusively British was
factually misleading, they most certainly viewed themselves as British
subjects. That view was patriotic, genuine, and a result of a choice.[17]

William began his formal studies in 1922 at Battersea Polytechnic. After
graduation he continued his studies at Birbeck College, London University, focusing on English language and literature. He received a First Class
Honors Degree in June 1927. Along the way, in May of 1927, he married
Hazel Kathleen Barr; they eventually had two daughters, but their marriage ended in 1936. This line of William's career indicated a bright and
intelligent mind, quite capable of impressive academic achievements.

William, however, was also developing a political career. On December
6, 1923, he joined the British Fascisti. This rather strange group was
founded by Miss R. L. Linton-Orman, and its primary goal was to prevent
a socialist revolution in Britain.[18] On the evening of October 22, 1924,
Joyce was in charge of the "I squad" of the British Fascisti. A public political activity was to take place in support of a political candidate for Lam-
beth North.[19] During the meeting, countergroups intervened, and Joyce
was attacked by an anonymous person who made a long cut on his face,
causing a very visible scar. In 1926 it was clear that the British Fascisti was
disintegrating. Although Joyce was given an opportunity to restructure

the group, he was too busy studying for final exams and making an income as a tutor. Although Joyce chose at this time to pursue an academic career, he was not finished with political action.

In March of 1928 he applied for a job in the Foreign Office but failed the review process and was rejected. At the same time, he also tried to join the Conservative Party. By that time, Joyce must have already possessed some strong opinions. The Conservative Party was not very open to extreme anti-Semitic fascists like himself. After two years of trying to exert influence there, he quit.[20] In July 1933 he joined the British Union of Fascists (B.U.F.), headed by Oswald Mosley.[21] In the autumn of that same year, Joyce was already deputizing at meetings for Mosley. Joyce quickly established himself as an asset and a capable, aspiring politician. He was certainly considered a very good orator.

Anticipating the possibility of a trip to Berlin with Mosley to meet in person the new German führer, Adolf Hitler (never to be actualized), Joyce applied for a British passport. In his application, Joyce stated that he was British by birth, a clear and obvious lie.[22] In July 1933 he was granted the requested passport.[23] In 1934 he was promoted to Director of Propaganda for the B.U.F. His paid appointment in the B.U.F., and later promotion, enabled him to leave the Victoria Tutorial College, and he abandoned his doctoral program at King's College.[24] "Throughout 1934, Joyce remained, next to Mosley, the most powerful figure of the B.U.F. in the popular imagination."[25] However, the two developed personal reservations toward each other.[26] Among other things, Joyce exhibited extreme patriotism (he insisted, for example, that "friends stand to attention and sing 'God save the King' at informal evening parties at his home") and overt hatred for Jews and capitalism.[27]

Joyce was not successful in the March 1937 elections for London County Council. A month later, Mosley "purged" Joyce and a close associate of his (John Beckett) from the B.U.F.[28] Joyce then founded his own party, the National Socialist League, with its paper *The Helmsman*.[29] The party had only a small number of recruits. In February 1937, Joyce married Margaret Cairns White, a B.U.F. member.[30] During 1938–1939, Joyce called publicly for a pact with Hitler (and Italy) and for active discrimination against Jews.[31]

The events preceding World War II began to reduce the choices Joyce had. In March 1938, Austria was annexed to Germany (the *Anschluss*). In March 1939, Hitler took over Czechoslovakia, and a British pact with Poland followed. It was clear that a major war was in the making. Joyce's British political fantasy had very little chance of materializing, and he had to make a choice. He could not join the British in their fight against Nazi Germany, and he could not opt out by declaring himself a conscientious objector. Moreover, Joyce truly believed in Hitler. Although the Joyces considered going to Dublin, they decided eventually to go instead to Berlin.[32] On August 24, 1939, Joyce applied for a renewal of his old passport, again stating falsely that he was British by birth.[33] The passport was renewed on that day. On August 26, 1939, the Joyces left England and arrived in Berlin the next day. Five days later, Hitler invaded Poland, and on September 3, England and France declared war against Nazi Germany.

Selwyn points out that when the Joyces arrived in Berlin, "they were uninvited, unexpected, without a single close friend or any means of subsistence."[34] However, it is equally true that prior to their coming to Berlin, they asked a friend, John MacNab, to check the potential response to a request from the Joyces to become naturalized German citizens.[35] MacNab brought back a favorable response. That meant, simply put, that the Joyces were welcomed in Nazi Germany. Joyce met his German contact—Christian Bauer—in the Ministry of Propaganda.[36] Although it turned out that Bauer was not a very reliable person,[37] Joyce nevertheless found employment in that ministry, making radio broadcasts to the United Kingdom. "Within three months, the refugee from England had become the known and acknowledged assistant of two of the greatest powers in the land."[38]

Although at first there were doubts about Joyce's ability as a broadcaster (his voice test was not very good), he did eventually end up broadcasting in English for Nazi Germany. He became, both in person and on the radio, an avid and enthusiastic supporter of Hitler's National Socialism.

It must be stated that Joyce was not the only English broadcaster.[39] Preceding him was another Englishman, Norman Baillie-Stewart.

As early as 14 September 1939, Jonas Barrington in the *Daily Express* described this voice that called from Germany, though in the first instance it probably belonged to Norman Baillie-Stewart: "He speaks English of the Haw-Haw, dammit-get-out-of-my-way variety, and his strong suit is gentlemanly indignation." On 18 September "Lord Haw-Haw of Zeesen" was formally christened in the same newspaper, the name soon becoming exclusively attached to the tones of William Joyce. In radio music-hall, the Western Brothers introduced a new comic song on the topic of "Lord Haw-Haw of Hamburg"[40]

By October 3, 1939, the voice on Radio Hamburg had been publicly identified as that of Joyce, and British intelligence positively identified Joyce in his broadcast of August 2, 1940.[41] Eventually, Joyce was the one identified as "Lord Haw-Haw," and he even identified himself as such in the transmissions. Furthermore, "Joyce was denounced as Lord Haw-Haw in the House of Commons as early as 23 May 1940 by the Member for Wolverhampton, G. Le M. Mander."[42]

During this time, Joyce applied for German citizenship and changed his name to Wilhelm Froelich. He became a German citizen on September 26, 1940. In early 1940, he also wrote a political manifesto, in English, in the form of a 50,000-word book, titled *Twilight over England*. The book was published (100,000 copies) in September 1940 in Berlin.[43] Sales of the book were slow, and many copies were sent to POW camps. An instructive fact is that on the first page of the author's preface, Joyce expresses no doubt as to how the British people (for whom the book was meant) would view him. There, in the very first paragraph, he characterizes himself as "a daily perpetrator of High Treason."[44]

The book is not an impressive tribute to Joyce's academic ability. It is full of stereotypical, historically unfounded statements supporting Nazi views. A whole chapter in the book concerns the Jews, who are found by him to be guilty of almost every possible crime.

It is evident that Joyce's career as the English loudspeaker for Nazi propaganda was meteoric. Joyce was not only rewarded by honor and prestige but also was paid very well. "He was to be the best-paid of the broadcasters, and, far more important, he was acknowledged as the English voice of Berlin."[45] Joyce did a good job—so much so that the Nazis awarded him the Kriegsverdienstkreuz 1st Class (War Merit Cross) in 1944. Charman, who wrote the introduction for the Imperial War Museum's edition of Joyce's book, could not help but notice that the same award was bestowed in January 1945 to Joseph Kramer, known as "the beast of Belsen."[46]

Some Notes on His Transmissions

Joyce's transmissions focused on two issues. The first was the encouragement of different groups in England to revolt against the legitimate British government of "Mr. Bloody Churchill," in his terminology. He "believed wholeheartedly in rousing the British people to revolution."[47] In this respect, Joyce helped to create the illusion of a fifth column by suggesting that a ghost army was waiting in the shadows, ready to strike. The second was the presentation of a fanatic who loathed England, with a "savage contempt . . . for Churchill."[48] Joyce did not just play the role of a broadcaster. He planned the transmissions, was deeply involved in their content, and spent time trying to persuade British POWs to join him. Some, in fact, did.

To get a sense of the characteristic quality of Joyce's transmissions, let us examine two illustrations. As usual, my approach to these illustrations is that of a contextual constructionist—I present both the constructions and the facts.

The *Admiral Graf Spee*. The first transmission concerns what has become known as the Battle of the River Plate. That battle took place on December 13, 1939.

The Nazi pocket battleship *Admiral Graf Spee* was commanded by Captain Hans Langsdorff and had a crew of 1,100.[49] This pocket battleship was sent to the South Atlantic seas, arriving in September 1939. Her orders stipulated that she was to hunt and sink Allied commerce. In two months of raiding, that pocket battleship was effective in sinking at least nine ships (totaling 50,089 tons). The British Admiralty could not allow such hostile high seas activities to continue unchallenged. A battle force naval squadron consisting of the heavy cruiser *Exeter* and the light cruisers *Achilles* and *Ajax*, commanded by Commodore Sir Henry Harwood, hunted down the Nazi ship.[50] The three British warships found the *Admiral Graf Spee* on December 13, 1939, and engaged her in the battle that has become known as the Battle of the River Plate.

They surrounded the Nazi ship and launched at her one salvo after the other. Clearly, the Nazi ship had superior guns (11-inch), but it was inferior in speed to both light cruisers. Captain Langsdorff focused his main armament against the most powerful of the three—the *Exeter*—and hit her quite badly. At the end of the battle the *Exeter* listed 7°–10° to starboard and was three feet down in the bows. She was steered by a boat compass, and all her guns were out of action. Her bridge was destroyed, and sixty-one officers and men were killed and twenty-three were wounded. The battle continued to rage for fourteen hours, and the *Admiral Graf Spee* was not doing badly. However, Captain Langsdorff made a fatal mistake by underestimating his chances in a continued battle against the three cruisers. He disengaged and found asylum in the neutral port of Montevideo.

Despite his request to stay in Montevideo for fifteen days to allow for necessary repairs, only a three-day stay was approved. Captain Langsdorff was led to believe, falsely, that a large and formidable British naval force was waiting for him outside the harbor. He decided, with the full knowledge and approval of the highest echelons of the Nazi government, to scuttle the ship. On Sunday, December 17, 1939, at 18:00, the *Admiral Graf Spee* moved out and stopped, and her crew abandoned her; then a series of explosions turned the ship into a flaming wreck.[51] Three days later, Captain Langsdorff, wrapped in the flag of the old Imperial German Navy, shot himself.[52] The symbolic value of the Nazi defeat was great. It was considered to be a moral boost for the British, and it shattered the myth that the Nazi pocket battleships were invincible. What did Lord Haw-Haw have to say about this bitter Nazi defeat?

On December 17, 1939, Radio Hamburg made its triple "Germany Calling" announcement followed by the "You are about to hear the news in

English," read by William Joyce. Here is what he had to say about the Battle of the River Plate:

> The *New York Times* reports the British cruiser *Exeter* has been run aground near port Stanley near the east coast of the Falkland Islands. This American newspaper states that the *Exeter* has been so severely damaged by the artillery of the *Admiral Graf Spee* that it is impossible to make this ship seaworthy again. As some of the guns of the *Exeter* are still in working order, the British admiralty obviously intends to make use of the hulk as an additional coast battery at Port Stanley.[53]

Not a word about the real defeat.

Let us examine the actual fate of the *Exeter*. This heavy cruiser survived the Battle of the River Plate. In fact, there is a photograph of H.M.S. *Exeter* sailing into her home port of Plymouth on February 15, 1940.[54] Among those cheering crowds waiting to greet the *Exeter* was Winston Churchill, who was there, he said, "to pay my tribute to her brave officers and men."[55] After being repaired, the *Exeter* joined Allied operations in convoys and other actions in the Dutch East Indies. She was hit badly during the Battle of the Java Sea but was able to limp back to Sourabaya.[56] After being repaired, the *Exeter* tried to escape to Colombo. As she was sailing, she was intercepted by a Japanese naval force that consisted of powerful cruisers. In the battle that developed, the *Exeter* was hit in such a way that all power failed, the main armament was put out of action, and fires raged. Realizing that his ship could no longer fight, Captain Gordon decided to sink her. The order to abandon ship was given after all measures were taken to assure that the ship would indeed dive to the bottom. The *Exeter*'s career ended when she plunged into the South Java Sea on March 1, 1942.[57]

The Invasion of Norway.   A second example concerns the Nazi invasion of Norway (April 9, 1940). In a transmission from April 1940, Lord Haw-Haw talks about the occupation of Norway. He states that the attack against Norway and Denmark is advancing according to plan, that the landing and occupation of Denmark were uneventful, and that the campaign against Norway met no significant resistance on the beach. Only near Oslo were there a few incidents, but Oslo was now occupied. He then goes on to quote the appeal of the German minister for Norway to the Norwegian government to avoid resisting Germany because it was "senseless." "Germany does not intend to infringe on the territorial integrity or political independence of the kingdom of Norway either now or in the future."[58]

Joyce ignored the brutal Nazi occupation of Norway and the hypocrisy of "political independence." Furthermore, the German Navy sustained serious damages in the operation, and its operational ability was significantly reduced. The Norwegians put up a courageous defense, and the Nazi conquest of Norway was certainly not a picnic.

William Joyce's personal life was not smooth. His first marriage dissolved into nothingness. Now, in Berlin, his second wife was having a hot love affair with a younger man. The traitor Joyce was thus betrayed on the personal level.[59] In August 1941, William Joyce sued his wife Margaret for a divorce on the grounds of infidelity. Margaret responded by stating that her husband abused her by losing all respect for her.[60] It was clear that the marriage came to a dead-end. Divorce was granted. Following the divorce in court, the two newly divorcees displayed an emotional outburst and fell into each other arms outside the court. They went to have a meal at the Kaiserhof. Later that day they each went his and her separate ways.[61] The two remarried again in February of 1942.[62]

Last Radio Recordings from Lord Haw-Haw

War hostilities ended May 7, 1945, and Joyce's last recording for a radio broadcast was made on April 30, 1945.[63] In that broadcast "Joyce insisted that the sole cause of war in 1939 was the German wish that the city of Danzig—racially and politically German and part of Germany until 1919—should be returned by Poland."[64] Had Danzig, according to this idiotic and malicious, not to mention historically wrong, version, been given to Germany, World War II would have been prevented.[65] In that transmission, Joyce also talked about Germany:

> I'm talkin' to you about Germany. That is a concept that many of you have failed to understand. . . . Here we have a united people. . . . They are not imperialists, they do not want to take what doesn't belong to them. All they want is to live their own simple lives, undisturbed by outside influences. That is the Germany that we know.

Of course, Joyce conveniently forgot to mention that a simple, undisturbed life was all that millions of Jews, Gypsies, Poles, Russians, Czechs, Danes, Norwegians, French, British, and others also wanted. The recording ends with, "Germany will live . . . Heil Hitler! . . . Farewell." There is a qualitative difference to this recording. Joyce sounds tired and his speech is clearly slurred.[66]

Tony Geraghty reported in 1974 that this last "transmission" was never actually transmitted. Geraghty notes that Joyce drank too much during

the recording, and his Nazi superiors decided not to transmit the recording because it was too obvious from the voice that something was very
wrong. The recording itself was found in the archives of Radio Luxembourg.[67]

The Capture of Joyce

"By the end of March the Joyces were lodged in the little town of Apen . . .
in the former Grand Duchy of Oldenburg."[68] Plans were made to trans-
port the Joyces by U-boat to the Irish Republic, where it was felt they
could live safely. However, by May 1945, this plan was simply not feasible.[69] Another plan was to escape through German-occupied Denmark to
neutral Sweden. The Joyces were put in Hamburg, and Joyce was given a
false passport under the name of Wilhelm Hansen.[70] However, the rapid
collapse of the shattered Third Reich left the Joyces with very few choices.
Joyce decided to go back to Flensburg, near the Danish border.[71]

> On the evening of 28 May 1945, Joyce was walking through a wood which
> overlooked the harbor. He was alone. Ahead of him he saw two English offi-
> cers who were apparently gathering firewood. They belonged to the Recon-
> naissance Regiment of the Royal Armoured Corps. . . . One of the officers
> was Captain Lickorish, and the other was Lieutenant Perry. Joyce could have
> passed on his way without attracting their attention. Instead, he waved a
> hand, speaking to them first in French. Then he called out helpfully in Eng-
> lish, "There are a few more pieces over here." He was walking away again
> when the two officers overtook him. Lieutenant Perry said, "You wouldn't
> happen to be William Joyce, would you?"
>
> The question was almost superfluous, for as Captain Lickorish said later,
> he had already recognized the voice as "that of the announcer or speaker on
> the German radio."
>
> Joyce stopped, put his hand into his pocket, looking for that faked pass-
> port which identified him as "Wilhelm Hansen." (Selwyn 1987:162)

The two British officers were alert. They suspected that the man in front
of them may try to pull a gun on them. Thus, as Joyce was reaching into
his pocket, Lieutenant Perry—in a hurry—got hold of his revolver and
fired low. At this close range, the bullet hit Joyce in his right thigh and
passed to his left. He fell crying in his confusion "my name is Fritz
Hansen." Captain Lickorish went to the wounded man searching for a
weapon. He found none, but did find two passports: one for "Wilhelm
Hansen" and the other, a military passport for "William Joyce." Joyce was
taken to the nearest Danish frontier post. Interesting that Joyce was not
thinking of a gun. He thought that the British officers suspected that he

William Joyce, accompanied by two guards, on the grounds of the Luneberg hospital to where he was taken after he was wounded during his arrest.

SOURCE: *Alan Wharam,* Treason: Famous English Treason Trials *(Phoenix Mill, England: Alan Sutton, 1995), p. 169.* Photo from Times Newspapers Ltd.

was about to use a poison vial. The story of the capture, and wounding, of Lord Haw-Haw made its way quickly to the news.[72]

A historical irony can be found in the Wiener Library, London. In the archives held there, Mr. Simmon, from the *Jewish Chronicle*, notes that Lieutenant Geoffrey Perry was Jewish.[73] His original name was Pinschewer, and he had lived in Berlin prior to his immigration to England in 1935. At the time of the report, he was described as working for the British Association of Publishers.[74]

The Trial

The next chapter in Joyce's life was his transfer to England, interrogation, and trial. Along the way he was treated for his wounds. Joyce was cooperative, and despite warnings, he "was a compulsive talker."[75] The British press easily defined Joyce's activity in Radio Hamburg as treason and Lord Haw-Haw as a traitor.

Selwyn points out that before Joyce was brought back to England, the Treason Act (1945) was amended. The law of 1695 required two witnesses to an act of treason "or else two acts of treason each vouched for by a separate witness. This safeguard was now abolished, and in Joyce's case the prosecution offered only one clear act of treason vouched for by one witness."[76]

Joyce was charged with high treason for his transmissions and for becoming a German citizen in 1940. The issue of his original citizenship was a serious one. It was difficult, if not impossible, for a British court to convict an American citizen turned German citizen on a charge of treason to Britain. Thus, the case is an empirical illustration of the need to establish that a traitor is a member of the group being betrayed. The prosecution claimed that obtaining a British passport (under false claims) put Joyce under British jurisdiction and made him a British citizen, requiring from him the duty of faithfulness.[77]

Joyce pleaded "not guilty." As far as he was concerned, he did not betray anyone. He never hid his fascist views, and when war broke out, he did as his belief required. However, his defense was based on the claim that the British court had no jurisdiction because he was a non-British citizen. That did not work. Joyce was also bothered by the possibility that a "predominantly Jewish jury" would judge him.[78]

The trial began in September 17, 1945, and lasted three days. "The trial of Lord Haw-Haw had caught the imagination of the world's press."[79] Joyce could answer affirmatively to the charge that he had never been a British citizen. However, he did feel himself to be British and had lived in Britain for thirty years. Thus, it was possible that treason could be invoked between September 18, 1939, and September 26, 1940 (when he became a German citizen). As Selwyn points out, "it was far from clear that an American subject in Germany could be guilty of treason against England, a country which he had left and to which he had no intention of returning."[80] However, it is equally true that "William Joyce had broadcast repeatedly and unrepentantly on behalf of the Nazi regime, undermining British morale by every means at his disposal."[81] Joyce's blatant and repeated radio messages threatening Britain with destruction and defeat, accusing the second-front of being "Jewish inspired,"[82] and inciting citizens with calls of "Lay down your arms! Resistance is useless!"[83] illustrate this charge dramatically.

The jury found Joyce guilty on the charge of high treason in twenty-three minutes of deliberations. His case came before the Court of Criminal Appeals on October 30, 1945. The hearing lasted for three days, and the problem of Joyce's nationality was a crucial one. On November 7, 1945, the appeal was rejected. The case was then appealed before the House of Lords on December 10, 1945. The discussions ended on December 13, and on December 18, it was announced that the appeal was rejected there as well.[84]

There were letters and appeals to the British authorities not to execute William Joyce. Documents released in 1995 by the Public Record Office "disclose a file of letters, telegrams, and petitions 3 inches thick urging George IV, Clement Attlee, the prime minister, and Chute R. Ede, the Home Secretary, to be lenient with a man who earned historical notoriety as the broadcaster Lord Haw-Haw." The Duke of Bedford wrote to Attlee:

> I gather he has never been charged with betraying military secrets. . . . I must say that I feel his execution would be an act of quite unjustifiable vindictive severity involving a not inconsiderable degree of hypocrisy as well. . . . Although in his frequent use of the term "Jewish," he displayed the exaggerated bigotry characteristic of anti-Semites, Joyce, when telling the British people in his broadcasts that their real enemies were the international financiers, spoke no more than the truth.[85]

Execution

William Joyce, known as "Lord Haw-Haw," was hanged in the early hours of the morning of January 3, 1946, at Wandsworth Prison. As Selwyn indicates, even on this day, he still had some devotees praying for him. Joyce's last letter to his wife stated: "I salute you, Freja, as your lover forever! Sieg Heil! Sieg Heil! Sieg Heil." He added the German call of the battalion to which he was recruited to defend Berlin's Wilhelmplatz district against the advance of the Red Army.[86] According to Selwyn:

> At 1 P.M. the BBC Home Service reported the execution at Wandsworth and the last public message of the man who had been hanged.
> "In death, as in this life, I defy the Jews who caused this last war, and I defy the power of darkness which they represent.
> "I warn the British people against the crushing imperialism of the Soviet Union.
> "May Britain be great once again and in the hour of the greatest danger in the West may the standard of the *hakenkreuz* [Swastika] be raised from the dust, crowned with the historic words '*Ihr habt doch gesiegt.*' [You have conquered nevertheless].
> "I am proud to die for my ideals; and I am sorry for the sons of Britain who have died without knowing why." (Selwyn 1987:7–8)

As Selwyn points out, although Joyce was convicted of treason on a grand scale, "he died without remorse, writing his last 'Sieg Heil!' not twenty minutes before the hangman entered the condemn cell" (p. 8).

Thus, very clearly, until his very last moments Joyce regretted nothing and had learned nothing. He remained loyal to his fallen idol, Adolf Hitler, and the abominable National Socialism to the end.

Some Historical Ironies

History can play some sardonic tricks. Recall that Joyce was captured and shot in the leg by a Jewish refugee from Germany. Another irony occurred years after his execution. One of Joyce's daughters from his first marriage—Heather Iandolo—became a regular visitor to the Shabbat morning service in the Chatham Synagogue. According to the *Jewish Chronicle*, the last time sixty-six-year-old Heather saw her father was when her parents were divorced (1936).[87] She was then seven years old. Mrs. Iandolo was reported as having a "cherished and warm regard for Jews," unlike her father. She visited Israel twice, and her daughter spent two years in an Israeli kibbutz.

The Impact of Lord Haw-Haw's Transmissions

Were Joyce's transmissions effective?

Selwyn quotes a confidential report of the BBC issued on March 8, 1940:

> [The report] was based on interviews with a random sample of 34,000 people. Of every six interviewees, one was a regular listener to William Joyce and four listened to him from time to time. The figures were unexpectedly high and not made more palatable by the discovery that it was the politically better-informed and the young who listened to Hamburg Radio regularly. These were also identified as people who did not easily believe in the myth of the British Empire united against a common enemy but, said the report, who knew quite well that a good many of its people had no enthusiasm for such a war.[88]

A quarter of the sample surveyed in December 1939 stated that they had listened to William Joyce the day before; 58 percent stated that they found Joyce to be fantastically funny; 50 percent just listened so that they would have something to talk about; 38 percent found Joyce amusing; 29 percent wanted to hear the German version of events; 26 percent wanted the news that the BBC did not give them; 15 percent thought he was a good broadcaster; 9 percent found BBC boring; and 6 percent admired Joyce's broadcastings. Most in the sample did not think it was unpatriotic to listen to Joyce. However, Selwyn also states that "in the BBC survey, 22 percent of those questioned said that they never listened to Radio Hamburg or any of the other German stations, because their wireless sets were simply not powerful enough to pick them up."[89] These numbers stand in contrast to other relevant figures: 23 million regular listeners to the BBC, and 10 million occasional listeners (to the news).[90] Clearly, at least in the early years of the war, many people in Britain chose to expose themselves to the propaganda transmissions from Germany.

Other Broadcasters

The impressive works by Edwards (1991) and Bergmeier and Lotz Rainer (1997) document the extent to which the Nazis utilized radio transmissions to non-Germans as a way to spread their version of reality. Edwards discusses at length American broadcasters (whom he refers to as "radio traitors") in the service of the Third Reich, such as Jane Anderson, Max Otto Koischwitz, Robert H. Best, Douglas Chandler, and Donald Day (and a few others).[91] Bergmeier and Lotz Rainer's 1997 work surveys the more general radio propaganda transmissions of Nazi Germany. Edwards concludes that, much like Joyce, most of the American broadcasters lost their loyalty to the United States years before World War II began. The number of such people, though not large, was significant.

Some Notes on This Case

Leaving aside the fine legal distinctions concerning citizenship, who and what exactly did Joyce betray? He was a significant force in the Nazi propaganda campaign, but he did it out of his own free will and out of a deep conviction in the Nazi cause, which he never hid. Was his execution an act of vengeance? I have no doubt that it was, although in the present politically correct terminology, the more accurate term would be "justice was served." This raises a more general question regarding the issue of what should be done with the leaders of defeated enemies after a conflict. Kilroy's 1994 play about Lord Haw-Haw deals with this issue.

Although I am not entirely convinced that conceptually (not technically or legally) the charge of treason in Joyce's case is simply constructed, deception was involved on several levels. Joyce's main effort was to persuade Allied soldiers and citizens to change sides. In other words, Joyce was committed to persuading the opponents of Nazi Germany to alter their moral boundaries, to violate their loyalty and commitment, to betray trust. Although the charge of treason as applied to Joyce himself is not simple, he was most certainly calling on others to betray their country. That call puts Joyce in a very questionable moral position. Moreover, Joyce's transmissions were based on half-truths, and falsehoods. Thus, Joyce's fight was based on deception while pretending to be an "honest" ideological opponent. In short, he was a liar at the very least.

The Case of Iva Toguri—Tokyo Rose

During the war in the Pacific, thousands of American soldiers were exposed to a bright, clear, and rather sexy voice transmitting to them daily from Japan. They came to call the female broadcaster Tokyo Rose. In at least two World War II submarine movies, Tokyo Rose is featured as submariners listen to her transmissions (in the 1943 *Destination Tokyo* the submariners ridicule the transmissions, and in the 1958 *Run Silent, Run Deep* these transmissions are used to help make an important operational decision).

In these transmissions, contemporary music was played, news was announced, and American soldiers were urged not to fight. The main purpose of these transmissions, obviously, was to erode the morale of American soldiers. For those Americans fighting the Japanese in the Pacific, Tokyo Rose was a very familiar voice, and according to many sources, they seemed to enjoy the program. Thus, instead of demoralizing the soldiers, her transmissions may have achieved the opposite effect. The question regarding the identity of Tokyo Rose is a thorny one. Several Japanese-American women were employed as broadcasters. However, one of them—Iva Ikuku Toguri D'Aquino (born in 1916)—was put on trial for treason in 1948. She became identified with the voice of Tokyo Rose.

Iva was an American citizen of Japanese parents. Her father, Jun Toguri, came to the United States in 1899 when he was seventeen, intending to find employment as a farmworker. On June 8, 1907, when Jun was twenty-five years old, he returned to Japan to find himself a bride. Although he was traveling with a Japanese passport, he was able to secure himself a Canadian passport as well. This passport guaranteed that he could return to North America whenever he so wished. In Japan he married nineteen-year-old Fumi Iimuro. After the marriage, he returned to the United States alone. It took six years before he could afford to bring his wife to America. In the meantime, he visited Japan, and Fumi gave birth to a son (Fred—born in 1910). Iva was born in Los Angeles, on July 4, 1916, and another sister was born later. Jun was determined to Americanize his children. They were discouraged from learning or using Japanese and were strongly encouraged to adopt American ways of life.

Iva was successful in her schooling, and in 1933 began her study of zoology at UCLA. Having completed her degree in 1936, she planned to enter medical school. However, Iva's aunt, Shizu, was seriously ill, and Iva's parents decided to send her to Japan to help her aunt. When Iva left America on July 1, 1941, for Yokohama, Japan, she had only a certification of identity and was instructed by the U.S. Immigration and Naturalization Service in Los Angeles to get her passport from the U.S. consulate in Yokohama. Iva arrived in Yokohama on July 24, where her relatives met her and took her to Tokyo. Iva, barely able to speak Japanese and fully Americanized, found it difficult to adapt to Japanese life.

Moreover, material shortages were an integral part of life in Japan. Iva clearly missed the United States and expressed her longing in letters and talks with her family. On September 8, 1941, she applied for an American visa. So unhappy was Iva that in November 1941 she called her father and told him that she wanted to return to the United States right away. Her father cabled her a few days later, instructing her to board a Japanese-owned passenger ship that was scheduled to leave Yokohama on December 2. The cable arrived one day before the departure of the ship, but Iva was unable to get all the documents necessary before departure. However, it did not make much difference. The Japanese attacked Pearl Harbor on December 7, and the ship that she would have taken to the United States was instructed to return to Japan. The declaration of war meant that Iva was prevented from going back to the United States.

Like other Japanese American families, her family in the United States was interned in a camp (her sick mother died in the process). Iva's money was running out, but her family in the United States could no longer help. Despite all this, she did try to find ways to return, thinking that an internment camp was better than remaining in Japan. Unfortunately, she simply could not afford a detoured sailing route to the United States (she had to first go to a third country, for example, India, and from there to the United States). For all practical purposes, Iva, without a U.S. passport and with close family ties in Japan, was stuck in Japan. She had to deal with the authorities to get rationing cards, work, and other essentials for survival. Obviously, the attention of the Japanese security service was focused on her (as well as others in similar situations).

In desperate need of income, she joined in June 1942 the Japanese national news agency. Her job was to monitor and transcribe English-language radio transmissions from such places as Hawaii, Australia, India, and China. There she met Felipe d'Aquino, an English speaking-man, five years younger than Iva, and the son of a Japanese mother and a Portuguese father. A pacifist, he offered her emotional support and identification. Eventually the two were married. Despite her attempts to survive, her income was barely sufficient, and she was deprived of a food rationing card. It did not take long for her, on a starvation diet, to become very sick, and she was consequently hospitalized for six weeks. Ironically, on October 22, 1942, American officials notified the Swiss consulate that Iva was entitled to a passport and that she could return to the United States. No indication exists that the Swiss mission ever contacted Iva with this news.

Looking for a job, she responded to an advertisement in the *Nippon Times* for employment as a part-time typist in English for Tokyo Radio, and she was accepted for the job. Sometime during November 1943, she was told that she was being considered for a position as an announcer for a radio program put together by POWs. Although she was reluctant at first, she was pressured, threatened, and eventually coerced into taking the job. She later met Australian major Charles Hugh Cousens, British-born and a graduate of Sandhurst, who was a radio personality in Sydney radio before the war and very well known.

Cousens had joined the Australian army and had fought as a commander of an infantry battalion in Malaya. He became a POW after the fall of Singapore. Like Iva, he was sick with dysentery. Once the Japanese discovered who he was, they began a long process of pressuring him into broadcasting for them. He resisted at first but eventually agreed to transmit POW messages. That was only the beginning. Soon he was asked to do more. In June 1942, Cousens was flown to Tokyo. Howe's 1990 work points out that Cousens agreed to transmit because he was planning to sabotage the transmissions from the inside. He began transmitting, at first imitating Japanese pronunciation. Eventually, in August 1943, he chose Iva to join him as an announcer. Howe, again, points out that this choice of an inexperienced announcer indicates the subversive intentions Cousens may have had and that Iva was party to. According to Howe, Cousens's choice of Iva meant that the transmissions were much less professional, effective, influential, or useful. Under Cousens's guidance, Iva began transmitting on Tokyo Radio, and in March 1943, Tokyo Radio began its "Zero Hour," in which Iva's voice became even more pronounced as Tokyo Rose. It is important to emphasize that there were other POWs who participated in the transmissions. Howe's 1990 work makes it abundantly clear that Iva Toguri and Major Cousens (and others) were coerced into their roles.

Once the war was over and Japan surrendered, U.S. journalists went to Japan searching for interesting stories. Two of them found Iva Toguri and, after talking with her, constructed her as *the* Tokyo Rose. This exposure eventually led to her arrest, trial, and imprisonment in 1948.[92]

Iva was found guilty of treason, sentenced to ten years in prison, and fined $10,000. She was released after six years in prison, and on January 19, 1977, President Gerald Ford granted her a pardon (on his last day in office).

Whether Iva Toguri was *the* one and only Tokyo Rose is a secondary issue. Even if she was not the sole female transmitter, she did transmit propaganda for the Japanese against the United States. However, Iva Toguri's actions are not equivalent to those of William Joyce. When the war began, she was trapped in Japan against her will. She did not identify at all with Japan, was coerced into broadcasting, and—if one is to trust her (and Cousens's) account—the intention was to sabotage such transmissions by making them funny and discreditable.

The fact was that Iva, born American and feeling American, transmitted propaganda with the purpose of demoralizing American soldiers. Were her transmissions successful? This is a difficult question. From the available anecdotes, it is possible to conclude that the transmissions did not seem to affect soldiers in the battlefields. Did she have a choice? She may have, to some extent, but one needs to remember the context in which she operated; one of those choices was starvation. Howe (1990) asserts that her behavior can be thought of as resembling the mentality in *The Bridge on the River Kwai*. The answer is not simple. One cannot state that, like William Joyce, she willingly conspired against the United States. Her actions were motivated by coercion, starvation, and fear. Does this make her less of a traitor? That she was coerced into broadcasting certainly makes her offense lighter. Did she violate trust and loyalty? As an American citizen, and furthermore, one who loved her life in the United States, the answer is that she indeed violated the trust and loyalty expected of a citizen—trust and loyalty that, by her own accounts, she felt very strongly about.

The case involving Iva Toguri raises issues concerning individuals who are forced to collaborate with an opponent of their country. Through such collaboration, they may be able to minimize damage or subvert the enemy's efforts. However, as we saw in the cases of collaboration in Europe, choosing this line of behavior is opting to walk a very narrow and slippery tightrope. Some tangible gains may be made in the short run, but such behavior remains morally questionable afterward and is open to contradictory interpretations. The basic reason is that such behavior always involves manipulation, deceit, concealment, and secrecy. Those choosing collaboration must take into consideration that such courses of action have a very high probability of being interpreted in a very unfavorable light. Cases such as Sacha Anderson (see Chapter 3) and Harold Cole (see Chapter 5) illustrate how manipulation, double meanings, stealth, and dishonesty pervade the double game of collaboration and underscore the difficulty of maintaining moral boundaries when such a course is chosen.

Concluding Discussion

The two "radio traitors" we focused on in this chapter illustrate some important points. To begin with, they were both regarded as traitors. It is not too difficult to show that, structurally, in both cases violations of both trust and loyalty led to that judgment. However, closer examination of the moral content of the cases reveals that the reality was much more complex. Iva Toguri and William Joyce are two very different cases.

Joyce developed an early affinity for fascist ideologies. He was not forced to join Nazi Germany; his commitment to Nazism was given freely, and he embraced it enthusiastically because it provided him a compatible political, social, and personal identity. Indeed, he wanted Britain to become another Nazi state. Much like Quisling and Degrelle, he did not "collaborate" with the Nazis. He saw himself as part of National Socialism and dedicated himself to the Nazi cause. As pointed out earlier, Joyce never hid his sympathies; he wanted to realize his dream of a Nazi Britain. In this respect, the question of Joyce's citizenship is irrelevant. Joyce's *identity* was that of a Nazi, and his actions conformed to his identity. From a British-American point of view, he was indeed a traitor. Joyce even conceded this in his book. In structural terms from all points of view, he violated the trust and loyalty required of him to the Anglo-American symbolic moral universe. In terms of content, the Nazis did not see him as a traitor because they thought that his move was morally justified. A non-Nazi examination of the way in which his treason was committed (publicly) and its content leads one to conclude that Joyce elected to identify himself with the morally wrong. Thus, we have here an illustration for the theoretical argument presented in the first chapters of the book—a structural betrayal, but one that is interpreted differently in varied contexts.

Iva Toguri presents a different case altogether. Clearly, she was forced into the role of Tokyo Rose and never developed a Japanese identity or identified with Japan's World War II moral and political views. But she did violate the trust and loyalty to her country—the United States. However, given the situation that she was trapped in, what real choices did she have? In other words, Toguri faced more or less the same choices that many European collaborators faced.

Thus, the structural mirrors reflecting the image of traitor for both Toguri and Joyce hide a complex reality and context in which they both can be understood as violating some forms of trust and loyalty. In that respect, the universal structure of betrayal exists in both cases. However, when we examine the circumstances of those breaches, their content, and how they were constructed, the label of treason becomes interpretively problematic.

8

Intellectual Betrayal:
Ezra Pound and Knut Hamsun

Intellectual support for the Nazi cause is an interesting issue. Two of the most prominent literary men of the century lent open and public support to the Nazi cause—Ezra Pound and Knut Hamsun. In this chapter, we shall explore the case of Pound and, more briefly, that of Hamsun. It is quite significant that after World War II ended, both men were diagnosed by professionals as suffering from some form of "mental illness."

Ezra Pound

Ezra Pound, one of the most distinguished twentieth-century American poets, played a morally questionable role before and during World War II. His anti-Semitism and disenchantment were an old story, long before the war. Indeed Selwyn points out that "some of his most famous lines from *Hugh Selwyn Mauberly* had denounced the futility of fighting Germany."[1]

Pound was born in Hailey, Idaho, on October 30, 1885, and raised in Wyncote (close to Philadelphia). He graduated from Hamilton College in 1905 and finished his M.A. degree at the University of Pennsylvania in 1906. Winning a fellowship in the same year, he left the United States to go to Europe to study Romance languages. However, his fellowship was terminated after only seven months, and he had to return. He next took a teaching position at Wabash Presbyterian College in Indiana (1907), but it did not take stormy Pound more than a few months to decide to leave again for a career as a poet in Europe. In 1908 he arrived again in Europe, this time in Gibraltar, and began to travel (covering large distances by walking), settling eventually in Venice. It did not take Pound long to enter and become part of literary circles in different cities across Europe and in London. During 1924, he and his wife (Dorothy, whom he married in 1914) settled in Rapallo, Italy, where he was to stay for quite some time.

During these years, Pound's main activity was focused on promoting several young literary figures, but he was also producing his own work.[2] In Rapallo, Pound focused on

> his labyrinthian life-work, the cantos, a kind of a journey through the story of mankind. . . . In cantos XIV–XV, Pound directly attacked war profiteers, high finance, politicians and imperialists alike, as well as all liars, orators and preachers. Because many banks were owned and managed by Jews, Pound developed a blind hatred of them.[3]

In April 1939, Pound visited the United States, hoping to meet President Roosevelt. He wanted to persuade him not to get the United States involved in another European war, but the president would not see him. The trip was a part of a significant personal effort by Pound to lobby in any way he could to prevent the United States from entering the war in Europe. In letters he wrote that the Jews were responsible for the war. Pound's version was that the war benefited the Jews because it enabled them to take control of the metals market.

Pound decided to stay in Rapallo when the United States joined the war effort against Nazi Germany.

> From the start of the war, when Italy still held "non-belligerent" status, Pound canvassed Italian radio officials to let him go on the air to address the American people. Eventually, beginning on 23 January 1941, he was given a ten-minute slot every three days in the "American Hour." This marked the beginning of an unprecedented one-man peace movement. To record his talks, Pound had to travel from Rapallo to the Italian capital. For each broadcast he was paid the equivalent of fifteen dollars. In his broadcasts, Pound blasted the "money hungry" Americans for sending aid to Britain, warned against the cost of intervention in terms of lives and blood: "For God's sake, don't send your boys over here to die for the Shell oil company and the Jewish war profiteers." He blamed the Jews for most of the wars in history, and held forth on just about anything that popped into his mind.[4]

Pound did his best to support fascist Italy's war effort, as he felt comfortable with that fascism.[5] Though he did not give up his American citizenship, he nevertheless preached against his country's policy, siding with its enemies, in the midst of a war. As the war progressed, he focused more and more on what he saw as the "communist menace."[6] Although Pound's activity was problematic before the Japanese attack on Pearl Harbor and the declaration of war by the United States, its treasonable nature became obvious after that declaration of war. Had Pound given up his U.S.

citizenship, or kept quiet after Pearl Harbor, his activities might have been overlooked. After all, the U.S. declaration of war (followed by Hitler's declaration of war on the United States) drew very sharp and clear moral boundaries between the two sides. Pound made his choice. He preferred to trust fascism and to be disloyal to the United States and the Allies. Three days after Pearl Harbor, Pound resumed the transmission of anti-U.S. and anti-Semitic propaganda. In his transmissions, he continued to attack his home country in a most vicious way.[7] For example, here is what he said on February 14, 1942: "That any Jew in the White House should send American kids to die for the private interests of the scum of the English earth . . . and the still lower dregs of the Levantine . . . "[8]

Moreover, Pound sought out and corresponded with another famous "radio traitor"—Lord Haw-Haw. Although William Joyce's responses to Pound were somewhat reserved, Pound wrote Joyce long and detailed letters. And although Pound continuously solicited Joyce's responses and wrote to him frequently, Joyce—for all practical purposes—politely ignored this flood. However, neither forgot to sign their letters with the "Heil Hitler" ending.[9]

On July 26, 1943, "a federal grand jury in Washington indicted Ezra Pound . . . on charges of wartime treason." Pound's response to these charges is instructive. He "received the news with disbelief, and sent a letter to Washington arguing that the simple fact that someone expresses his personal views could not possibly be taken as evidence of treason."[10]

Following the Allied invasion of Italy and the surrender of the Nazi army in Italy on May 2, 1945, a few partisans located Pound, captured him, and gave him to the U.S. counterintelligence unit in Genoa.[11] Pound was arrested and held in a military prison near Pisa. He was then sixty years old. His health, and perhaps his psychological well-being, was failing. The physical conditions of his imprisonment were difficult. For example, he was kept in isolation; his belt and laces were taken away; there were guards present around the clock; and the lights were never shut off. After being exposed to these conditions for three weeks, Pound began to complain about nightmares and hallucinations. He lost both his appetite and some weight. A local psychiatrist who examined him did not find any cause to diagnose him as mentally ill but recommended transferring the pro-Nazi poet to the sick bay. There, Pound continued his work on the *Cantos*.[12]

In November 1945, Pound was put on an airplane and sent to the United States. Although he was charged with treason and the chances for a conviction were high, a well-publicized trial was considered a problematic situation. A well-known poet who had identified publicly with fascism a long time before the war and who had broadcast propaganda from Italy seemed like a possibly explosive mix. The day was saved by some mental health professionals who suggested that Pound's experience in prison may have made him mentally unbalanced and therefore unfit to stand trial.

Julien Cornell, who was Pound's lawyer, wrote a book (1966) about the "trial." He admits that the charge of treason against Pound was made because of Pound's Italian radio transmissions, which aided and comforted the enemy at some very critical moments of the war for the Allies. However, he claims that Pound's own response to the charge of treason was that "the treason was in the White House, not in Rapallo."[13] Before any trial into the nature of the accusations could actually begin, Pound's lawyer chose a defense that would rest in showing that Pound was mentally ill and, hence, unfit to stand trial.

If Cornell could get his client certified as "insane," the embarrassment of trying the famous poet would be avoided, as well as the danger of his being declared a traitor and possibly shot as such. Although the stigma of madness is perhaps not any better than that of badness, it would absolve Pound of responsibility for his dubious wartime actions; but most important of all, it would get Pound out of the danger zone of a potential death sentence. To accomplish this goal, Cornell demanded that the issue of Pound's sanity be settled. The court agreed. Thus, four psychiatrists were assigned to examine Pound. Three were appointed by the government: Dr. Marian King (age fifty-six), Dr. Joseph L. Gilbert (age fifty-five), and Dr. Winfred Overholser (age fifty-one); one was appointed by the defense: Dr. Wendell Muncie (age forty-eight). Having examined Pound, these four psychiatrists concluded that he was "insane and unfit to stand trial." They submitted their report to the court on December 14, 1945. In it they wrote the following:

> In our opinion, with advancing years his personality, for many years abnormal, has undergone further distortion to the extent that he is now suffering from a paranoid state which renders him mentally unfit. . . . He is . . . insane and mentally unfit for trial, and is in need of care in a mental hospital.[14]

This unanimous report left very little choice for the jury and the judge. The "trial" ended on February 13, 1946, when the federal jury accepted the psychiatrists' judgment and concluded that Pound was "mentally unsound" and "was unfit to stand trial."[15]

One must note that the only issue in this procedure, which Cornell refers to as a "trial," was whether Ezra Pound was fit to stand trial, that is, an issue of sanity. This, amazingly, does not prevent Cornell from giving the impression that there actually was a trial and from stating that Pound was not found guilty because his crime was never proven. One needs to read this outrageous statement a few times to understand this technical hocus pocus. In any event, Judge Law, who presided over the sanity procedure, sent Pound to St. Elizabeth's Hospital for the mentally ill. As Cole's review (1983) notes, Pound

> had frequently participated in Italy's shortwave broadcasts to North America, making speeches that were not only full of praise for Mussolini and Hitler but outspokenly opposed to America's wartime purposes and its political leadership. The Constitution defines treason as "levying war" on the United States or "giving aid and comfort" to its enemies, and Pound certainly did the latter in his broadcasts.

It thus seems fairly reasonable to assume that had Pound been tried, he would have been convicted of treason.

Structurally, there can be little doubt that Pound was a traitor. Pound, a citizen of the United States, chose to stay in Italy during the war because he sided with Italy against the United States, and he willingly made radio transmissions for Italy against his home country. He violated the trust of his country and was most certainly disloyal. However, from a moral point of view, one must note that Pound's pro-fascist and anti-Semitic views had been established much earlier. He did not side with fascist Italy out of convenience or some form of tangible inducement or pressure. Pound seems to have genuinely believed in the fascist and Nazi ideology. In this sense, he resembles the "patriotic traitors" described by Littlejohn (1972).

Those interested in how the psychiatric evaluation was made and what Pound did at St. Elizabeth's will find the answers in Torrey's instructive (1984) work. A psychiatrist at St. Elizabeth's Hospital, Torrey was in a strategic position to evaluate the situation. He states, very clearly, that Pound was never mentally ill and that he continued to work during all of his stay at the hospital. Torrey documents, in detail, the collaboration between Pound and the psychiatrists and how they created the deception that Pound was crazy. Having examined Pound's wartime activities, Torrey believes that these activities should be seen as treason.[16] What Cornell refers to as the "trial," Torrey refers to as the "non-trial."[17] Torrey states that the psychiatrists who examined Pound felt that they saved the great poet from social degradation and possibly a very harsh sentence. Furthermore, according to Torrey, Pound cooperated fully in this charade and did his best to give a "show" that would persuade the psychiatrists that he was insane.[18] Torrey confirms that Cornell's strategy was very successful. Pound was not branded as a traitor, he was able to continue his work, and those who knew him did not think for a minute he was crazy. Torrey found Pound to be eccentric,

Pound gives the fascist salute on arrival in Naples on July 9, 1958, after being released from the mental hospital.

SOURCE: *E. Fuller Torrey,* The Roots of Treason: Ezra Pound and the Secret of St. Elizabeth *(New York: McGraw-Hill, 1984). Photograph attributed to Wide World Photos.*

racially bigoted, and rather oblivious to social norms, but he felt that Pound was definitely not crazy. During Pound's stay at St. Elizabeth's, he expressed consistent fascist tendencies, praised Mussolini,[19] and continued with his extreme anti-Semitism.[20]

Pound was visited daily by his wife, Dorothy. Many literary friends visited him as well, and he managed to conduct an extensive correspondence. The lobby for Pound's release was meanwhile gaining momentum. Ernest Hemingway's comment after receiving the 1954 Nobel Prize for literature that indeed it was Ezra Pound who deserved the prize helped, too. The pressure achieved its desired result, and at the age of seventy-two, in April 1958, Pound was released, having never been put on trial for treason. In June of the same year, he and his wife left the United States for Brunnenburg in South Tyrol. Pound died on November 1, 1972, at the age of eighty-seven in Venice, fourteen years after his release from St. Elizabeth's Hospital.[21]

Knut Hamsun

It is noteworthy, and significant, that the winner of the Nobel Prize for literature in 1920, the Norwegian author Knut Hamsun (described by many as a literary giant), was also a Nazi sympathizer.

Hamsun was born on August 4, 1859. He had had a harsh childhood and was employed as an occasional worker. He traveled throughout the United States, taking on several different jobs. In 1890 his novel *Hunger* appeared (translated into German in 1891) and was followed by more stories. He won the 1920 Nobel Prize for literature for his masterpiece, *The Growth of the Soil* (published in 1917 and translated into German in 1918). Between 1927 and 1933, Hamsun produced the Vagabond Trilogy. Hamsun's work displays some unmistakable characteristics: an appreciation of the simple life, a closeness to nature, and a strong tone of anti-American and antitechnological civilization. Hamsun's expressed positions were consistently hostile to both Britain and the United States. He disliked parliamentary methods of government and what he defined as "a lack of culture" in the United States. Also, the process of industrialization was not to Hamsun's liking, and he was all in favor of a rural way of life.

These themes made Hamsun's work quite popular among Hitler's youth movement. Hamsun was not indifferent to German National Socialism and did not hide his view that he saw in Nazism an antidote to Anglo-American materialism. This, naturally and inevitably, led him to Quisling and his fascist party.[22] He joined Quisling's political cause, gave him a solid endorsement (October 17, 1936), and was thus the most distinguished individual to support that Norwegian Nazi. In endorsing Quisling, Hamsun exclaimed, "If I had ten votes, he [Quisling] would receive them."[23] Although Hamsun joined Quisling rather early, he remained committed to Quisling even during some difficult times and refused to break away from him, despite requests to do so.[24] Following the German invasion and occupation of Norway (1940), Hamsun had no hesitation in calling upon Norwegians to terminate resistance because, like Quisling, he believed that Norway had an advantaged position in a Nazi-ruled Europe.

Hamsun was accepted for an interview by Hitler (in Vienna in 1943) and expressed open support for him. He urged Hitler to remove the Nazi commissioner of Norway—Terboven—but Hitler was not moved by his appeal. Terboven served his purposes, in spirit and in practice, much better than either Hamsun or Quisling ever could.[25] Despite his disappointment in the meeting with the führer, his public support for Hitler did not waver.[26]

Moreover, Hamsun was hosted by Dr. Goebbels—the Third Reich master propagandist—in his Berlin home on May 19, 1943. Hamsun and

Goebbels seemed to admire each other and apparently enjoyed each other's company. After Hitler's suicide, Hamsun created an emotional eulogy in his memory.[27]

Hamsun, clearly, went further in supporting Nazism than Pound. Both men, however, felt committed to an ideology that, to them, made sense, described the kind of world they wanted to live in, and set acceptable moral and political boundaries

It is interesting to note that Hamsun, like Ezra Pound, was subjected to psychiatric examinations after the war. Professor Gabriel Langfeldt, a leading Norwegian psychiatrist, diagnosed him as not responsible enough to stand trial on charges of treason. Based on this diagnosis, the Norwegian authorities "concluded that Hamsun was not mentally competent to be prosecuted. The outcome of this case, however, was that the novelist at the age of ninety mustered his 'permanently impaired mental faculties' to write his final masterpiece, part fiction and part autobiography, in which he attacked Dr. Langfeldt."[28] Hamsun, it must be noted, refused to be declared mentally ill and was fully prepared to pay for his wartime activities.[29]

Nevertheless, Hamsun was denounced and fined after the war for his friendliness toward Germany. He had publicly supported the Nazis, had written articles for them, and had helped recruit Norwegians for their cause. His version of his trial, *On Overgrown Paths,* was published in 1949 (and translated into German in 1950).[30] This was his last book. It is interesting to note that during his trial, Hamsun tried as best he could to minimize his connections with Nazi Germany and his support for Quisling and denied that he caused any real damage.[31] Hamsun died on February 19, 1952.

It is worth noting that although Hamsun was the most prominent Norwegian to publicly support the Nazi cause and Quisling, he was not the only one. Such individuals as Kirsten Flagstad, world-famous Wagnerian soprano, and Christian Sindig, an eminent composer, were involved in similar activities.[32]

Concluding Discussion

There are several issues that require our attention at this point: The first is a puzzle; the second is the nature of the betrayal here, and the third is the processing of deviance in the cases of Pound and Hamsun.

There is a puzzle behind the "intellectual betrayal" of Ezra Pound and Knut Hamsun. Both Pound and Hamsun were famous and gifted literary men, and so one wonders how these incredibly fertile and creative minds, so sensitive to human nuances and with such a powerful control of language, could lend such strong support to totalitarian ideologies founded on the oppression of the human spirit and the hatred of large collectives of humans. Of course, poets and authors are not immune to overinflated egos or idiosyncratic or eccentric behavior. However, one asset they must possess is a sensitivity to the "human condition," a mature perspective of the complexity of human culture. It is difficult to understand how the works of Pound and Hamsun could have been created without this sensitivity, sympathy, and compassion. To illustrate just a limited sense of that power, I quote one of Pound's short poems:

A Pact

I make a pact with you, Walt Whitman—
I have detested you long enough.
I come to you as a grown child
Who has been a pig-headed father;
I am old enough now to make friends.
It was you that broke the new wood,
Now is a time for carving.
We have one sap and one root—
Let there be commerce between us.[33]

In this poem one can see animosities of the past, ambivalence, reconciliation, remorse, and hope for a better future. Pound's alignment with fascism and Nazism does not fit with the sensitivity revealed here. Coles's 1983 review expresses a similar amazement at this enigma.

Pound's and Hamsun's affinity for fascism and Nazism is part of a larger puzzle. Many intellectuals have aligned themselves with questionable characters and oppressive ideologies. At issue is whether an intellectual's political ideology should play a part in our attitude toward his or her work, and if so, how. The debate requires a moral judgment, but it need not detract from the admiration, or criticism, of the works of the person in question.

The failure to detect the evil nature of fascism and Nazism by two such gifted individuals is an enigma, but it also requires a moral judgment of these two intellectuals who are viewed by many as giants of the human spirit—Pound, perhaps, more so than Hamsun.[34] One must concede that these two great men made a choice. No one forced their hand. They freely elected to side with fascism and Nazism a long time before the war began. Regardless of the quality of their work, this was—first and foremost—a moral choice.

The debate of whether Pound's work should be separated from his political and moral views was reignited in 1999. A report by Dinitia Smith in the *New York Times* (October 23) informed readers that the dean of the

Cathedral of St. John the Divine—the Very Reverend Harry S. Pritchett Jr.—overruled a decision by a group of prominent American writers to honor Ezra Pound with a place in the Poets' Corner of the cathedral. He justified his decision by stating that Pound's destructive anti-Semitic writings and broadcasts from fascist Italy during World War II caused too much pain. Reverend Pritchett's decision was clearly a moral judgment.

Structurally, the nature of treason in Pound's and Hamsun's acts is clear. They violated the trust invested in them by free democratically elected governments and violated their loyalty to these regimes. In other words, Pound and Hamsun stood up against the sovereignty and interests of their countries, as defined by democratically elected governments. However, one must concede that their own views were not very sympathetic to democracy, and they were drawn to the totalitarian and repressive ideologies represented by Hitler and Mussolini. In this sense, they remained faithful to their views, much like other European collaborators mentioned earlier, such as Quisling, Mussert, and Joyce. Once again we see how the structure of betrayal materializes, and how its moral content and context can be interpreted differently.

Finally, the way in which social control agencies processed the deviance presented by Pound and Hamsun is similar. Both were discredited as mentally ill. Thus, one could infer that they were not responsible for their wartime activities, which, through this rationale, become invalidated—a rather ad hominem escape route. Obviously, the construction of Pound and Hamsun as irresponsibly "ill" makes one question the validity of this judgment. Judging by Fuller Torrey's 1984 work, the validity of Pound's "illness" is rather questionable.

An added note here must be focused on the advantages and disadvantages of viewing both Pound and Hamsun through a medical prism rather than through a moral one. I must confess that, for reasons stated in Chapter 1, I believe that the moral prism is more valid in these cases. The political choices of Pound and Hamsun must be judged for what they were—as moral decisions. That choice, during World War II, implied an affinity with fascism and/or Nazism. That moral preference needs to be assessed from a moral point of view. One can and should expect such gifted individuals to be more compassionate than to identify with worldviews that are extreme, racist, full of hatred, simplistic, and militaristic. The implication of this stand to their works is a different, but related, issue. Would it be easier to evaluate Pound's and Hamsun's works if we were to assume that they were mentally ill rather than morally wrong, or vice versa?

9

Edward VIII:
A Traitor Monarch?

The Riddle

The popular image of King Edward VIII is primarily a romantic one.[1] It is of a popular king who preferred love to power, who left his role as the king of England in December 1936 in favor of living with the woman he fell in love with—Mrs. Wallis Warfield Simpson.

Edward VIII's story is an instructive historical tale because of the crucial question of whether he was a traitor. It has been virtually impossible to find direct and "official" evidence of betrayal by Edward VIII in the written literature. However, some of the most important aspects of the case have been concealed. One needs to read the literature very carefully to find those telltale bits and pieces of information about a possible treason. However, a London Channel 4 television program transmitted in 1995 and titled *Secret Life: Edward VIII—The Traitor King* made it very clear that, in fact, Edward VIII was a traitor.[2]

The Channel 4 program indicated that new information supported their view that Edward VIII was a traitor and that his affair with Mrs. Simpson was used by politicians as a face-saving justification for yanking him out of his throne. The program implied that this new information was concealed by both the British government and the royal family in order to prevent a colossal embarrassment. Winston Churchill, who apparently knew about Edward VIII's treacherous actions, preferred not to disclose the facts to the public for the same reason, and because he was deeply convinced of the vitality and necessity of the monarchy. Brown notes that Churchill was determined to "clip the tongue and hobble the feet of . . . the Duke of Windsor."[3]

Thus, we are dealing with two stories here. The first has to do with the factual basis for the claim that Edward VIII was a traitor. The second has to do with the possible cover-up of any traces of treason on part of Edward VIII. In the following narrative, I have tried to integrate several sources to examine the possible betrayal by King Edward VIII.

It is important to note that Channel 4 was not the first to question the behavior of Edward VIII (later Duke of Windsor). Quite a few authors and researchers have examined, in more or less direct ways, the same issue.[4] What the Channel 4 program did was to clarify and focus many of the questions in such a manner that the viewer was left gasping at the old and new revelations. And yet confirming the information provided by Channel 4 in other sources is difficult and makes the claim that Edward VIII was a traitor problematic. Indeed, sources confirm that Edward VIII behaved erratically and childishly, was irresponsible, could not be trusted with classified military information, and leaned rather strongly toward fascism and Hitler. These are troublesome qualities, but did that make him a traitor?

The Beginning

Edward VIII (Duke of Windsor, among other titles) was born June 23, 1894, the eldest son (out of four) of George, Duke of York (who later became King George V) and Princess Mary of Teck (later Queen Mary). He became heir to the throne in May 1910. He was trained for the Royal Navy (1907–1911) and was commissioned in the army's Grenadier Guards after the beginning of World War I (August 6, 1914). Edward had much affection and natural sympathy for Germany. His mother's family had deep roots in Germany, and he spent much time there. German was also a language he liked and felt comfortable with.

The outbreak of World War I in 1914 meant that Edward had to make some tough decisions. Although he was prevented from being placed in an actual combat role, it seems that whatever duties he was assigned to he performed in an acceptable manner. After the war ended, he toured extensively the areas controlled by the British Empire. He was a handsome and popular king in the making. Following the illness of his father in 1928, his interest in national issues grew. In the early 1930s, his interest and involvement in trying to find solutions for the unemployed increased significantly. His influence was beneficial, and his popularity in the early 1930s soared. In 1930 Edward was given Fort Belvedere by King George V. There he developed the art of gardening and harbored a social circle of friends. Although the American ambassador told Roosevelt that Edward was "surrounded by a pro-German cabal," Ziegler claims that there is scant evidence for this.[5]

During this time, Edward developed a distaste for royal rituals and had several affairs with married women.[6] These indiscretions were never publicized, but his assistant private secretary—Sir Alan Lascelles, appointed at the end of 1920—was disturbed by what he considered to be his immoral behavior (and wrote about it to his wife). Edward's continued irresponsible behavior caused their relationship to deteriorate, and in 1927 Lascelles asked for an interview with Stanley Baldwin, then the prime minister, regarding the issue. He told Baldwin about the deteriorating morality of Edward and added that "the Heir Apparent, in his unbridled pursuit of wine and women, and whatever selfish whim occupied him at the moment, was rapidly going to the devil, and unless he mended his ways, would soon become no fit wearer of the British Crown." Baldwin agreed with him.[7]

In 1930 the future king met the ambitious and outspoken Mrs. Simpson, an acquaintance that would prove fateful. Wallis Warfield Simpson was divorced from a U.S. Navy lieutenant in 1927 and married Ernest Simpson in 1928. The couple were part of the prince's social circle of friends. It so happened that by 1934 the prince was madly in love with Mrs. Simpson. However, King George V died (January 20, 1936) before the prince could discuss the matter with him.

By 1933 Hitler had risen to power in Germany. Edward felt that Hitler's performance with the German economy was outstanding; it appeared that he had led Germany out of economic depression and provided employment to the German masses. Edward became convinced that England should support Hitler by, among other things, giving him a friendly and congratulatory hand. Also, the memories of the horrors of World War I were still very fresh, and the desire to avoid a replay of such a calamity must have played a strong role in Edward's conciliatory mood toward Hitler. He chose to ignore the potential meaning of Hitler's massive program of rearming Germany and its obvious implications. In fact, in June 1935, in a speech to the Royal British Legion, the prince advocated an alliance between Germany and Britain. The speech was very well received in Germany.[8] Edward's father, King George V, was furious. He accused his son of behaving in an unconstitutional way because he was involving himself in foreign affairs and making pro-German statements. More than one source states that shortly before his death, the ailing king noted that once he was dead, his successor son would ruin himself within a year.[9] Actually, it took Edward much less than a year to fulfill his father's prophecy.

It should be noted that British appeasement toward Germany in the 1930s had deep roots.[10] Moreover, fascism did win some genuine converts. For example, a rather famous member of the British aristocracy—Unity Mitford—was an admirer of Hitler and Nazism.[11] Britain also had a fascist movement, which tried to win converts.[12]

Edward's reaction to his father's illness and death led to the final break with Lascelles. The news of King George V's grave condition reached his son while he was on a safari trip in South Africa. His reaction was disbelief, and he viewed the news as an "election dodge of old Baldwin's" (Bradford 1989:167). According to Lascelles:

> Then for the first and only time in our association, I lost my temper with him. "Sir," I said, "the king of England is dying; and if that means nothing to you, it means a great deal to us." He looked at me, went out without a word, and spent the remainder of the evening in the successful seduction of a Mrs. Barnes, wife of the local Commissioner. He told me so himself next morning.[13]

Despite a good start in late 1920, Lascelles became so disillusioned with Edward that he resigned about eight years later. In 1935 he was asked to rejoin Edward's entourage—which he reluctantly did. Both he and Baldwin felt that the prince was childlike and somehow did not mature.[14]

Edward VIII as King

Following the death of King George V, Edward VIII became king on January 20, 1936. Edward VIII's behavior was not that expected from a king.[15] Moreover, as he began to exercise his new role, he began to try to persuade the royal family to accept Mrs. Simpson. At that time, she was involved in securing a divorce from her husband and had in fact received a preliminary decree of divorce on October 27, 1936. However, Edward's attempts in this regard were met with fierce resistance. The idea of having a foreigner as the king's wife was very problematic.

At King George V's funeral, Charles Edward (uncle of Edward VIII), Duke of Saxe-Coburg and Gotha, an overt pro-Nazi and a member in the Nazi Party (as well as a senior officer in the S.A.), showed up in a Nazi uniform.[16] Moreover, Coburg wrote a detailed report to Hitler and Joachim von Ribbentrop (German ambassador at large) relating that he had had lengthy and frank discussions with Edward VIII, in which the king told him that "an alliance Germany-Britain is . . . an urgent necessity and a guiding principle for British foreign policy."[17] Although some cast doubt on the accuracy of Coburg's report, he did point out that Edward VIII saw a German-British alliance as something important and desirable. The issue of Edward VIII meeting Hitler also came up, and the new king certainly expressed his wish to meet the führer, using Coburg as a mediator. Edward VIII was thus giving clear signals of his intention to play an active role in British foreign policy. Coburg, who was an enthusiastic Nazi sympathizer, did not hesitate to pass the new king's preferences on to Berlin.[18]

The Nazis took these reports very seriously, and Ribbentrop noted that he "was convinced Edward VIII was 'a kind of English National Socialist, with strong concern for the social problems of his country and warm sympathy for an understanding with Germany.'"[19] Although the new king was advised against making political statements, this warning was apparently ignored. Costello states that Edward VIII most certainly wanted to develop directly, or influence indirectly, foreign policy toward Nazi Germany.[20]

Thomas states that Hitler was concerned about a new war with Britain and tried repeatedly, through various diplomatic channels, to initiate contacts with the British royal family in order to forge some sort of an understanding or alliance with Britain.[21] The memories of the terrible human loss during World War I underlay the feelings of many British citizens that a new war had to be averted, perhaps at any cost. This sentiment explains, at least in part, what has become known as the "appeasement" policy of the 1930s. Thomas points out that direct diplomatic channels between Edward VIII and the Nazis were kept open through several channels (including Simpson).

It is instructive to look at another relevant report:

> Sir Orme Sargent of the Foreign Office at the end of 1936 recorded a conversation in which he was told of Ribbentrop's belief that the real reason for the abdication was neither moral nor constitutional but political: "Mr. Baldwin's real motive was . . . to defeat those Germanophile forces which had been working through Mrs. Simpson and the late King with the object of reversing the present British policy and bringing about an Anglo-German détente." Hitler also was said to be very distressed by the abdication, "since he had looked upon the late King as a man after his own heart and one who understood the Führer-prinzip and was ready to introduce it into his country.". . . In December 1936 the German Ambassador was personally instructed by Hitler to do all he could to prevent the abdication.[22]

Ziegler is quick to point out that the German Foreign Office was completely misguided about interpreting Edward VIII's views and intentions. However, even from this report it is clear that at the very least Mrs. Simpson was a Nazi sympathizer, as her frequent visits to the German embassy indicate. It may be that the Nazis were misguided about the magnitude and depth of Edward VIII's sympathies, but not about their nature or direction. In fact, Ziegler notes that German ambassadors to Britain in the early 1930s were instructed to "cultivate him" and that the future king (then the Prince of Wales) clearly expressed pro-German views.[23] Moreover, German reactions to the October 1937 visit of King Edward VIII to

Germany were very positive, and Hess, Goering, and Ribbentrop very much hoped "to see Edward VIII remain on the throne."[24]

In March 1936, Hitler took quite a risk when he decided to occupy the demilitarized Rhineland.[25] This occupation was a blatant violation of pacts Germany signed. What was Edward VIII's reaction to Hitler's entry into the Rhineland? He gave clear and unequivocal support for a "no reaction" response and to appeasement.

Albert Speer recalls that on March 7, 1936—the day German troops marched into the demilitarized Rhineland—Hitler rode a special evening train to Munich, anxiously awaiting reports of other countries' reactions to his invasion. "At one station a message was handed into the car. Hitler sighed with relief: 'At last! The King of England will not intervene. He is keeping his promise. That means that it can all go well.'"[26] One is left wondering, What promise was Hitler referring to? When was it made? Regardless of the king's actual ability to influence the government, there is little doubt that his voice carried at least *some* weight. Speer is quick to point out that any "military intervention would have probably required the King's approval," and knowing that the king of England was, at the minimal level, an appeaser wanting a "peaceful solution" most certainly lifted Hitler's mood.[27]

Brown is much blunter. He quotes Ambassador Leopold von Hoesch's telegram to Ribbentrop of March 11, 1936, in which the ambassador wrote that he found much understanding for the Nazi point of view from the court and that the court instructed the government that "no matter how the details of the affair are dealt with, complications of a serious nature are in no circumstances to be allowed to develop."[28] This message obviously helped to calm the highest Nazi officials. Their peace of mind following Hitler's aggression "was attributable to the influence of the King of England."[29] Bradford corroborates this point: "There is evidence . . . from captured German documents that the King put pressure on the government against going to war over Germany's take-over of the Rhineland in March 1936."[30]

Thomas asserts that Edward VIII told German ambassador Leopold von Hoesch directly that there would be no war as a result of the German aggression.[31] The act of passing "highly sensitive military information, obtained by virtue of [the King's] privileged position, to a foreign power was nothing less than high treason."[32] However, it must be remembered that the British government at that time was not eager to go to war. Churchill, who advocated armed opposition to the German move, and his supporters were labeled "warmongers" by Chamberlain and Baldwin.[33] However, even the pro–Edward VIII biographer Ziegler points out that following the illegal remilitarization of the Rhineland, Edward VIII called von Hoesch and told him: "I sent for the Prime Minister and Gave him a piece of my mind. I told the old so-and-so that I would abdicate if he made war. There was a frightful scene. But you needn't worry. There won't be a war."[34]

It became obvious that Edward VIII wanted to express himself politically and was determined to do so. The king's political activity—in both content and structure—caused much concern. He was clearly out of line constitutionally, intervening in matters he should not have; and he was sympathetic to Nazi Germany. As Bradford points out, the main issue was not whether the king was pro-German—many people in Britain were pro-German—but that he was acting in an unconstitutional manner.

On August 11, 1936, Joachim von Ribbentrop became the German ambassador to Great Britain.[35] Evidently, Ribbentrop and Mrs. Simpson were close friends and spent a great deal of time together.[36] It seems obvious now that Mrs. Simpson was telling Ribbentrop what she must have heard from Edward VIII (before and after he became the king) about his briefings from British prime minister Baldwin. Thus, Ribbentrop must have known the content of the discussions in the British cabinet. As it became evident that both Mrs. Simpson and Edward VIII were leaning strongly toward Nazi Germany, Edward VIII was perceived more and more as a security risk, and the British foreign office was withholding certain documents from him.[37]

As it was revealed much later, during the spring and summer of 1936 a group of powerful and influential British officials were uniting against Edward VIII, because they felt that he was unfit to rule. The Dominion nations were consulted on whether they would accept Mrs. Simpson as queen, and the answer received was a clear "no." According to Channel 4, it was becoming obvious that the antipathy toward Mrs. Simpson could be used to get rid of a very problematic king. By September 1936 Neville Chamberlain agreed to the plan. Bradford points out that the anti–Edward VIII conspiracy had also gained some support in the United States,[38] and the Windsors themselves may have begun to lean toward it, too.

The opportunity was fast approaching. In October 1936, Mrs. Simpson began formal divorce proceedings. So desperate were the conspirators against Edward VIII that a rumor about a secret file ("the China dossier") was fabricated and circulated.[39] The rumor implied that Mrs. Simpson had enjoyed an exotic sex life in the 1920s in connection with luxurious brothels in the East.[40]

Baldwin told Edward VIII that Mrs. Simpson was unacceptable as queen to him, his government, the Dominion nations, and the British Empire. Edward VIII searched in vain for ways to bypass this problem.[41]

Since no solution could be found to this romantic quagmire, Edward made a choice: He gave up his position as king in order to remain with Mrs. Simpson. He submitted his abdication on December 10, 1936. Parliament endorsed the instrument of abdication on December 11, and in a radio broadcast that evening, Edward explained that he found it impossible to act as king without the support of the woman he loved. He therefore chose love over power. His brother George VI was appointed king. Edward VIII reigned as king between January 20 and December 10, 1936, a short period of eleven months. Edward left England that night for Austria, where he waited for Mrs. Simpson's divorce to become final. On June 3, 1937, Edward and Mrs. Simpson were married at Candé, France. No representatives of the royal family were present. George VI made Edward VIII the Duke of Windsor and his wife the Duchess of Windsor, but he refused to allow her to use the title Her Royal Highness. Edward became very angry and upset about this.

It is interesting to note Thomas's 1995 hypothetical scenario. What might have happened if Edward VIII had been king when Nazi Germany invaded Poland in September 1939? It is possible that such an opinionated king would have intervened in Britain's foreign policy and refused to go along with the ultimatum given to Nazi Germany following that invasion, or refused to later declare war on Nazi Germany. That could have created a major constitutional crisis in Britain: a cabinet that was determined to go to war, and a king who refused to sanction that move. Such a crisis, however, was averted when Edward abdicated the throne.

A major tenet in Thomas's work is that although Edward left England, he most certainly expected to return to the throne.[42] Moreover, the Nazis not only were interested in getting a pro-Nazi king back on the throne but were probably involved in plots to facilitate that event.

Although Edward was happy with Wallis, abdication created three central problems that were to haunt him for years to come. First, his financial resources after abdication were—in his own mind—unsatisfactory. Second, he very desperately wanted Wallis Simpson to be recognized as Her Royal Highness, in other words, to receive the honor that he felt she deserved, but that honor had been refused. Third, he wanted to be involved in matters of state and may have expected to play an active part in British diplomacy. He was placed, however, in a very minor position, and he felt that his wishes to be involved were, for all practical purposes, ignored.[43]

Post-Abdication

The whereabouts of the Duke of Windsor during the period of World War II is an interesting, important, and thorny issue. Between 1936 and 1938 the couple lived mostly in France and visited several European countries.

One of the individuals with whom the Duke of Windsor associated was Charles Bedaux, a French millionaire with worldwide industrial interests, including some strong connections in Nazi Germany. Bedaux was an advisor to Hitler in the Vichy government and was probably involved in Nazi Germany's war effort. He was later imprisoned by the Allies in North Africa under charges of treason and of trading with Nazi Germany.[44] Bloch points out that Bedaux committed suicide in an American prison in 1944, but that in 1961 the French government "formally absolved [him] of any treasonable wartime conduct."[45] Bedaux played a crucial role in arranging the Duke of Windsor's trip to Nazi Germany and his personal meeting with Adolf Hitler. He was also involved in arranging the duke's visit to the United States. Although perhaps at the beginning the duke was not aware of Bedaux's connections in Nazi Germany,[46] he could not have possibly missed it later. It is clear that Bedaux tried to move the duke further toward the direction of Nazi Germany.

Bedaux recruited another millionaire into the duke's social circle—the Swedish Axel Wenner-Gren. This man was an arms dealer close to Reichsmarschall Hermann Goering and a Nazi sympathizer.[47] Although the official version downplays, and perhaps even questions, the fact that the Duke met Wenner-Gren before 1940,[48] the Channel 4 documentary stated that evidence indicates that the two had already met in 1937 in Paris. According to this version, it was Wenner-Gren who gave, in person, to the Duke of Windsor a personal invitation from Adolf Hitler to visit him in Germany. And Ziegler concedes that the Paris meeting was documented in Wenner-Gren's diary.[49] However, in an interestingly discrediting fashion, Ziegler characterizes the meeting as "brief" and states that in that "brief" meeting the two "presumably" discussed the idea of supporting an international organization that would coordinate "all the various peace movements." It must be said that discussing "peace" with Hitler at this point in time could only mean support for Hitler's expansionist intentions. Furthermore, when Wenner-Gren later met the duke in Nassau, he noted in his diary that the duke "remembers very well our conversation in Paris,"[50] which tends to contradict the notion that it was a "brief" and supposedly insignificant meeting.

The Duke of Windsor began to plan his trip to Germany. The news about this planned visit was most unpleasant to the British government. It created questions about the Duke of Windsor's possible ambitions to return to the political arena and most certainly constituted an intervention in British foreign policy at a very difficult moment. Indeed, Bloch notes that both Churchill and Beaverbrook tried to persuade the duke not to visit Germany, but their efforts failed. On October 3, 1937, the duke released a press statement, which announced that the Windsors were going to visit both Germany and the United States "for the purpose of studying housing and working conditions."[51]

The Nazis did not fail to grasp the meaning of such a trip and presented it as an unofficial state visit aimed at promoting an agreement be-

The Windsors meet Hitler, 1937.
SOURCE: Ma'ariv, *December 5, 1996. Photo from Associated Press archives.*

tween Germany and Great Britain. It is certain that the duke hated World
War I, and it is possible that the ex-king felt that he could persuade Hitler
to prevent another war. Also, it was obvious that the Nazis were going to
give him the red carpet treatment, and he may have missed that kind of
public respect. The Nazis, evidently, had other ideas. They had long believed that the ex-king and Mrs. Simpson were sympathizers and thought
that they could use the duke in promoting a peace accord to their advantage, and not just in Europe.

Visiting Nazi Germany

The Duke and Duchess of Windsor arrived at the Friedrichstrasse Station
in Berlin on October 11, 1937, as Hitler's guests. Their visit to Nazi Germany lasted until October 23. Their official host was Dr. Robert Ley (in

charge of labor). Brown quotes the *New York Times* report that on two separate occasions the duke gave what appeared to be the Nazi salute (on one occasion, to Hitler himself). Although the tour plan was exhausting, the Duke apparently enjoyed his visit tremendously.[52] Nazi officials paid him considerable respect, and the Windsors also met Goebbels, Goering, Hess, and Ribbentrop.

According to the Channel 4 documentary, the idea of mounting support for Hitler was discussed when the duke visited the home of Rudolf Hess on October 22, 1937. It turns out that Hess and the duke shared some points of views: They were against communism, and they both wanted peace. The idea was to promote a world peace, dominated by a Nazi army and with Britain's empire intact. The United States was supposed to remain outside Europe. Edward was supposedly told that when such a peace prevailed, he would return to the throne.

The duke's visit to Germany included listening to music and visiting the S.S. training center and a concentration camp (although it is quite certain that he was unaware of the atrocities committed there). The height of the visit, no doubt, was a one-hour personal meeting (and tea) with Adolf Hitler at Berchtesgaden on October 22. The Channel 4 documentary showed a photograph of a smiling Hitler with the Windsors.[53] Although Hitler refused to talk directly to the duke and used an interpreter, he most certainly assumed that the duke shared the Nazi worldview.[54] That an official visit by the duke and duchess at that time could be, and was, interpreted as giving support to Nazi Germany is clear. Ziegler, who wrote the official biography of Edward VIII, notes that "the worst that can be said about the German visit is that the Duke closed his eyes to most of what he did not wish to see, and allowed himself to be paraded as an admirer of the economic miracle and as tacitly condoning the brutal side of the social experiment."[55]

Bradford and the Channel 4 documentary provide a less innocent interpretation and some very real concerns regarding the potential political implications of that tour.[56] One cannot simply excuse a visit to a dictator like Hitler, not even in 1937, as expressing innocent interests in examining what may have looked like some economic "miracle" (which, in reality, it was not). Moreover, in a world where Hitler's fascism was ideologically competing with other political ideologies (communism, democracy, even monarchy), lending Hitler support and legitimacy by visiting him and his nation had some very clear and loud moral and political implications, especially when the visitor was the former king of England.

Trusting the Duke

Quite a few British officials were suspicious of the political aspirations of the duke, both before and after the 1936 abdication. As tension was mounting in Europe, both the British and the Americans became concerned about the Duke's indiscretion with classified military and political information. One incident took place in 1937, two years before World War II began. An American low-level diplomat, George Messersmith, met the duke in Vienna in 1937. Messersmith told the duke about a train accident that had occurred. In the course of the story it was revealed that the Americans had broken a secret military code of the Axis powers. The Duke of Windsor did not keep his mouth shut but told the story at a dinner party given by an Italian diplomat. Messersmith reported the incident. This seemed to confirm the suspicion that the duke could not be trusted.[57] As we shall see, there were several other incidents, too.

The Verdun Radio Transmission

Another problematic event involving the Duke of Windsor occurred in the spring of 1939, just a few months before the war began. A few days after King George VI and his wife embarked on a trip to Canada and the United States (May 5, 1939), the Duke of Windsor broadcast "an appeal for world peace directed at America from the famous First World War battlefield at Verdun."[58] Bloch notes that this was the last time the duke made a speech that millions of people listened to and that many received with enthusiasm.[59] The speech was made on May 8, which is the anniversary of the Battle of Verdun. The meaning of that broadcast, at that particular point in time, cannot be underestimated. Great Britain was on the brink of war with Nazi Germany, and the king was on his way to the United States on a very important mission.

The duke stated in his broadcast that as "a soldier of the last war" and in "the presence of the great company of the dead," he was making an appeal for world peace. It must be acknowledged that regardless of the duke's political convictions, his experience in World War I was such that he felt that preventing a replay of that war was worth almost anything. However, the thought that such a ruthless tyrant as Hitler could be so easily appeased was, at best, terribly naive.

Bradford notes the duke's rationale for the transmission: "I became convinced that Europe was headed down the slippery slope to war. Only the Americans had the influence to arrest the slide. That was why I decided to aim my appeal at them."[60] Ironically, there is not a shred of evidence that the duke was trying to persuade Hitler to stop his aggressive actions, which were the source of the conflict. In the duke's conversation with his wife after his personal meeting with Hitler, reported by the duchess in her autobiography, there was no mention of any such effort to avert war.[61] Thus, although the duke was calling for peace, he was in reality asking for appeasement (in that particular historical context, "peace" really meant "peace under Hitler's terms").

It is instructive to examine how Ziegler, Edward VIII's official biographer, interprets this broadcast.[62] According to Ziegler, the American radio network NBC "invited him to broadcast to the United States from Verdun after a visit to the battlefield. His speech was short, eloquent, uncontroversial and written entirely by himself."[63] Ziegler adds that "nobody else had offered him the chance or was likely to do so—least of all the British. It was hardly the Duke of Windsor's fault if the BBC refused to let the British people hear his words. He believed that he had something of real significance to say and that, coming from him, it might be listened to."[64]

Close reading of this passage reveals the speciousness of the argument. The facts are that the duke gave up power and influence once he chose Mrs. Simpson, yet he was trying to steer British policy from the backseat when he directly appealed to the American people. The duke was thus undermining British policy and intervening in the royal visit to the North American continent. Why should anyone be surprised that the BBC would not let the duke cast his defeatist, pro-Nazi Germany position? Besides, the duke most certainly had direct channels of communication to the British government, and he could have tried to persuade them directly. The Verdun broadcast was a blatant attempt to intervene in British policy by a man who—to a large extent—had given up that right. Clearly Ziegler assumes an innocent peace-seeking motivation behind the duke's broadcast to the United States, whereas Channel 4 and Bradford find that it was a treacherous and defeatist speech.

Ziegler notes that on August 25, 1939, the duke telegraphed Hitler: "Remembering your courtesy and our meeting two years ago, I address to you my entirely personal, simple though very earnest appeal for your utmost influence towards a peaceful solution of the present problems."[65] One must note the humble and apologetic position the duke assumes in begging Hitler. Hitler replied: "You may be sure that my attitude towards England is the same as ever. . . . It depends upon England, however, whether my wishes for the future development of Anglo-German relations materialize."[66] This message is chilling in its hypocrisy. Hitler at this point was about a week away from brutally violating Polish sovereignty; on September 1 he unleashed a devastating and ferocious blitzkrieg campaign against Poland, taking a gamble that the United Kingdom would not honor its last-minute guarantee of Polish independence (not to mention the violation of the ten-year nonaggression pact Hitler signed with Poland in 1934). Britain could tolerate no more and declared war on Germany on September 1, 1939.

The Windsors in France

When the war began, the Duke and Duchess of Windsor came home to England, but they returned to France on September 29. The duke was given a military appointment.[67] However, it was made clear to the duke that he could not possibly "be a free-lance in the war area."[68] The Channel 4 documentary stated that the duke devoted little time to his military assignment, preferring to spend most of his time in Paris with the duchess and his friend Bedaux, who paid the hotel bill of the royal couple. One gets a totally different impression from reading Ziegler's version.[69] According to Ziegler, the duke was active in touring the units and preparing reports. However, his insistence on acting independently became problematic.

Count Julius von Zech-Burkesroda, the German minister to the Netherlands, recognized very quickly that the duke was "disgruntled over the insignificance of his role."[70] Indeed, on October 16, 1939, the duke wrote that there was "no enthusiasm over this war."[71]

When Hitler was preparing his invasion into the Low Countries and France, he had several options: (1) attacking south through the Maginot Line; (2) attacking through Belgium and northern France; and (3) attacking through the Ardennes. The Channel 4 documentary stated that originally Hitler planned to use the second option, through Belgium and northern France. However, on January 10, 1940, a *Luftwaffe* airplane was forced to land in Belgium, and on it were documents with all the details of the planned German attack.[72] Although an attempt was made by a German officer to burn the documents, there was not enough time to do so, and the papers were captured by a local law enforcement officer.[73] Baudot et al. state that although the German invasion plans were communicated to the British and French governments, it did not make much difference.[74] It was assumed that these papers presented "a clumsy German attempt at deception." Unfortunately, these plans were genuine and authentic. Weinberg is more skeptical and is quick to point out that the German intention to attack leaked out continuously through various channels.[75]

Channel 4's version, however, integrates this incident with the duke's disloyal and untrustworthy behavior. Following the crash landing, according to the Channel 4 documentary, Hitler needed to find out whether his war plans had been compromised. Then, Count Zech, the German minister to the Netherlands, reported to Berlin that the duke had discussed in detail what would happen if Hitler invaded the Netherlands. According to Count Zech, the duke stated that his information was based on documents found in a German airplane that made a crash landing in Belgium. Obviously, the duke had been briefed by non-German intelligence sources. Channel 4 stated that this was exactly what Hitler was waiting for. He altered his war plans and instructed his forces to use the third option instead. That plan was considered impractical by the Allies because it was felt that it was not possible to move armor through the Ardennes. However, Hitler believed that it was possible. Instead of launching an attack through the Low Countries, the Nazis penetrated the Ardennes on May 10, 1940, with a force of seven panzer divisions, driving across Belgian and Luxembourgian borders along the narrow Ardennes roadways. Like a hot knife cutting butter, the Nazi advance was extremely swift, and within two days they reached the Meuse River. On May 12, the Nazi military machine was threatening Paris. As Costello points out, "it is now possible to develop a convincing case that an intelligence leak leading back to the Duke of Windsor may have played a significant part in prompting Hitler to order his generals to change their battle plan."[76] According to Brown, who wrote the biography of "C" (British chief of intelligence in World War II), "that leakage from the Duke to Zech through intermediaries was again plain treachery."[77]

The Windsors in Spain and Portugal

The Channel 4 documentary stated that not only was the duke a hopeless talker, but as the Nazi invasion progressed, he left his post and traveled with the duchess to southern France to rest, and later to Spain and Portugal. Channel 4 pointed out that the duke's only real choices were to remain in his military unit or to return to England. Leaving his post to travel throughout southern Europe was reason enough for a court-martial on a charge of desertion, a charge that any other officer would have had to face. Brown is more blunt: "The duke abandoned his post without permission, a court-martial offense, and fled to the south of France to rejoin the duchess at their villa on the Riviera."[78] Ziegler quotes Metcalfe who stated that the duke had to remain with his unit and expressed his fear that the duke might "do *anything*—anything *except* the right thing. . . . He talks of having done enough!"[79] Thomas offers a different interpretation for the duke's rather strange behavior:

> Believing that the fall of France was imminent, he knew if he remained at his post, he would be ordered back to England where he ran a very real risk that his involvement with Bedaux had been reported and he would be branded a traitor. By making his way to the south of France, he was not fleeing the German advance as has often been suggested, but putting himself out of reach of the British.[80]

Again, Ziegler offers a somewhat different version.[81] He asserts that although the duke went to southern France with the duchess, he returned to Paris by May 22. Since he was given virtually nothing to do, he left Paris to rejoin the duchess. In a draft of a message to the duke that Churchill prepared to telegraph on July 1, 1940, he wrote: "Already there is a great deal of doubt as to the circumstances in which Your Royal Highness left Paris." However, Churchill decided to cut out this sentence. Ziegler leaves the reader with the clear impression that the duke had little choice: "The Duke left Paris with the approval, indeed the relief of the Military Mission. . . . To say that the Duke had deserted his country when he had nothing to do in Paris, and had been told to leave by his superior officer, was obviously unfair."[82] The Channel 4 documentary dramatized this issue by pointing out that while thousands of refugees were forced to leave their homes, the Duke and the Duchess of Windsor were bathing in the sun. The Germans invaded France, and on June 21, 1940, France surrendered. Most British citizens chose either to escape to Dunkirk or to Britain.

The Duke of Windsor chose Spain. The Windsors arrived in Barcelona late on the night on June 20, 1940, where they stayed for two days, and then continued to Madrid, arriving there on June 23. They resided at the Ritz Hotel, suite 501. Spain, one must remember, was under the dictatorship of Generalissimo Franco. Although Franco declared Spain to be neutral in the war, there is little doubt concerning Spain's sympathies. Spain was clearly allied with Hitler. Moreover, Madrid was a city of conspiracies, full with spies and intrigue. The choice of Spain as a refuge looks indeed strange. After all, the Windsors could get to Dunkirk and from there back to England. In any event, the time was not an easy one for Britain, and the evacuation from Dunkirk, heroic and magnificent as it was, did not change the overall bleak picture.

It may be that the duke felt more secure in Madrid, and he may have hoped to be able to influence some sort of a peace settlement by keeping in touch with the Germans. Regardless of the duke's feelings, as England and Germany were entering the war, the Windsors found themselves welcomed by Franco in neutral (but sympathetic to Hitler) Spain. The duke was still bitter about having to abdicate the throne, angry that Mrs. Simpson was not given HRH status, and upset for not being given a position of power and influence. Moreover, it was quite obvious that he was far from antagonistic toward Hitler. Further, he might have genuinely felt that nothing was worth another world war and that if appeasing Hitler was the way to avoid it, he was willing to go along. That the Windsors had chosen Spain at this particular time must have caused alarm in the British government and raised suspicions in the court of King George VI.

An equally plausible interpretation for the duke's behavior was that he was trying to gain time, hoping perhaps to be able to press the British government to give him an appropriate position, to give official recognition to Wallis, and—possibly—to leave the door open for negotiations with the Nazis. The duke's behavior most certainly was not characteristic of a man who decided to give up his throne and sink into a comfortable life with the woman he loved.

From the time of the duke's arrival in Madrid (June 23), an interesting exchange developed between Churchill and the duke regarding the duke's choice of residence. The Channel 4 documentary stated that the real struggle during this time was the battle between Churchill and Hitler for the duke's loyalties. The Germans wanted to keep him in Spain so that they could negotiate with him; Churchill wanted him back in England.

Moreover, the British ambassador to Spain, Sir Samuel Hoare, believed that the war was either lost or unwinnable and that a negotiated peace should not be ruled out. That view was close to the duke's,[83] and the duke had no reservations sharing his pro-German views with others, including Americans. The American ambassador to Spain, A. W. Weddell, sent a report to Washington, D.C., on July 2, 1940, in which he noted:

> [The duke] declared that the most important thing now to be done was to end the war before thousands more were killed or maimed to save the faces of a few politicians. . . . These observations have their value, if any, as doubtless reflecting the views of an element in England, possibly a growing one, who find in Windsor and his circle a group who are realists in world politics and who hope to come into their own in event of peace.[84]

Even Ziegler, who is sympathetic to the Windsors, notes that to support appeasement in June 1940 could be forgiven, but "to say it openly to a representative of a foreign, even if friendly power, was to say the least indiscreet." As Ziegler points out, so damaging were these talks between the duke and Ambassador Hoare, as well as the duke's public expressions supporting appeasement, that the ambassador telegraphed London (on June 30, 1940) and urged the government "to contradict German propaganda saying that Hoare and the Duke were carrying on negotiations for peace."[85] The results of these activities were obvious. Waller notes that "German Ambassador Eberhard von Stohrer . . . had high hopes when he reported to Hitler: 'Windsor has expressed himself in strong terms against Churchill and against the war.'"[86] Bradford adds that if indeed the documents regarding the duke's expressions against Churchill and the war are true, then the duke was "contemplating something very like treason."[87]

On June 19, 1940, Churchill stated in the cabinet that "steps must be taken to ensure the Duke's safe return."[88] Ziegler quotes Alexander Cadogan, permanent undersecretary at the Foreign Office, commenting on June 19, 1940, on the Windsors in Spain: "The quicker we get them out of the country the better. But I'd sooner send them to a penal settlement.

He'll be the Quisling of England when Germany conquers us and I'm dead."[89]

Indeed, British ambassador Hoare contacted the Windsors and "hastened to inform them that the Prime Minister attached great urgency to their return to England and wanted them to go on immediately to Lisbon, where, on their arrival, two flying-boats of Coastal Command would be sent to take them home. He told them too, that the Duke of Westminster had offered them the use of his house, Eaton Hall, near Chester."[90] On June 24, 1940, the duke replied to Churchill that he was not returning, and opened a process of negotiation in his letter about the position he wanted to be given once he returned, stating, in addition, that a position outside England might be preferable. Churchill replied on June 26 that such negotiations would be better held *after* the duke had returned to England. The duke refused, stating that he would return only *after* these negotiations had been successfully accomplished (including giving the duchess an HRH status and exemption from some taxes). Ambassador Hoare found himself in the midst of these negotiations and added in one of his communications the bizarre idea that giving the duke a "command at sea" might be a solution.[91]

These negotiations were taking place just after France had collapsed and the completion of the May 26–June 4 Dunkirk evacuation. Churchill was trying to cope with a very difficult and complex situation. That these negotiations with the duke were taxing his precious time is obvious. Moreover, the trivial demands the duke was making on the prime minister in a time of national crisis reveal the nature and magnitude of the duke's abominate position. Even sympathetic Ziegler must admit that the duke was "badgering the Prime Minister," that his position was "inexcusable," and that his "sense of proportion . . . had failed him."[92]

The Channel 4 documentary is more blunt. According to the program, the Duke knew fairly well that he was making demands that Churchill could not have possibly met. Moreover, the program stated that at that time there was a small, but not insignificant, pro-peace (or appeasement) movement in England, which was lobbying for a negotiated settlement with Hitler. Indeed, Bradford notes: "In November Horace Wilson, the most influential man in Whitehall, told Monckton that the only real worry as far as the Government was concerned was that the Duke's return to England might be exploited by extremist groups, which he undoubtedly meant to include Sir Oswald Mosley's fascist blackshirts, who had supported Edward VIII over the Abdication."[93] Churchill must have been concerned that the duke would spearhead that movement. And the Windsors had already proven in Madrid that they were willing to speak out very loudly for appeasement and against Churchill.

On June 25, 1940, Churchill wrote back to the duke: "Your Royal Highness has taken active military rank, and refusal to obey direct orders of competent military authority would create a serious situation. I hope it will not be necessary for such orders to be sent. I most strongly urge compliance with wishes of the Government."[94] The threat of a possible court-martial implied in Churchill's firm message is quite clear. And the threat worked. A few days later the Windsors left for Portugal. They arrived in the Lisbon area on July 3, 1940.

However, before leaving Spain, the duke made some damaging statements. Mr. Weddell, the American ambassador to Spain, wrote to the State Department that he had heard the duke saying that the only thing to do was to achieve "a peace settlement with Germany."[95] The anti-British nature of these statements is unquestionable.

While negotiations were going on between Churchill and the Duke of Windsor, the Germans were forming their own plots.[96] Ziegler states that the duke was unaware of these plots, but the Germans were not mistaken in assuming that the duke represented a political force that was sympathetic to their cause.

The Germans were trying to determine how best to utilize the duke's political sympathies. Several researchers point out that the Germans, headed by Ribbentrop on this issue, made several contingency plans focusing on moving the duke to their side.[97] In Ziegler's terms, the Germans wanted "to keep the Duke of Windsor in Europe, and make use of him as a tool of their policy."[98] At first, attempts were made to persuade the Spaniards to keep the duke in Spain for as long as possible. These efforts failed, but before the duke left Madrid, he made some rather strong statements against Churchill to German ambassador von Stohrer.[99]

The move to Lisbon did not silence the Windsors. "An American diplomat in Lisbon, H. Claiborne Pell, reported to Washington [July 20, 1940] that 'the Duke and Duchess are indiscreet and outspoken against the British Government.'"[100] Brown is more specific about the nature of the duke's statements in Portugal: "The Duke was soon reported to have stated that England 'faced a catastrophic military defeat, which could only be avoided through a peace settlement with Germany.'"[101]

According to the Channel 4 documentary, King George VI was aware of the political threat posed by the Duke of Windsor, because regular intelligence reports received from Madrid indicated the duke's disloyal position. The Channel 4 program stated that King George VI's private secretary, Alexander Hardinge of Penshot, wrote a secret report to the king in which he states that the Nazis were planning to overthrow King George VI and reseat Edward VIII as king. That scenario reflected the Nazi evaluation of the extent to which they could expect the duke to side with them if and when they conquered England.[102] The secret Nazi plan to detain the duke in Europe and their contingency plan to restore him as king of England show that they viewed the duke as a potential collaborator. As Ziegler points out, the duke's behavior gave them good reason to think so.[103]

In Portugal, the Windsors resided in the villa of a rich banker, Ricardo Espírito Santo Silva, at Cascais (a few miles outside Lisbon). Various sources note that Santo was a Nazi informant, sympathizer, and supporter.[104] And, again, the duke did not hide his views. On one occasion the duke was heard (this time by an informant to Marcus Cheke, a British embassy clerk) predicting that Churchill's government would fall and that Labour would form a new government that would negotiate peace with the Germans. In this scenario, King George VI would abdicate the crown and the duke would be restored to the throne: "Britain would then lead a coalition of France, Spain, and Portugal, and Germany would be left free to march on Russia."[105]

Another rather strange event took place while the Windsors were in Portugal. According to the Channel 4 documentary, the Duchess of Windsor left some personal items in her Paris apartment when the royal couple fled south. She instructed her maid to travel to Paris and retrieve these personal belongings. Paris, however, was then occupied by the Nazis, and the duke had to obtain special permission and documents for the trip of the maid. Who did he apply to? The Gestapo. All this occurred after Dunkirk, of course. Thus, the Windsors were in contact with the enemy, making requests and asking for special favors. Sarah Bradford comments that this was "extraordinary."[106] She also reports that in response to a request from the duke while he was in Madrid, "the Germans agreed to keep watch on the duke's Paris house."[107] Donaldson confirms this rather bizarre incident, adding that a telegram was sent by von Stohrer (German ambassador to Spain) to Berlin explaining that the maid's trip to Paris could be used to help postpone the Windsors' departure.[108] Indeed, after the war ended, the Windsors returned to Paris and found that "their house in the Boulevard Suchet had been undisturbed during the war, all their possessions were unharmed, and their caretaker even informed them that, when a pair of boots belonging to Major Gray Phillips had been taken, he had complained to the *Kommandantur* who had them returned with apologies."[109]

Although the Duke of Windsor has been portrayed by some as a devout peacenik (even at the price of appeasing Hitler), another incident shatters that illusion. The Nazi air force, the *Luftwaffe*, took an active and effective part in the Nazi military campaign, which led to the British evacuation at Dunkirk, and Nazi bombers were constantly attacking British (and other) ships engaged in the evacuation and other operations.[110] On July 10, 1940, Baron Oswald von Hoyningen-Huene, the German ambassador to Portugal, "told Ribbentrop that the Duke spoke freely in favor of compromise and said that the bombing of England would soon make it ready for peace."[111] "The Duke believes with certainty that continual heavy bombing will make England ready for peace." In other words, the duke made the fantastically absurd suggestion that the aerial heavy bombardment of Britain was for Britain's own good. Ambassador Hoyningen-Huene's report further states that the duke "intends to postpone his journey . . . at least until the beginning of August, in a hope of a change in his favor. He is convinced that had he remained on the throne, war could have been avoided and describes himself as a firm supporter of a peaceful compromise with Germany."[112]

Bradford too does not fail to note that this German document implies that the duke was trying to delay his departure from Portugal, hoping that events would turn in his favor.[113] That could only mean, in the relevant context, a radical change in British policy and the recall of the duke to England to assume a powerful position (presumably king). Thus, the peace-loving Duke of Windsor recommended heavy bombardment of his own country—all for the sake of peace, of course. One cannot avoid Thomas's acid note: "There is no record that he ever suggested to Churchill that bombing Germany would have a similar effect."[114] Such statements make it plainly clear whose side the duke was on. And such violations of trust and loyalty are indicative of genuine treason.

Meanwhile, the Nazis were busy making their plans to keep the duke in Europe (and, if necessary, to kidnap him).[115] One of these plans called for the return of the duke to Spain. The plan was that during a hunting campaign near the Spanish border, the Windsors would cross the border secretly and ask for asylum in Spain. There, according to the Channel 4 documentary, the Windsors would live in a castle owned by Count of Montarco. The count was instructed to prepare the castle for the royal couple. The plan called for the duke to use the castle as the place from which he would announce his disengagement from the British government and call for peace. In that public announcement, preferably in a radio transmission, the duke was supposed to publicly reject the British war policy and sever ties with his brother the king. Ribbentrop thought that intimidating the duke and making him feel that Portugal was unsafe would help to realize this plan.

Ribbentrop's man for the job was the S.S. officer Walter Schellenberg. Schellenberg hired individuals to break the windows of the duke's home by throwing rocks, which achieved some effect of intimidation. Moreover, he had a message delivered to the duke's home in which it was stated that the British secret service was planning to assassinate him.[116] Schellenberg states that he was working under Ribbentrop's instructions and that his goal was to bring the Windsors into the Nazi area of influence.

Angel de Valesco, a Spanish agent who was working at the time for the Nazis, was sent to Portugal to help bring the duke back to Spain. Valesco appeared on the Channel 4 documentary and stated that when he met the duke at the villa, "the Duke was trembling, the poor man. There were times when he didn't know what he was saying. He knew what he wanted to say . . . but could not say it properly. So when anyone asks me what I think about that interview . . . what I say is, 'The man was confused, he was trembling. He did not know what would happen next.'"

The duke was under the surveillance of British agents in Lisbon, and Churchill knew the dangerous and precarious position the duke was in. Indeed, even Ziegler, who tries his best to present the Duke of Windsor in the best possible light, has no choice but to acknowledge that "a report from a representative of the British Secret Service in Lisbon said that the Germans had recently approached Bedaux and asked him to establish whether the Duke of Windsor would be prepared to become King in the event of a German victory. Bedaux declined."[117] Bradford summarizes the "Quisling activities" of the duke in Spain and Portugal by stating that "from the moment of his arrival on 23 June, the Germans in collaboration with the Spanish Government contemplated using him as a weapon either in the event of a successful invasion of England or, possibly, in peace negotiations, detaining him in Spain with or without his co-operation."[118]

The problematic nature of the duke's activities did not escape British intelligence. Indeed, Bradford points out that the duke made statements against Churchill and the war and that the chief of British intelligence was discussing the "Quisling activities" of the duke (in Madrid and Lisbon as well).[119] At the very least, the Duke showed practically no support for his country at a time when it was most needed.

Meanwhile, in London, various options were considered for the duke's future. Both Churchill and King George VI felt that bringing the duke back to England was a bad idea. In fact, the king wrote, "My brother has behaved disgracefully."[120] Bradford adds that on July 10, 1940, the king was "amused at C's [head of British Intelligence] report of the Quisling activities of my brother."[121] Apparently, the king wanted to project in public the impression that his brother's activities were nonthreatening. Eventually, Churchill decided to offer the duke the position of governor and commander in chief of the Bahamas. Although some concerns were raised that the duke might use this position to plot against Churchill, he brushed these concerns aside. He did warn the duke, in a letter, to be very careful about what he said as a representative of the British Crown.[122] However, even this decision was fraught with difficulties. London was concerned that the duke might change his mind and, instead of going to the Bahamas, might decide to go back to Spain, where he could launch a peace initiative. British ambassador Samuel Hoare, concerned about such an event, wrote in July 26, 1940, that an effort must be made to prevent the duke from coming back to Spain.[123]

As concern about the duke's intentions was mounting in London, Walter Monckton—the duke's good friend—was asked to go to Lisbon and talk to him. Monckton arrived in Lisbon on the evening of July 28. Like Valesco, he found a demoralized duke who did not really believe that the British secret service was planning to assassinate him, but was a little unsure about it. He also suspected that the Germans might try to assassinate him once he arrived in the Bahamas, and he was not too keen to return to Spain. According to the Channel 4 program, Monckton carried with him a letter warning the duke about making contradictory statements about the British government's policy. It may be that Monckton had some harsher things to say, too. Monckton's presence in Lisbon had its effect. After his arrival, concern regarding the duke's actions diminished. On August 1, 1940, the Windsors boarded *Excalibur* at 15:00 and sailed to the Bahamas.[124]

It is interesting to note that on the same day, Hitler issued his Directive 17 on the planned Nazi invasion of Britain. Preparations for the invasion by the army were to be completed by September 15, and the operation was to take place September 19–26. The order was to be given about fourteen days after the main *Luftwaffe* offensive had begun.[125] *Luftwaffe* attacks on British shipping in the English Channel increased in intensity between August 1 and 11, and on August 11 Weymouth and Portland were bombed from the air; Portsmouth was bombed the next day. The Battle of Britain had begun. On August 15, the *Luftwaffe* flew almost 1,800 sorties, and the British Royal Air Force (R.A.F.) almost 1,000. The advice given by the Duke of Windsor to bomb England was being ruthlessly executed.

A revealing communication from the duke to his brother, King George VI, dating July 23, 1940 (just prior to his departure from Portugal), testifies to his state of mind then. In that telegram, the duke "urged the King to end the war, telling him to dismiss the Cabinet and replace it with one headed by the elderly but still active Lloyd George, which meant dismissing Churchill, the leader of a democratically elected Government."[126] In the context of events between September 1939 and the summer of 1940 (and the insatiable German aggression prior to September 1939), this suggestion could only be interpreted as a strong pro-Nazi stand, one that was completely contrary to the stance of Churchill's government.

One final note here is that when the Nazis realized that the duke might leave European soil, they clearly tried to change his mind even about leaving Portugal, mostly by talks with Santo Silva, the owner of the villa where the Windsors stayed. According to the Channel 4 documentary, the duke told his landlord that he could not disobey the instructions he received from London because it "would disclose his intentions prematurely." In other words, the duke may have had a plan that he thought he could operationalize from the Bahamas. This interpretation receives support from reports by Santo and Hoyningen-Huene that the duke wanted, explicitly, to keep his German contacts open. The duke may have wanted to keep all his options open in case Britain lost the war.[127] Almost all sources seem to agree that while the Windsors were in Spain and Portugal, the Nazis were working frantically on plans aimed at keeping the Windsors in Europe.[128] At the farewell party for the Duke of Windsor in Portugal, the duke assured the Germans "of his 'deepest sincerity and expressed admiration and sympathy for the Führer.' Moreover, Windsor said 'he could, if necessary, intervene from the Bahamas.'"[129]

The Windsors in the Bahamas

Those thinking that the Duke of Windsor was harmless in the Bahamas were about to face an unpleasant surprise. The Windsors arrived in the Bahamas in the middle of August 1940.[130] Their stay in the Bahamas had some interesting problematic aspects. One of the first incidents was the duke's wish to spend a total of about £7,000 to renovate the Government House. When Churchill saw the duke's first demand for an initial £5,000 from public funds in Britain, his comment was, "Comment is needless." Such a demand in the midst of a costly war was, at the very least, insensitive. The *Daily Tribune* pointed out that with that kind of money, another hurricane could be purchased to defend Buckingham Palace from bombing.[131]

Swedish industrialist Axel Wenner-Gren resided in the Bahamas when the duke arrived there. The duke had already met with Axel Wenner-Gren in Paris. There seems to be little doubt that the Americans and the British viewed Wenner-Gren as a Nazi sympathizer or worse. Even Ziegler concedes that British intelligence intercepted a letter sent to Wenner-Gren from a friend in Rio de Janeiro prior to the duke's arrival in Nassau telling Wenner-Gren that he should expect the arrival of "a new and interesting family ... who ... hold sympathetic understanding for totalitarian ideas."[132] However, Ziegler dismisses the letter as a "cryptic" message and asserts that Axel Wenner-Gren was interested only in "peace." The duke, however, had been warned by Lord Halifax, then British ambassador to the United States, that Wenner-Gren "was not a suitable companion" for him. The duke responded by questioning Lord Halifax's advice and demanded to know exactly on what grounds the suspicions against Wenner-Gren were based.[133] Of course, the suspicions were based on intelligence evaluations, which could not possibly be revealed to the duke in full, given his past behavior. However, there can be no doubt about two facts. One, the duke was explicitly warned against associating with Wenner-Gren, and two, he rejected the advice and kept close ties with Wenner-Gren. In 1941 the Americans put Wenner-Gren on a list of persons who were to be treated as "enemy aliens." Up to that point, the duke could refuse the advice of his own government and maintain close ties with Wenner-Gren, but that position was insupportable after Wenner-Gren was defined as an "enemy alien" by the Americans.[134]

More light about British fears of the association between Wenner-Gren and the Duke of Windsor is shed by Brown:

> On several occasions in 1942 and 1943, Churchill expressed anxiety that a U-boat, acting under the control of the *Southern Cross's* [Wenner-Gren's yacht] powerful wireless station, would land an armed party in the Bahamas and spirit the duke and duchess away to Germany. Churchill therefore ordered that a platoon of British troops be stationed around the Windsors' home in Nassau.[135]

Although the duke wanted to visit the United States and meet with President Roosevelt, Britain was—obviously—not too thrilled about this prospect.[136] However, the duke did meet with Roosevelt in Miami aboard the *Tuscaloosa* on December 13, 1940. Ziegler notes that Roosevelt was "dismayed by the gloom which [the duke] radiated and his obvious belief that the United States would shelter in isolationism." Ziegler notes that a second meeting with Roosevelt (October 4, 1941) was marked by a more positive spirit.[137] The Windsors sailed back on Wenner-Gren's yacht, the *Southern Cross,*

> to spend Christmas among what was, according to American intelligence, his circle of men like Mooney, an anti-British Irish American traveling with authorization from Goering to make piece with Hitler, and Alfred P. Sloan, chairman of General Motors, another Hitler sympathizer. During this period the Duke is alleged to have had several conversations on the subject of peace with Nazi Germany.[138]

One must remember that during this period, Nazi Germany was involved in a vicious battle against Britain in both air and sea.

Thus, while in the Bahamas, the duke was maintaining contacts with people who were under very strong intelligence suspicions of being Nazi sympathizers. Among these associates the duke could freely ventilate his political and moral views, and through them he could send the Nazis signals that they should not forget him. It was a way of keeping his options open. The verbal context for such discussions was that the duke was interested in pursuing a "peaceful" solution to the conflict in Europe. However, given the nature of Hitler's regime, "peace" could only be interpreted as concession to a racist, ruthless, and deceptive tyrant who could not be appeased. Moreover, for a former British king to have held such views in late 1940 was ethically very questionable.

One reason that the British were not too keen about the Duke of Windsor making visits to the United States and meeting with high-ranking U.S. officials must have been that they felt he could not be trusted to represent their interests in a forceful, loyal, and meaningful way. Developments in the inner political arena of the United States in 1940–1941 heightened that mistrust. At issue was the pending legislation for the Lend-Lease Act, whereby the United States would provide aid to nations fighting Germany and Italy (and later Japan). During December 1940, President Roosevelt was lobbying for passage of the bill, against the pressure of American isolationists. A long and bitter debate raged about the type and degree of U.S. involvement in the war. After much debate, the bill was submitted to Congress in January 1940. Roosevelt received solid support from the Democrats, and it passed the House on February 8, 1941 (260 votes to 165) and the Senate on March 8, 1941 (vote was sixty to thirteen). Thus, the months of February–March 1941 were crucial for decisions made regarding the nature of U.S. involvement in World War II. The duke was not unaware of this debate. An incident much like the duke's Verdun radio transmission in the spring of 1939 was about to unfold.

In either December 1940 or February of 1941,[139] the Duke of Windsor gave an interview to Fulton Oursler, a journalist for the American magazine *Liberty* and a friend of President Roosevelt. The interview was published first in *Liberty* on March 12 and later in the London *Sunday Dispatch* (March 16, 1941). Bradford's version is that the duke gave his interview to Oursler on February 6, 1941, only two days before the bill passed the House. The timing of the interview could not have been worse from a British point of view. What did the Duke tell Oursler? Bradford states that in the interview the duke appeared to "advocate a negotiated peace and advised America under no circumstances to enter the war."[140] Ziegler expands a bit on the impression that emerged from the interview:

> The Duke . . . saw no hope of a British victory. Nor was there hope of a change of heart in Germany. "You cannot kill 80m Germans and since they want Hitler, how can you force them into a revolution they don't want?" The only hope was for a Pax Americana: a peace imposed upon a discredited Europe by the New World, which would restore a measure of sanity to international relations. "The Duke of Windsor has given an interview to a magazine in the U.S.A. in which he pretty frankly disclaims all chance of an English victory," Goebbels is supposed to have commented, adding that they would not use it in their propaganda for fear of discrediting the speaker.[141]

Ziegler adds that the duke "claimed to have had many words put into his mouth." Churchill was not the type to watch this treacherous interview and keep quiet. Indeed, he was furious. Ziegler notes, "Whatever was meant, . . . Churchill . . . said the Duke's words would certainly be interpreted as 'defeatist and pro-Nazi, and by implication, approving of the isolationist aim to keep America out of the war.'"[142] Churchill "advised" the duke to seek advice before making public statements and used the opportunity to demand that the duke sever his contacts with Wenner-Gren as well.[143] The duke was a bit belligerent and exchanged some telegrams about these issues with Churchill. The Nazi attack on Russia on June 22, 1941, but much more so, the December 7, 1941, Japanese surprise attack on Pearl Harbor, shattered completely any hope the duke might have kindled of keeping the United States out of the war.

By the time the Channel 4 documentary program was taped, Oursler had died. The producers thus interviewed his son. He told the British television crew that the interview with the duke had been conducted on December 19, 1940. In that interview, the duke stated that the United States should not enter the war, that it would be a tragic event if "Hitler would be overthrown," that "Hitler was the right and logical leader of the German people," and that it was "unfortunate" that he had never met Hitler (an obvious lie; the duke met Hitler in October 1937), who, in his view, was "a great man." According to Oursler's son, the duke told his father that if Roosevelt would make a move toward peace, the duke would support that move immediately. Such a move, the duke is reputed to have said, would start a revolution in England and would force peace. Oursler's son states that his amazed father returned to the hotel, finding it difficult to believe what he has just heard. He thought that the duke wanted his treacherous sentiments to be passed on to Roosevelt. According to Oursler's son, his father saw Roosevelt and told him about the interview. Oursler's son states that Roosevelt told his father that nothing was surprising in those days and that some upper-class people in Britain wanted to appease Hitler and stop the war. The interview was eventually published in March 1941, having been heavily censored. In this respect, the duke's claim that the article had not quoted him correctly was correct.

Brown, author of the biography of the chief of British intelligence during the war, reinforces Oursler's revelations. According to Brown, the duke "made little secret of his sympathies" and told "a prominent American visitor" that it was "too late for America to save Democracy in Europe" and that it was better for America to "save it in America for itself." Moreover, Brown adds:

The Duke was said to have written highly compromising letters to Hitler personally, ones that escaped the British censorship but were known to have

been delivered. The Dutchess too, was being watched by the FBI, for as Assistant Secretary Adolf Berle recorded in his diary on September 20, 1940, the
eve of the day scheduled for the invasion of England: "Tamm, of the FBI,
came down. They have uncovered some correspondence which looks as
though the Dutchess of Windsor was in constant communication with
Ribbentrop. . . . It looks as though there has been some intriguing. . . . Maybe
the Dutchess would like at long last to be Queen.[144]

Following the end of the war, the Windsors lived mostly in Paris, with
the duke occasionally visiting Britain. There are reports that he was involved in some rather questionable dealings in currency during and after
the war.

The Coverup

One last episode involves an attempt to cover up the treacherous nature
of the Duke of Windsor's activities during the war. According to the
Channel 4 program, the British royal family asked art historian Anthony
Blunt (at that time, working for British intelligence) to help them hide the
duke's pro-Nazi wartime activities.

In July 1945, Blunt traveled to Germany, supposedly to retrieve some
innocent letters. But according to the Channel 4 documentary, this was a
cover-up. Blunt's real mission was to retrieve (and destroy) documents
pertaining to the Duke of Windsor, for example, the transcripts of his conversation with Hitler in October 1937. Bradford refers to the so-called
Marburg File, which is the record of Hitler's conversations with foreign
statesmen, stating that no record exists of Hitler's conversation with the
Duke of Windsor.[145] Moreover, the contents of the file that relates to the
duke's activities in Lisbon in July 1940, clearly a damaging file, were
taken and classified as "secret" by the Allies. Bradford adds that the
Americans were persuaded to keep these documents secret.[146]

According to the Channel 4 program, Blunt was highly successful in his
mission. The documents that he brought back with him are locked up in
Windsor Castle for 100 years. Waller confirms that documents relating to
the Windsors are sealed in British top secret files until the twenty-first
century.[147] Moreover, the Channel 4 documentary, relying on John
Costello, claims that MI6's (external British intelligence) archives have
more information about the duke's treacherous behavior during World
War II. Ziegler concedes that Blunt and Owen Morshead (the Windsor li-
brarian) went to Europe and visited both Germany and Holland in a nonsecret mission to retrieve some letters and relics.[148] Ziegler denies categor-
ically the existence of a cover-up.

It is perhaps no coincidence that Anthony Blunt himself was a traitor and one of Britain's most famous spies of the twentieth century. A book about his treachery has been written by John Costello.[149] Other sources tend to support, some very strongly, the coverup version. Brown, for example, is convinced that the "lost" documents, which showed "evidence of treasonable communication between Windsor and Hitler . . . and the ex-kaiser, . . . almost certainly existed."[150] The coverup story, obviously, supports the idea that the royal family had something very serious to hide regarding the behavior of the duke during World War II.

Those familiar with the Windsors' story were not surprised at the Channel 4 documentary. What this program did was to assemble, in a focused short presentation, the facts supporting the idea that the Duke of Windsor was a traitor. Clearly, Waller is grossly understating the truth when he says that, at the very least, "the Duke of Windsor was frankly an embarrassment to the British government."[151]

It is obvious that much of the Duke of Windsor's behavior can be easily interpreted as treachery. There is no doubt that he sympathized with the Nazis, associated with Nazi sympathizers, and was quite indiscreet in airing his views and in guarding secret intelligence information that reached him. Prominent researchers of World War II confirm this. Weinberg has no doubt that the Duke of Windsor "and even more his wife, had displayed strong pro-German sentiments."[152] Costello confirms this[153] and adds that the duke "admired Hitler's leadership."[154] Weinberg adds that "the evidence is clear that he seriously considered working with the Germans and, in fact, remained in contact with them for some time *after* going to the Bahamas."[155]

Concluding Discussion

This case is interesting and instructive in terms of treason. To begin with, it involves the well-known sympathy of the Duke of Windsor (and his wife) for the Nazis, as well as his public statements (for example, his visit with Hitler, the Verdun radio transmission, the cable to his brother, the interview with Oursler), which clearly reflect his consistent advocating of an "appeasement" solution to the conflict. Although unpleasant and morally wrong, this sentiment, in the context of the early to mid-1930s, could not possibly be considered treason. In this respect, the duke was no different than many others in the early 1930s who were faced with the choices of fascism, Nazism, democracy, and communism, not to mention monarchy. However, as the outcomes of these choices became clearer, particularly with the evident military expansionist policy of Nazi Germany and its blatant and hateful racism, and as it became clear that a second world war was in the making, the moral meaning of these choices could no longer be ignored.

Hitler's invasion of Poland in September 1939, and the following ultimatum and declaration of war by Britain, settled the questions of trust and loyalty in a swift and decisive way. Either one was with England or against England. The Windsors' overt behavior prior to August 1, 1940, was certainly not one of solid support for Britain. Even after August 1 (when the Windsors departed for the Bahamas), the duke continued to maintain his contacts with the Nazis and made statements aimed at preventing the United States from entering the war.

One can concede that the Duke of Windsor was interested in preventing the war. However, to achieve this goal he was ready to appease Hitler (although he must have known that Hitler's appetite was insatiable). Thus, under the rhetoric of "peace," he provided support for one of the most brutal and wretched regimes in the history of this planet. Moreover, when one examines those aspects of his behavior that were not overt, but apparently quite well known to Allied intelligence, the allegations of distrust and disloyalty become much more serious.

The Duke of Windsor's continued unhappiness with the royal family, who refused to grant HRH status to the woman he married, and his clear sympathy for Hitler combined to create an explosive concoction. It is clear that Churchill, a firm believer in the monarchy, spent a great deal of time and energy keeping the Duke of Windsor in check. In the middle of a war, he sent letters and friends, conducted surveillance, and exiled the duke to the Bahamas to contain his questionable loyalty and untrustworthiness.

It is, perhaps, appropriate to end this part by reviewing the summary of the Channel 4 documentary. It argued that the Duke of Windsor accepted the Nazis' proposal to head Britain under German tutelage, a kind of a Vichy government. Doing that simply meant helping the Nazis and "working with the enemy." The program implied that he also helped German espionage efforts and that on the diplomatic level he tried to convince President Roosevelt to press a "peace" agreement between Nazi Germany and England. In reality, suggesting "peace" at that point in time could only mean a British capitulation and a collapse of Churchill's policy. It was also suggested that at one time Roosevelt proposed assassinating the duke, but the British would not allow that. The royal family must have felt that to divulge his activity to the public would hurt the monarchy. Some friends of the Duke of Windsor argued that he was convinced that Britain was close to losing the war and that a worldwide Nazi regime would be established. If such a scenario was about to happen, the duke was convinced that he was going to "save" the remnants—a rationalization of several collaborators during the war years (for example, Pétain). Although the British people and the Duke of Windsor denied the treacherous nature of his behavior, there are some very serious doubts regarding his loyalty to and trust in Britain at its most difficult moments. The Channel 4 documentary implies that, perhaps, he should have been charged with treason.

Clearly, there are compelling reasons to suspect that the duke violated loyalty to his government and the trust invested in him by his government (not to mention his people). His activities certainly bring him very close to the definition of traitor. The fact that many of his activities were conducted in secret further supports the charge.

However, an important ingredient in betrayal, turncoating, did not take place here. Of the three elements necessary to define the duke as a traitor (violating trust, violating loyalty, and turncoating), only two seem to have been present in his behavior, thus making the charges made by the Channel 4 documentary at least partially substantive. The duke most certainly violated both trust and loyalty on more than one occasion. He is situated rather well within the boundaries of being a traitor. However, his behavior did not illustrate the full extent of treason. One major element, that is, siding unequivocally and openly with the Nazis is missing. The lack of such a move makes labeling the Duke of Windsor a traitor more difficult. This case alerts us to the fact that sometimes the potential traitor walks a very thin line, just on the verge of treason.

This case certainly adds to our understanding of treason by illustrating that treason is not a discrete variable but a continuous one. The depth and intensity of treason varies. Gathering adequate information is crucial, too, especially in cases where concealment took place. For example, the unknown implications of the duke's meeting with Hitler and the secreting of the records of that meeting leave too much important information out of the picture. If and when this information becomes available, more light will pour on this puzzling case.

The Duke of Windsor died in 1972. He never faced directly, or provided persuasive accounts for, the nature of his questionable behavior before, during, or after World War II. There are many uncertainties in regard to the facts of this case. Because no explicit and open records exist, one must read the relevant texts very carefully to reach a conclusion. The important lesson from this is that one can be a "traitor" and, at the same time, camouflage it quite effectively. There are several contributing factors to this situation: politics, leadership, identity, and loyalty.

The first is politics. There were powerful actors who had an interest in concealing the Duke of Windsor's true support for Nazi Germany. The

German cause was better served by having the duke appear to be a loyal and trustful British citizen. This mask aided them in gaining access to the higher echelons of the British political system, and kept a potential Pétain-like collaborator in stock, without discrediting him. The British political system had no interest in exposing the duke's real preferences and sympathies because that would only have caused divisiveness in their efforts to deal with the conflict. Finally, as the war progressed and Germany was losing, the duke himself had no reason to clear the fog surrounding his unethical behavior. What some journalists, intelligence officers, and politicians knew was squelched quite effectively after the war. Blunt's postwar mission to Germany to retrieve the potentially incriminating transcripts of the Hitler-Duke conversations assured secrecy. The interests of various political actors thus coincided in this case and helped to obfuscate the reality of treason with a mask of loyalty and trust, seasoned with the duke's resentment that he was not being given the respect he deserved. Such a deceptive political game, particularly in the context of World War II, was not unique to the case of Edward VIII. This type of game is typical of politics, where interests create a game of masks for public consumption, camouflaging a reality of immorality and, in this case, of treasonable behavior.

A related topic is the nature of leadership. Clearly, leaders from all sides faced the dilemma posed by the duke's questionable behavior and participated in this game of masks versus reality. For the reasons stated above, none of the major political or military leaders came out in the public arena and exposed the duke's behavior for what it was. The Nazis were planning to coerce the duke into defection, but when this secret plan collapsed, they did not expose it in public. Similarly, Churchill, who had to allocate precious time from his busy schedule to deal with the duke, kept quiet about the problem. However, this did not prevent him from intervening forcefully and decisively by telling the duke what was appropriate and what was not. There is no doubt that despite the secrecy and potential embarrassment posed by the duke's behavior, Churchill projected reliable, credible, and solid leadership in this case. The lesson here is clear. Once Churchill and the Nazis clearly defined their interests, based on a specified moral symbolic universe, appropriate leadership styles and decisions followed.

The last two topics are those of identity and loyalty. The most important issue is the way in which the Duke of Windsor saw his identity—politically, socially, and culturally. As we saw, from very early on, the duke felt a kinship with Nazi Germany and was probably willing to cooperate and collaborate with the regime. In this respect, he was probably closer to Laval[156] or Pétain, rather than Quisling, Degrelle, or Antonescu.

Had the Nazis successfully invaded Britain, the duke would have been useful to the Germans as the new king. This type of a split identity was characteristic of not only the duke. In Europe, one leader after another whose countries were occupied by the Nazis faced a similar dilemma. However, the Duke of Windsor had shown clear signs of his political preferences by the early 1930s. What was he to do? His British government was pursuing a policy that he did not like, and Nazi Germany's victory was not guaranteed. Thus, while expressing dissatisfaction and expounding pro-German sympathies in private, he managed to maintain a public facade of loyalty to the Crown, with no small help from Churchill and others in the government. The loyalty issue was a by-product of the conflict that the duke helped into being. Was he completely loyal to Churchill's Britain? Not quite. Did he make a full switch of loyalty to Germany? Not quite. In other words, the duke never crossed, unambiguously, moral boundaries. When such a crossing seems to have occurred, its true nature was denied, or it was interpreted in morally neutral terms, or the crossing itself was obfuscated. In several instances, understanding the nature of the duke's violations of trust and loyalty required that we present the alternatives he faced. In other instances, the nature of the act was evident in itself.

Overall, this case provides a portrait of a man in a high political position who was apparently torn among his desire for peace at almost any cost, his loyalty to Britain, and his love and appreciation of Germany. Situations of conflict are typical arenas for antagonistic loyalties, indecisiveness, playing one game in public and another in private, and thus keeping as many options open as possible (for example, see Admiral Darlan's behavior). This type of behavior may actually be more pronounced in individuals in high positions because there is more at stake. Thus, walking the tightrope of conflicting loyalties, not fully committing oneself to any one side, constructing various masks of behavior in public and concealing others is often typical of such situations.

Finally, one must add that this morally dubious behavior involves an intricate play of fabrication, concealment, and ambiguity. Consequently, separating fact from fiction, the real from the false, creates problems not just for contemporaries, but for later generations and researchers as well. Because the Duke of Windsor appeared to have honored his loyalty to the Crown, deconstructing his betrayal requires delving into the details of his actions. Not only was the Duke of Windsor presenting a public image of loyalty and trust in Britain, while engaging in activities that were clearly damaging the British cause, but he was also enmeshed in indecisiveness itself.

10

The Case of Malinali Tenepal— Malinche

This sixteenth-century case of betrayal is complicated and fascinating, and known very well in Mexico, but much less so elsewhere. This case involves the story of the Conquest of Mexico led by Hernán Cortés (1485–1547) in the sixteenth century. Prevailing historical accounts state that in that conquest, Cortés was helped by a local woman named Malinche. She has become a symbol of treason. In Mexico today, "to be called a malinchista is to be called . . . a traitor. . . . La Malinche . . . has become a symbol. . . . [She] is for the most part portrayed as the perpetrator of Mexico's original sin and as a cultural metaphor for all that is wrong with Mexico."[1] Even the house where she lived with Cortés in Mexico City (57 Higuera) is shunned.

The historical narrative of the Spanish Conquest of Mexico is not a simple account. The story itself is based mostly on Spanish sources, that is, the victors telling their version of the events. Moreover, the various narrators had their own agendas and interests to present and defend, and thus one should approach the popular and accepted historical narrative with that in mind. To complicate matters a bit further, there is no consensus about all the details. In the narrative below, I have tried to present the more or less accepted view. Recently, Hassig's challenging 1996 work has cast some serious doubts on this accepted history. I will present Hassig's views later.

The Background

In 1511 Hernán Cortés and Diego Velázquez sailed from Spain to conquer Cuba. Following that endeavor, Cortés was chosen to lead an expedition to the Yucatán peninsula in early 1519; he was thirty-three years old. After a delay to adequately supply his forces, he left Cuba on February 18. His military strength at the time of departure included the following: eleven

Montezuma II meets Hernán Cortés. Malinche is standing behind Cortés. Recorded in the Lienzo de Tlaxcala.

SOURCE: *Nigel Davies,* The Aztecs: A History *(New York: G. P. Putnam's Sons, 1973).*

ships (15 according to some sources), about 550 soldiers,[2] and 150 sailors.[3] He had ten heavy guns, four lighter pieces called falconets, a fair amount of ammunition, and sixteen horses. Not a very impressive force in Western military terms.

In March 1519, the small squadron arrived at an island off the coast of Yucatán called Cozumel. There, Cortés tried to find and rescue two survivors of a Spanish shipwreck in 1511, who were being held by the local people. Although his attempts failed, he nevertheless used his stay in Cozumel to resupply his ships.

At the beginning of March, the ships left Cozumel. They did not travel far. A leak in one of the boats forced them to return to the same port. Upon returning, they met one of the Spanish captives, Gerónimo de Aguilar. During the time Aguilar had been stranded on Cozumel, he became familiar with the Mayan dialects of Yucatán, which made him an ideal candidate for interpreter. Another major advantage, perhaps more important, was that he had not really integrated into the local culture. He wanted to rejoin his original Spanish culture. Cortés provided Aguilar with exactly the opportunity he wanted. This is an important point, because another Spanish sailor who survived the shipwreck, Gonzalo de Guerrero, had become completely naturalized and absorbed into the local culture and showed no interest in rejoining Cortés.[4] Once the repairs of the ship were completed, Cortés and his fleet sailed again on March 4. The next point of landing was near a coastal area known as Tabasco (on about March 22). The town that was to become the focus of battle was Potonchan. From now on, a clash of two cultures was to unfold.

The Aztec empire, which dominated Mexico, was then ruled by Montezuma (sometimes called Moctezuma) II. The Aztecs based their rule on a taxation system that was highly coercive and on a blood-thirsty religious belief system. Their lust for human sacrifices is well documented. Some reports (probably exaggerated) state that the Aztecs once made 80,000 human sacrifices in four days. The amount of coercion and pressure required to supply the Aztec priests with the humans needed for the ritual sacrifices must have been enormous.

Moreover, at the time of the conquest, the Aztec system was characterized by a high degree of conflict. Montezuma II was both an admirer of power and a firm religious believer. He also expected the return of a legendary god—Quetzalcoatl, the Plumed Serpent—whose comeback was based on both prophecies and omens. There are indications that when the news of Cortés's landing reached Montezuma II, he believed these white Spaniards to be the gods he was waiting for.[5] This belief was a fateful mistake. It was going to cost him his empire and his life.

In military terms, Cortés had about 550 soldiers, some horses, and some technologically advanced weapons (armor and firearms). This relatively modest force was about to bring down a mighty empire. Militarily, it is conceivable that had Montezuma II been more determined, assured, and not so hesitant, his vast superiority in manpower, knowledge of the terrain, and better intelligence could have translated into a defeat of Cortés. At least, he could have made the price of conquest so high that it would have become impractical for Cortés to continue. But Montezuma was not blessed with these attributes. His opponent, Cortés, was a determined, decisive, cunning, and ruthless commander. He knew how to create opportunities and took advantage of them when they were present. In this clash, the fate of the Aztecs was sealed. Hassig discusses a number of explanations for how and why it was possible for so few Spaniards to defeat so many Aztecs.[6] He also adds that Cortés did not land into a vacuum. He found himself in the midst of military and political conflicts among the various groups that formed the Aztec empire. Some of these groups most certainly used Cortés and his forces for their own purposes.[7]

The first battle began in March 1519 around Potonchan.[8] There, defiant Indians were mounting their forces against Cortés. They "consisted of five squadrons of eight thousand men each."[9] Cortés had "a force of three hundred Spaniards" with horsemen and cannons.[10] In the fierce battle that ensued, Cortés's forces won. Having conquered Potonchan, Cortés left on April 17 to continue the Conquest of Mexico.

Enter Marina

Another important event took place in Potonchan. Before the Spaniards left, they acquired twenty (nineteen, according to some versions) women slaves. One of these women—Malinche—is the focus of this narrative.[11]

Cortés next landed near what we now know as Vera Cruz, on April 21, 1519. Cortés realized that Aguilar could not provide interpretative assistance because he was ignorant of the spoken language.[12] Unlike the Mayan dialect used in Tabasco, the area where Cortés landed was under Aztec influence, and the spoken language was Nahuatl. At that point, Cortés was informed that one of the female slaves was a native Mexican and understood the language. The name given to that female slave was Marina. In Vaillant's 1962 book on the Conquest of Mexico, figure 28 shows the Spaniards landing at Vera Cruz, and at the right side of the drawing one can see Marina "exercising her diplomacy on a native."[13]

When Marina was brought to Cortés she was between fourteen and nineteen years old.[14] Because Marina never left anything in writing about her life, her personal history prior to her life with the Spaniards is not entirely clear, but what follows is based on existing evidence. It is believed that her original name was Malinali Tenepal. Her first name is like the twelfth day of the twenty-day Aztec month. The second name possibly hints at a person who talks a lot, and with animals.

Malinali was said to have been born in Painalla in the province of Coatzacualco, on the southeastern borders of the Mexican empire.[15] Malinali was a native speaker of Nahuatl. Although details about the social status of her family of origin are unclear, it is claimed that she was the daughter of a local chief (*cacique)* who died while she was still young.[16] Her mother, Cimatl, soon remarried another *cacique*. A son was born of this new marriage. Cimatl feared that Malinali might stand in the way of her half-brother inheriting the position of chief. According to this version, she sold Malinali secretly to some traveling traders of Xicallanco. To conceal this, she pretended that Malinali died. In fact, she used the dead body of a child of one of her slaves to show that Malinali was dead.[17] The traders sold Malinali, again, to the *cacique* of Tabasco, who gave her to the Spaniards. Johnson suggests that the name the Spaniards gave her—Marina—was a Spanish approximation of Malinali. The locals, however, might have found the Malinali-Marina names too difficult, and they called her Malinche (the suffix "che" indicated respect).[18] Thus, when Malinali was given to Cortés, she was a "slave in Potonchan in the Chontal Maya-speaking area of Yucatan."[19]

Marina was fluent in Nahuatl, her mother's tongue, and her stay in Tabasco gave her a good knowledge of Mayan, too. The use of Marina and Aguilar as interpreters worked this way: Marina talked Nahuatl with the Aztecs. She then translated it to Mayan for Aguilar, and he translated it into Spanish. Eventually Maria knew enough Spanish so that this cumbersome translation was no longer necessary. Clearly, the Aguilar-Marina combination was a phenomenal advantage for Cortés.[20]

Various sources state that Marina looked different than the other female slaves; she was more distinguished and beautiful,[21] as well as "intelligent."[22] She is described as "clever and seemed sometimes humane. Tradition says that she was 'beautiful as a goddess.'"[23] When the female slaves were given to Cortés, he first gave Marina to one of his good friends, Alonso Hernández de Puertacarrero.[24] However, as Marina settled into her new role as interpreter, Cortés realized that she was one of his major assets. Marina "could not only tell Cortés what the words meant, but could also explain Indian attitudes, expressions, gestures, acts, and reactions. She was sensitive to everything that went on, an acute observer."[25] Puertacarrero was soon sent to Spain on Cortés's flagship, heading a mission to give the Spanish king his share of the accumulated treasures.[26] Marina "rode behind Cortés on his horse, stood beside him in the field, shared his bed at night and later bore him a son."[27] Marina, thus, was not just a technical linguist advisor to Cortés. She was the cultural expert whose advice to him was the tool that made a crucial difference in Cortés's ability to conquer Mexico. In this respect, Marina shifted her trust and loyalty from her local cultural matrix to the Spanish conquistadors.

At Vera Cruz, Cortés destroyed his ships, so that his men would not consider retreating to Cuba on the march inland to the Aztec capital. Many sources note how indispensable Malinche's advice and assistance were on the march. Along the way, Cortés learned about the cruelty of the Aztecs, their demands for taxes, and their capture of prisoners to be sacrificed to the Aztec gods in Tenochtitlán. Many Indian tribes were unhappy with Aztec rule and were waiting for an opportunity to free themselves from the Aztec yoke. Marina stepped way beyond the technical role of a translator as she assumed the role of cultural interpreter and advisor. Her cultural knowledge enabled Cortés to take advantage of opportunities about which he would not have known without Marina's guidance. This advantage was magnified by the inner divisions and conflicts among the different Indian groups and by Montezuma's apparent ambivalence about how to deal with Cortés.

Two additional events are worthy of mention. One was Cortés's encounter with the Tlaxcaltecs. The Tlaxcaltecs were no great admirers of the Aztecs. Yet they fought Cortés with determination and courage, causing him considerable damage.[28] Eventually, they became his allies. Indeed, figure 32 in Vaillant's book shows Cortés meeting Tlaxcaltec high dignitaries with Marina doing the interpretation.[29]

The second event is that during Cortés's march to the Aztec capital, Tenochtitlán, he went to see the Cholollans, who were allies of Montezuma and the Aztecs. Cortés and his soldiers entered Cholollan, while his Tlaxcaltec escort waited outside the city. The story goes that while in the city, Malinche found out that the Cholollans were preparing an ambush for Cortés and that a big Aztec army was waiting just outside Cholollan. She told Cortés about it, and he prepared his own ambush. The next day, under the pretext of some fabricated excuse, he convened the Cholollan nobility and soldiers into a central court, and there, unprovoked and in a coordinated act, his soldiers massacred them all. This signaled the beginning of a larger massacre of the Cholollans in the streets, in which the Tlaxcaltecs took an active part. Clearly, in this tale Malinche is credited with betraying a local plan to ambush Cortés and finish him off. Here is how Johnson describes the event:

> [Marina] had been approached by a Cholulan woman who admired her and wanted her to remain in Cholula and marry one of her sons. She was urged to accept in order to save her own life, because the Spaniards were soon to be attacked. The Cholulan woman knew because her husband, a chief, had been given a golden drum by the Aztecs as an inducement to take part in the assault. Marina pretended to agree and begged for time, saying she would have to find someone to carry her personal goods, her clothes and the jewelry, and she persuaded the older woman to wait in her quarters while she did so.
>
> When Cortés heard Marina's story, he seized a priest and, through Marina's interpretation, forced a confession out of him that confirmed the story.[30]

Davies questions the validity of the Cholollan conspiracy against Cortés, calling it unrealistic.[31] From this point on, Cholollan served as a model of obedience and loyalty to Cortés.[32] It must be emphasized that the question of whether there actually was a Cholollan conspiracy against Cortés is not as important as Malinche's role in exposing such a conspiracy, whether real or imagined. The fact is that Malinche emerges as the one who betrayed the Cholollans. The massacre at Cholollan was—as Prescott points out—to remain a "dark stain on the memory of the Conquerors"[33] and "one of the most controversial events in Cortés' life."[34]

And Malinche has certainly been portrayed as having played a central role in that event.

Davies reports on another possible betrayal by Malinche during the expedition to Honduras..

> Cuauhtémoc [Montezuma's successor] was compelled to accompany his master [Cortés] on this ill-fated adventure. . . . During the long march, on the pretext of an alleged plot, Cortés ordered Cuauhtémoc and the cacique of Tacuba to be hanged. According to native sources, Cuauhtémoc was the victim of mere calumny. One wonders why Doña Marina, still acting as interpreter, could not, had she wished, have ascertained the real truth. Before the former ruler was hanged, he exclaimed: "O Malinche, for many days I have understood that you would condemn me to this death, and have known your false words, for you kill me unjustly."[35]

The rest of the historical narrative is well known. Cortés continued his conquest of Mexico. He reached Tenochtitlán in November 1519. Later, Montezuma was killed, Tenochtitlán destroyed, and the conquest expanded to Honduras and Guatemala. When Vaillant shows the conquest of Tenochtitlán, he produces a drawing in which "Cuauhtémoc, who conducted the defense of Tenochtitlán, is received with all the honors of war by Cortés and his consort, Marina. . . . With this event, the Mexicans were finished."[36]

Militarily and politically, the Conquest of Mexico is most certainly one of the most fantastic and extraordinary tales in history. In it, a rather small military force, fighting its way in an unknown territory, conquered and, in fact, eliminated the entire Aztec empire.

The role of Marina in this conquest is portrayed, repeatedly, as crucial. When Montezuma met Cortés, Marina (and Aguilar) translated. Critical conversations between the two were translated by Marina, too.[37] Indeed, plate 62 in Vaillant's 1962 book shows the meeting of Montezuma and Cortés with Marina standing right behind Cortés. Vaillant states that "Marina's value to Cortés cannot be underestimated."[38]

Cortés's official wife—Catalina—eventually arrived in Mexico. Within three months of her arrival, she was dead, officially from asthma. However, Catalina's mother accused Cortés of participating in her daughter's murder by strangling her.[39] Although Cortés had several women (including one daughter of Montezuma), Marina bore him a son—Martín. Although historically and biologically inaccurate, this son is credited as the first mestizo. Thus the Spanish Conquest of Mexico not only was a military-political conquest, but it "was followed by a biological conquest that would create a mestizo society."[40]

During the course of the expedition to Honduras, Cortés eventually "arranged and supervised a marriage between his faithful interpreter, diplomatic advisor, and mistress, Marina, and Juan de Jaramillo. Jaramillo was drunk at the time, and many of the Spaniards were secretly critical of Cortés for his treatment of the woman who had not only made his conquest possible, but had also borne him at least one child. Despite her marriage, Marina continued to serve Cortés as an interpreter."[41]

Both Collis and León-Portilla write about Marina's courage and describe how in difficult moments of despair and danger, such as during the Tlaxcaltec attack, Marina showed no fear.[42] Their accounts support the position that Malinche's role was predominantly one of cultural mediator, not just technical translator.

Collis adds that "near Tlaxcala there is a volcano which in Cortés's time was called Matlalciuatl (the Dark Green Woman). The divine denizen of this mountain was afterwards identified with Doña Marina and the mountain is now called Malinche, her name."[43] That Marina displayed authoritarianism in her dealings with the Aztecs is also clear from another drawing in Vaillant's book. In the illustration, Marina gives an order to an Aztec to do something, and that Aztec, to use Vaillant's own explanation, "complies with ill grace."[44]

Marina joined Cortés on his last trip to Honduras. Aguilar had died by then,[45] but Marina could now speak Spanish. Johnson describes how during that expedition she was reunited with her mother:

> During her last service to Cortés—an interpreter during the March to Honduras—Marina had a reunion with her mother, who had sold her to slave traders years earlier. The mother, by now Christened Marta, and her son Lázaro were brought to the Spaniards' camp at Coatzacoalcos. The older woman and the young man were trembling with fear. But Marina forgave her mother, treated both of them with kindness, and loaded them with gifts.[46]

It appears that in her later years Marina enjoyed a high income from the estates given to her by Cortés. She had townhouses in Mexico City, a country house in Chapultepac, and a garden in Coyuacen.[47] However, little else is known of her life.

> Beyond the fact that she bore a daughter to Juan de Jaramillo, little more is known of Marina, except that her death occurred around 1540. In 1605 Don Fernando Cortés, son of the illegitimate Don Martín Cortés, addressed a memorial to the Spanish court detailing the services his grandmother had performed during the Conquest. With that the record, official and otherwise, of Malinali, Marina or Malinche ends. The name Malinche, however, unhap-

pily lives on in Mexican slang as a pejorative term for persons who betray their nation and heritage.[48]

There is little doubt that although Malinche was a heroine for the conquistadors, she was considered an archetypical traitor by many Mexicans. The popular narrative of the conquest leaves very little doubt as to Malinche's crucial role in that conquest. Even Hassig admits that the Marina is "widely regarded . . . to have played a vital role in the conquest of Mexico [and] La Malinche has become a major motif in Mexican literature."[49] It is easy to understand why Malinche is considered a traitor. Although she most definitely seems to have had some very good reasons for violating trust in, and loyalty to, her native culture, that does not seem to change the image. Thus, we have a woman who was considered a hero during the colonial period, but following the War of Independence (1821), "she was increasingly regarded as a traitor, a whore, and a racial turncoat who collaborated with the Spanish invaders."[50]

Hassig's Challenge

In a powerfully argued and persuasive 1996 paper, Hassig attacks the accepted popular narrative about Malinche. Hassig is no amateur. He has published two major books focusing on the Aztecs and the Conquest of Mexico.[51] In his 1994 short history of the Spanish Conquest, Hassig, contrary to other researchers, plays down Malinche's role. For example, his description of the events in Cholollan does not even mention Marina.[52] Hassig does not fail to notice that (a) the history of the Spanish Conquest is typically known from Spanish sources, and (b) very little factual information is known with any degree of certainty about Malinche. He points out, for example, how even information about her background is meager. Hassig summarizes the importance of Malinche in Mexican history in three areas: (1) she is considered to be the mother of the mestizo race; (2) she acted as a cultural interpreter for Cortés and thus facilitated the Conquest of Mexico; and (3) she is "credited with saving the Spaniards by learning of the Chololtec plans to massacre them, warning Cortés" (p. 2). Hassig then takes these three popular beliefs, one by one, and shatters their validity.

In brief, the first claim, says Hassig, cannot be factually true. "The Spaniards were given numerous Indian women before the pregnancy of Marina. . . . Thus Marina was not the mother of the first recognized mestizo" (pp. 2–3). As to her role as cultural interpreter, Hassig admits that indeed she must have acted as a translator, but the importance of her role— he claims—is greatly exaggerated. Hassig claims that "the pivotal translator in the early days of the Conquest was not she but Aguilar" (p. 4).

Also, he challenges the accepted version that she quickly learned Spanish and thus the need for another translator was significantly diminished (p. 4). Moreover, Hassig points out that Malinche's social position was such that her ability to act as a cultural interpreter was probably very low, or none at all (p. 5). In other words, her knowledge about, and ability to comprehend, the geopolitical intricacies of the culture was very minimal, to say the least.

The Cholollan massacre, according to Hassig, is the most significant intervention by Malinche. Hassig easily discounts her role there. He points out that there is no tangible evidence that the Cholollans were indeed preparing any ambush for Cortés. Hassig points out that once Cortés's forces began the conquest, he became entangled in local politics among various Indian groups. The massacre at Cholollan can, and should, be understood within this context. Basically, Hassig argues that the Tlaxcaltecs and Cortés conspired together to massacre those Chololtecs who were siding with the Aztecs against the Tlaxcaltecs and Cortés. Cortés, in this context, is viewed as having been manipulated by the Tlaxcaltecs to help them as their ally, against part of the Chololtecs. "In a single stroke, Cortés killed the king, much of the political leadership, and the cream of the Chololtec army. After the massacre, Cortés appointed a new king and forced an alliance between the Tlaxcaltecs and the Chololtecs."[53] Hassig also discards Malinche's story about being asked to marry a local as highly improbable.

Moreover, Hassig argues that although the Chololtecs posed no threat for Cortés, they did pose a political challenge to the Tlaxcaltecs. Thus the massacre in Cholollan must be interpreted as an inner conflict within its political context in central America. "In short, the Tlaxcaltecs had the most to gain by defeating Cholollan, since they were the most significant military threat the Chololtecs faced. . . . [A] massacre of the Chololtec leadership would serve Tlaxcallan's interests, removing those who betrayed them while strengthening those out of power who were sympathetic to the Tlaxcaltecs."[54]

Hassig is convinced that "the Tlaxcaltecs were almost certainly the masterminds of this event,"[55] and "Cortés's own massacre was both premeditated and coordinated with the Tlaxcaltecs."[56] He thus completely discards Marina's role as the "discoverer" of the supposed Cholollan "plot" against Cortés.[57] However, it is clear that placing Marina in the central role of betraying the Cholollan plot to ambush Cortés—thus leaving Cortés little choice but to launch a preemptive strike—removes the responsibility for the massacre from Cortés and casts Marina into the uncomfortable heroine/traitor role.

About Marina, Hassig concludes: "Her role as a translator was real, but she was neither unique nor irreplaceable. But what of her role in warning Cortés of the planned ambush in Cholollan? Except for Cortés's word, there is no evidence of such a plot."[58] He also points out that whereas the "earliest chronicles pay [Marina] the least attention, over time her role became more certain, defined, and important. . . . From brief references to her in the earliest accounts, she grows and is fleshed out (invented?), both as a person and as a participant."[59]

The question of betrayal is also addressed by Hassig:

> The ultimate betrayal in the Conquest does not belong to Marina and what she may or may not have done but, rather, to those who accept the "facts" of the Conquest, and Marina's role in it, from a Spanish perspective. . . . The facts of Marina's life are not what is important here; it is how her life was used in support of a particular view of history. . . . Thus, the post-colonial reassessment that dismissed Marina as a heroine and reconceived her as traitor was not the daring revisionism it seems. It did not reassess the role of Marina, but merely shifted her position within the Spanish-authored history that this reinterpretation accepts unquestioningly. Marina as traitor did not break free of the conqueror's vision; it merely shifted its emphasis and continued the collaboration.[60]

Very strong words indeed.

Furthermore, Hassig points out that the consensus "view of the Conquest has grown largely from the five major first-hand accounts of the Conquest, plus that of López de Gómara."[61] He directs our attention to the fact that these narratives were written by nonobjective observers.

Concluding Discussion

We currently have two very different accounts about Malinche. One, the popular and accepted view, tells her story from the Spanish point of view. In it, she is portrayed as a heroine by the Spaniard conquistadors. Following the colonial period, she was regarded as a traitor. The essence of this contradictory perception is a matter of who views her. The acts attributed to her by the Spaniards constructed her as a heroine. The very same acts, viewed by the Mexicans, made her a racial and cultural traitor, violator of the trust and loyalty of her people. Malinche is an excellent example of how the very same actions, examined from different points of view, give rise to the heroine/traitor dichotomy. This is a prime illustration of how the interpretation of the moral content of treason is totally dependent on political context and on the *structure* of betrayal.

Then along comes Hassig, who challenges all that. In his interpretation, the role of Malinche was extremely exaggerated. The real treason, according to him, is to trust the historical narrative of the conquest, as given by the victors.

The important point for our purposes is not whether Hassig is right or wrong. The sociological and historical fact is that Malinche was indeed socially constructed as both a heroine and a traitor. Whether that construction is historically accurate does not concern us here. Much like other national myths, such as Israeli myths,[62] the myth of the Blitz,[63] and the Masada myth,[64] the narrative of Malinche gained a life of its own as a national symbol. Malinche is a classic case of the social construction of national consciousness.

The case involving Malinche fits our theoretical approach very nicely. Cortés and Malinali were from entirely different symbolic moral universes. When they met, Malinali must have been quick to appreciate the power of Cortés, as well as the opportunities presented by this fateful meeting. Cortés was quick to capitalize on Malinali's evident lingual talents and probably her natural intelligence and quick grasp of the local geopolitical situation. For Cortés and his Spaniards, there could only be appreciation for her. Indeed, from their perspective, she was a heroine. She made a complete move to their side—psychologically, politically, and physically. It was a genuine case of turncoating. For postcolonial Mexico, Malinali was viewed with scorn as a traitor, as the woman who enabled Cortés to conquer and alter Mexico—politically, socially, culturally, and physically. The power to decide the nature of the symbolic meaning of Malinali's actions is obvious here, too.

Was the moral construction of Malinali as a traitor by postcolonial Mexico justified? They certainly had the power to construct her as a traitor, but the moral basis of their judgment is rather shaky. The people whose trust and loyalty Malinche violated and supposedly betrayed had enslaved her. The question of whether a slave can "betray" those who enslaved her remains a rather thorny issue when viewed from a Western symbolic moral universe.

Moreover, Malinali was not the only one to collaborate with the conquistadors. Hassig points out that the Totonacs, Tetzcocas, Chalcas, and, of course, the Tlaxcaltecs all took the side of the Spaniards.[65] If Cortés and his limited military power could overcome Montezuma, it was in no small measure because of the local help he received. For example, the Tlaxcaltecs were mighty allies. And it is not too difficult to realize that the motivation of a slave to help people who, to a large extent, freed her and offered her a lifestyle she could not possibly have had as a slave, was strong and probably even justified. The social construction of Malinali as first a hero and later a traitor reflect changes in the complex structure and moral content of Mexican society, as well as the changes in power configurations in that society. The acts Malinali supposedly committed were not, in themselves, inherently treacherous. In deciding whether she was a traitor, one must first answer the questions, who trusted her? Who was expected to trust her and why? Who was she supposed to be loyal to and why? Even if the popular version of the events leading to the massacre at Cholollan (contested by Hassig) is valid, to conclude that she "betrayed" any Indian in Cholollan must be viewed as a controversial statement.

Clearly, Malinali crossed cultural boundaries. She moved from being loyal to her own cultural heritage to a hostile culture whose representatives came to Mexico on a voyage of conquest and exploitation. Can a slave be defined as a traitor if that slave goes against her captors? Although Malinali sided with the victors, when she joined them, it was not clear that they would indeed win. Moreover, it is possible that her joining Cortés provided the Spaniards with an indispensable assistance, which increased their chances of winning.

Politically, Malinali, the slave, converted from the Aztec-dominated culture to a different culture. Her identity must have been transformed as well, as she adopted and embraced the ways of life of the conquering Spaniards. These transformations obviously culminated in a changed direction of trust and loyalty for her. As we have seen in previous chapters, Malinali's account is not atypical. Vlasov is a comparable example.

The generalization from this case is as follows. We had one culture, dominated by a powerful, abusive, and divisive regime that supported disunity, rivalry, and conflict. Many individuals were quite unhappy and wanted to get the oppressive yoke off their backs. Then a foreign power invaded the territory, threatened the powerful hegemony of the local regime, and searched for local support. This situation is analogous to many other similar invasions throughout history.

Such events may encourage individuals to redefine the boundaries of their symbolic moral universes; trust and loyalty may shift, and conversion and turncoating from one culture to another may take place. Very much in C. Wright Mills's spirit, the political, social, and cultural upheaval may translate to the personal level with the forming of new identities, and those new identities support the upheaval. This case illustrates that individuals who experience such transformations of their identities risk being socially constructed as "traitors." Furthermore, as Ducharme and Fine showed in their 1995 study of Benedict Arnold, and Hassig in this case, as the concepts of loyalty and trust change their meaning, and different groups of people construct different meanings for national consciousness, the images of betrayal and heroism also change. We can certainly expect that when similar conflict situations arise, individuals like Malinali and Vlasov, who straddle the line between hero and traitor, will emerge. The non-European case of Malinali supports the power of the generalizations of the analytical conceptualization created here.

11

Treason in Judaism and Israel

So far we have examined quite a few cases of betrayal in Europe and North America. It is, perhaps, only fair that I complement these cases by examining a few famous cases of traitors from Israel and the history of Judaism, since I come from that cultural context. Although quite a few cases can be found in Black and Morris's 1991 work, and West even devotes a whole chapter to Israeli cases,[1] I would like to present a somewhat different selection of cases, based on the analytical approach presented in this book.

Like other cultures, Judaism had its share of traitors. I describe below a few of the more famous characters, the period in which they acted, and the meaning of their actions. This, by no means, is an exhaustive list and is meant for illustrative purposes only. As we shall see, periods of turmoil, of debate about the meaning and nature of moral boundaries and their enforcement, are periods when the issues of trust and loyalty emerge. When cultures are experiencing processes of disintegration, reintegration, and change, the issue of moral boundaries is at the forefront. These are periods when individual members are required to decide who they are, who or what they identify with, and which side they stand with. Typically, it is during periods of such unrest and turmoil that we find our traitors.

Elsewhere in this book I have mention some biblical cases of betrayal. The first case I discuss here takes place in the last period of the second Jewish temple.

Josephus Flavius and Yochanan Ben-Zakkai

During A.D. 66–73 the Jews revolted against the Roman conquest of Israel (referred to at that time as the Roman province of Judea).[2] The initiative of a small number of people, the Jewish revolt against the Roman Empire was doomed to fail. What has become known as the Great Revolt was in fact a majestic military, social, and political failure of the Jews. The last effort by the Roman imperial army against the Jewish rebels of the Great Revolt was the destruction of Masada in A.D. 73.[3] Although Jewish resistance against Rome did not end in this revolt (the Bar Kokhba revolt erupted again about sixty years later), the Roman victory against the rebels was decisive, and the second Jewish temple was destroyed and reduced to ashes. However, out of this destruction arose a new form of Judaism, not nationalistic but rather spiritual. In many significant aspects, this was the birth of Orthodox Judaism.

That period gave rise to two very famous figures who defected to the Romans. One is a person who became, perhaps, the best-known traitor in Jewish history—Josephus Flavius; the other was Rabbi Yochanan Ben-Zakkai who is credited with establishing Orthodox Judaism, a form of Judaism that prevailed until 1948, when a new Jewish state, and hence a renewed Jewish national culture, was established by secular Jews.

Joseph Ben-Matityahu, later known as Josephus Flavius, was born in Jerusalem in A.D. 37 to a priestly family. He was not an enthusiastic supporter of the Great Revolt. However, when the Great Revolt began, at around A.D. 66, he became the governor of the Galilee and was charged with the important responsibility of defending it. In A.D. 67, the major fortress in the Galilee—Yodfat (Jotapata)—fell. The last few survivors, including Josephus, decided to commit suicide. Josephus managed to trick the others, and he and another person remained as the last ones alive. At that point, Josephus persuaded the other man that they should both surrender to the Romans. Josephus was apparently a skillful man, and he struck a relationship with the commander of the Roman forces, Vespasian. Among other things, Josephus supposedly told him that he would become emperor. Vespasian indeed later became the Roman emperor.

Regardless of how historically accurate this story is up to this point, it is clear that Josephus then went to Rome where he became a Roman citizen and an official historian. He married four times and probably died sometime around A.D. 100.[4] As a result of Joseph Ben-Matityahu's betrayal in Yodfat and his defection to the Romans, he has been viewed by many as one of the most pronounced traitors in Jewish history. What is regarded as his act of betrayal is accentuated even further because of his ineffective defense of the Galilee. However, this man wrote the only book available about the period. It is a strange situation indeed that we have to form an opinion about the behavior of Jews during those fateful years, based on information provided by a Jew who is viewed by many as a traitor to his own culture and people.

In 1998 there was an interesting twist related to Josephus Flavius and treason. The head of Israeli premier Binyamin Netanyahu's chambers in

1998 was a man named Uri Elitzur. Elitzur has been identified with the Israeli religious right, living in and supporting Israeli settlements in the occupied West Bank. He has been politically involved and even edited the settlers' extreme right weekly magazine *Nekuda*. In 1998 Netanyahu's government was involved with the Palestinian Authority in negotiations that were aimed at giving them more territory for continuation of the Middle East peace process.

For many settlers, giving any of the territories to the Palestinians is considered a "no-no." Elitzur seemed to support Netanyahu's position that some territorial concessions were unavoidable. Consequently, some settlers distributed pamphlets in which Elitzur was renamed "Josephus Flavius"—in other words, stating that he was a traitor. Sure enough, Netanyahu, as well as other settlers, denounced these pamphlets. Since the Rabin assassination, Israel has indeed become very sensitive to name-calling.[5]

Josephus Flavius was not the only one guilty of betrayal in that era. Another rather famous man defected from the Jewish camp to the Romans and is generally not viewed as a traitor at all. That man was Rabbi Yochanan Ben-Zakkai who, like Josephus Flavius, lived and died during this cataclysmic period for the Jewish people. Ben-Zakkai escaped from Jerusalem, probably in A.D. 69, in the middle of Vespasian's spring offensive in the north, and found refuge with the Romans.[6]

Like many other contemporary Jews, Yochanan Ben-Zakkai kept a healthy and sober degree of skepticism in the face of increasing levels of military-political activism, zealot fervor, and false messianism. Clearly, he was not a fan of either the Zealots or the Sicarii[7] and questioned the wisdom of challenging the might of the Roman Empire. The case of Yochanan Ben-Zakkai not only raises the issue of possible alternatives to the Great Revolt but also provides a comparison to Joseph Ben-Matityahu (Josephus Flavius).

Like Josephus Flavius, Ben-Zakkai disagreed with many of the stated goals of the Jewish Great Revolt.[8] Being in his sixties when he defected, he apparently found common ground with Vespasian (who was more or less his age), chief commander of the Roman military machine that was crushing the Jewish rebellion (and on his way to becoming emperor of the Roman Empire). Vespasian granted Ben-Zakkai his wish to establish a small center, with a few Jewish scholars, to study and continue developing spiritual Judaism. The place Ben-Zakkai was sent to was Yavneh. There Yochanan Ben-Zakkai was successful in establishing a renewed branch of spiritual Judaism. As so many have pointed out, despite his defection, Ben-Zakkai is definitely *not* considered a traitor. His way led to a renewed type of Jewish life, and his challenge of the rebels' decision to confront the Roman Empire is frequently presented as an alternative to the rebellion. Apparently, both Ben-Zakkai and Josephus Flavius objected to the rebellion against the Romans. Whereas Josephus probably left Judaism altogether, went to Rome, and adopted a Roman lifestyle, Ben-Zakkai did not leave and remained Jewish to his last day.

Many individuals take Ben-Zakkai as an illustration of what could have been the alternative to the rebellion against the Romans, that is, instead of decimation and destruction on a mass scale, a renewed and meaningful Jewish life that enabled Jews to fulfill their religious and cultural aspirations without endangering what was most cherished to them.[9]

The Josephus-Ben-Zakkai contrast is used continuously in political and moral debates in modern Israel. For example, Israel Eichler, editor of the Haredi[10] weekly *The Haredi Camp*, wrote in his magazine that one needs to remember the hoodlums who, during the days of the second temple, brought destruction to the land (despite their good intentions). He contrasted them with Yochanan Ben-Zakkai, whom he called a Jewish holy scholar and righteous man who surrendered to the Romans and went to Galut in Yavneh. Eichler was quick to point out that Ben-Zakkai was the one to be credited with the survival of the people of Israel since then (A.D. 69–70).[11]

There are many interesting parallels between Ben-Zakkai and Josephus. Both were from the in-group; both lived in the same period and under similar circumstances; both left their people in a most difficult time. However, Ben-Zakkai is portrayed as continuing to be part of his people and helping in its revival. Josephus left his people completely to become something else. The violation of trust and loyalty by Josephus, as well as his turncoating, thus holds an altogether different meaning than that of Ben-Zakkai. It is thus Josephus who is remembered as a defector and traitor. Indeed, Ladouceur notes that Josephus is "usually regarded as an opportunistic traitor."[12]

The *Judenrat*

Our next case took place about 1,870 years after the Great Revolt. *Judenrats* were the councils of Jews set up as the governing bodies of the various ghettos constructed by the Nazis throughout Germany and occupied Europe during World War II. These councils represented the Jews in the Nazi regime, and the Nazi orders concerning Jews were funneled through these councils. The Nazis certainly used these councils to help them control the Jewish population. Many Jews view these councils with scorn and disgust because, to them, they represented a form of collaboration with the Nazis and in fact the councils helped the Nazis exterminate Jews. Judenrats, for many Jews, have become synonymous with betrayal and collaboration with the enemy. Thus, the *Judenrat* suggests the existence of an *organization* that, by nature, is regarded as treacherous, as opposed to the individual traitor.

Those Jews who were active in the *Judenrats* faced an impossible situation. It is inconceivable that they *wanted* to help the Nazis exterminate the Jews, and many of them probably thought that by participating in these councils they could mitigate the evil wrath of the Nazis and perhaps even save life (including, of course, their own and their families). Unfortunately, the nature of the Nazi occupation and extermination plan was such that these Jewish councils could not really do much to alleviate the situation in a significant way.[13]

Pre-Israel Cases of Betrayal

Before the state of Israel was established in 1948, secular Zionism developed a determined drive to establish a nation-state. That effort began in the last decades of the nineteenth century. The major political struggle was to secure the legitimacy of a new Jewish state by the major world powers. Another political and military struggle was with the emerging Arab national movement.

However, there were several conflicting ideological streams within secular Zionism, which differed on a variety of issues: How should the British Mandate occupation of Palestine (which lasted from 1917 until 1948) be dealt with? What role should the Arabs play? What should be the social and political shape of the emerging state? Beginning in the 1920s, there emerged three main prestate underground Jewish groups who practiced direct action: (1) Hagana, (2) Etzel ("Irgun"), and (3) Lehi (also known as the "Stern Gang"). These groups were unequal in size, with differing ideological stands on a variety of issues; sometimes they cooperated, and at other times they competed with one another.[14] At times, the hostility of these groups to one another reached lethal proportions; sometimes one group viewed members of the other group(s) as "traitors" and persecuted and even killed them. From the large number of such cases, some quite fascinating, I shall discuss only two.[15]

The Case of Israel De Hahn

Israel De Hahn was born in the small Dutch town of Smilda to an Orthodox Jewish family on December 31, 1881. His father was active in the life of the local Jewish community but was not doing very well economically and turned into a very bitter person. Israel's sister, Carey, was born less than a year before him, on January 21, 1881. Carey and Israel were apparently gifted and very talented children. As they grew up they turned their backs on Orthodox Judaism.

At the age of nineteen and having finished school, Israel De Hahn decided to move to Amsterdam and to become completely secular. There he studied law and, at the age of twenty-one, received his doctorate degree. In Amsterdam he also joined the socialist party. De Hahn's political and academic career in Amsterdam was strong and stable. There were also indications that he was developing (or actualizing) a homosexual identity. Despite this, De Hahn got into a problematic and stormy marital relationship with a Christian physician named Johanna Van Marsphain. De Hahn traveled to Russia several times, and apparently his experiences in Russia, and of Jewish life there, persuaded him to return to Orthodox Judaism. Later he decided to immigrate to Palestine.

In February 1919, De Hahn left his family in Amsterdam and began his long journey to Palestine. On his arrival, he settled in Jerusalem. Although De Hahn obviously moved to Palestine out of a Zionist ideology, he very quickly became disillusioned with the local Zionist political and social leadership. He drifted slowly into the circles of the most extreme anti-Zionist Jewish Orthodox groups in Jerusalem. He later began to write for newspapers in Holland very critical essays about the Zionist enterprise in Palestine and got involved in local anti-Zionist activities. De Hahn's ideology crystallized in 1920, and during 1921 he attacked not only the Zionist elite but the new immigrants as well. For example, after the 1920 riots in Jerusalem, De Hahn supported the British governor of Jerusalem—Sir Ronald Storrs—when most of the Jewish community demanded his resignation. There were other anti-Zionist activities in which De Hahn was involved and which were regarded by contemporary and important Zionist figures as being pure treason, or close to it. These activities did not make De Hahn a very popular figure within the Yishuv (prestate [1948] Jewish community in Palestine).[16]

This process came to a peak when in 1922 some of these debates received public attention outside Palestine. Local newspapers (secular and religious) published pieces calling for vengeance against De Hahn for his activity. He began to receive threats, and in May of 1923 he received a direct death threat demanding that he should leave Palestine. All this did not stop De Hahn, and he continued his activities and published extremely critical essays abroad. De Hahn continued to receive written threats and warnings urging him to stop his activities.

On the evening of Monday, June 30, 1924, De Hahn went to pray in the synagogue that was located within the old structure of the Sha'arei Zedek hospital in Jaffo Street in Jerusalem. De Hahn left the synagogue at approximately 19:45. As he left the synagogue and was walking down the street, he was shot three times and died a few minutes later in the operating room of the hospital at the age of forty-three.

Although there were rumors that De Hahn's assassination was related to his alleged homosexuality, it became evident that the real reason was political. Although there are several opinions as to exactly who assassinated De Hahn, there is little doubt that a member of the Hagana did it, on explicit orders from the Hagana's leadership. It was a case of an ultra-Orthodox Jew who was perceived as threatening the secular Zionist effort to reestablish a Jewish state and who was thus defined by them as a "traitor," that is, as a person who violated what was seen by the Hagana as the values of Jewish trust and loyalty. It is quite obvious that De Hahn was assassinated because he was perceived as posing an immediate threat to a group of dedicated, active, and revolutionary Zionists who occupied important positions in the leadership of the Jewish community in Palestine.[17]

The Case of Yehuda Arie Levi

Yehuda Arie Levi, thirty-three years old and single, was a Sefardi Jew who came to Palestine from Italy. He was gifted with technical talents and when he joined Lehi he became the manager of the technical department. Levi served as a guide and teacher in Lehi's courses on explosives. An industrious and inventive fellow, Levi developed road mines, bullets, and igniting grenades. He showed an inclination toward the study of chemistry and was going to be sent to the United States as a representative of Lehi.

On November 29, 1947, the United Nations decided that the Jewish state would be established. This created a problem for Lehi. They had to decide whether to disband the organization and join the new emerging Jewish state or to continue to exist and operate as an independent organization. Originally Lehi's headquarters gave the order to disband, but the order was canceled within a month. That process left many members of Lehi totally confused.

Yehuda Arie Levi was one of those who decided to leave Lehi and join the Hagana. He contacted the Hagana's members and told them of his intentions. He did not keep his decision a secret and also told other members of Lehi about it. Lehi's headquarters sent a woman to talk to Levi to find out exactly what his intentions were and why. Despite the cancellation of the disbanding order, he insisted on joining the Hagana.

After the woman talked with Levi and reported to her superior, Lehi's members were instructed to avoid contacts with Levi and to excommunicate him. Most of his friends stayed away from him. Levi did not give up; he continued to voice his opinion and demanded an explanation from Lehi's command. A clarification was needed. The process of clarification turned very quickly into a "trial." However, even the "judges" could not find anything wrong in Levi's actions or words. The whole affair was turned over to Lehi's headquarters. There it was decided that he should be killed.[18]

At 6:30 on Thursday, January 15, 1948, about fifteen armed young males broke into Levi's apartment in Hayarkon Street in Tel Aviv and took Yehuda Arie by force with them. Although the exact details are not entirely clear, it appears that a few weeks after Levi's kidnapping, his family began to apply pressure on different political figures to help find their son. Even the Tel Aviv Rabbinate demanded to know where Levi's body was buried (after a rumor that he was killed was spread). And, indeed, his body was found later, with four handgun bullet holes in his chest.

An inner memo of Lehi told members that Levi was accused of violating the group's discipline, telling lies, demoralizing other members of Lehi, and disclosing secrets. He was brought before a special "court," found guilty as charged, and executed. Lehi members were told that this act could not be avoided.

On Friday, November 11, 1987, *Yediot Aharonot* published a long cover story on this case written by Amos Nevo. According to the report, on the day Levi was kidnapped by Lehi, he was put before a Lehi "court" and shot on the same day, after Yellin-Mor—one of Lehi's commanders—approved the verdict.[19] The actual assassin was interviewed, under the pseudonym "Ze'ev," and stated that he shot Levi because had he not, he would have been shot himself. "What could I do? Why did those who were the judges not prevent it? I received an order, and I shot, I could not refuse."[20] "Ze'ev" told Nevo that the order to shoot came from "Adam." The use of pseudonyms thirty-four years after the assassination and the reluctance to be exposed obviously indicate that those involved certainly do not feel comfortable with their actions.

On February 15, 1977, Levi's name was added to the list of Lehi's casualties. His family wrote on his tombstone that he was murdered by bad people ("Zedim"), which made some contemporary Lehi survivors (for example, Yazernitzki, Anshell Shpillman) quite angry. Shpillman told Nevo that in 1948 Lehi had no prisons, that Levi could not have been isolated, and that "there was no choice . . . the underground could not afford such anarchy. . . . That was a loss, a tragedy. But he [Levi] brought the death upon himself."[21]

Levi was not a "traitor" or a "squealer" in the stereotypical sense of the terms. He just wanted to transfer from Lehi to the Hagana on the reasoning that Lehi was about to become one with the new Jewish state. His execution cannot possibly be understood as anything other than a strong signal from Lehi's leadership to the other members, in a period of great confusion and contradictory messages and commands, that the coherent symbolic moral universe of Lehi was still intact and vibrant and that any-body willing to violate Lehi's moral boundaries would be punished se-verely. Levi refused to hide his opinions. That made his challenge to the moral boundaries even harder. His execution needed to be explained to Lehi's members—for exactly the same reason—to clarify and reify the moral boundaries in the most explicit manner.

Israeli Cases of Betrayal After 1948

After the establishment of the state of Israel in 1948, there were quite a few cases involving treason. The cases involving Va'anunu and Manbar were discussed elsewhere in this book. Here I describe a few more.

The Case of Captain Meir Tubianski

Short announcements in the Jewish daily press on July 20, 1948, informed the public that on June 30 an unknown spy was executed. The man who was killed was Captain Meir Tubianski—the only Israeli executed on charges of treason.

The Accusations.   The British Mandate over Palestine ended in May 1948, and the partition plan did not award Jerusalem to the Jews. A long and fierce battle over Jerusalem took place in 1948, and the Jewish portion of Jerusalem was under siege. The city was bombed and bombarded by the artillery of the Jordanian Legion, as well as exposed to the shooting of Arab snipers. Life in Jewish Jerusalem was under much pressure militar-ily, economically (food was rationed), socially, and politically. The Lehi, Etzel, and Hagana were active in defending the city. During the siege, ru-mors about spies, collaborators, informers, and traitors abounded, and the ugly ghosts of war poisoned the atmosphere. During 1948 Lehi alone assassinated four individuals in Jerusalem on suspicions of "espionage."

During the Arab siege of Jerusalem in 1948, the three underground Jew-ish organizations continually moved their headquarters and weapon shops. The Hagana's intelligence service, the Shai, headed at that time by Binyamin Gibly, became suspicious about the accuracy of the Arab ar-tillery in hitting targets that moved about the city (for example, weapons shops and headquarters). Gradually, suspicions focused on the Jerusalem Electric Company. The company had the addresses of all important places in the city, and some of its workers were in constant contact with the Arab side of the city, using their wireless transmitters (for legitimate reasons).

Suspecting that employees of the Jerusalem Electric Company were re-sponsible for the "accurate artillery," Etzel arrested five British clerks of the company and investigated them. The Hagana arrested Meir Tubianski.

Meir Tubianski held the rank of major in the British army during the Second World War. In June 1948, he was appointed the first commander of the newly established Israel Defense Forces (I.D.F.) camp in Schneler near Mea Shearim.[22] Since Tubianski did not succeed in this job, he was transferred to command the airstrips in Jerusalem.[23] However, in 1948, Tubianski was also an engineer and a senior official in the Jerusalem Electric Company. Members of the Hagana suspected that he gave important military addresses to his British colleagues in the Jerusalem Electric Company so that they could connect them to the electrical network. It was suspected that this information was then transmitted to the Arab artillery, which bombarded the new addresses. It must be noted that even if these suspicions were valid, Tubianski was clearly not guilty of deliberate espionage. If these headquarters and weapons shops, which were moving about the city, wanted electricity, someone had to get the addresses for the company to connect them to the electrical grid.

Tubianski was an old member (about twenty-two years) of the Hagana. In the early months of 1948, Isser Be'ery, the head of the Shai in Israel,[24] received information that Tubianski was providing hostile British clerks with information (which they supposedly passed on to the Arabs). Be'ery consulted with the head of the legal service of the newly formed I.D.F., then Abraham Gorally, and as a result, decided to arrest Tubianski. Be'ery later claimed that he understood from Gorally that he was allowed to establish a military court against Tubianski. On the very same day, Be'ery told the commander of the Palmach (originally, Hagana's military unit) about his suspicions. A written request was made to the Palmach's regional commander to assist Be'ery in any way possible.

The "Trial."   On Monday June 30, 1948, Be'ery sent one of his officers to arrest Tubianski, who was in Tel Aviv. Tubianski came willingly and without resistance. They left Tel Aviv at around 15:00. At around 16:00 Tubianski faced the charge of treason in front of a "military court" in the deserted Arab village of Beit Giz (on the road from Tel Aviv to Jerusalem). Three judges were appointed to hear the trial.[25] Tubianski was not allowed to prepare a defense or to consult with a lawyer. He was shown a list of the arms and ammunition shops/factories in Jerusalem of which he supposedly had given the addresses to his British superiors in the Jerusalem Electric Company.

To understand the specific charge we need some details. At that time Jerusalem had two different networks of electricity, one of which serviced the military and both of which were serviced by the Jerusalem Electric Company. The British manager of the Jerusalem Electric Company— Michael Bryant—may have known about the two electrical networks. It was claimed that during a conversation on June 16, 1948, Tubianski gave

Bryant the information. This conversation was open and was probably overheard by other Jewish workers. Because it was suspected that Tubianski was giving vital and secret information to a hostile British citizen, this information was passed on to the Hagana's intelligence unit. It needs to be noted that despite the insinuations, the information provided by Tubianski could have been obtained in other ways. Tubianski was also accused on charges that the information given on June 16 to Bryant was passed on to the Jordanian artillery.

When Tubianski heard the charges, he supposedly admitted giving Bryant the information, thereby indirectly admitting guilt. Although there is a version that he supposedly may have even said that he deserved a death sentence, a more reliable version is that he probably admitted giving the list of places that needed electricity on both networks in Jerusalem, but maintained that the information was given *only* so that these places could be connected to the network and receive electricity and not for reasons of sabotage. Nevertheless, the judges found Tubianski guilty of espionage and treason and sentenced him to death. On the same day he was arrested, at around 19:00, a firing squad shot Tubianski to death. The whole "trial," conviction, and execution took about three hours.

The Aftermath. Tubianski's wife, Chaya (Lena), was not told what had happened, but when she found out, she wrote to David Ben-Gurion (November 1948), demanding an explanation. Ben-Gurion instructed the army chief of staff to investigate. Consequently, Ben-Gurion wrote Tubianski's wife in December 1948 that "I checked the procedure of his trial and I found out that it was not in order, perhaps because the underground laws were still dominant in the army."[26]

On July 1, 1949, Ben-Gurion wrote again to Mrs. Tubianski that

> It was found that Meir Tubianski was innocent (and his execution) was a tragic mistake. . . . Attempting to rectify the tragedy, the chief of staff decided: 1. to give Meir Tubianski a rank of a captain; 2. to give him a full military burial; 3. to pay you and your son compensation. . . . Your husband made a mistake and perhaps a serious one, giving his British superior a list and did not think it would fall into the wrong hands. He admitted the mistake and regretted it, but he had no bad intentions and without intent there is no treason.[27]

Tubianski was buried in a full military service on July 7, 1949.[28]

On July 10, 1949, Isser Be'ery, then head of military intelligence and directly responsible for Tubianski's execution, was arrested and charged with the unlawful killing of Tubianski. The trial itself was open to the public and began in the district court of Tel Aviv on October 16, 1949, and lasted until October 30, 1949. On November 22, 1949, the verdict was given. The court stated specifically that no charges of treason against Tubianski were substantiated and that his execution was a fatal mistake.

The court stated that the use of the list Tubianski supposedly had given to his British superior as evidence lacked any basis. Furthermore, some questions were raised during the trial regarding the nature of the accusations against Tubianski. For example, between June 11 and July 7, a cease-fire was in effect, so the information supposedly given by Tubianski *could not* have served the Jordanian artillery. Moreover, there were some questions as to whether in fact the Jordanian artillery *was* so accurate.[29] In short, Tubianski was innocent of the charges of espionage and treason.

Tubianski's execution was attributed to Be'ery for three reasons: (1) Be'ery appointed three of his subordinates as judges in a "field military court" and told them that if they found Tubianski guilty they had permission to sentence him to death; (2) after the judges had found Tubianski guilty and sentenced him to death, Be'ery approved the sentence and verdict; (3) Be'ery ordered that a firing squad be assembled to carry out the court's decision. Be'ery was found guilty as charged and was sentenced to one day in prison.[30] Clearly the court was convinced that Tubianski was killed illegally but was equally convinced that Be'ery did not do what he did with a malicious intent.

The five British clerks kidnapped by Etzel in 1948 were given to the Hagana. Three were released for lack of evidence, two were charged with espionage. One (Hawkins) was found innocent, and the other (William Silvester) was found guilty. In an appeal to the Israeli Supreme Court, this individual was found not guilty and was consequently released.[31]

The Tubianski case left a scar in the moral fiber of Israeli society. Debates about it still rage.[32] Tubianski was the *only* person in the history of Israel who was executed on charges of treason, and the first person (out of two; the other was Adolf Eichmann) who was sentenced to death in Israel and actually executed.

The Tubianski case is significant and instructive. The "trial" and "court" represent the type of "justice" that prevailed among the three prestate underground Jewish organizations until 1948. The justice that emerged, crystallized, and prevailed after 1948 was based on open and formal procedures grounded on facts and due process and was radically different from the pre-1948 "justice." The Tubianski case was based on insufficient and inconclusive evidence, conjecture, pressure, a lack of procedures, and improper attention to basic rights of defendants, and there was no right of appeal. What was called a trial was not a trial in the sense that we all know and understand. Tubianski really did not have much of a reasonable chance to defend himself once the "trial" began.

Tubianski, a victim of circumstances beyond his control and of human error, fear, and viciousness, was certainly considered (wrongly) by his prosecutors to be a member of the collective who betrayed the trust invested in him and who was disloyal to his collective. This combination led to his definition as a traitor, with a tragic result.

The Case of Dr. Israel Kasztner

In March 1944 the Nazis invaded Hungary. Adolf Eichmann and his aides came to Budapest and began their preparations to activate the "final solution" for Hungarian Jews.

The Jews in Hungary were divided into several main groups. Many of them were, however, aware of what the Nazis were doing to European Jews. They tried to organize help and created a "saving committee."

One of the key members of the committee was Dr. Rudolf (Israel) Kasztner (born 1906). Kasztner was a local Zionist politician who found himself in the midst of something more dreadful than Dante's hell. He tried to negotiate with Eichmann and his group of killers and attempted to save as many Jews as he possibly could under the circumstances.

Kasztner was effective in securing the exit of what has become known as the "train of the prestigious" in June 1944. That was a train with 1,684 Jews aboard, which the Nazis allowed to leave Hungary for Switzerland, supposedly as a sign of "good will" and an indication of "intent." Kasztner was also involved in several other activities aimed at saving Jews[33]

On May 25, 1953, the legal advisor to the Israeli government accused, in criminal file no. 53/124, Malkiel Greenwald with defaming Dr. Kasztner.[34] At that time, Kasztner was the spokesman for the Israeli ministry of commerce and industry. Greenwald, in mimeographed letters, accused Kasztner of collaborating with the Nazis, helping in the final extermination of Hungarian Jews, helping a Nazi war criminal, and living on funds "confiscated" from Hungarian Jews. Greenwald called for the death of Kasztner because of his supposedly treacherous behavior. According to Greenwald's accusations, Dr. Kasztner actually helped the Nazis. The main claims were that the June 1944 train was a price the Nazis paid to buy Kasztner's silence in order to keep most Hungarian Jews unaware of what was really awaiting them and that Kasztner gained economically from the money confiscated from the Jews. These were certainly monstrous accusations.

In January 1954, the trial began in Jerusalem, and Greenwald hired Shmuel Tamir as his lawyer.[35] Tamir was very effective in converting the trial from a simple criminal case into a political trial, and Greenwald became the accuser rather than the accused. This trial was one of the most dramatic and painful trials in the history of Israel. It lasted from January

1954 to June 22, 1955. In the trial, the role of the Jewish leadership in Nazi-occupied Hungary in 1944 and in Palestine was examined with a magnifying glass.

Tamir implied that there were many different issues in which Kasztner was involved, and in which he basically acted as a collaborator with the Nazis, and hence he was a bona fide traitor. I shall mention them briefly. First, he maintained contacts with and negotiated with the Gestapo and the S.S. Second, he was involved in what later became known as the June 1944 "train of the prestigious." The implication was that the train was the price that Eichmann and his Nazi group paid for Kasztner's silence. Third, the Nazis allowed Dr. Kasztner to hide his Jewish identity in Budapest, and his behavior there, according to Tamir, was disgraceful. He did not wear a yellow Magen David, and he played cards with Nazis. Fourth, Kasztner selected Jews from the Kloj Ghetto over Jews from other places; 388 Jews from that particular ghetto were on the June 1944 train, and many of them were relatives of Kasztner. Fifth, Kasztner helped to turn Yoel Brand's mission into a failure. Sixth, Kasztner failed to alert and inform Hungarian Jews that they were not just being transported outside of Hungary to a new resettlement but that they were being transported to an extermination camp at Auschwitz. He also failed to warn Jewish leaders outside Hungary of the horrendous events. Seventh, in 1944 the British Army sent several British Jewish officer paratroopers to Hungary for intelligence purposes. Three of them—Hanna Senesh, Yoel Nusbacher (Palgi), and Peretz Goldstein—clearly intended to help organize the Jews into resisting the Nazis.[36] It was claimed that Kasztner was involved in the arrest of all three by the Nazis. Eighth, after the war ended, Kasztner testified in favor of S.S. officer Kurt Bachar. Ninth, Kasztner interfered with operations to save Jews in Europe. Tenth, Kasztner had personally used the money confiscated from Jews to live luxuriously in Switzerland.

On June 22, 1955, Judge Halevi, in a long and detailed verdict, determined that in fact Kasztner had cooperated with the Nazis and thus had helped indirectly in preparing the ground for the extermination of Hungarian Jews, and that he had helped ex-S.S. officer Kurt Bachar. The judge stated that the above tenth accusation was totally groundless. Judge Halevi stated in the verdict that when Kasztner had accepted "the gift" of the train, "he sold his soul to the devil."[37]

The trial in Jerusalem attracted much attention. On the night of March 15, 1955, an anonymous pamphlet was distributed in which one of the judges—M. Peretz—was accused of being biased and of cooperating with the old "leadership" so as to help "cover up" Kasztner's supposed "atrocities."[38] It is obvious that there were many people in Israel in the mid-1950s who were unhappy with Kasztner's activities during the period of the Holocaust and saw it as a major betrayal.

Eldad Sheib, who was one of the triumvirate that had previously commanded Lehi, had a newspaper called *Sulam* ("ladder" in Hebrew), which preached a right-wing national ideology. He also formed an organization called Hazit Hanoar Haleumit (in Hebrew, "the front of the national youth"), where small groups met and discussed various national topics. Eldad preached doing "something" about Kasztner.[39]

The transition of Israel to a state in the late 1940s and early 1950s was a problematic and painful process. Various political groups felt that the emerging state was not what they wanted and chose terrorism "to get their way." One of these groups was the right-wing Malchut Israel ("the Kingdom of Israel"), or, as it later became known as, the "Zerifin underground." That group was particularly active during 1952–1953. For example, on February 9, 1953, late at night, members from the group planted a bomb at the Soviet embassy, which was then located at 46 Rothschild Street in Tel Aviv. The bomb exploded and wounded some workers and caused much damage. Consequently, Moscow severed its diplomatic ties with Israel for about six months. The Israeli secret service began an investigation, exposed the group, and arrested about sixteen members. They were charged in a military court. Some were found guilty and sent to prison. Two members of that group were Ya'acov Herouti and Joseph Menkes, who were previously members of Lehi.[40] The lawyer for the defendants was again Shmuel Tamir. For lack of evidence, Menkes was not brought to court. Herouti received a ten-year prison sentence. In 1955 Herouti, and others, received state clemency and were released.

On Saturday night, March 2, 1957, Dr. Kasztner returned to his home in Tel Aviv from his work as the night editor of a local Hungarian language newspaper.[41] An anonymous male approached, identified him, and shot him three times with a gun. Dr. Kasztner was taken to a hospital where he fought death for about two weeks. He died on March 18. The Israeli secret service, headed then by Isser Harel, began an investigation. Very soon four suspects were arrested: Ya'acov Herouti, Joseph Menkes (thirty-eight years old), Ze'ev Ekstein (twenty-four years old), and Dan Shemer (twenty-three years old).[42] The police told the press on March 12, 1957, that they had solved the case.[43]

Although there were other individuals in the background,[44] only Menkes, Ekstein, and Shemer were indicted on May 28, 1957, for the assassination of Dr. Kasztner and for being members in a terrorist organization. Herouti was charged with membership in a terrorist organization. On January 28, 1958, in a different trial, Herouti was found guilty of producing the pamphlet mentioned above and was sentenced to eighteen months in prison. An appeal to the Israeli Supreme Court was not accepted. Menkes, Shemer, and Ekstein were found guilty of Kasztner's assassination. In responding to an appeal, the Israeli Supreme Court stated that it was Menkes who persuaded Ekstein to assassinate Kasztner and even gave him the gun to do it. The court stated that there was an underground organization that was responsible for the assassination. The three were convicted for their participation in a terrorist organization and received long prison sentences.

Meanwhile, the Israeli Supreme Court debated the original Greenwald-Kasztner trial. The five judges reconfirmed that Kasztner in fact helped S.S. officer Kurt Bachar by giving false testimony on his behalf. However, most judges rejected all the other accusations made by Greenwald as essentially baseless.

On May 23, 1960, Israel's prime minister—David Ben-Gurion—announced in the Israeli Knesset that Adolf Eichmann had been caught and would be put on trial in Israel. After a long and dramatic trial, Eichmann was executed. The Kasztner affair did not become a major issue in Eichmann's trial, but from the few references to it (and from interviews Eichmann gave to *Life* magazine), it appears that from Eichmann's perspective, Kasztner was obviously trying to save as many Jews as he possibly could. But it was also conceded that a by-product of that effort was the fact that Hungarian Jews were kept quiet. Kasztner's enigma, therefore, was not fully resolved.

Clearly, Ekstein, Shemer, and Menkes acted as a group. Their cohesion was partly integrated by their ideological conviction in what they viewed as Kasztner's guilt in collaboration with the Nazis. They were also united by a right-wing and nationalistic worldview that went back to Lehi and to Sheib's "Sulam" group. In fact, Sheib's club was located at Menkes's house.[45] Sheib's revolutionary right-wing propaganda no doubt helped to shape and crystallize the group into taking the lethal path leading to Kasztner's assassination.

The Greenwald-Kasztner trial and Kasztner's assassination served as hot platforms for moral debates. The Greenwald-Kasztner trial examined the nature and scope of the Jewish leadership's involvement and collaboration in helping to prevent (or helping to accomplish) the Nazis' extermination campaigns. The assassins' trial was used by Tamir and journalist Uri Avneri to claim that the Israeli secret service was behind Kasztner's assassination because it was too dangerous for the major political party—then Mapai—to leave Kasztner alive. Their version seemed to have been supported by the fact that the Israeli secret service had penetrated the Menkes-Ekstein group and that for a short while before the assassination, Ekstein had worked for the service. These claims were examined and dismissed.[46]

Furthermore, other works imply that at least in the Brand affair (discussed in Chapter 3), Himmler probably intended to negotiate a peace agreement with the Allies. In this context, Eichmann's "offer" to spare the

Jews in the "blood for trucks" deal was a by-product of that initiative. Bauer's work indicated that some essential parts in Brand's 1954 testimonies were not true and points to Tamir's questionable role in helping to amplify lies.[47]

The Kasztner affair continues to haunt Israeli society. Dinur asserted in a 1987 perspective on the case that Kasztner's actions during World War II in Hungary were aimed at saving as many Jews as possible and were distorted by Tamir's biased and one-dimensional interpretation. In 1994, historian Yechiam Weitz collaborated with Israeli TV in the production of a three-hour miniseries about the case, accompanied by three hours of prime-time televised discussions. In 1995 he also published a book on the topic.[48]

The Case of Udi Adiv and Dan Vered

Udi (Ehud) Adiv was a member of an Israeli Jewish-Arab ring of operators who provided Syrian intelligence with information. The ring was established by Daoud Turki, a nationalist and Communist Christian-Arab from Haifa. The common denominator between the Arab and the Jewish members of this ring of spies was their belief in socialism, with strong Maoist and Trotskyist tendencies. The Israeli secret service exposed the affair in December 1972 when details of the spy ring were leaked to the press. Although during the investigation more than thirty Arabs and about four Jews were arrested, clearly the most prominent left-wing Jew in the espionage net was Udi Adiv, as Black and Morris (1991:277–279) point out. He was twenty-six years old when he was arrested, an ex-member of the Gan Shmuel kibbutz, ex-paratrooper in the Israeli army who fought in the Six Day War, and a star basketball player. With him was Dan Vered, a twenty-eight-year-old mathematics teacher from Tel Aviv. In 1972, the exposure of this case of espionage created noisy echoes.

Adiv and Vered secretly visited Damascus and were trained in the basic skills of coding and the use of weapons and explosives. They also gave their hosts information.

Adiv later claimed that the information given was amateurish and not essential. He was indicted in court on charges of espionage and treason in a trial that began on February 25, 1973.

Turki (singing the International) and Adiv were found guilty of espionage and treason and sentenced in March 1973 to seventeen years in prison. Other members of the spy ring who were on trial (four, including Dan Vered) were sentenced to various punishments. Both Turki and Adiv served about twelve years, until 1985 when they were released. After his release, Adiv expressed regret for his acts, but not for his ideological views.

As Cromer (1998) points out, the case of Udi Adiv served as a point of clashing between two major symbolic moral universes in Israel. The religious one stated that Adiv, *the* archetype of a secular Jew—kibbutznik, paratrooper, secular, Zionist—has also become an archetype of a traitor. The implication was that secularism inevitably leads to betrayal, and hence sticking to orthodox religion was the solution. However, secularists pointed out that Adiv was an unrepresentative case (for example, Uri Illan, mentioned below, came from the same kibbutz as Adiv, was also secular, and is considered a genuine hero) and the orthodox version of Judaism did not provide an inoculation against treason or deviance.[49] It is, of course, no coincidence that treason provided the platform for the two major ideologies to clash. It does, after all, signify the boundaries of trust and loyalty. The debate between the secular and religious interpretations of Judaism, as focused on the case of Udi Adiv, was thus about the diagnosis of the case, its reasoning, its methods of correcting the deviance, its meaning and generalizability.

On April 10, 1975, while in prison, Adiv married Sylvia Klingberg, the daughter of a famous Soviet spy—Markus Klingberg (discussed in Chapter 3). Klingberg was imprisoned for penetrating Israeli high-security installations working in the area of chemical and biological warfare and providing his Soviet operators with the information he gathered there. In 1978 the two were divorced and married other partners.[50]

Both Adiv and Vered were members of the majority Jewish collective in Israel. Their decision to aid Israel's enemy, Syria, by providing it with information and undergoing training as spies reflected a decision to violate the trust invested in them by the state and their loyalty to that state. Adiv became the name associated with this spy ring and a synonym for treason.

The Cases of Amos Levinberg and Uri Illan

On the day that the 1973 Yom Kippur War began, October 6, the Israeli stronghold in the Hermon mountains, the Golan Heights, held close to sixty soldiers. At around 15:00, four Syrian helicopters carrying commando soldiers landed near the stronghold, attacked it, and overcame the Israeli soldiers. Eighteen Israeli soldiers died in that fierce battle; thirty-one were taken prisoner. Among the prisoners was Lieutenant Amos Levinberg. He was an intelligent young officer whose appetite for knowledge was voracious. Volunteering for a variety of duties, he had learned a lot about Israeli military. Levinberg, an obsessive collector of detailed information, was also gifted with a phenomenal memory. In fact, it was clear that he knew too much.

*Uri Illan. Photo by
Uri's sister Hanna.*

The Syrians have a reputation for their brutal treatment of POWs. However, it turned out that no such "treatment" was necessary for Levinberg. He provided the Syrians with all the information they wanted, and more. The military damage that Levinberg inflicted on Israel was substantial.

That Levinberg had a weak character is obvious. However, Israeli intelligence, which allowed him access to so much sensitive information (certainly way beyond his "need to know"), must share the blame.

When Levinberg returned from Syrian captivity, the extent of the disaster he helped into being became clear. He was ostracized as a traitor. Cohen quotes him as saying, "For years I wanted to die. I had a strong sense of betrayal, of guilt, but the guilt lies with whoever stationed me in the Hermon outpost."[51] In other words, given the breadth and depth of his knowledge, he should have been assigned to an outpost where the risk of him becoming a prisoner was not so high.

Was Levinberg a traitor? He was certainly a member of the in-group, and he violated the trust invested in him and compromised his loyalty to the state by giving so much information so freely to the Syrians. Did he have a choice? Had he been tortured, he could have died without disclosing anything, or he might have broken under torture and give all the information he knew anyway. The issue of what is expected of POWs in terms of disclosing information (and under what conditions) is a difficult and thorny question.

Uri Illan provides the opposite case—that of heroism. He was born in 1935 in the kibbutz of Gan Shmuel,[52] joined the Israeli Army in 1953, and was trained as a paratrooper. On December 8, 1954, Illan, three other soldiers, and an officer, were sent across the Syrian border in the Golan Heights to attach listening devices to Syrian telephone lines. They were all caught by the Syrians and placed in a Syrian prison. All the soldiers were subjected to psychological manipulation and torture. After a month, Illan committed suicide. His body was returned to Israel on January 14, 1955. When his body was examined, it was found that prior to his suicide he had placed little notes in his clothes and between his toes in which he wrote that he had not betrayed his friends. The notes also implied that he was under great stress and wanted revenge. The other four soldiers were returned to Israel on March 29, 1956, in return for forty Syrian soldiers. Two of the Israeli soldiers were court-martialed.[53]

It is appropriate to examine these cases because they shed light on a very particular type of behavior. Are POWs, under the credible threat of severe torture, or actually under such torture, still "required" to disclose basically nothing? If they do disclose information, should it be considered a "betrayal"? From the perspective presented in this book, the answer appears to be yes. However, the theoretical perspective we used have assumed that a decision to violate trust and become disloyal is not forced but a voluntary decision. When one is coerced to betray, sometimes brutally and under a threat of death, should we still consider our moralistic response to it, straight and simple, as noncoerced betrayal? My inclination is to respond in the negative. Perhaps the expectation that civilians, or soldiers, under such conditions, should keep quiet is an unrealistic expectation. The implications of this issue go beyond POWs being coerced to reveal military secrets. It has obvious implications for collaborators during World War II (and in other conflicts). The question we must ask ourselves is, what is the threat that the potential collaborator faces? Although the universal structure of violating trust and loyalty materializes in the cases of both collaborators and POWs who disclose military secrets, the circumstances may be such that the social and moral responses to such behaviors must be different than those of individuals who commit such violations under little or no threat or danger.

The Case of Derech Hanitzotz

In 1982 a monthly Israeli magazine, *Derech Hanitzotz* (in Hebrew, "the way of the spark") began to appear. The magazine reflected the views of a rather small group of Israeli leftists called Hanitzotz. In 1985 the magazine was upgraded to a biweekly and was published in both Hebrew and Arabic. It focused on reports and news about the Israeli-occupied territories and about the Palestinians. Roni and Ya'acov Ben-Effrat were paid employees, and Michal Schwartz (originally Arielli) worked as a volunteer. During 1988, about five individuals associated with *Derech Hanitzotz* were arrested. Rabchi El-Aruri, Arab editor of the Arab language version of the magazine, was arrested first (February 16, 1988); two days later (February 18) *Derech Hanitzotz* was closed by an administrative order. When the man in charge of issuing the order was asked to explain it, he responded that the magazine and its people had a connection to Nayif Hawatmeh, head of the Democratic Front for the Liberation of Palestine (DFLP), a terrorist organization. On April 15, 1988, Ya'acov Ben-Effrat was arrested, and on April 23, his wife, Roni, was arrested, too. Michal Schwartz was arrested on April 27. Other members of the group were Assaf Adiv (brother of Udi Adiv, discussed earlier) and Hadas Lahav, who were arrested in May 1988. All in all, five Jewish members and one Arab were arrested.[54]

The main charges against the individuals associated with *Derech Hanitzotz* were that they were in contact with a foreign agent and members in an illegal terrorist organization. The prosecution claimed that some time at the end of 1983 or early 1984, Michal Schwartz met in London with Salah Refat—a senior member in Nayif Hawatmeh's organization—and she was persuaded to join the organization. She was followed shortly by Roni Ben-Effrat. These individuals, together with Ya'acov Ben-Effrat, agreed with Hawatmeh's people that they would establish in Israel a Jewish-Arab political organization and would publish a newspaper, all financed by Hawatmeh's organization. Indeed, Schwartz and Ben-Effrat established in Israel a not-for-profit organization called *Hanitzotz* and published *Derech Hanitzotz*. Hawatmeh's terrorist organization, according to the prosecution, financed it all and provided guidelines for their activities. The report in *Ha'aretz* quoted anonymous sources in the state's prosecution, who noted that "it was decided not to accuse Schwartz and Ben-Effrat with treason because there is no solid evidence for such an accusation, which is difficult to prove in court."[55] The same report stated that although Hadas Lahav, Ya'acov Ben-Effrat, and Assaf Adiv were in custody, the specific accusations against them had not yet been established.

In short, the basic accusation against the Jewish members in *Hanitzotz* was that they cultivated contacts with Hawatmeh's group. Eventually, Israeli journalists were told that the nature of the evidence was such that individuals associated with *Derech Hanitzotz* were not going to be charged with treason, but with "membership in a foreign hostile organization" and with "contacts with a foreign agent."[56] Although technically none of these charges was direct treason, the subtext was certainly one of treason.

The implication was, clearly, that Jewish individuals associated with *Derech Hanitzotz* were conspiring with an Arab terrorist organization against the state of Israel. Violating trust and loyalty were certainly the issues here. Indeed, on May 23, 1988, Michal Schwartz and Roni Ben-Effrat, the two editors of *Derech Hanitzotz*, were formally accused in court of the above crimes. Eventually, each member of this group who was in custody was charged in court, was found guilty, and received a prison sentence.[57] By 1991 no Jewish member of the group remained in prison.

Two related events are well worth noting here. First, Michael Warshawski, who was involved in publishing a pamphlet of Hawatmeh's terrorist organization (but was not associated with *Derech Hanitzotz*), was also sentenced to a prison sentence.[58] Second, on October 3, 1989, a very famous Israeli "peacenik"—Aibi Natan—was sentenced to six months in prison for meeting Yasser Arafat, chairman of the Palestine Liberation Organization, which was viewed then as a terrorist organization.[59] Later that month, Aibi Natan refused to express "regret" for meeting Arafat in return for "clemency."[60]

Clearly, Jewish members of *Hanitzotz* were considered to be members of the in-group who violated their loyalty to the state and the state's trust in them by conspiring with a hostile organization.

The Case of Victor Ostrovsky

Victor Ostrovsky was born in Edmonton, Canada, on November 28, 1949, to a Canadian father and an Israeli mother. Victor's parents separated when he was a young child. He was raised in both Canada and Israel as a Zionist. When he was eighteen, he joined the Israeli army where he served for three years in the military police as an officer. After his release from the army in November 1971, he returned to Canada, but after five years he returned to Israel, in May 1977, and joined the navy (he served in submarines). In April 1979, while still in the Israeli navy, the Israeli secret service, the Mossad, initiated an interview with him to determine whether he was interested in joining its ranks. Victor was indeed interested. The process was long, and the April 1979 interview was just the beginning. In 1981 he left the navy and tried to start a business as a graphic artist. The business was not very successful. In October 1982, the Mossad contacted him again, and more interviewing followed. He passed the entry examination, and in February 1984 he began his career with the Mossad. For two years he was trained for, and eventually participated in, an operation that eventually failed (March 1986). Consequently, he was fired.[61] He left Israel and eventually settled in Canada with his wife, Bella, and two daughters.

It is difficult to know what exactly drove Victor to his next act—his hurt feelings from being fired from the Mossad, or as he likes to put it, his concern for Israel. In any event, he decided to write a book spelling out everything he knew about the Mossad. He did that with the aid of a professional journalist, Clair Hoy, and in 1990 the Toronto-based publishing house, Stoddart, published their book, *By Way of Deception: A Devastating Insider's Portrait of the Mossad*, with Hoy as the first author. The book is, indeed, a pretty devastating critique of the Mossad from a knowledgeable insider. Israel's attempts to prevent the publication of the book failed. Although there are quite a few books on the Israeli Mossad (including some by one of its legendary commanders—Isser Harel), Ostrovsky's book is different. Unlike other books, it attempts to hide nothing. It exposes the structure of the Mossad, the names of units, commanders, operatives, modes of recruitment and training, as well as modes of operation. It appears to be a very accurate, reliable, and believable book. Indeed, at a price of $26.95 Canadian, it must have been considered an almost free gift by any of Israel's enemies. By publishing this book and spilling out his knowledge, Ostrovsky violated his oath and agreement to the Mossad to keep secret the knowledge he gained from Mossad. That meant that a member of the group violated the trust in him and his loyalty by providing classified information in a discrediting way to whoever could afford the price of the book. Not surprisingly, the book sold very well, thus providing Ostrovsky a comfortable existence. There can be little doubt that Ostrovsky is considered a bona fide traitor by many Israelis.

The Assassination of Yitzhak Rabin (November 4, 1995)

The reason for delving into this case is that Rabin was defined by his assassin (and not only by him) as a traitor.[62] Israelis and Palestinians have been engaged in a bitter and bloody conflict for many years. Israeli Jews who tend to accept at least some of the moral arguments made by the Palestinians (typically found in the so-called Israeli left) run a serious risk of being referred to as "traitors" by other Israeli Jews (typically from the so-called Israeli right, or Israeli religious right). The main reason is that in a conflict situation, the issues of trust and loyalty are seen as polar and contradictory. Such questions as, "Are you with us or against us?" and "Can we trust you?" become crucial. These questions are interpreted to mean whether a person can be trusted to identify with the interests of a specific ethnic or religious group in a way that the majority of (or powerful) members in that group see as legitimate. Such a conflict raises the possibility for different people to define interests and loyalties in different ways and claim loyalty to and trust in altogether different sets of values, for example, those promoting peace and/or liberal secularism versus continued conflict and/or conservative orthodox religious interpretation of Judaism. This conflict spawned great debate regarding the nature of treason, and the assassination of Israeli prime minister Yitzhak Rabin occurred in precisely this context.

As in other cases of assassination by Jews, the killing of Rabin had a strong political-ideological background.[63] Rabin was killed because of his moral political position, his power, and his acts. This assassination was committed with a carefully premeditated intention and not out of any momentary rage. Assassinating Rabin was thus the end product of a long process that Yigael Amir, the murderer, was going through. This process not only provided the context within which Amir was persuaded that Rabin had to be killed, but it was also the context that provided Amir with the rhetoric of justification that Amir was to use. As in other similar cases, this assassination was committed by an individual belonging to the same ethnic, or cultural, group as that of the assassin, that is, a Jew killing another Jew.

Rabin's assassin was a member of a group. In this context, we must make a distinction between two groups. The first one is the small and immediate group within which Amir interacted intensely. Members of this immediate and intimate group were the ones with whom Amir shared his innermost thoughts, ideas, and intentions. This was a group of young, observant Orthodox Jews, with extreme militant right-wing ideology embedded within a politically conservative religious worldview. It was this group's feedback that Amir heard, and it was these people who provided Amir's moral, psychological, political, and practical support (for example, his brother or Margalit Har Shefi).

This rather small group was immersed in the subculture of a much larger political, religious, and ideological milieu from which this small group drew its inspiration, ideas, support, and the powerful rhetorical and psychological devices with which it interpreted and shaped its worldview in a specific way.

This rather large group itself was also part of a broader spectrum of groups and movements on the right side of the political map of Israel in 1995 that shared a common worldview of Israel. Their views were similar on important issues regarding the interpretation of Israel's political and ideological past and future, and many of them shared the same set of priorities regarding policy and ideology. The psychological trick that enabled so many members of these groups on the religious right-wing side of Israeli politics to socially construct Rabin, a democratically elected prime minister, as a "traitor," a "collaborator," or even a "terrorist" and a "killer" could be performed only within this context. That is, the political steps that Rabin and his government took in a courageous and risky attempt to reach a political settlement with the Palestinians were not at all liked by these members, who preferred to define this as "treason." One cannot, and should not, avoid stating that a very similar social dynamic was operating in another famous case of assassination, that of Dr. Israel (Rudolf) Kasztner, discussed earlier.

As in other cases of Jews assassinating other Jews, Yitzhak Rabin, along with the ministers in his government, was exposed—for a very long period of time—to unrestricted, inflexible, and constant instigation from many elements in the Israeli right. This campaign was focused on constructing Rabin as a genuine traitor. These elements used a campaign of vile propaganda that was meant to destabilize and delegitimize a freely and democratically elected government, and much of their deceitful propaganda was personally directed at Rabin. Rabin was presented as a traitor and a collaborator with the Palestinians, and threats were made that in due time he would be judged a criminal, much like other well-known traitors, such as Vidkun Quisling, Lord Haw-Haw, and others who were put on trial and executed. Rabin's government was portrayed as the Judenrat, and he and his ministers were compared to the Vichy government. The rhetoric used was cynical, emotional, poisonous, and sophisticated and it created a depressing atmosphere of hatred, of verbal (and nonverbal) violence and abuse. In such an atmosphere, and in the eyes of many people, Rabin was seen as stigmatized, deviant, and estranged. In other words, he became the "other," external to the group. A danger to the group. In fact, surveys and polls made before the assassination showed that his popularity had declined very significantly. Simple, superficial, and deceitful slogans, whose explicit goal was the delegitimization of Rabin and his government, appeared on houses, on bumper stickers, in newspapers, and at crossroads. When individuals from the left (for example, from the Peace Now movement) tried to stage counter-demonstrations, they were cursed at, spit on, and were frequently severely beaten by hooligans from the right.[64]

Two illustrations epitomize the situation. A few weeks before Rabin's assassination, some leaders from the Israeli right staged a demonstration in downtown Jerusalem (Zion square), and the head of the right-wing opposition, Mr. Benyamin Netanyahu, made a speech. During that event, some members of the right put up a very big photo-montage (clearly visible in televised reports of that event) where one could easily see Rabin in a Nazi military uniform (either S.S. or Gestapo). The size of this abomination is indeed incredible. That any Jew could even think about, much less so do, something like this is instructive. The second illustration is a testimony to the media by Leah Rabin after the assassination. Leah told reporters that sometime before the assassination she returned home. As happened before, demonstrators from the right staged a demonstration in front of her house, cursing her and her husband. However, the "new" element in this particular demonstration was that some demonstrators threatened that after the elections, she and Yitzhak would be put on trial "like Mussolini and his mistress" after the end of World War II. To those of us who need a reminder, let me point out that sixty-two-year-old Benito

Mussolini, Italy's fascist dictator since 1922, and his young mistress, Clara Petacci (twenty-five years old), were caught by partisan forces near Lake Como on April 27, 1945. They were court-martialed and shot the next day, together with sixteen other fascist leaders. On April 29, their bodies— hanging by the heels—were displayed in Milan.[65] These two associations (as well as those made to Quisling, Lord Haw-Haw, and others) were made in the most brutal way possible, as if there was anything there at all which made these comparisons viable. Thus, these hate crimes, preceding the actual assassination, turned Rabin—in the minds of many Israelis— into a traitor to his people, a collaborator, and a stranger. This campaign of instigation and vilification—as in other cases—created the necessary social and psychological background required for the assassination.

It is well worth noting that the word "instigation" need not be interpreted in its narrow or technical sense. The phenomenon of instigation against Rabin was much broader. It involved a very different political and ideological worldview than the one held by Rabin. This worldview provided the analytical framework within which the translation and creation of the concrete expressions of instigation and hatred were made meaningful.

Furthermore, Amir was an observant Orthodox Jew, who chose to study at the only religious (Orthodox) university in Israel (Bar Illan) and identified himself with the Israeli right. His act of assassination brought into focus a possible theocratic justification for the assassination. That a religious Jew, identified with the right, assassinated a secular Jew, from the left, could hardly have escaped attention. Moreover, Amir stated that he received religious justification for his act. The works of Shteinberg (1996) and Efendowitz (1997) point out the religious context of the assassination, with Efendowitz noting that *the* major lesson from the assassination was that its major motive was religious.

This is the place to note that elements in the Jewish Israeli right have no monopoly, or exclusive rights, over campaigns of instigation and hatred like those preceding the assassination of Rabin. In other historical periods, the direction of hatred and instigation was reversed.[66] However, since at least the early 1980s, the ideological campaign of instigation, delegitimization, and hatred of elements in the Jewish Israeli right (many of whom are Orthodox Jews) against the left (many of whom are secular) was a clear background for a number of acts of terror. Let me give just a few illustrations.

On the evening of February 10, 1983, during a demonstration of the Peace Now movement, a hand grenade was thrown into the crowd and exploded. Ten demonstrators were wounded and Emile Greenzweig, thirty-three years old, was killed. Yonah Avrushmi was accused and found guilty of murdering Greenzweig. On October 28, 1984, a nineteen-year-old AWOL soldier, David Ben-Shimol, fired a stolen "Lau" antitank guided missile into an Arab bus in Jerusalem, near the Cinematheque. One Arab was killed, and ten others were wounded. On April 22, 1985, a group of three Jews—Danny Eisenman (twenty-seven years old), Gil Fux (twenty-one years old), and Michal Hallel (twenty-five years old)—murdered an Arab taxicab driver, Hamis Tutanji (thirty-two years old), in revenge for an Arab terrorist act of murdering a Jewish taxicab driver—David Caspi—a few days earlier. In February 1994, Dr. Baruch Goldstein, a physician, entered the tomb of the fathers ("Me'arat Hamachpela," in Hebrew) in Hebron, a holy place for Jews and Arabs, with an M-16 automatic rifle, and opened fire on Moslem worshipers. Twenty-nine Arabs were killed, and 125 wounded. In May 18, 1995, Haniel Koren, a twenty-two-year-old soldier, entered a church in Jerusalem, poured turpentine and tried to set the place on fire. On May 21, he entered a church in Jaffo and opened fire. Luckily, in both cases no one was injured. Although Koren stated that the reasons for his acts were "religious," it was Avrushmi who stated clearly that the reason for his act was the instigation he was exposed to.

There can hardly be a doubt that those committing the above-mentioned acts of terror were affected by the atmosphere of hatred created by the propaganda and instigation coming from elements in the right, which tended to describe anything with which they disagreed as "betrayal" or "treasonous." Thus, members of Peace Now were defined as "traitors." This atmosphere of intolerance and hatred served as the background for Yigael Amir's assassination of Rabin.

The assassin's motivation was to stop the peace process in which Rabin was involved and to avenge Rabin's betrayal, as seen from the assassin's right-wing religious Orthodox worldview. From the assassin's point of view, his murderous act was politically and ideologically justified. This justification was established within the social network in which he lived and functioned, and which supported him. These two groups, the general and the specific concrete, formed the social structures that provided the assassin the psychological and rhetorical devices that not only helped him orient himself to the act but also gave him the motivation and the will to commit this act of political murder.

In this respect, the similarity between the assassination of Yitzhak Rabin in 1995 and the murder of Haim Arlosoroff in 1933 is striking.[67] In both cases, the murder exposed the deep and hateful cleavages dividing the right and the left in Jewish Israeli society. In both cases, the murder became the focal point for the political and ideological breaking of different population groups. Heilbruner (1995) points out the similarities between the assassination of Rabin and the atmosphere of extreme instigation and accusations of betrayal by the extreme right in Germany, which led to the assassination of Walther Rathenau, the German foreign minister, on June 24, 1922.

As in other cases of political assassination, and certainly from the point of view of the assassin and those who support or identify with him, it can be claimed that what is operative here is an alternative system of justice. The assassin feels that he cannot get political justice for a prime minister whom he views as a traitor. He thus resorts to assassination in order to achieve justice. Furthermore, the violence of the act calls attention to his political, religious, and ideological views. In just this manner, Prime Minister Rabin, not protected as he should have been, was shot and killed by Amir on Saturday evening, November 4, 1995, in Tel Aviv.

Concluding Discussion

In some respects, the inspiration for writing this chapter came from such previous works as those by Archer (1971), O'Toole (1991), and Weyl (1950). The idea of looking at one culture, historically, and examining cases of betrayal and treason there is interesting and suggestive. It allows an in-depth view of the different cases and, perhaps, opens an opportunity for making some cultural generalizations.

The first observation that needs to be made is that, like other cultures, both Judaism and Israel have their share of traitors. In this respect, Judaism does not present a different case than other cultures. It is certainly not free of traitors. This observation, coupled with the discussion about infidelity, reinforces the conclusion that betrayal is not a dramatically rare event. On the contrary, it is nearly an everyday, almost routine event.

Second, in all the cases we examined, the issue of crossing the boundaries of symbolic moral universes on issues of trust and loyalty was the core structural issue that determined the construction of the relevant individuals as traitors. That was clear, case by case.

Third, examining the cases revealed the difference between the image of an individual as a traitor and the reality behind it. In each of these cases, the politics of identity and the context played a major role. The cases of Josephus Flavius and Yochanan Ben-Zakkai show how two contemporaries coped with a similar context, and with similar choices; one kept his Jewish identity, whereas the other chose to transform. One has been constructed and commemorated as a hero, the other as a traitor. In a similar way, Amos Levinberg and Uri Illan both faced a difficult, torturous captivity. Whereas Illan chose not to reveal what he knew, Levinberg revealed everything he knew. Again, Illan is constructed as heroic, Levinberg as a traitor. The murders of De Hahn and Levi provide us with an excellent illustration for the cultural antagonism of conflicting identities. De Hahn represented everything the Hagana was against. Levi represented independence and the freedom to embrace a new identity that was supposed to emerge with the creation of a new Jewish state. Lehi's leaders could not accept it. The Judenrat is remembered as a treacherous organization. However, examining the context in which it functioned softens this image. There were several cases of assassination that resulted from the construction of the victims as traitors. Israel De Hahn, Yehuda Levi, Israel Kasztner, and Yitzhak Rabin were all killed because individuals and groups were convinced that they violated their loyalty and trust in such a profound manner that the only remedy was to kill them.[68] However, in each of these cases, a close examination reveals that the assassins were insensitive to complex situations and ignorant of the facts, not to mention lacking in compassion and mercy. In no case is this as clear as in the case of the unnecessary, unjustified, and hurried execution of Captain Meir Tubianski.

Fourth, in this chapter we examined some organizations that were defined as treacherous—the *Judenrat* and *Derech Hanitzotz*. One can add to this the small groups of activists that were behind the treachery of Udi Adiv and Dan Vered, as well as the ones behind the assassinations of Kasztner and Rabin. This is an interesting phenomenon because it implies that cultures may have organizations whose goal is to violate the trust and loyalty of the mainstream morality of these cultures, by presenting and reinforcing a different morality. There is one major difference between the Judenrat and the other organizations, and it has to do with context and choices. Unlike membership in the other organizations, the membership of the Judenrat was under conditions of extreme stress and threat, and joining the organization was not made from a stand of full free will and choice. Moreover, the choice and consent of many individuals who served in the Judenrats were not fully informed regarding the real intentions of the Nazis. However, the common denominator of these organizations is that their actions were defined as treacherous. One needs to remember though that in all these cases, the construction of these organizations as inseminators of betrayal is not universally shared.

The more general conclusion is that it may not be uncommon to find an ideological group behind the traitors. To counterbalance the possible existence of a fifth column, a cold war, or espionage, nations have created state-sponsored organizations that recruit, operate, and support traitors. The case of the Israeli-operated spy (traitor to the United States) Jonathan Pollard is a good example.

Fifth, examining the personal motivation of traitors has provided some interesting clues. The historical context played a major part in the traitors' choice of actions and their direction (for example, Levinberg, Ostrovsky). Traitors also used historical context to justify their acts.

Finally, although application of the universal structure of betrayal—that is, the violation of trust and loyalty—enabled us to explain the different cases presented in this chapter, it was morality that was crucial in constructing the cases as betrayals. Without morality as a criterion, no meaningful interpretation could have been accomplished.

Conclusion

Was Delilah a traitor? Can such figures as Quisling, Vlasov, Benedict Arnold, Judas, Malinche, Lord Haw-Haw, Ezra Pound, Stauffenberg, Edward VIII, Josephus, Pollard, and Kasztner be all lumped together in one category as traitors? If so, in what sense?

This book was never intended to be a comprehensive encyclopedia of betrayal. Its major purpose was to develop a conceptualizing apparatus that would help us better understand the nature of betrayal. Hopefully, this goal has been achieved. However, writing or reading a dry document, highly abstracted, about betrayal is a punishment undeserved by anyone. Thus, throughout the book, we examined numerous cases, some very detailed, of betrayal. All these individual real-life stories helped us to weave our more general sociological treatise on betrayal.

Throughout this book we examined a great number of cases involving various forms and manifestations of betrayal. We saw that it is possible to classify many of the cases into analytical categories. Examining all these cases, one needs to ask, When is the likelihood of invoking the label "traitor" increased? Although this label is context and situation dependent, it also has a social structure. This structure emerges when we examine carefully the type of violations that invoke this term. This examination reveals that the probability of invoking this term is increased significantly whenever specific boundaries of symbolic moral universes are crossed.

The method we used consisted of examining diverse behaviors, in different time periods and cultures, trying to crystallize the common analytical core behind the different empirical manifestations of betrayal without losing the cultural mosaic itself. This method involves two interesting and contradictory processes. On the one hand, it decontextualizes the cases by lumping so many cases and contexts together. On the other hand, it enhances the importance of context by examining the specific content that elicits the societal response of "traitor" or the more specific form referred to as "treason."

Our examination of the behaviors of a considerable number of individuals and groups, in different time periods and cultures, reveals that the varieties of the behaviors that are viewed as betrayal provide a fascinating, rich, and stimulating mosaic. This variety has a common core that, at the minimal level, can be characterized as follows. Betrayal is a behavior that, first of all, involves a social interaction, presumed or directly observed, of individuals who are perceived to share the same cultural heritage and similar cultural goals.

In addition, there are some main elements that must be present to invoke the term "traitor." To begin with, attribution of betrayal occurs when two major violations of expectations occur: violation of trust and violation of loyalty. These violations by an in-group member typically invoke the accusation of the deviant violator as a traitor. The more serious and threatening these violations are perceived to be, the higher the likelihood of invoking the label. When no such violations exist, the charge of betrayal is weakened considerably. For example, a spy who pretends to be someone he or she is not can hardly be accused of "betraying" a collective he never belonged to. Third, betrayal means that a person from the in-group defaults on his or her moral obligations and commitments to the group and crosses the boundaries of the group or dyad. In other words, some actual turncoating must take place in addition to the aforementioned violations. This added element inevitably increases the probability of finding the person to be a traitor. Finally, when violations of trust and loyalty occur, accompanied by turncoating and committed in stealth or secrecy, the label of "traitor" is practically unavoidable. In such cases, the term "traitor" is used regardless of the power configuration. Interestingly enough, these cases are mostly concentrated in the interpersonal level. Such actions as those committed by strike violators and police informers also tend to fall in this category.

Our examination of the different forms of betrayal makes one conclusion very clear. Betrayal is not a rare occurrence. It takes place in numerous areas of our life, almost on a daily basis. Betrayal, in other words, is quite prevalent; most of us have experienced at least one form of it, most likely more than once.

Analytically speaking, although betrayal is a multidimensional phenomenon, the two most crucial variables that distinguish betrayal from other forms of human behavior are violations of trust and loyalty. However, these two variables are not discrete but continuous. Betrayal involves behaviors that are spread on a qualitative spectrum, varying in terms of perceived severity.

One of the important distinctions is whether the betrayal is personal or collective. Within these two types, we have even finer distinctions. For example, people seem to differentiate between a "one-night stand" and a long-lasting affair. Moreover, a further distinction within a "one-night stand" concerns the motivation and context of the act, for example, whether money was used to obtain sex. If we are examining betrayal on the collective level, then questions of motivation, context (for example, industrial espionage in peacetime versus military espionage in wartime), and inflicted damage become crucial.

For both types of betrayal—personal and collective—the issue of stealth or open behavior is another significant variable. One reason why this distinction is so important is that violating trust and loyalty in secrecy typically involves deceit. Thus, issues of dishonesty, pretense, lying, and making other people believe in a false reality come into play.

Another dimension involves threat potential. When a large organization such as a state is being threatened by a structural violation of trust and loyalty (for example, treason), especially during periods of conflict, its reaction will be severe. Betrayal on the interpersonal level (for example, infidelity) also typically yields strong emotional reactions, as identities are being seriously challenged and threatened.

To summarize, "traitor" is a general name referring to an individual who violates trust and loyalty in a variety of circumstances and contexts. Traitors can be found in interpersonal, group, organizational, or national contexts. The term "traitor" refers to a person who is perceived to be a bona fide member of the same collective, or group, as those whose trust and loyalty the traitor compromises. That is, a strong assumption about a common and shared cultural heritage (past, present, future, common goals, language, values, norms, worldviews) exists between the traitor and the betrayed. Added to this basic structure of violation are issues that can solidify, or weaken, the application of the term "traitor" in specific cases. These issues include the following: Were the violations committed in secret? Were the victims of the violations specific individuals, groups, organizations, or countries? Did the violations involve deception? Was the threat potential of the violation large or small? Moreover, the nature and circumstances of betrayals have been used to determine the proper societal reactions to such actions.

Following the tradition of contextual constructionism, we first established the facts and the characterization of betrayal. Once we exposed the universal structure underlying betrayal, we could move on to the construction. It became clear that although the universal structure of violations could be rather easily identified in each case we discussed, there were several other important related issues. These issues are relevant to the construction of the term "traitor" and its application in different contexts. First and foremost is the issue of morality.

Basic questions of boundaries and power lie at the heart of betrayal. When the term "betrayal" is invoked, the issue of moral boundaries is not

far behind. The main reason is that issues of loyalty and trust are fundamental moral issues. Facing these issues requires making decisions regarding loyalty and solving similar questions regarding trust. In each
case discussed in this book, issues of morality determine the ethical judgment of the case in question.

Morality, however, like deviance, is highly influenced by power. Specific moral claims, and the consequent social reactions to those claims, de-
pend on power and its usage. Invoking the possibility of betrayal thus always involves examining challenges to both morality and power.
Moreover, when secrecy is involved in the betrayal, an element of deceit
is added to the mix, and thus an additional moral issue compounds an already complex situation. Power relations are also magnified here, as the
issue of who has the power to deceive who and why is at the forefront as
well. Obviously, one result of this is that invoking and validating the existence of betrayal almost guarantees a harsh societal response.

A distinction between the universal social structure of betrayal and its
specific moral content was made throughout the book. Discussing moral
issues requires paying some attention to those making the moral diag-
noses, including the author of this book. Moreover, these moral stands
gain importance because labeling any specific person as a traitor is—like
it or not—passing a moral judgment. Of course, it is irresponsible to make
overgeneralizing statements. For example, although it is easy to determine whether an act of betrayal was committed on the personal level or
on the collective level, punishment is typically much more severe for betrayal on the collective, or national, level. If we confine ourselves just to
the issue of treason, and we remind ourselves of such individuals as
Quisling, Lord Haw-Haw, Ezra Pound, and Malinche, it may become
quite difficult to decide who was a bona fide traitor and who or what they
betrayed. A person with a Nazi worldview would definitely not view
Quisling or Lord Haw-Haw as traitors. To my mind, the issue of morality
and power is indeed crucial.

Black's theory of social control is appropriate here, at least from the
point of view of those labeled "traitors."[1] Black bases his approach on the
concept of "self-help criminal justice." He argues that the main reason
that offenders involve themselves in deviant and criminal behavior is not
that they want to violate norms or laws. Rather, these offenders feel that
they achieve justice by breaking some rules. According to Black, these deviants are involved in a process of exercising social control either by forcing the culture in which they live to recognize their claims or by getting
justice for what they define as their own cause. From this intriguing perspective, traitors can indeed be viewed as being involved in the pursuit of
"justice"; however, it is "justice" according to their own criteria.

There is another major issue involved here, and that is the issue of the type of identities that emerge from betrayal. C. Wright Mills alerts us to the fact that personal biographies, and consequently identities, are linked intimately to social and historical processes. Nowhere is this process clearer than in the cases of treason. Traitors facing competing symbolic moral universes have to make a choice. Such a choice can make them heroes for one universe but despised and detested traitors for another. Consider individuals such as Malinche, John André, Nathan Hale, and a large number of others. Moreover, the very selection of specified cases as traitors reflects a moral choice that accepts the construction of particular individuals as traitors as opposed to heroes. We live within cultures, and as Wright Mills points out, we cannot escape the cultural context. However, we need to be aware of this, so that we can develop a better understanding of betrayal. The identities that various traitors embraced, and those given them after the fact, were all embedded in specific political and, even much more so, moral contexts.

This observation necessarily brings me to the next point, which involves masks and reality. In an interesting fashion, this also connects us to contextual constructionism. Once we have ascertained the basic facts of the case, we can unfold the social (and moral) construction of betrayal. Then we can contrast the reality with the construction. In fact, we repeated this exercise numerous times throughout our analysis. Although it is an almost classical exercise in contextual constructionism, it is also an exercise in debunking and tends to color research with a subversive hue, which it should.

The identities of traitors are thus a reflection of the political and social contexts in which they live and function. In this sense, one can ask, To what degree are these identities genuine? Are they part of the empirical and factual substratum or are they socially and morally constructed? In the context of World War II, these questions help us draw a line between genuine collaborators and true believers (for example, Quisling, Seyss-Inquart, Degrelle, Vlasov, and Joyce) and opportunistic collaborators, faking loyalty and trust. The issue of fact versus construction, truth versus falsehood, and empirical versus mythical is thus cutting across not only the macro social and cultural level but also the level of individual identities. This conclusion stems not only from C. Wright Mills's formulations but also from symbolic interaction. That, perhaps, should not really surprise us. Contextual constructionism is grounded rather strongly in symbolic interaction.

Deviance (and crime), as argued elsewhere, needs to be understood within central cultural contexts.[2] Indeed, betrayal, as a form of deviance, is intimately connected to both loyalty and trust and to membership in groups. This means that issues of betrayal always involve central processes of change and stability in the moral and social boundaries of collectives of people and hence in their sense of belonging and identity. It is no wonder then that issues involving betrayal are often emotionally explosive and typically give rise to moralistic discourses.

Treason, perhaps not surprisingly, is the most complex betrayal. When all the major elements that define betrayal exist (violations of trust and loyalty by a member of the in-group, secrecy, and turncoating), the likelihood for a consensual definition of betrayal is rather high. When the element of stealth disappears, and individuals who are branded as traitors are simply those with different political views, the power configurations play a major part, and the nature of "treason" becomes problematic and debatable (for example, Quisling, Lord Haw-Haw, Pétain, Vlasov, Pound, and Malinche). If and when such "traitors" are brought to trial, one can expect a harsh sentence, but one can also expect that the accused will not accept the verdict as valid. Moreover, the issue of treason will always elicit a debate regarding the proper dividing line between legitimate dissent and violation of trust and loyalty or even giving aid and comfort to the enemy. What exacerbates this problem these days is that the boundaries between "friend" and "enemy" may be blurring, as even "the other" may be difficult to discern. Postmodernism, by nature, blurs the boundaries between diverse symbolic moral universes, and hence sharp distinctions may become difficult to maintain.

The various definitional elements presented here can be used to delineate the moral boundaries between different forms and manifestations of betrayal. The term "betrayal" refers to a large number of types and categories representing a wide spectrum. Although there is a universal social structure behind these different manifestations, the specific content of different types of betrayal needs to be assessed in different ways. I hope that we now possess the analytical tools for conceptualizing this fascinating form of human behavior in a way that is true to its rich and complex nature.

Notes

Chapter 1

1. See short report in *Newsweek*, December 29, 1996, p. 22, and a review of the case by Ronen Bergman in *Ha'aretz's* supplement, December 11, 1998, pp. 59–62. The charge Gil faced in court was espionage related and dealt with individuals who give information that is meant to harm and damage the state's security. On the verdict, see *Ma'ariv*, March 25, 1999, pp. 12–13; and *Yediot Aharonot*, same date, p. 19.

2. See Black and Morris 1991:400–409; Gutman 1995; Rachum 1990; and Raviv and Melman 1990:278–300.

3. See Ben-Yehuda 1985; and Zerubavel 1991.

4. See Ben-Yehuda 1985, 1989.

5. Landa 1994; Fukuyama 1995; Eisenstadt and Roniger 1984; and Seligman 1997 examine these issues.

6. See Goode and Ben-Yehuda 1994 on moral panics. In a way, this interpretation can also help us understand the modern quest for religion and the revival of interest in religions, new and old, as well as in magical and fantasy solutions. The major failure here is the liberals' failure to educate people to cope and live with empirical and spiritual uncertainties.

7. See Fletcher's intriguing 1993 work.

8. See Polmar and Allen 1997:573–574; Gilling and McKnight 1995; and Toscano 1990. See also *Yediot Aharonot*, March 13, p. 5. A group of British and other people created a support group for him, demanding, among other things, that he be treated as any other prisoner; see *Ha'aretz*, April 10, 1998, p. B3; and *Tel Aviv*, September 27, 1996, pp. 53–58. In 1998, this group (the Israeli committee for Mordechai Va'anunu and for a Middle East free from atomic, biological, and chemical weapons) published a book expressing its views, *Va'anunu and the Bomb* (in Hebrew).

9. See *Ha'aretz*, April 17, 1998, p. A8.

10. *Yediot Aharonot*, July 17, 1998, p. 2. See also Maron 1998a. For more details, see *Yediot Aharonot*, November 24, 1999, pp. 1–11.

11. *Ma'ariv*, July 17, 1998, p. 3. Manbar's accounts received wide publicity in October 1998, when Illana Dayan's TV Channel 2 program "FACT" provided a forty-eight minute documentary on this affair. It is worth noting that another Israeli—Hertzel Rad—was found guilty and convicted in 1995 on charges of espionage for Iran, too. He was sentenced to six years in prison, half of which were conditional. He was released from prison in March 1997.

12. See Amit 1992:372–409.

13. Judges, chapters 13–16. See also Bower 1990:2–3; and Seth 1972:150–153.

14. Judges, chapters 4–5; see also Heaps 1969:39–42.

15. See report in *Newsweek*, vol. 128, no. 12 (September 16, 1996), pp. 36–37.

16. For example, see *Evening Standard*, September 17, 1996, front page.

17. For example, Cardinal Winning, leader of the Roman Catholic Church in Scotland.

18. See *Evening Standard*, September 20, 1996, pp. 1, 5.

19. The newspaper paid the couple £15,000 (equivalent, at that time, to about US $23,000). The interview was quoted widely by the BBC, too.

20. For short summaries see the September 30, 1996, issues of *Time*, p. 24, and *Newsweek*, p. 6.

21. See *Evening Standard*, October 8, 1996, and the BBC1 18:00 news on that day, and *The Times*, October 9, 1996, p. 10.

22. *Evening Standard*, July 2, 1997, p. 4. See also Ku 1998.

Chapter 2

1. Granting an illegal pass to a ship—the *Charming Nancy*.

2. Brandt 1994:188–189.

3. See Polmar and Allen 1997:32.

4. Lentz 1988:xvii; and Polmar and Allen 1997:24.

5. There are numerous works about Benedict Arnold. See Arnold 1979; Bakeless 1998; Boylan 1973; Decker 1932; Flexner 1991; O'Toole 1991:55–59; Polmar and Allen 1997:32; Randall 1990; Sellers 1930; Seth 1972:28–32; Wallace 1954, 1978; and Weyl 1950:44–59. My favorite two items are Brandt's (1994) excellent and very well-written account and Ducharme and Fine's (1995) critically penetrating analysis of the images of Benedict Arnold.

6. Lentz 1988:xvii; O'Toole 1991:22–24; Polmar and Allen 1997:250; and Seth 1972:285–287. For a critical evaluation of Hale's mission, see Bakeless 1998:110–122.

Chapter 3

1. See the *Newsweek* issue of September 30, 1996, which was devoted to the general issue of infidelity. On adultery in China, see *Newsweek*, August 24, 1998, p. 24. Malaysia's punishment consists of six floggings, three years in prison, or a fine of around $1,190. Malaysia utilizes "Modesty Guards," whose job is to find people who are involved in illegal sex in hotels and public parks. See *Yediot Aharonot*, "24 Hours," supplement, August 23, 1998, p. 6.

2. For example, see Lawson 1988.

3. See Norton and Hastings 1997.

4. *Newsweek*, September 30, 1996, p. 40.

5. This case is described in Chapter 1.

6. See *Newsweek*, September 30, 1996, p. 38.

7. Ibid., p. 40.

8. Ibid.

9. Chapter 10, pp. 287–307.

10. See also Ofir-Shacham 1998.

11. Norton and Hastings 1997.

12. Shenhar 1998. See also Muhlbauer and Zemach 1991:138–141; Nardi 1996:42–45; and Shemer 1992:266–267.

13. Horowitz and Ben-Arie 1998:14; and Weitz 1998. See also contemporary newspaper coverage, for example, *Yediot Aharonot*, January 15 and 17, 1993; in both cases coverage begins on front page.

14. See *Yediot Aharonot*, "24 Hours," supplement, August 23, 1998, p. 6.

15. For a short review of an international list of infidelities and adulteries by celebrities, see Kobi 1998.

16. See *The Times*, October 9, 1996, front page.

17. See *Newsweek*, December 8, 1997, p. 22.

18. Horowitz and Ben-Arie 1998:14.

19. See *Ma'ariv*, October 11, 1996, magazine *Weekend*, pp. 30–31; and Horowitz and Ben-Arie 1998.

20. See *Newsweek*, August 20, 1998, pp. 12–21, 25–39.

21. July 3, 1997, p. 8.

22. "Operation Drumbeat," which began in January 1942; see Blair 1996:508–526; Gannon 1990; and Hickam 1989.

23. See Blair 1996:559.

24. See Volkman 1994:56–80.

25. Dobson and Payne 1986:288–289; and Polmar and Allen 1997:158, 374, 508.

26. Aldrich worked in CIA headquarters. In more than a decade of treacherous activity, he betrayed at least eleven CIA agents to the Soviets, of which at least four were executed (Richelson 1995:422).

27. Polmar and Allen 1997:21–22, 443–444.

28. Alias Walter G. Krivitsky, born 1898. See Deacon 1987:202–203; Dobson and Payne 1986:175–176; and Polmar and Allen 1997:318.

29. Volkman 1994:77.

30. Lentz 1988:79; and Polmar and Allen 1997:319.

31. Polmar and Allen 1997:107.

32. Volkman 1994:77.

33. See also Bower 1990:60–67; Friedrich 1972:100–103; and Richelson 1995: 94–96.

34. For example, see Richelson 1995:95; Smith 1976; Weinstein 1978; and Weinstein and Vassiliev 1999.

35. See Polmar and Allen 1997:263; and Scott 1996.

36. Scott 1996:31.

37. Ibid.

38. Polmar and Allen 1997:263, 575–578; and Richelson 1995:224–225. For more on Venona, see Haynes and Klehr 1999.

39. Polmar and Allen 1997:263.

40. Scott 1996:31.

41. See also Friedrich 1972:103–104; and Weyl 1950:424–441 for shorter reviews.

42. In its most intense form, this war lasted from the early 1950s to the late 1980s, a period of about forty years. See Whitcomb 1998. See also Weinstein and Vassiliev 1999; and Friedman 2000.

43. See Deacon 1987:301–302; and Polmar and Allen 1997:239.

44. Penkovsky 1965; Polmar and Allen 1997:429–431; Richelson 1995:274–282; and Volkman 1994:23–30.

45. Polmar and Allen 1997:239.

46. *The Report of the Royal Commission*, 1946:11.

47. See Sawatsky 1984 (who conveys how difficult it was to cope with Gouzenko); and Seth 1972:270–278.

48. See Deacon 1987:316–317; Polmar and Allen 1997:270–272; and Wise 1988.

49. See Bower 1990:141–151; King 1989; Richelson 1995:91–94; and Sinclair 1986 for the political and academic (as well as sexual) contextualization of campus cultures in which this ring developed. See also Winks's 1987 more general approach.

50. Deacon 1987:334–336; Dobson and Payne 1986:205–208; and Polmar and Allen 1997:347–349.

51. Dobson and Payne 1986:41–44; and Polmar and Allen 1997:90–91.

52. Costello 1988; Penrose and Freeman 1986; Polmar and Allen 1997:77–78; and Volkman 1994:17–22.

53. Also known as the "third man," see Page, Leitch, and Knightley 1969; Philby 1969; and Volkman 1994:8–16.

54. Sometimes referred to as the "fifth man"; Dobson and Payne 1986:46–47; Polmar and Allen 1997:97; and Richelson 1995:93–94, 136, 185.

55. Dobson and Payne 1986:217–220; Polmar and Allen 1997:358–359; and Seth 1972:388–391.

56. Dobson and Payne 1986:193–194; and Polmar and Allen 1997:341.

57. He also had an affair with Maclean's wife—Melinda—which began in 1964.

58. Polmar and Allen 1997:433–436.

59. *Newsweek*, September 8, 1997, p. 42.

60. See also Bulloch 1966:158–168; and Pincher 1987:197–224.

61. Dear and Foot 1995:297.

62. There are several books and studies written about this affair. For concise accounts, see Gutman 1995:265–278; Melman and Raviv 1989:68–70; and Schiff and Haber 1976:400–402.

63. For example, see Bearse and Read 1991; Polmar and Allen 1997:309–310; Volkman 1994:77; and Selwyn 1987:115–119.

64. Polmar and Allen 1997:65–66, as well as Seth 1972:317–319, provide good summaries. There are several spying episodes in the Bible. One is about Joseph's brothers, who say that they came to Egypt to search for food, but Joseph accuses them of being spies. A second episode involves a command by the Almighty to Moses to send spies into Canaan. Moses sends twelve spies and when they return after spending forty days on their mission, their reports are mixed and even contradictory. Only two of the spies recommend an invasion; the rest warn of big troubles ahead. The Israelites panic, but the Almighty, who feels that this panic reaction indicates little faith in Him, punishes them by keeping them from the

Promised Land for forty years. A third episode involves Joshua sending two spies to Jericho. There, the spies, who practice the world's second-oldest profession, meet Rahab, a practitioner of the world's oldest profession. She manages to save the spies from an informer working for the king of Jericho. During the Israelites' successful attack and conquest of Jericho, Rahab's household is spared. Surely these stories have some interesting lessons for today.

65. For example, Bower 1990:282–298; Howe 1986; and two fictional movies about her called *Mata Hari*, one made in 1932 (starring Greta Garbo in the title role) and one in 1985 (with Sylvia Kristel in the title role).

66. "Cicero," was the code name for Elyeza Bazna, who spied for the Nazis in the British embassy in Turkey in World War II; for short descriptions, see Deacon 1987:170; Polmar and Allen 1997:121; and Seth 1972:126–129.

67. For example, see Volkman 1994:260–280.

68. See Deacon 1987:96–97; Polmar and Allen 1997:161; and Seth 1972:143–149.

69. See Johnston 1998.

70. See Polmar and Allen 1997:442–443, for a short description of the case, and Vinitzky-Seroussi 1999 and Zelizer 1999 for an analysis of the public debate that followed and its implications. Hillel Cohen (1998) confronted Pollard's lawyer, Lary Dav, with parts of the events described here. Dav's response was that Pollard never contacted the South African embassy and never received large sums of money. Dav's version is that Pollard received a low salary, which, at its peak, reached no more than $1,500 a month and that his motivation was ideological. Dav also stated that he had heard about a secret Swiss bank account Pollard supposedly had, but neither he nor Pollard had ever seen it. Obviously, Dav's interest is in representing his client in the most positive light possible. For example, ideological motivation appears better than financial greed. Another spy for Israel, Icebrandt Smith (renamed Avner Shamir in Israel), who operated in Holland, was also caught, but unlike Pollard, he was allowed to leave the country and chose to move to Israel; see Melman 1998.

71. See Black and Morris 1991:226–229; Deacon 1977:79–91; Eisenberg, Dan, and Landau 1978:65–133; Melman and Raviv 1989:165–169; Polmar and Allen 1997:128; Raviv and Melman 1990:143–146; Segev 1986; and Steven 1980:199–206. Many sources couple the description of Eli Cohen's activities with those of another Israeli implanted spy, the German-born Israeli Wolfgang Lotz, who operated in Egypt under an assumed identity. Again, Lotz cannot be referred to as a traitor.

72. Black and Morris 1991:164. For more on Beer, see Beer 1956–1957, 1966 (written in prison and brought to press by Amikam Gurevitz); Black and Morris 1991:158–166; Harel 1987:93–168; Melman and Raviv 1989:122–125; Polmar and Allen 1997:54–55; and Raviv and Melman 1990:98–100. On the influence of the Beer case on an inner cultural dispute within Israel, see Cromer 1985.

73. See Raviv and Melman 1990:102–103.

74. Prange 1984; and Whymant 1996.

75. For example, see Codevilla 1992; Deacon 1987; Dobson and Payne 1986; Knightley 1986; Laqueur 1985; Polmar and Allen 1997; Richelson 1995; Sarbin, Carney, and Eoyang 1994; Seth 1972; Volkman 1994; and West 1993.

76. For example, see Stohl 1989.

77. *Abwehr* was the German military intelligence organization headed by Admiral Canaris from 1935; see Zentner and Bedurftig 1997:2–3. On the double-cross system, see Masterman 1972; and Polmar and Allen 1997:173–174.

78. I am deeply grateful to Joanna Michlic-Coren, who not only suggested this type of betrayal but read this section very carefully and made some very useful and constructive comments and suggestions.

79. See Noakes and Pridham 1988, vol. 3:667–705. On the Pact of Steel, see Toscano 1967.

80. See Laqueur 1976:135–139.

81. Heinz-Dietrich Lowe in Dear and Foot 1995:250. It is estimated that there were about 7,800,000 Soviet POWs, about 2,800,000 of whom died while in Nazi captivity; see Baudot et al. 1989:395–396.

82. For example, see Bethel 1995; and Tolstoy 1979.

83. See Kersten 1991; and Steinlauf 1997, ch. 3.

84. See report in *Ha'aretz*, June 3, 1998, p. B5, based on a report in the *Guardian* from May 25.

85. Robinson 1996:280–281.

86. For more on whistle-blowing, see Akerstrom 1991:43–51; Bok 1993; DeMaria 1992; Glazer and Glazer 1989; Greenberg and Baron 1997; Near and Miceli 1985, 1992, 1997; "Nice Guys Finish Last," a 1994, 55 minute television documentary produced and directed by Nicholas Adler and Caroline Sherwood, Australian Film Corporation and Titus Films; Miethe 1998; Robinson 1996:273–288.

87. Glazer and Glazer 1989:252–255.

88. For example, see *Ha'aretz*, January 23, 1996, p. A6.

89. *Ha'aretz*, November 11, 1995.

90. Some examples of the consequences of whistle-blowing in Israel include the following: (1) A tester in the ministry of transportation who warned that road tests of motorcyclists were faulty was fired (*Ha'aretz*, June 30, 1998); (2) An adviser to fire departments was fired after warning that many hospitals were dangerous firetraps (*Davar*, September 18, 1995); (3) A security officer who complained about fiscal mismanagement in the municipality of Lod was transferred to an inferior job (*Ha'aretz*, August 22, 1997); (4) A woman who exposed in public that vegetables were being falsely marketed as "organic" and that the marketing organization was deceiving the public was isolated and persecuted, along with members of her family (various reports in the press in the summer of 1997). The Ogen Association was established in Israel to help whistle-blowers. It was established by a woman who had exposed mismanagement and was then committed, wrongly, to a mental hospital, following a complaint by the organization that her behavior was erratic. Her suffering was so great that it propelled her into public efforts on behalf of whistle-blowers. For more on whistle-blowing in Israel, see Bar-Ulpan 1997; and Verner 1992.

91. Robinson 1996:274–275.

92. See Leach 1995:1.

93. Ibid.,2.

94. See Rolef 1988:130–131.

95. July 26, 1997, p. 4.

96. From the Canadian *The Globe and Mail*, August 15, 1997, p. A13.

97. Nettler (1982:50) is one of the few who include a discussion of conversion within the context of an interpretation of treason.

98. *The* (London) *Times,* July 6, 1996, pp. 1–2.

99. Abu-Tuema 1995:18.

100. Pincher 1987:127.

101. Gray 1994:147. Gray refers to Casement as a "traitor."

102. For short descriptions of the case, see *Encyclopedia Britannica*, 1980, *Micropaedia,* vol. 2, p. 608; Pincher 1987:xvi, 4, 108, 127; and Polmar and Allen 1997:103. For a longer account, see Gwynn 1931. Ingliss 1973 and Wharam 1995:156–165 focus on the trial. Allegations of homosexual behavior were involved in this case, too, and some accounts state that this may have created a prejudiced atmosphere against Casement.

103. Polmar and Allen 1997:103.

104. Geva's military and political superiors included the chief of staff, Rafael "Raful" Eitan, Minister of Defense Ariel Sharon, and Prime Minister Menachem Begin.

105. Schiff and Ya'ari 1984:264–266.

106. The dean of faculty was Professor Gershon Ben-Shachar (from the department of psychology). Departmental chief administrator was Mrs. Osnat ("Ossie") Ben-Shachar.

107. The president at that time was Professor Hanoch Gutfreund (from the department of physics).

108. Quoted in Archer 1971:62. See also Rosenbloom's 1998 work, which examines, among other issues, the effectiveness of strikebreakers. Rosenbloom's study is focused on the recruitment of strikebreaking labor from outside the striking group. His conclusion is that recruitment and usage of strikebreakers significantly impacted strike efforts in such sectors as the cotton textile industry, mining, iron and steel production, the cigar industry, and in the railroad industry.

109. This part is based on my 1993 book, *Political Assassinations by Jews: A Rhetorical Device for Justice* (Albany: State University of New York Press), pp. 26–30. Used with permission from SUNY Press.

110. See Rapoport 1971:3–4.

111. See Rapoport 1984; and Hurwood 1970:13–16.

112. For example, see Ben-Yehuda 1993:102–106; see Ben-Yehuda 1995 for summaries on the Sicarii and Masada.

113. For example, see Hodgson 1955; and Lewis 1967.

114. Lewis 1967:20.

115. For example, see Lewis 1967:12; Rapoport 1984; and Ford 1985:100–104.

116. Rapoport 1984.

117. For more on the Assassins, see Ford 1985:96–104; Franzius 1969; Hammer 1835; Hodgson 1955; Hurwood 1970:5–13; Lerner 1930; Lewis 1967; and Wilson 1975:15–301.

118. Rapoport 1971.

119. Or like fifth column saboteurs (discussed in Chapter 5).

120. Lentz 1988:78–79.

121. Ben-Yehuda 1993.

122. Published originally in 1903 and made into a movie in 1984.

123. Lentz 1988:48; and Polmar and Allen 1997:110.

124. Collins was murdered because some rebellious forces thought that he presented a political threat for the Irish Rebellion (Lentz 1988:47–48). An impressive 1996 movie titled *Michael Collins* was made on the controversy.

125. See Seth 1972:150–153 on Delilah. See Bower 1990; and Polmar and Allen 1997:266, on "honey traps" or sex traps.

126. The case is described in fuller detail in Chapter 1. For the specific subplot involving "Cindy," from Va'anunu's point of view, see *Yediot Aharonot*, January 24, 1997, Saturday Supplement, pp. 10–11. This story had an interesting twist in April 1996. Uzi Mahaneimi—a journalist working for the *Sunday Times*—managed to locate and expose the real "Cindy." He found out that her real name was Sheryl Ben-Tov, where she lived, and talked with her. Because of this exposure, the head of Israel's military intelligence (AMAN), Shlomo Gazit, told journalists that the state of Israel should consider charging Mahaneimi with treason, or something similar; see *Ma'ariv*, April 11, 1997, p. 6.

127. See Colton and Vanstone 1997, alas methodologically weak.

128. For example, see Ben-Yehuda 1985, 1986; Kohn 1986; and Pallone and Hennessy 1995.

129. The description is based on my 1993 book, *Political Assassinations by Jews: A Rhetorical Device for Justice*, pp. 201–202, 208, 283.

130. *Sefer Toldot HaHagana*, vol. 3, part 1:562–563.

131. See Braham 1981; Hilberg 1985, vol. 2:796–868; and Laqueur 1980.

132. See Bauer 1982:148–191; and Wyman 1984:244.

133. Bowyer Bell 1987:95; Katz 1966:185; Bauer 1982:148–191; and Hadar 1971.

134. Brand 1957:155. See also Brand 1960:49–79; Niv 1965–1980, vol. 4:80–81; Ayalon 1980; Rosenfeld 1955; Bauer 1982: 148–191; and Hadar 1971.

135. For example, see Hadar 1971; and Bauer 1982:134–191.

136. Brand 1957, 1966, 1974.

137. See Wyman 1984:243–245.

138. Ibid.

139. See Marx and Fijnaut 1995.

140. For examples, see Marx and Fijnaut 1995; and Staples 1997.

141. See Black and Morris 1991:156–167; Harel 1987; Melman 1998; and Melman and Raviv 1989:122–129, 236–243.

142. See Black and Morris 1991:148–149; and Melman and Raviv 1989:126–128.

143. Black and Morris 1991:149.

144. Ibid., 442–443; and Melman and Raviv 1989:243. See also *Yediot Aharonot*, September 4, 1998, p. 4, and *Ma'ariv*, same date, p. 7.

145. Black and Morris 1991:443; see also Melman and Raviv 1989:241–243. Kalmanovitch was later deported to Russia.

146. *Ha'aretz*, December 12, 1997, p. 1.

147. See *Ha'aretz*, June 4, 1993, pp. A1–3; *Kol Hair*, June 4, 1993, pp. 46–51; *Yediot Aharonot*, June 4, 1996, pp. 2–3; *Yediot Aharonot*, Supplement, October 22, 1993, pp. 14–15, 17.

148. And a hefty fine of $250,000. See Blum 1987; Earley 1988; and Polmar and Allen 1997:585–588.

149. Polmar and Allen 1997:21–22; and Weiner, Johnston, and Lewis 1995.

150. See Deacon 1987:263–265; Dobson and Payne 1986:4–5; Polmar and Allen 1997:3–4, 447; and Seth 1972:9–15. On Gary Francis Powers and the U-2 incident, see Beschloss 1986; Polmar and Allen 1997:448, 561–563; Richelson 1995:264–268, 293–294; and Seth 1972:465–489.

Chapter 4

1. *Oxford English Dictionary*, 2nd ed., vol. 8 (Oxford: Clarendon Press), pp. 458–459.

2. *Encyclopaedia Hebraica*, vol. 7 (Jerusalem: Encyclopedia Publishing), pp. 603–607 (Hebrew).

3. *Encyclopaedia Britannica*, vol. 22 (London: Encyclopaedia Britannica, 1956), pp. 435–438.

4. *Micropaedia*, vol. 10 (London: Encyclopaedia Britannica, 1974), p. 103.

5. Ploscoe 1934:93. It is interesting that the 1968 edition does not have treason listed in it.

6. And possibly a few others; see Stone 1988.

7. Jiordano Bruno died for challenging the Ptolemaic worldview and the morality that supported it; Galileo also suffered because of this worldview. Freud's psychoanalytic theories, which revolutionized psychology and psychiatry and enriched other disciplines, were originally criticized heavily on moral grounds. For more on these issues, see Ben-Yehuda 1985.

8. *Encyclopaedia Britannica*, vol. 22, p. 435.

9. Ploscoe 1934:93.

10. Nettler 1982:35; and Hurst 1983:1559.

11. *Encyclopaedia Britannica*, vol. 22, p. 436.

12. For example, Andreyev 1987; Conway 1993; Hoidal 1989; Johnson 1990; Lottman 1985; Randall 1990; and Selwyn 1987.

13. For example, Pincher 1987; Weyl 1950; and West 1995.

14. For example, Boveri 1956; Bulloch 1966; Klement 1984; Littlejohn 1972; O'Toole 1991; Weale 1994; and West 1964.

15. For example, Archer 1971:3; Hagan 1989, 1997; Pincher 1987; and West 1995.

16. Archer 1971.

17. The case is that of William John Vassall—a British Admiralty clerk whose espionage caused much damage. For details, see Bulloch 1966:152–153; see also West 1995:65–69.

18. See Bergmeier and Lotz Rainer 1997; and Weale 1994.

19. See Polmar and Allen 1997:451–452; Knightley and Kennedy 1987.

20. West 1985:361–370.

21. See Kooistra's 1989 work on criminals as heroes. On a related case, see Campbell 1977.

22. See Akerstrom 1991:52; and Hagan 1989, 1997.

23. Pincher 1987:xv.

24. Ibid., 1–14, 22.

25. Ibid., 22–23.

26. Friedrich 1972:83, 93.

27. Ibid., 91–92.

28. Ibid., 224.
29. Ibid., 89.
30. Ibid., 188.
31. Nettler 1982:35.
32. Ibid., 42.
33. As do Hurst's 1983 and Ploscoe's almost legal-technical 1934 presentations.
34. Archer 1971:10–11; and Weyl 1950:22.
35. Archer 1971:16.
36. Ibid., 22–23.
37. Weyl 1950:161. See also Archer 1971:31–37; and Weyl 1950: 110–162.
38. Archer 1971:38–47; and Weyl 1950:163–211.
39. Archer 1971:48–51; and Weyl 1950:212–237.
40. Archer 1971:51–54; and Weyl 1950:238–261.
41. Archer 1971:48–62; and Weyl 1950:262–302.
42. Detailed in Klement 1984, ch. 7:187–217.
43. Ibid., 217.
44. Archer 1971:62–63.
45. Ibid., 63–68.
46. Quoted in ibid., 70.
47. Ibid., 72.
48. Weyl 1950:304. See also Archer 1971:69–75; Weyl 1950:303–316; White 1957; and Witcover 1989.
49. Archer 1971:116. On Kuhn and the Bund, see Higham 1985; Parrish and Marshall 1978:221, 349; and Weinstein and Vassiliev 1999.
50. Archer 1971:76–118; Higham 1985; and Weyl 1950:317–341. See also the relevant parts in Weinstein and Vassiliev's fascinating 1999 book.
51. Archer 1971:116.
52. Ibid., 76–77.
53. See also Weyl 1950:317–341.
54. Archer 1971:115–116; Blair 1996:603–605; Hickam 1989:248–252; and Weyl 1950:347–356.
55. Archer 1971:106–118.
56. Ibid., 117.
57. Ibid., 143–154. See also Weinstein and Vassiliev 1999.
58. Archer 1971:155–166.
59. On the historical inaccuracies of the 1966 movie, see Marius 1995:70–73. See also Ackroyd's 1998 superb and vivid biography.
60. On the movie's historical inaccuracies, see Fraser 1995.
61. See Ash 1990; and Mackay 1995.
62. For a short review, see Weyl 1950:13–20.
63. For more on traitors and their executions in England in the eighteenth and nineteenth centuries, see Gatrell 1996:298–321.
64. See, for example, Hagan 1989, 1997.
65. For example, the cases of the German White Rose and of Captain Meir Tubianski.
66. For example, see Bergesen 1977.

67. See Ben-Yehuda 1985:23–73; Briggs 1996; Klaits 1985; Levack 1987; and Quaife 1987.

68. See Ploscoe 1934; and Hurst 1983.

69. Hurst 1983:156.

70. *Times Literary Supplement*, February 16, 1996, p. 36.

71. This connects this work more explicitly to works by such scholars as Erving Goffman, Anselm Strauss, and Gustav Ichheiser (1970).

Chapter 5

1. For reviews, see Dear and Foot 1995; Parrish and Marshall 1978; Weinberg 1994; Wheal, Pope, and Taylor 1995; and Young 1981. Baudot et al.'s 1989 *The Historical Encyclopedia of World War II* even devotes some decent space to treason within the context of World War II (p. 457). It points out that the sharp clash between such extreme ideologies as fascism and communism created clear boundaries and made usage of the term "treason" meaningful.

2. For Cole's story, see Murphy 1987. For Suzanne Warren's side, see Young 1959.

3. Polmar and Allen 1997:209. For an interesting discussion of saboteurs in the United States during World War I, see Witcover 1989.

4. See Baudot et al. 1989:432–434; and Foot 1984.

5. Kessler 1991:144.

6. See Pryce-Jones 1976; Shermer 1971; and Weyl 1950:317–341.

7. The Office of Strategic Services—a U.S. intelligence and sabotage organization—was created by President Roosevelt on June 13, 1942, and abolished by President Truman on January 12, 1946. In July 1947 Truman established the Central Intelligence Agency (CIA), which in many respects continued the work of the OSS. For a short review, see Polmar and Allen 1997:408–410.

8. Polmar and Allen 1997:209–210.

9. White's work (1957) continues this argument into the 1950s. His work is focused on sabotage by the communists during the cold war, but the cases examined in the book are instructive because they show how difficult it is to discern whether certain incidences were actually the result of saboteurs' work. Among them he notes the burning of the Reichstag on the night of February 27, 1933, for which the Dutch Van der Lubbe was blamed and condemned to death. It is actually quite reasonable to assume that the Nazis themselves were behind that fire, which was used to consolidate Hitler's grip on Germany (for a short description, see Snyder 1976:286–289). In addition, White mentions the "mysterious" mid-air explosions of the British-designed and manufactured Comet jet. We now know that these accidents were due to a fatal design flaw and metal fatigue and did not result from sabotage. See also M. R. D. Foot in Baudot et al. 1989:423–424.

10. See also Archer 1971:81–93; Breuer 1989; and Weyl 1950:317–341.

11. See Polmar and Allen 1997:395–396, and the discussion in Chapter 6.

12. For example, see Hoettl 1953.

13. See De Jong 1950, 1956. For a general review, see Baudot et al. 1989:163–164.

14. See Snyder 1976:141–142; and Zentner and Bedurftig 1997:396. See also Smelser's 1975 study of the Sudeten problem.

15. See *Ha'aretz*, July 7, 1997, p. A2, and a penetrating documentary by Gil Sedan from Israeli TV's Channel 1 on this topic on July 6, 1997, titled "The Story of Three Ex-collaborators," produced by Yarin Kimor.

16. See Gilbert 1963; and Zentner and Bedurftig 1997:34–35.

17. Warmbruun 1963:272–275.

18. Typically called *Judenrats*. See Trunk 1972 [1977]; and Zentner and Bedurftig 1997:43.

19. From Louise De Jong's introduction to Warmbruun's 1963 book, p. v.

20. See Baudot et al. 1989:102–109; and Zentner and Bedurftig 1997:149–151.

21. See Seth 1956, which provides details about resistance in Norway, Greece, Denmark, Luxembourg, Holland, Yugoslavia, Belgium, France, and Italy. See also M. Baudot's more general view in Baudot et al. 1989:410–414.

22. See Rings 1979 for different patterns of collaboration.

23. Parrish and Marshall 1978:563; Snyder 1976:320; Hans Umbert in Dear and Foot 1995:90–93, see also p. 998; Young 1981:589–90; Zentner and Bedurftig 1997:872–873.

24. Beneå later fled first to the United States and then to England, where he became the voice of Free Czechoslovakia. See Zentner and Bedurftig 1997:77.

25. Dear and Foot 1995:521; Snyder 1976:134; Wheal, Pope, and Taylor 1995:204–205; and Zentner and Bedurftig 1997:175–176.

26. Mastny 1971:223.

27. Weinberg 1994:518.

28. Dear and Foot 1995:521; Parrish and Marshall 1978:255; Wheal, Pope, and Taylor 1995:204–205; and Zentner and Bedurftig 1997:375.

29. Assor 1997:63–64.

30. See H. Bernard in Baudot et al. 1989:129–130; and Paul Latawski in Dear and Foot 1995:279–280.

31. MacDonald and Kaplan 1995:60.

32. See Trunk 1972, [1977]; and Zentner and Bedurftig 1997:43.

33. The discovery of the bodies was made on April 12, 1943. For more on this, see Paul 1991; Wittlin 1965; and Zaslavsky 1999.

34. Sword, in Dear and Foot 1995:644, 646.

35. Claus Bjørn in Dear and Foot 1995:293–295; Littlejohn 1972:53–82; Wheal, Pope, and Taylor 1995:125–126; and Zentner and Bedurftig 1997:191.

36. See Novick 1968:184, on sentencing and ratios; and Baudot et al. 1989:401, on the executions.

37. Heavy water is an important component in the production of atomic energy.

38. Special Operations Executive was a British secret service aimed at subversive warfare in enemy-occupied territory; see M. R. D. Foot in Dear and Foot 1995:1018–1022, and his own 1984 book.

39. See Dear and Foot 1995:1244–1245; Gallagher 1975; and Kurzman 1997. For a more general context, see also Bernstein 1995, particularly pp. 25–27; Brooks 1992; Cruickshank 1986; Walker 1989; and Weinberg 1994:568–570. The 1965 British motion picture *The Heroes of Telemark*, filmed on location, depicts these actions.

40. Olav Riste in Dear and Foot 1995:818–823; Wheal, Pope, and Taylor 1995:339–340; and Zentner and Bedurftig 1997:652–654.

41. Hoidal 1989:159.

42. Ibid., ch. 5.

43. For example, the May 21, 1936, "battle of Gjøvik," which involved street fighting following an inciting speech by N.S. members. These members were attacked and beaten, and after more than seven hours of fighting they were able to free themselves only because state police troops were sent to Gjøvik; ibid., 229.

44. Ibid., 236–237.

45. Ibid., ch. 8.

46. Ibid., 314.

47. Ibid., 319–320.

48. Their first meeting was on December 14, 1939, and their last in January 1945.

49. Wistrich 1984:313; and Zentner and Bedurftig 1997:946–947.

50. Hoidal 1989:473.

51. Ibid., 473–474.

52. Ibid., 499–500.

53. Ibid., ch. 15.

54. Ibid., ch. 18.

55. Quoted by Hoidal 1989: 717.

56. Hoidal 1989:773–774.

57. Novick 1968:187.

58. Baudot et al. 1989:401.

59. For more on the Quisling affair, see Dahl 1999; Hewins 1965 (albeit controversial); Hoidal 1989; Parrish and Marshall 1978:512–513; Zentner and Bedurftig 1997:744, 946–947. On Norwegian collaboration, see Littlejohn 1972:1–52.

60. Baudot et al. 1989:153–160; and Dear and Foot 1995:346.

61. Dear and Foot 1995:701; and Zentner and Bedurftig 1997:563.

62. Martin Conway in Dear and Foot 1995:121; see also Conway's much fuller 1993 work; J. Gerard-Libois in Baudot et al. 1989:53–56, 134; Littlejohn 1972:131–184; and Zentner and Bedurftig 1997:75–76.

63. Quoted in Snyder 1976:62; see also Zentner and Bedurftig 1997:187, 801–802.

64. Snyder 1976:62; Conway, in Dear and Foot 1995:289.

65. Quoted by Snyder 1976:62.

66. See Archer 1971:128 and Novick 1968:187 on the numbers of arrestees, and Novick 1968 on the population ratio. The number of executions is given in Baudot et al. 1989:401.

67. From the Allied point of view, the Dutch underground was one of the most effective in Europe. See Warmbruun 1963:275–282.

68. Hirschfeld's 1988 work states that they won only 0.2 percent of the votes.

69. Foot in Dear and Foot 1995:782–786; Hirschfeld 1988; Rings 1979:94–99; Wheal, Pope, and Taylor 1995:324–326; and Zentner and Bedurftig 1997:613.

70. Snyder 1976:239; and Zentner and Bedurftig 1997:613.

71. Parrish and Marshall 1978:563; Rings 1979:197–198; and Warmbruun 1963:206.

72. In Dear and Foot 1995:783; see also M. R. D. Foot in Baudot et al. 1989:349–350; Littlejohn 1972:83–129; Hirschfeld 1988; and Warmbruun 1963.

73. *Yediot Aharonot*, September 26, 1996; Foot in Dear and Foot 1995:782; and Warmbruun 1963:165–184.

74. See Archer 1971:128 on the number of arrestees and Novick 1968:187 on the sentences given and the population ratio. Number of executions is given by Baudot et al. 1989:401.

75. Dank 1974:12–13.

76. Quoted from Dank 1974:13.

77. See Roderick Kedward in Dear and Foot 1995:407–408. See also Littlejohn 1972:185–290.

78. Quoted in Dank 1974:25; see also P. M. H. Bell in Dear and Foot 1995:426–431 (on de Gaulle and Free France); E. Pognon in Baudot et al. 1989:181–183 (on de Gaulle) and 167–168 (on Free France). On aspects of the Pétain–de Gaulle contrast, see Tournoux 1964.

79. Daladier served as premier three times (the latest term being 1938 through March 1940) and as minister of war from 1936 to 1940.

80. Parrish and Marshall 1978:148–149, 527–528.

81. Quoted in Dank 1974:294. For more on Pétain's trial, see Roy 1968.

82. See also Dear and Foot 1995:396–398, 876–877; E. Pognon in Baudot et al. 1989:386–388; Roy 1967; and Zentner and Bedurftig 1997:702–703.

83. Assor 1997:84–95; Dear and Foot 1995:673; and Zentner and Bedurftig 1997:528–529.

84. Gordon 1980:326.

85. See Dear and Foot 1995:396–398; Gordon 1980; Hirschfeld and Marsh 1989; and Kedward and Austin 1985.

86. For example, see an agonizing account of some such cases in Dank 1974:139–158.

87. See Hirschfeld in Dear and Foot 1995:246–249.

88. Selwyn 1987:220; see also Baudot et al. 1989:61.

89. Selwyn 1987:214.

90. See Dank 1974:322. I am not sure that the numbers were lower in the Soviet Union.—N.B.Y.

91. Archer 1971:128.

92. Novick 1968:187.

93. Ibid., 218–219.

94. Ibid., 204.

95. Ibid., 187.

96. See also M. Baudot's lucid summary in Baudot et al. 1989:402–403.

97. Quoted from the section "A Touch of History," p. 17, from *Vichy Guide*, published and distributed by the Tourist Office. I used the pamphlet I received in the hotel I was staying in—Les Celestins—in June 1998.

98. For more on the Vichy government, see Paxton 1972 and the illustrative book by Azéma and Wieviorka 1997.

99. See Baudot et al. 1989:173–175; Roderick Kedward in Dear and Foot 1995:405–407; Kedward 1993; and Schoenbrun 1990.

100. On July 3, 1940, the French fleet was destroyed by the British in operation *Catapult* at Mers el Kébir. The "battles" began June 24–26 and lasted into July 4. For more, see Dear and Foot 1995:739–740; Parrish and Marshall 1978:400; Tute 1989; Weinberg 1994:145–146; and Wheal, Pope, and Taylor 1995:300–301.

101. According to Boveri (1956:129), Darlan was much closer to Pétain personally than Laval.

102. Boveri 1956:129.

103. Operation Torch, commanded by Eisenhower. See Dear and Foot 1995:813–818; Parrish and Marshall 1978:468–469; and Wheal, Pope, and Taylor 1995:633.

104. Wheal, Pope, and Taylor 1995:11, 345.

105. See Parrish and Marshall 1978:150–151, 211–212; and Wheal, Pope, and Taylor 1995:122, 172–173.

106. From a 1942 letter to Roosevelt quoted by Boveri 1956:132.

107. Wheal, Pope, and Taylor 1995:469.

108. Verrier 1990:19.

109. Parrish and Marshall 1978:74.

110. Wheal, Pope, and Taylor 1995:122.

111. Ibid., 188.

112. Boveri 1956:126–134.

113. Quoted in Boveri 1956:131.

114. Boveri 1956:132–133.

115. Parrish and Marshall 1978:150–151; see also Assor 1997:96–107. On Churchill and de Gaulle, see Kersaudy's 1982 work.

116. See Bunting 1995; Cruickshank 1975; Dear and Foot 1995:202; Parrish and Marshall 1978:112; Sinel 1969; Toms 1967; and Wheal, Pope, and Taylor 1995:90.

117. See, for example, *Newsweek*, International Edition, December 14, 1998, pp. 22–28.

Chapter 6

1. Tomasevich 1975:460–463. See also Dedijer 1992; Martin 1978; Milazzo 1975; and Roberts 1973. For a more general background, see Parrish and Marshall 1978; Zentner and Bedurftig 1997:1072–1073; and Cohen 1996. On atrocities, see Tomasevich 1975:256–261; and Cohen 1996.

2. See Baudot et al. 1989:372, 484; Cohen 1996:88–91, 100–106; Dear and Foot 1995:869; Wheal, Pope, and Taylor 1995:116, 490; and Zentner and Bedurftig 1997:694, 985.

3. See Dennis Deletant in Dear and Foot 1995:954–959; and Zentner and Bedurftig 1997:809–810.

4. Dear and Foot 1995:45; Parrish and Marshall 1978:22; and Young 1981:523–524. For a more general discussion about Romania in this context, see H. Bernard in Baudot et al. 1989:417–420; and Zentner and Bedurftig 1997:33.

5. Mayer 1977:246; Parrish and Marshall 1978:416, 561, 660; Wheal, Pope, and Taylor 1995:496; Young 1981:606–607; and Zentner and Bedurftig 1997:997.

6. Andreyev 1987:37.

7. Ibid., 37.

8. Dear and Foot 1995:914.

9. Mayer 1977:246.

10. Wheal, Pope, and Taylor 1995:376–377.

11. The Yalta Conference took place in February 1945 and was the second meeting of Churchill, Roosevelt, and Stalin.

12. Keegan 1978:214; Parrish and Marshall 1978:660; Wheal, Pope, and Taylor 1995:496; Young 1981:606–607; and Zentner and Bedurftig 1997:997. On the more general issue of collaboration in the Soviet Union, see Littlejohn 1972:291–334.

13. Andreyev 1987:3.

14. Burton 1963:125.

15. Ibid., 126.

16. Andreyev 1987.

17. Ibid., 2.

18. Ibid., 7.

19. Andreyev in Dear and Foot 1995:1247–1248.

20. Keegan 1978:214; see also Young 1981:607.

21. See Koch 1989; McKale 1974; Muller 1991; and Zentner and Bedurftig 1997:999–1000.

22. Snyder 1976:153; and Zentner and Bedurftig 1997:425–426, 430–431.

23. See Koch 1989.

24. Snyder 1976:153.

25. Zimmermann 1986:27.

26. Ibid., 9–11.

27. For example, see Baudot et al. 1989:183–186; Benz and Peble 1997; Dear and Foot 1995:477–478; Fest 1996; Graml, Mommsen, Reichhardt, and Wolf 1970; Hamerow 1997; Hedley 1986; Hoffmann 1977, 1988; Klemperer 1994; Leber 1957; Mason 1978; and Zimmermann 1986 for general reviews. On the July 20, 1944, conspiracy, see Baigent and Leigh 1994; Forman 1973; Galante 1981; Kramarz 1967; Manvell 1971; Whalen 1993; and Williams 1976.

28. Bayles 1945; Dulles 1947; Dumbach and Newborn 1986; Hanser 1979; Neumann 1945; and Zentner and Bedurftig 1997:1045–1046.

29. Quote is from Dumbach and Newborn 1986:179–180. On Freisler, see Koch 1989:136–138; and Zentner and Bedurftig 1997:295–296.

30. See Wheeler-Bennett 1967.

31. Dear and Foot 1995:478; see also Kershaw 1987, chapter 8.

32. For more and fuller details, see Baigent and Leigh 1994; Dear and Foot 1995:478; Fest 1996; Forman 1973; Friedrich 1972:104–108; Galante 1981; Kramarz 1967; Manvell 1971; Mason 1978; Parrish and Marshall 1978:601–602; Snyder 1976:332; Whalen 1993; Wheal, Pope, and Taylor 1995:252–253; and Zentner and Bedurftig 1997:971–973. On equating "loyalty" with "honor" in the S.S., see Williamson 1995; and Zentner and Bedurftig 1997:682. This was an instructive exercise in rhetoric because it evaded the direct moral issue, which is "loyalty to what" (or "to whom").

33. On Bonhoeffer, see Dear and Foot 1995:152; Parrish and Marshall 1978:74; Snyder 1976:34–35. See also *New York Times*, August 16, 1996, p. A2. On Niemoller, see Hadley 1995:70–71; and Zentner and Bedurftig 1997:647–648.

34. Baudot et al. 1989:202; Parrish and Marshall 1978:239–240; Snyder 1976:121–122; and Zentner and Bedurftig 1997:351–352.

35. The *Abwehr* conducted German military intelligence and counterintelligence; it was created after World War I. For short descriptions, see Winfried Heinemann's discussion in Dear and Foot 1995:1–3; and Zentner and Bedurftig 1997:2.

36. Assor 1997:141–187; Colvin 1957; Dear and Foot 1995:189–190; Hohne 1979; Parrish and Marshall 1978:102; Snyder 1976:49–50; Zentner and Bedurftig 1997:125–126.

37. Dear and Foot 1995:251–252.

38. See Dear and Foot 1995:257; and Hicks 1995.

39. See Brackman 1987; and Chang 1997.

40. See Gold 1996; and Williams and Wallace 1989.

41. The march followed the fall of Bataan, a small area on the western side of the main Philippine island of Luzon, on April 9, 1942.

42. See Dear and Foot 1995:115; Knox 1981; and Stewart 1956 (for one soldier's illustrative account).

43. Wheal, Pope, and Taylor 1995:49–50, 220.

44. Lyman P. Van Slyke in Dear and Foot 1995:215–216, 222–223; see also pp. 660–661 on the Kwantung Army and p. 916 on Pu-Yi.

45. Dear and Foot 1995:916.

46. See also Pu-Yi 1987; and Bernardo Bertolucci's 1987 movie *The Last Emperor,* which won nine Academy Awards.

47. Baudot et al. 1989:112–115.

48. See Polmar and Allen 1997:243–247.

49. Johnson 1990:164–168.

50. See Seth 1972:591–594; and Bower 1990:127.

51. Seth 1972:591–594; and Bower 1990:127.

52. See Seth 1972:595–596; quote from Bower 1990:129.

53. A picture of the stamp can be found in Polmar and Allen 1997:421, 447, along with similar stamps featuring other spies (for example, Abel, Philby, and Nathan Hale).

54. See Knightley 1986:192–3; and Laqueur 1985:236.

55. Richelson 1995:90. For more on Sorge, see Bower 1990:121–129; Deacon 1987:241–243; Dobson and Payne 1986:297–299; Knightley 1986:185–193; Parrish and Marshall 1978:580; Polmar and Allen 1997:523; Prange 1984; Richelson 1995:89–91, 113–115, 124–125; Seth 1972:583–596; Snyder 1976:325; Volkman 1994:112–120; Whymant 1996.

56. Johnson 1990:2.

57. Ibid.

58. Ibid., 35.

59. Ibid., 35–36.

60. Ibid., 36.

61. West 1995:277–278; West argues that this ideological line was adopted by Agnes as a result of her meeting Laipat Rai, an Indian nationalist, at Columbia University.

62. West 1995:277–278; and Polmar and Allen 1997:517–518.

63. Johnson 1990:198.

64. Ibid.

65. Ibid., 11.

66. Ibid., 12.

67. Ibid., 200–215.

68. See Clayborne Carson in Dear and Foot 1995:632–634. This is also the place to call attention to Shibutani's 1978 fascinating work.

69. See Tanaka 1997.

70. Keegan 1978:77; Parrish and Marshall 1978:186; and Weinberg 1994:504.

71. See Weinberg 1994:898.

72. Ibid., 504.

73. Keegan 1978:77.

74. *The Record of Collaboration of King Farouk of Egypt with the Nazis and Their Ally, The Mufti.* The official Nazi Record of the King's Alliance and of the Mufti's Plans for Bombing Jerusalem and Tel Aviv. Memorandum submitted to the United Nations, June 1948, by the Nation Associates, New York.

Chapter 7

1. See Weyl 1950:361–373; and Edwards 1991.

2. Weyl 1950:388.

3. Edwards 1991; and West 1987.

4. Weyl 1950:361–373; and Archer 1971:119–128.

5. Edwards 1991:99–114.

6. On Wodehouse, see the *Globe and Mail*, Sept. 17, 1999, p. A16; Edwards 1991:32; and Bergmeier and Lotz Rainer 1997:112–114.

7. On "Axis Sally," see Bergmeier and Lotz Rainer 1997:126–130; Edwards 1991:88–93, 97–98; and Weyl 1950:376–382.

8. Edwards 1991:41–56; and Weyl 1950:374–376.

9. See Cole 1964; Selwyn 1987; and Wharam 1995:166–172.

10. Selwyn 1987:13.

11. Selwyn 1987.

12. Cole 1964:21.

13. Ibid., 23.

14. Ibid., 24.

15. Ibid., 26.

16. Both Cole (1964) and Selwyn (1987:16, 22) derive this conclusion.

17. See Cole 1964:26–29; quote is from p. 29.

18. Ibid., 29.

19. Ibid., 30.

20. Ibid., 35.

21. See Shermer 1971.

22. Cole 1964:41.

23. This passport—based on falsified information—would eventually be used by the British prosecution as an indication of Joyce's professed loyalty and his breach of it. It would mean Joyce's death.

24. Selwyn 1987:41.
25. Ibid., 43.
26. Charman 1992:vii.
27. Ibid.
28. Ibid.
29. Cole 1964:72–81.
30. Ibid., 66.
31. Charman 1992:vii.
32. Cole 1964:84–85.
33. Ibid., 85.
34. Selwyn 1987:76–77.
35. MacNab visited Berlin in the summer of 1939; see Cole 1964:82–83.
36. Bauer was the one who gave MacNab positive reassurances about their acceptance.
37. Cole 1964:93–95.
38. Selwyn 1987:93; Selwyn refers to Goebbels and Goering.
39. See Bergmeier and Lotz Rainer 1997; Edwards 1991; and West 1987.
40. Selwyn 1987:91–92.
41. Ibid., 124.
42. Ibid.; see also Cole 1964:110–119.
43. Selwyn 1987:105. The book, by the way, was reproduced in English by the British Imperial War Museum in 1992.
44. P. 7 in the 1992 reprint of his book published by the Imperial War Museum.
45. Selwyn 1987:130.
46. Charman 1992:xii.
47. Selwyn 1987:111.
48. Ibid., 112.
49. The Germans built three such pocket battleships. They were designed to be more powerful than cruisers and faster than battleships. The *Admiral Graf Spee*'s technical specifications matched the above goal. It was launched in 1934, with six 11-inch guns as main armament, eight 6-inch guns, eight 19.7-inch torpedo tubes, and an impressive cruising speed of 26 knots.
50. The *Exeter* was built in 1931 with six 8-inch guns as main armament, eight 4-inch guns, and a top speed of 32 knots. The *Achilles* was a New Zealand cruiser. Its main armament consisted of eight 6-inch guns, and it had a top speed of 31.25 knots. The *Ajax* was a Royal Navy cruiser completed in 1934. It had eight 6-inch and four (later eight) 4-inch guns and eight 21-inch torpedo tubes.
51. See Wheal, Pope, and Taylor 1995; and Pope 1956.
52. Snyder 1976:126.
53. Tape #13438 in the Imperial War Museum, London. The r's in "Admiral Graf" were pronounced as German rolling r's.
54. *The Drama of the Graf Spee*, 1964:xxvi; see also Tonks 1971:20.
55. Tonks 1971:17.
56. January–February 1942; see Parrish and Marshall 1978:320–321.
57. Tonks 1971; Wheal, Pope, and Taylor 1995:511.
58. Tape no. 4859, in the Imperial War Museum, London.
59. Cole 1964:186–187.

60. Ibid., 195.
61. Ibid., 196.
62. Ibid., 205.
63. Selwyn 1987:152.
64. Ibid., 156.
65. Hitler's territorial expansionist intentions (including world domination) were laid out in his *Mein Kampf*, and his taking of Austria and Czechoslovakia is proof enough that whatever he could not achieve by politics, he took by military force. It is important to make this point clear because a somewhat similar claim was made by Kilzer (1994).
66. Tape no. 5224/1, Imperial War Museum, London.
67. See also Weale 1994:185.
68. Selwyn 1987:150.
69. Cole 1964:229.
70. Selwyn 1987:151.
71. Ibid., 160; see also Charman 1992:xii; and Cole 1964:244–247.
72. Selwyn 1987:162–163.
73. May 28, 1976, Bibliographical Archive G15, reel 27.
74. See also Selwyn 1987:163; Charman 1992:xiii; and Cole 1964:247.
75. Selwyn 1987:168.
76. Ibid., 170.
77. Charman 1992:xiii-xiv.
78. Selwyn 1987:179.
79. Ibid., 180.
80. Ibid., 190–191.
81. Ibid., 189.
82. Radio transmission from April 11, 1943.
83. Selwyn 1987:107.
84. Charman 1992:xiv.
85. *The Times*, February 8, 1995.
86. Selwyn 1987:4.
87. *Jewish Chronicle*, February 17, 1995, p. 10.
88. Selwyn 1987:108–109.
89. Ibid., 118–119.
90. See Charman 1992:ix.
91. Bergmeier and Lotz Rainer (1997:45–83) add several more names to the list.
92. Full details are provided in accounts by Duus 1983 and Howe 1990. For shorter accounts, see Archer 1971:122–123; Baudot et al. 1989:456; Dear and Foot 1995:1119; Parrish and Marshall 1978:632; Weyl 1950:382–388; Wheal, Pope, and Taylor 1995:467; and Young 1981:602–603.

Chapter 8

1. Selwyn 1987:219.
2. Bergmeier and Lotz Rainer 1997:73–74.

3. Ibid., 74.

4. Ibid., 75.

5. Redman 1991.

6. See Pound 1978.

7. Torrey 1984:161. The anti-Semitic tone in his transmissions in 1941 was very salient. Casillo (1988) points out that Pound's anti-Semitism emerged from his work and his mind. Although it diminished later, it remained a major theme in his transmissions; see Carpenter 1988:594–597. Carpenter points out that Italian officials were puzzled by Pound's motives and were concerned that his transmissions might be using a code to pass information to the Allies, that is, that Pound may have been a spy (p. 597).

8. Torrey 1984:161.

9. See Carpenter 1988:592–596: and Bergmeier and Lotz Rainer 1997:75–79.

10. Bergmeier and Lotz Rainer 1997:77.

11. Ibid.

12. Ibid., 77–78.

13. Cornell 1966:vii.

14. In Torrey 1984:196.

15. Cornell 1966:44.

16. Torrey 1984:155–176.

17. Ibid., 177–218.

18. Ibid., 195.

19. Ibid., 225–226.

20. Pound tended to deny his anti-Semitism when confronted with it. See Ibid., 226–227. See also the excellent review in Coles 1983.

21. Bergmeier and Lotz Rainer 1997:78–79; and Selwyn 1987:219–220. For short accounts of the case, see Boveri 1961:182–188; and Weyl 1950:400–411. See Heymann 1976 on Pound's personal history; see Korn 1985 on Pound's usage of history.

22. Zentner and Bedurftig 1997:379.

23. Quoted in Hoidal 1989:236, 803, n57 and n58.

24. For example, in June 24, 1937. See ibid., 272 and 808, n179.

25. Zentner and Bedurftig 1997:379.

26. Boveri 1961:197.

27. Assor 1997:26–28.

28. Hoidal 1989:743.

29. Boveri 1961:199.

30. Zentner and Bedurftig 1997:379.

31. Boveri 1961:198–199.

32. Littlejohn 1972:31.

33. *Personae: The Collected Shorter Poems of Ezra Pound* (New York: New Directions, 1926), p. 89. I am very grateful to Declan Spring, editor, New Directions, New York, who granted me permission to quote the poem.

34. Pound's affinity for fascism did not fail to attract attention. For examples, see Carpenter 1988:566–597; Casillo 1988; Chace 1973; and Redman 1991.

Chapter 9

1. This includes a 1980 biographical movie titled *Edward and Mrs. Simpson,* starring Edward Fox and Cynthia Harris.

2. The British television documentary program on King Edward VIII was transmitted on November 16, 1995. The executive producers were Sally Woodward and David Hart. The program was directed by David Hart and Nick Read. I shall refer to this program here as Channel 4.

3. Brown 1987:272.

4. For example, see Bloch 1988; Bradford 1989; Costello 1988; Higham 1988; Parker 1988; and Thomas 1995.

5. Ziegler 1990:268–269.

6. See Bradford 1989:125–127.

7. Bradford 1989:166.

8. Thomas 1995:41.

9. Channel 4, 1995.

10. See Gilbert 1963; and Morris 1991.

11. Pryce-Jones 1976.

12. See Shermer 1971 for a short review; see also Chapter 7 on radio traitors and Lord Haw-Haw.

13. Quoted in Bradford 1989:167.

14. Ziegler 1990:163.

15. Bradford 1989.

16. Ibid., 164; and Costello 1988:449.

17. Brown 1987:181–182, 678.

18. Ziegler 1990:267; Bradford 1989:165; and Costello 1988:451.

19. Ziegler 1990:268.

20. Costello 1988:449.

21. Thomas 1995:28–30.

22. Ziegler 1990:268.

23. Ibid., 207–208.

24. Ibid., 391.

25. The agreement was achieved within the framework of the 1925 Locarno Pacts.

26. Speer 1971:113.

27. Ibid.

28. Brown 1987:183.

29. Ibid., 184.

30. Bradford 1989:165.

31. Thomas 1995:69–70.

32. Ibid., 70.

33. Ziegler 1990:270.

34. Ibid. This telephone conversation was overheard and reported by Fritz Hesse, a press attaché in the German embassy.

35. Ribbentrop was later appointed foreign minister of the Third Reich (on February 4, 1938).

36. See Higham 1988. Brown (1987:179) notes that "C," chief of the British Secret Intelligence Service (SIS), was quite concerned about the relationship between Mrs. Simpson and Ribbentrop.

37. Bradford 1989.

38. Ibid., 283–284.

39. See Ziegler 1990:224.

40. For a statement that there was no fabrication and that, in fact, Mrs. Simpson *had* such a past, see Thomas 1995:37, and Higham 1988.

41. For example, he suggested that Mrs. Simpson give up some significant rights as queen; see Bradford 1989:182–186.

42. Thomas 1995:88.

43. See Bloch 1988.

44. Bloch 1988:108; Bradford 1989:441; and Channel 4, 1995.

45. Bloch 1988:108.

46. Ziegler 1990:362.

47. See Higham 1985:15, 45, 160, 164–170; for a rather strange and dissenting view, see Ziegler 1990:456.

48. Ziegler 1990:454–459.

49. Ibid., 455.

50. Quoted in ibid., 456–457.

51. Bloch 1988:112.

52. Brown 1987:186. For more, see Bloch 1988:113; and Ziegler 1990:391.

53. More pictures can be seen in Bryan and Murphy 1979 (Morrow edition), eighth picture page following page 320 (Hitler shaking the hand of the Duchess); Donaldson 1974, first picture page following page 324 (Hitler shaking the Duchess's hand and Nazi officials escorting the Windsors); Thomas 1995, third picture page following page 128 (the Windsors leaving Berchtesgaden, with Nazis saluting in the back). With the exception of one insignificant picture of the Windsors meeting with Josef Terboven, the Nazi Gauleiter of Essen (on April 24, 1940, he was appointed Reich Commissioner of Norway, a position he held until the end of the war and that he executed with ruthless brutality), Ziegler (1990) provides no pictures of the October 1937 visit to either Germany or Berchtesgaden (picture page before page 319).

54. See Ziegler 1990:392.

55. Ibid., 392–393.

56. Bradford 1989:254–257.

57. Channel 4, 1995.

58. Bradford 1989:285.

59. Bloch 1988:136–139; see there the transcript of the speech on pp. 313–314.

60. Bradford 1989:286.

61. See her book, *The Heart Has Its Reasons* (London: Landsborough, 1956), pp. 268–269. The duchess states that visiting Hitler was a last-minute, unplanned event and that her husband refused to discuss with her the contents of his meetings with Hitler. Her version is that the duke told her that during the one-hour meeting with Hitler, it was Hitler who did most of the talking, focusing on "what he's trying to do for Germany and to combat Bolshevism" (p. 269).

62. Ziegler 1990:398–400.

63. Ibid., 398.

64. Ibid., 399.

65. Ibid., 400. This cable was sent about a week before Hitler's invasion of Poland, which marked the beginning of World War II, more than three months after the Verdun broadcast.

66. Ibid., 401.

67. The duke was assigned to the command of Major General Sir Richard Howard-Vyse, headquartered at Vincennes; ibid., 406–407.

68. Ibid., 406.

69. Ibid., 406–413.

70. Ibid., 414.

71. Ibid., 415.

72. Different sources vary slightly about the exact date.

73. The incident is referred to as the "Mechlin Incident." Young (1981:46), Baudot et al. (1989:313), and Weinberg (1994:11) all confirm the story about this forced landing of a German plane. Breuer (1997:14–18) provides more details. He identifies one of the two German officers on the airplane as army officer Major Helmuth Reinberger. No name of the pilot is given. Reinberger tried to burn the documents in front of the Belgian investigating officer, Captain Emilio Rodrigue. Major Reinberger threw a batch of papers, which he had been carrying under his gray coat, into the burning stove in the room where he was waiting to be interrogated. Captain Rodrigue rushed to the stove and got the papers out (p. 15). Breuer dates the incident to January 10, 1940.

74. Baudot et al. 1989:313.

75. Weinberg 1994:11.

76. Costello 1988:452.

77. Brown 1987:679.

78. Ibid., 273; see also Kessler 1991:143.

79. Ziegler 1990:416.

80. Thomas 1995:181.

81. Ziegler 1990:416.

82. Ibid., 417.

83. Ibid., 421. Hoare was a strong supporter of Chamberlain's appeasement policy; see Baudot 1989:224.

84. Quoted in Donaldson 1974:364.

85. Ziegler 1990:421.

86. Waller 1996:168.

87. Bradford 1989:578.

88. Quoted in Ziegler 1990:421.

89. Ibid., 420.

90. Donaldson 1974:359.

91. Ziegler 1990:422–423.

92. Ibid., 423.

93. Bradford 1989:341.

94. Quoted in Bradford 1989:576.

95. Brown 1987:273.

96. For example, see Bloch 1984, 1988:165–169.

97. For example, see Bloch 1984; Bryan and Murphy 1979:422–436 (Morrow edition); Donaldson 1974:359–377; Kessler 1991:146; Kilzer 1994:240–247; Schellenberg 1965:66–80 (including the publisher's strong disclaimer on pp. 66–67); Thomas 1995; and Ziegler 1990:423–436.

98. Ziegler 1990:423.

99. Ibid., 424. Ziegler attempts to discredit this report.

100. Waller 1996:168.

101. Brown 1987:273.

102. See Ziegler 1990:434.

103. Ibid., 424.

104. For example, Channel 4, 1995; Brown 1987:273; and Ziegler 1990.

105. Ziegler 1990:425.

106. Interview in Channel 4 program, 1995.

107. Bradford 1989:578.

108. Donaldson 1974:368, 376.

109. Ibid., 391.

110. Miller 1995:80.

111. Ziegler 1990:425. Again, Ziegler tries to discredit the report.

112. Quoted in Thomas 1995:204, and in Channel 4, 1995.

113. Bradford 1989:579.

114. Thomas 1995:204.

115. Brown 1987:273–276; and Costello 1988:453–454.

116. Ziegler 1990:431; Brown 1987:275; Kessler 1991:152–159; and Schellenberg 1965:66–84.

117. Ziegler 1990:459.

118. Bradford 1989:578.

119. Ibid.

120. Ibid., 577.

121. Ibid., 578.

122. See ibid., 576; see also Ziegler 1990:426–427. The warning letter is reproduced in Brown 1987:275.

123. Ziegler 1990:432.

124. Ibid., 432–433. Brown (1987:275–276) notes that in fact Schellenberg's mission failed and that following the fiasco in Lisbon, Schellenberg fell ill as a result of "a severe case of liver or gall bladder poisoning, an episode from which he never recovered and from which he died young. He always insisted that he had been poisoned by the British secret service." Schellenberg died at the age of fifty-two.

125. See Young 1981:69.

126. Thomas 1995:205.

127. See Ziegler 1990:433–434.

128. Brown 1987:272–276; Thomas 1995; and Waller 1996:167–173.

129. Costello 1988:454.

130. Ziegler 1990:442.

131. Ibid., 443.

132. Ibid., 455.

133. Ibid., 457.

134. Ibid., 458.

135. Brown 1987:681.

136. Bradford 1989:583–584; and Ziegler 1990:464–483.

137. Ziegler 1990:461.

138. Bradford 1989:584.

139. Bloch (1988:186) states that it was in December. Bradford (1989:584) states February as the date of the interview.

140. Bradford 1989:584.

141. Ziegler 1990:460.

142. Ibid.; see also Bloch 1988:186–190.

143. Bradford 1989:585.

144. Brown 1987:276.

145. Bradford 1989:425.

146. Ibid., 165.

147. Waller 1996:171.

148. Ziegler 1990:550.

149. See John Costello, *Mask of Treachery* (New York: William Morrow, 1988); see also Penrose and Freeman 1986. Costello (1988:469) even implies that Blunt's intimate knowledge of the nature of the contacts between the Duke of Windsor and the Nazis during World War II, gained through his mission to retrieve the relevant documents in Europe, gave him a powerful insurance policy against being punished by the British for his treachery. The fact is that when the British became aware of Blunt's treachery, he was not punished accordingly.

150. Brown 1987:683. See also Bradford 1989:563–564; Costello 1988:443–471; and Rusbridger 1989:183.

151. Waller 1996:168.

152. Weinberg 1994:143.

153. Costello 1988:448.

154. Ibid., 449.

155. Weinberg 1994:144.

156. The Duke of Windsor probably met Laval in December 1935. The purpose of that alleged meeting was, supposedly, to discuss and solidify support for British nonintervention in the Italian invasion of Abyssinia in 1935. Again, the duke was sympathetic to a fascist regime's expansionist policy. See Ziegler 1990:210–211.

Chapter 10

1. Kraus 1997:A4.

2. Hassig (1994:47) states that there were 450; other sources place the entire number of Spaniards at 508.

3. Plus "two hundred Indians . . . and a few Indian women for menial offices"; Prescott 1925:124.

4. Johnson 1977.

5. Hassig 1994:54.

6. Hassig 1996:13.

7. Ibid.

8. Thomas 1993:169–171.

9. See Prescott 1925:136. Please note that he cautions against attributing too much credibility to numbers.

10. Hassig 1994:50.

11. Ibid., 51, 163–164; and Thomas 1993:171.

12. Prescott 1925:140.

13. Vaillant [1944] 1962:242.

14. Davies 1973:243.

15. Johnson 1977:43. Others give different localities for her place of birth; see Hassig 1996:1.

16. See Gruzinski 1992:79.

17. Johnson (1977:43) states that, in fact, a slave's daughter was actually killed for this purpose.

18. See Gómara 1964, chapter 26. There are different versions regarding her enslavement; see Hassig 1996:1.

19. Hassig 1996:1.

20. See Davies 1973.

21. For example, see Hunter 1990:9; and Davies 1973:238.

22. Dorner 1972:72.

23. Thomas 1993:172.

24. Thomas 1993:172.

25. Johnson 1977:44.

26. Ibid., 44, 64.

27. Ibid., 44.

28. See Hunter 1990:14.

29. Vaillant [1944] 1962:246.

30. Johnson 1977:93.

31. Davies 1973:252. See also Hunter 1990:15; Prescott 1925:238–244; and Thomas 1993:260–262.

32. Johnson 1977:94.

33. Prescott 1925:244.

34. Thomas 1993:262.

35. Davies 1973:288. See also Thomas (1993:594), who does not mention Malinche in this context.

36. Vaillant 1962, fig. 50, p. 260.

37. Davies 1973:263; Hunter 1990; Johnson 1977:116; León-Portilla 1990:65; and Thomas 1993.

38. Vaillant 1962:247.

39. Hunter 1990:23.

40. Johnson 1977:179.

41. Ibid., 192; see also Prescott 1925:597.

42. Collis [1954] 1994:97; and León-Portilla 1990:69.

43. Collis 1994:233. The volcano La Malinche is located 120 kilometers east of Mexico City, 25 kilometers northeast of Puebla. Its elevation is 4,461 meters.

44. Vaillant 1962, fig. 34, p. 247.

45. Collis 1994:235.

46. Johnson 1977:221–222. See also Prescott 1925:596–597.

47. Collis 1994.

48. Johnson 1977:222.

49. Hassig 1996:1.

50. Ibid., 1, 17.

51. See Hassig's 1988, 1992, and 1994 works.

52. Hassig 1994:78–80.

53. Ibid., 80.

54. Hassig 1996:11.

55. Ibid., 12.

56. Ibid., 16.

57. Hassig (1996:16) indeed offers a few possible explanations as to why Marina was "credited" with the "discovery" of the Cholollans' plot.

58. Hassig 1996:15.

59. Ibid., 16–17.

60. Ibid., 18.

61. Ibid., 6–7; quote is from p. 6.

62. See Zerubavel 1995.

63. Calder 1992.

64. Ben-Yehuda 1995.

65. Hassig 1996:17.

Chapter 11

1. West 1995:351–366; Ostrovsky and Va'anunu star in that chapter. The topic of treason has traditionally attracted much attention in Israel. Cromer has done some academic work on both the case of Israel Beer (1985) and on Adiv (1986). In the daily popular press, Maron (1998b) drafted one the more analytically confused and contradictory but colorful pieces. He surveyed some of the traitors (Udi Adiv, Yoseph Amit, Israel Beer, Markus Klingberg, Shimon Levinson, Nachum Manbar, Victor Ostrovsky, and Mordechai Va'anunu), making the factually unsubstantiated claim that they all did what they did because of what he referred to as a problem of "lost honor." That is, all these traitors felt that people did not give them the honor (or respect) they deserved.

2. Part of the description of this case is based on Ben-Yehuda 1995:48–49.

3. See Ben-Yehuda 1995.

4. For short biographical sketches of Josephus Flavius—the man, his deeds, and his writings—see Encyclopaedia Judaica, 1971, vol. 10, pp. 251–264; and Jewish Encyclopedia, vol. 7. For more on Josephus's writings, see Aberbach 1985; Feldman 1984; Flusser 1985; Hadas-Lebel 1994; Rajak 1983; Rapoport 1982; Stern 1987; Stone 1984; and Thackeray 1968. There are literally thousands of works about Josephus Flavius, and it is impossible, and counterproductive, for this short review to delve into all of them. Nevertheless, the curious reader is referred to Feldman's summarizing works from 1984 (about 1000+ pages) and 1986 (about 700 pages).

5. See Ha'aretz, June 15, 1998, p. A3; and Yediot Aharonot, June 22, 1998, p. 5.

6. There are several versions concerning his escape. See Ber 1970–1971:175–190; Kaminka 1943–1944; Lewis 1975:20–21; Zerubavel 1980:107–116; and Kedar 1982:59–60. For more readings on Ben-Zakkai and Yavneh, see Alon 1967:219–252; Ben-Dov 1990; Hadas-Lebel 1994:112–115; *Encyclopedia Hebraica* 1967–1968, vol. 19, pp. 346–349; *Encyclopedia Judaica* 1971, vol. 10, pp. 148–154; Goren 1987; and Neusner 1970.

7. The Zealots and the Sicarii were Jewish ideological and political groups that existed during the time of the Great Revolt.

8. See Stern 1984:320–345.

9. For an interesting discussion about the Masada-("death, destruction") Yavneh ("life") contrast, and its possible implications for Judaism generally and contemporary Judaism particularly, see Weiss-Rosmarin 1966. See also Ben-Yehuda 1995:49, 331, n. 39.

10. Haredi is the ultra-Orthodox version of Judaism.

11. Segal 1996.

12. Ladouceur 1987:95.

13. See Snyder 1976:184; and Trunk 1972, 1977.

14. For a short description of the historical development of these groups and the historical context, see Ben-Yehuda 1993:79–97.

15. For a fuller discussion, see Ben-Yehuda 1993, upon which the description of these cases is based.

16. He alienated mostly the non-ultra-Orthodox community, but some members of the ultra-Orthodox community, too. Socially, this put De Hahn in a questionable position within local contemporary Jewish networks.

17. For a fuller summary of the case, see Ben-Yehuda 1993:137–140.

18. Probably by the two leaders of Lehi at that time—Yellin-Mor and Shaib.

19. See Nevo 1987.

20. Ibid., 21.

21. For a fuller summary of the case, see Ben-Yehuda 1993:252–254.

22. Schiff and Haber 1976:222–223.

23. Shealtiel's testimony, *Ha'aretz,* October 19, 1949, p. 2.

24. The Shai was the intelligence service of the Hagana. In June 1948 it was replaced by three different units: military intelligence (headed by Isser Be'ery and Chaim Herzog); inner intelligence service (headed by Isser Halperin and Yoseph Israeli); and external political intelligence service (headed by Reuven Shiloach).This structure was later changed again. As is clear, the case of Tubianski occurred during a period of structural uncertainty, when Israel as a state was emerging and when its intelligence community was in the process of being formed. See Ben-Yehuda 1993:438, n. 115.

25. Be'ery appointed himself as a prosecutor. He appointed as judges Binyamin Gibly, Avraham Kidron, and David Caron. No legal (or other) defense was appointed for Tubianski.

26. *Ma'ariv,* July 5, 1949, p. 2.

27. Tubianski's file in the *Ha'aretz* archives.

28. *Ha'aretz,* July 5, p. 1; July 7, p. 1; July 8, p. 1, 1949.

29. *Ha'aretz,* October 26, 1949, p. 2.

30. See also Bar-Zohar 1970:39–45; Harel 1989:113–137; and *Ha'aretz*, November 23, 1949.

31. Katz 1966:427.

32. For example, Gutman 1995:160–169; and Teveth 1992.

33. For example, Kasztner was involved in Yoel Brand's mission to the West, mentioned elsewhere in this book. This was the famous diabolical "blood for trucks" "offer" from the Nazis; Jews were to be traded for trucks from the Allies.

34. See Harel 1985:113–125.

35. Tamir was earlier a member of Etzel, and in the late 1970s he became Israel's minister of law.

36. *Sefer Toldot HaHagana* (The History of the Hagana), vol. 3, pt. 1, pp. 635–640.

37. See Rosenfeld 1955:415.

38. Harel 1985:106.

39. See Ibid., 47–48, 145–147.

40. See ibid., 55–73, for a short account.

41. At 8 Shderot Shmuel Street

42. See *Ha'aretz*, March 7 and 11, 1957.

43. See *Ha'aretz*, p. 4.

44. Such as Tamir, Rumak, and Sheib.

45. Harel 1985:138.

46. See Black and Morris 1991:153–156; Harel 1985; and Margalit 1982.

47. See Hadar 1971; and Bauer 1982:134–191.

48. See Gutman 1995:187–196. For a fuller summary of the case, see Ben-Yehuda 1993:278–284.

49. For a short description, see Schiff and Haber 1976:495. See Cromer (1986, 1998) on the societal reactions to this case.

50. Sylvia married in Paris, Adiv in Israel. See *Ma'ariv*, August 4, 1993, p. 2; *Yediot Aharonot*, Supplement, August 6, 1993, pp. 1–3, 23.

51. Cohen 1993:55.

52. This is the same kibbutz that Udi Adiv and Assaf Adiv (discussed next) came from.

53. See Schiff and Haber 1976:38; *Ha'aretz*, January 16, 1955, p. 1; Granot 1981:39–43; and Melman 1999.

54. *Ha'aretz*, May 6, 1988, p. B2.

55. *Ha'aretz*, May 24, 1988, p. 1.

56. *Ha'aretz*, May 3, 1988, p. A1, and May 19, 1988, p. A12.

57. Michal Schwartz was sentenced to eighteen months in prison; Ben-Effrat to thirty months; and Assaf Adiv to twenty months.

58. *Ha'aretz*, November 20, 1989, p. 13.

59. In addition, he was handed a twelve-month prison sentence conditional upon abstaining from similar activities for the next three years.

60. See *Ha'aretz*, October 4, 1989, p. 3, and October 29, 1989, p. 3.

61. For an interview with the man who fired Ostrovsky—David Arbel—see *Ma'ariv*, May 5, 1998, weekend supplement, pp. 12–80. Arbel claims that Ostrovsky provided inaccurate accounts and concocted blatant lies. Consequently, "it was necessary to fire him" (p. 12).

62. This passage is partially based on Ben-Yehuda 1997 and 1998.

63. Ben-Yehuda 1993.

64. See for example Karpin 1999; and Sprinzak 1999.

65. See Ford 1985:286–287; and Lentz 1988:101–102.

66. An example is the so-called Season—during the early 1940s. For a short description, see Ben-Yehuda 1993:210.

67. Haim Arlosoroff was a major Jewish political figure in Palestine at the time. See Ben-Yehuda 1993:140–143.

68. As pointed out in my 1993 book, there are several other cases, for example, Michael Schnell and Chaya Zeidenberg, among others.

Conclusion

1. See Black 1983, 1984a, 1984b.

2. See Ben-Yehuda 1985.

References

Hebrew books are identified as such by (Hebrew) at the end of the reference. The titles of books written in Hebrew are translated into English by the author, except in those cases where an English title is provided by the publisher.

Aberbach, Moses. 1985. "Josephus and His Critics: A Reassessment." *Midstream* 31 (no. 5):25–29.

Abu-Tuema, Haled. 1995. "The Mufti of Jerusalem: Accepting Israeli Citizenship Is Treason." *Jerusalem*, August 18, p. 28 (Hebrew).

Ackroyd, Peter. 1998. *The Life of Thomas More*. New York: Doubleday.

Aho, James A. 1994. *This Thing of Darkness: A Sociology of the Enemy*. Seattle: University of Washington Press.

Akerstrom, Malin. 1991. *Betrayal and Betrayers: The Sociology of Treachery*. New Brunswick, N.J.: Transaction Publishers.

Allen, Robert L. 1989. *Port Chicago Mutiny*. New York: Warner Books, Amistad Books.

Alon, Gedaliah. 1967. *Studies in the History of Israel*. Tel Aviv: Hakkibutz Hameuchad (Hebrew).

Amit, Moshe. 1992. *A History of Classical Greece*. Jerusalem: Magness Press (Hebrew).

Anderson, Benedict. 1991. *Imagined Communities: Reflections on the Origin and Spread of Nationalism*. London: Verso.

Andrew, Christopher, and Vasili Mitrokhin. 1999. *The Mitrokhin Archive: The KGB in Europe and the West*. London: Allen Lane, Penguin Press.

Andreyev, Catherine. 1987. *Vlasov and the Russian Liberation Movement: Soviet Reality and Emigré Theories*. Cambridge: Cambridge University Press.

Archer, Jules. 1971. *Treason in America: Disloyalty Versus Dissent*. New York: Hawthorn Books.

Arnold, Isaac N. [1880] 1979. *The Life of Benedict Arnold*. New York: Arno Press.

Ash, Marinell. 1990. "William Wallace and Robert the Bruce: The Life and Death of a National Myth." In *The Myths We Live By*, edited by Samuel Rapael and Paul Thompson, pp. 83–93. London and New York: Routledge.

Ash, Timothy Garton. 1994. *In Europe's Name: Germany and the Divided Continent*. New York: Vintage Books.

Assor, Reuven. 1997. *Traitors in the Second World War*. Tel Aviv: Yaron Golan (Hebrew).

Ayalon, Amos. 1980. *Timetable*. Jerusalem: Edanim Publishers, Yediot Aharonot Edition (Hebrew).

Azéma, Jean Pierre, and Olivier Wieviorka. 1997. *Vichy, 1940–1944.* Paris: Perrin (French).

Baigent, Michael, and Richard Leigh. 1994. *Secret Germany: Stauffenberg and the Mystical Crusade Against Hitler.* London: Penguin Books.

Bakeless, John Edwin. [1959] 1998. *Turncoats, Traitors, and Heroes: Espionage in the American Revolution.* New York: Da Capo Press.

Baker, Robin. 1996. *Sperm Wars.* England: Fourth Estate.

Banai, Ya'acov. 1958. *Anonymous Soldiers.* Tel Aviv: Hug Yedidim (Hebrew).

Bar-Ulpan, Dina. 1997. *A Conceptual Framework to Study Whistleblowing in Israeli Organizations.* M.A. Thesis. University of Tel Aviv (Hebrew).

Bar-Zohar, Michael. 1970. *Issar Harel and Israel's Security Services.* Jerusalem: Weidenfeld and Nicolson (Hebrew).

Baudot, Marcel, Henri Bernard, Hendrik Brugmans, Michael R. D. Foot, and Hans-Adolf Jacobsen. 1989. *The Historical Encyclopedia of World War II.* New York: MJF Books.

Bauer, Yehuda. 1982. *The Holocaust: Some Historical Aspects.* Jerusalem and Tel Aviv: Moreshet; Institute on Contemporary Judaism, Hebrew University; Sifriat Poalim (Hebrew).

Bayles, William. 1945. *Seven Were Hanged.* London: Victor Gollancz.

Bearse, Rsay, and Anthony Read. 1991. *Conspirator: The Untold Story of Churchill, Roosevelt, and Tyler Kent, Spy.* London: Macmillan.

Becker, Howard S. 1963. *Outsiders.* New York: Free Press.

Beer, Israel. 1956–1957. *In the Circle of Security Problems.* Tel Aviv: Sifria La'am, Am Oved (Hebrew).

———. 1966. *Israel's Security: Yesterday, Today, Tomorrow.* Tel Aviv: Amikam (Hebrew).

Ben-Dov, Meir. 1990. "From Jerusalem to Yavneh: A Day After the Destruction." *Ha'aretz,* August 3, p. B4 (Hebrew).

Ben-Yehuda, Nachman. 1985. *Deviance and Moral Boundaries.* Chicago: University of Chicago Press.

———. 1986. "Deviance in Science: Towards the Criminology of Science." *British Journal of Criminology* 26 (no. 1):1–27.

———. 1989. *The Politics and Morality of Deviance: Moral Panics, Drug Abuse, Deviant Science, and Reversed Stigmatization.* Albany: State University of New York Press.

———. 1993. *Political Assassinations by Jews: A Rhetorical Device for Justice.* Albany: State University of New York Press.

———. 1995. *The Masada Myth: Collective Memory and Mythmaking in Israel.* Madison: University of Wisconsin Press.

———. 1997. "Political Assassination Events as a Cross-cultural Form of Alternative Justice." *International Journal of Comparative Sociology* 38 (no. 1–2):25–47.

———. 1998. "Political Violence: Political Assassinations as a Quest for Justice." In *Crime and Criminal Justice in Israel: Assessing the Knowledge Base Toward the Twenty-First Century,* edited by Roberet R. Friedmann, pp. 139–181. Albany: State University of New York Press.

———. Forthcoming. *Archaeology, Politics, and Deception: The Excavations of Masada.*

Benz, Wolfgang, and Walter H. Pehle, eds. 1997. *Encyclopedia of German Resistance to the Nazi Movement.* New York: Continuum.

Ber, Yitzhak. 1970–1971. "Jerusalem During the Days of the Great Revolt." *Zion* 36:127–190 (Hebrew).

Bergesen, Albert J. 1977. "Political Witch Hunts: The Sacred and the Subversive in Cross-national Perspective." *American Sociological Review* 42:220–233.

Bergmeier, Horst J. P., and E. Lotz Rainer. 1997. *Hitler's Airwaves: The Inside Story of Nazi Radio Broadcasting and Propaganda Swing.* New Haven and London: Yale University Press.

Bernstein, Jeremy. 1995. *Hitler's Uranium Club: The Secret Recordings at Farm Hall.* With an introduction by David Cassidy. Woodbury, N. Y.: American Institute of Physics.

Beschloss, Michael R. 1986. *Mayday! The U-2 Affair: The Untold Story of the Greatest U.S.-U.S.S.R. Spy Scandal.* New York: Harper & Row.

Best, Joel. 1993. "But Seriously Folks: The Limitations of the Strict Constructionist Interpretation of Social Problems." In *Constructionist Controversies: Issues in Social Problems Theory,* edited by Gale Miller and James A. Holstein, pp. 109–127. New York: Aldine de Gruyter.

Best, Joel, ed. 1989. *Images of Issues: Typifying Contemporary Social Problems.* New York: Aldine de Gruyter.

Best, Joel, ed. 1995. *Images of Issues: Typifying Contemporary Social Problems,* 2nd ed. New York: Aldine de Gruyter.

Bethell, Nicholas. 1995. *The Last Secret: Forcible Repatriation to Russia, 1944–1947.* London: Penguin Books.

Black, Donald. 1983. "Crime as Social Control." *American Sociological Review* 43:34–45.

Black, Donald, ed. 1984a. *Toward a General Theory of Social Control,* 2 volumes. New York: Academic Press.

Black, Donald. 1984b. "Crime as Social Control." In *Toward a General Theory of Social Control,* vol. 2, pp. 1–27. New York: Academic Press.

Black, Ian, and Benny Morris. 1991. *Israel's Secret Wars: The Untold History of Israeli Intelligence.* London: Hamish Hamilton.

Blair, Clay. 1996. *Hitler's U-Boat War: The Hunters, 1939–1942.* New York: Random House.

Bloch, Michael. 1984. *Operation Willi: The Plot to Kidnap the Duke of Windsor, July 1940.* London: Weidenfeld and Nicolson.

———. 1988. *The Secret File of the Duke of Windsor.* London: Bantam.

Blum, Howard. 1987. *I Pledge Allegiance . . . The True Story of the Walkers: An American Spy Family.* New York: Simon and Schuster.

Bok, S. 1993. "Whistleblowing and Professional Responsibility." In *Ethical Theory and Business,* edited by Bowie E. Norman and Tom L. Beauchamp, pp. 261–269. Englewood Cliffs, N. J.: Prentice-Hall.

Boveri, Margret. [1956] 1961. *Treason in the Twentieth Century.* Translated from German by Jonathan Steinberg. London: Macdonald.

Bower, Donald E. 1990. *Sex Espionage.* New York: Knightsbridge.

Bowyer Bell, J. 1987. *Fighting Zion*. Jerusalem: Achiasaf (Hebrew).

Boylan, Brian Richard. 1973. *Benedict Arnold: The Dark Eagle*. New York: W.W. Norton.

Brackman, Arnold C. 1987. *The Other Nuremberg: The Untold Story of the Tokyo War Crimes Trials*. New York: Quill, William Morrow.

Bradford, Sarah. 1989. *King George VI*. London: Weidenfeld and Nicolson.

Braham, Randolph L. 1981. *The Politics of Genocide: The Holocaust in Hungary*. New York: Columbia University Press.

Brand, Hansy, and Yoel Brand. 1966. *The Devil and the Soul*. Tel Aviv: Ledori (Hebrew).

Brand, Yoel. 1957. *On a Mission for the Condemned to Death*. Tel Aviv: Ayanot (Hebrew).

———. 1974. "Testimony in the Trial of Eichmann." In *The Legal Advisor to the Government Against Adolf Eichmann*, Testimonies (B), pp. 869–909. Jerusalem: Publication Service, Mercaz Hahasbara (Hebrew).

Brandt, Clare. 1994. *The Man and the Mirror: A Life of Benedict Arnold*. New York: Random House.

Breuer, William B. 1989. *Hitler's Undercover War: The Nazi Espionage Invasion of the U.S.A.* New York: St. Martin's Press.

———. 1997. *Unexplained Mysteries of World War II*. New York: John Wiley & Sons.

Briggs, Robin. 1996. *Witches and Neighbours: The Social and Cultural Context of European Witchcraft*. London: HarperCollins.

Broad, W. J., and N. Wade. 1982. *Betrayers of Truth*. New York: Simon and Schuster.

Brooks, Geoffrey. 1992. *Hitler's Nuclear Weapons: The Development and Attempted Deployment of Radiological Armaments by Nazi Germany*. London: Leo Cooper.

Brown, Anthony Cave. 1987. *"C": The Secret Life of Sir Stewart Graham Menzies, Spymaster to Winston Churchill*. New York: Macmillan.

Bryan III, J., and Charles J. V. Murphy. 1979. *The Windsor Story*. London: Granada (and New York: William Morrow). There are differences between these two editions.

Bulloch, John. 1966. *Akin to Treason*. London: Arthur Barker.

Bunting, Madeleine. 1995. *The Model Occupation: The Channel Islands Under German Rule, 1940–1945*. London: HarperCollins.

Burton, Robert Bentley. 1963. *The Vlasov Movement of World War II: An Appraisal*. Dissertation. American University, Washington, D.C.

Calder, Angus. 1992. *The Myth of the Blitz*. London: Pimlico.

Campbell, Rodney. 1977. *The Luciano Project: The Secret Wartime Collaboration of the Mafia and the U.S. Navy*. New York: McGraw-Hill.

Carpenter, Humphrey. 1988. *A Serious Character: The Life of Ezra Pound*. Boston: Houghton Mifflin.

Casillo, Robert. 1988. *The Genealogy of Demons: Anti-Semitism, Fascism, and the Myths of Ezra Pound*. Evanston, Ill.: Northwestern University Press.

Chace, William M. 1973. *The Political Identities of Ezra Pound and T. S. Eliot*. Stanford: Stanford University Press.

Chang, Iris. 1997. *The Rape of Nanking: The Forgotten Holocaust of World War II*. New York: Basic Books.

Charman, Terry. 1992. "William Joyce, 'Lord Haw Haw,' 1906–1946: A Biographical Introduction." Introduction to *Twilight over England*, by William Joyce, pp. v–xix. London: Imperial War Museum reprint of 1940 edition (Berlin: Internationaler Verlag).

Codevilla, Angelo. 1992. *Informing Statecraft: Intelligence for a New Century*. New York: Free Press.

Cohen, Avner. 1998. *Israel and the Bomb*. New York: Columbia University Press.

Cohen, Erik, and Eyal Ben-Ari. 1991. "Hard Choices: The Sociological Analysis of Value Incommensurability." *Human Studies* 16:267–297.

Cohen, Hillel. 1998. "Did Pollard Spy for South Africa Too?" *Kol Hair*, July 24, p. 27 (Hebrew).

Cohen, Philip J. 1996. *Serbia's Secret War: Propaganda and the Deceipt of History*. College Station: Texas A&M University Press.

Cohen, Ran. 1993. "The Man Who Knew Too Much." *Jerusalem*, September 15, pp. 54–56 (Hebrew).

Cohen, Stanley. 1985. *Visions of Social Control*. Cambridge: Polity Press.

———. 2000. *States of Denial*. Oxford: Polity Press.

Cole, J. A. 1964. *Lord Haw-Haw and William Joyce: The Full Story*. London: Faber and Faber.

Coleman, James S. 1990. *Foundations of Social Theory*. Cambridge and London: Belknap Press of Harvard University Press.

Coles, Robert. 1983. "The Roots of Treason: Ezra Pound and the Secret of St. Elizabeth's." *New York Times*, October 23, 1983 (Book Review).

Collis, Maurice. [1954] 1994. *Cortés and Montezuma*. London: Robin Clark.

Colton, Matthew, and Maurice Vanstone. 1997. *Betrayal of Trust: Professionals Who Sexually Abuse Children*. New York: New York University Press.

Colvin, Ian. 1957. *Hitler's Secret Enemy: Admiral Canaris—Patriot or Traitor?* London: Pan Books.

Compton-Hall, Richard. 1991. *Submarines and the War at Sea, 1914–1918*. London: Macmillan.

Conway, Martin. 1993. *Collaboration in Belgium: Leon Degrelle and the Rexist Movement, 1940–1944*. New Haven and London: Yale University Press.

Cook, J., and T. Wall. 1980. "New York Attitude Measures of Trust, Organizational Commitment, and Personal Need Nonfulfillment." *Journal of Occupational Psychology* 53:39–52.

Cornell, Julien. 1966. *The Trial of Ezra Pound: A Documented Account of the Treason Case by the Defendant's Lawyer*. London: Faber and Faber.

Coser, Lewis. 1956. *The Functions of Social Conflict*. New York: Free Press.

Costello, John. 1988. *Mask of Treachery*. New York: William Morrow.

Cromer, Gerald. 1985. "The Beer Affair: Israeli Social Reaction to a Soviet Agent." *Crossroads* 15:55–75.

———. 1986. "'Secularization Is the Root of All Evil': The Response of Ultra-Orthodox Judaism to Social Deviance." *Proceedings of the 9th World Congress on Jewish Studies* (August 1985), 2nd Division, vol. 3 (August 1985):397–404. Jerusalem: World Association for Jewish Studies.

———. 1998. "Udi Adiv." In *The Writing on the Wall: Constructing Political Deviance in Israel,* by Gerald Cromer, pp. 110–168. Ramat Gan: Bar-Illan University Press.

Cruickshank, Charles. 1975. *The German Occupation of the Channel Islands.* Oxford: Oxford University Press.

———. 1986. *SOE in Scandinavia.* Oxford: Oxford University Press.

Dahl, Hans Fredrik. 1999. *Quisling.* Cambridge: Cambridge University Press.

Dan, Uri. 1998. "And Then, in the Morning, the Iraqi MiG Landed in Israel." *Ma'ariv,* Rosh Hashana Supplement, September 20, pp. 4–7 (Hebrew).

Dank, Mitton. 1974. *The French Against the French: Collaboration and Resistance.* London: Cassell.

Dasgupta, Partha. 1988. "Trust as a Commodity." In *Trust: Making and Breaking Cooperative Relations,* edited by D. Gambetta, pp. 49–72. New York: Basil Blackwell.

David, Saul. 1995. *Mutiny at Salerno: An Injustice Exposed.* Washington, D.C.: Brassey's.

Davies, Nigel. 1973. *The Aztecs.* London: Abacus.

Deacon, Richard. 1977. *The Israeli Secret Service.* London: Sphere Books.

———. 1987. *Spyclopedia.* London: Futura.

Dear, I. C. B., and M. R. D. Foot, eds. 1995. *The Oxford Companion to the Second World War.* Oxford and New York: Oxford University Press.

Decker, Malcolm. [1932] 1960. *Benedict Arnold: Son of the Havens.* Tarrytown, N.Y.: Antiquarian Press.

Dedijer, Vladimir. 1992. *The Yugoslav Auschwitz and the Vatican: The Croatian Massacre of the Serbs During World War II.* Buffalo, N.Y.: Prometheus.

De Jong, L. 1950. *The German Fifth Column: Myth or Reality?* Amsterdam: The Netherlands State Institute for War Documentation.

———. 1956. *The German Fifth Column in the Second World War.* Translated from the Dutch by C. M. Geyl. London: Routledge and Kegan Paul.

De-Maria, William. 1992. "Queensland Whistleblowing: Sterilizing the Lone Crusader." *Australian Journal of Social Issues* 27 (no. 4):248–261.

Dennistone, Robin. 1997. *Churchill's Secret War: Diplomatic Decrypts, the Foreign Office, and Turkey, 1942–1944.* New York: St. Martin's Press.

Dimbleby, Jonathan. 1997. *The Last Governor: Chris Patten and the Handover of Hong Kong.* London: Little, Brown.

Dinur, Dov. 1987. *Kasztner: New Light on the Man and His Activities.* Haifa: Gestlit (Hebrew).

Dobson, Christopher, and Ronald Payne. 1986. *The Dictionary of Espionage.* London: Grafton Books.

Donaldson, Frances. 1974. *Edward VIII.* London: Book Club Associates.

Doran, Jamie, and Piers Bizony. 1998. *Starman: The Truth Behind the Legend of Yuri Gagarin.* London: Bloomsbury.

Dorner, Jane. 1972. *Cortez and the Aztecs.* London: Longman.

Drama of Graf Spee and the Battle of the River Plate: A Documentary Anthology, 1914–1964. 1964. Compiled by Sir Eugen Millington-Drake; forward by Admiral of the Fleet Earl Mountbatten of Burma; preface by Admiral of the Fleet Sir Philip Vias. London: Peter Davies.

Ducharme, Lori J., and Gary Alan Fine. 1995. "The Construction of Nonperson-hood and Demonization: Commemorating the Traitorous Reputation of Benedict Arnold." *Social Forces* 73 (no. 4):1309–1331.

Dulles, Allen Welsh. 1947. *Germany's Underground*. New York: Macmillan.

Dumbach, Annette E., and Jud Newborn. 1986. *Shattering the German Night: The Story of the White Rose*. Boston: Little, Brown.

Dupuy, Ernest R., and Trevor N. Dupuy. 1970. *The Encyclopedia of Military History from 3500 B.C. to the Present*. London: Macdonald.

Durkheim, Emile. 1933. *The Division of Labor in Society*. New York: Free Press.

Duus, Masayo. 1983. *Tokyo Rose: Orphan of the Pacific*. Translated from the Japanese by Peter Duus. New York: Kodansha International.

Earley, Pete. 1988. *Family of Spies: Inside the John Walker Spy Ring*. New York: Bantam Books.

Edwards, John Carver. 1991. *Berlin Calling: American Broadcasters in Service to the Third Reich*. New York: Praeger.

Efendowitz, Avner. 1997. "Give Back to God That Which Is God's." *Ha'aretz*, May 16, p. 7B. (Hebrew).

Eisenberg, Dennis, Uri Dan, and Eli Landau. 1978. *The Mossad*. New York: New American Library.

Eisenstadt, S. N., and Luis Roniger. 1984. *Patrons, Clients, and Friends: Interpersonal Relations and the Structure of Trust in Society*. Cambridge: Cambridge University Press.

Ekman, Paul. 1992. *Telling Lies: Clues to Deceit in the Marketplace, Politics, and Marriage*. New York: W. W. Norton.

Farren, Harry Desmond. 1940. *Sabotage: How to Guard Against It*. New York: National Foremen's Institute.

Feldman, Louis H. 1984. *Josephus and Modern Scholarship, 1937–1980*. New York and Berlin: Walter de Gruyter.

————. 1986. *A Supplementary Bibliography*. New York: Garland.

Fest, Joachim. 1996. *Plotting Hitler's Death: The German Resistance to Hitler, 1933–1945*. Translated by Bruce Little. London: Weidenfeld & Nicolson.

Fletcher, George P. 1993. *Loyalty: An Essay on the Morality of Relationships*. New York: Oxford University Press.

Flexner, James Thomas. 1991. *The Traitor and the Spy: Benedict Arnold and John André*. Syracuse: Syracuse University Press.

Flusser, David. 1985. *Josephus Flavius*. Tel Aviv: Ministry of Defense, Transmitted University (Hebrew).

Foot, M. R. D. 1984. *SOE: An Outline History of the Special Operations Executive, 1940–1946*. London: BBC.

Ford, Franklin L. 1985. *Political Murder: From Tyrannicide to Terrorism*. Cambridge: Harvard University Press.

Forman, James. 1973. *Code Name Valkyrie: Count von Stauffenberg and the Plot to Kill Hitler*. New York: S. G. Phillips.

Franzius, Enno. 1969. *History of the Order of Assassins*. New York: Funk and Wagnalls.

Fraser, Antonia. 1995. "Anne of the Thousand Days." In *Past Imperfect: History According to the Movies,* edited by Mark C. Carne, pp. 66–69. London: Cassell.

Friedman, Norman. 2000. *The Fifty-Year War: Conflict and Strategy in the Cold War.* Annapolis, Maryland: Naval Institute Press.

Friedrich, Carl J. 1972. *The Pathology of Politics: Violence, Betrayal, Corruption, Secrecy, and Propaganda.* New York: Harper and Row.

Friedrichs, David O. 1996. *Trusted Criminals: White-Collar Crime in Contemporary Society.* Belmont: Wadsworth.

Fukuyama, Francis. 1995. *Trust: The Social Virtues and the Creation of Prosperity.* New York: Free Press.

Galante, Pierre. 1981. *Operation Valkyrie: The German Generals' Plot Against Hitler.* New York: Dell Books.

Gallagher, Thomas. 1975. *Assault in Norway: Sabotaging the Nazi Nuclear Bomb.* New York: Bantam Books.

Gambetta, D. G. 1988. "Can We Trust Trust?" In *Trust: Making and Breaking Cooperative Relations,* edited by D. Gambetta, pp. 213–237. New York: Basil Blackwell.

Gannon, Michael. 1990. *Operation Drumbeat.* New York: Harper and Row.

Gatrell, V. A. C. 1996. *The Hanging Tree: Executions and the English People, 1770–1868.* Oxford: Oxford University Press.

Geraghty, Tony. 1974. "Joyce's Last Tape." *The* (London) *Times,* April 21, 1974.

The German Fifth Column in Poland. 1940. London: Hutchinson & Co. Published in London for the Polish Ministry of Information.

Getty, Arch J., and Oleg V. Naumov. 1999. *The Road to Terror: Stalin and the Self-Destruction of the Bolsheviks, 1932–1939.* London and New Haven: Yale University Press.

Giddens, Anthony. 1991. *Modernity and Self Identity.* Stanford: Stanford University Press.

Gilbert, Martin. 1963. *The Appeasers.* London: Weidenfeld and Nicolson.

Gilling, Tom, and John McKnight. 1995. *Trial and Error: Mordechai Vanunu and Israel's Nuclear Bomb.* London: HarperCollins.

Glass, Shirly. 1998. "Vows Which Were Violated." *Psychology Today: Soul, Body, and Spirit,* July–August, 17:28–43 (Hebrew).

Glazer, M. P., and P. M. Glazer. 1989. *The Whistleblowers.* New York: Basic Books.

Glenton, Bill. 1986. *Mutiny in Force X.* London: Hodder and Stoughton.

Gold, Hal. 1996. *Unit 731 Testimony.* Tokyo: Yenbooks.

Gõmara, Francisco López de. 1964. *Cortés: The Life of the Conqueror by His Secretary.* Los Angeles: University of California Press.

Good, D. 1988. "Individuals, Interpersonal Relations, and Trust." In *Trust: Making and Breaking Cooperative Relations,* edited by D. Gambetta, pp. 131–185. New York: Basil Blackwell.

Goode, Erich. 1989. "The American Drug Panic of the 1980s: Social Construction or Objective Threat?" *Violence, Aggression, and Terrorism* 3 (no. 4):327–348; reprinted in *International Journal of the Addictions* 25, no. 9 (1990):1083–1098.

———. 1997. *Deviant Behavior,* 5th ed. Englewood Cliffs, N.J.: Prentice Hall.

Goode, Erich, and Nachman Ben-Yehuda. 1994. *Moral Panics.* Oxford: Blackwell.

Gordon, Bertram M. 1980. *Collaboration in France During the Second World War*. Ithaca and London: Cornell University Press.

Goren, Rabbi Shlomo. 1987. "A Lone Fighter for Peace: Was Rabbi Yochanan Ben-Zakkai Alone in the Struggle for Peace with the Romans?" *Ha'aretz*, August 4, p. 20 (Hebrew).

Graml, Hermann, Hans Mommsen, Hans-Joachim Reichhardt, and Ernst Wolf. 1970. *The German Resistance to Hitler*. Berkeley: University of California Press.

Granot, Oded. 1981. *Intelligence*, a volume in *Tzahal Bechelo: Encyclopedia for Army and Security*, edited by Yaacov Erez and Ilan Kefir. Tel Aviv: Revivim, *Ma'ariv* (Hebrew).

Gray, Edwyn A. 1994. *The U-Boat War, 1914–1918*. London: Leo Cooper.

Greenberg, Jeremy, and Robert A. Baron. 1997. *Behavior in Organizations*. London: Prentice-Hall.

Greenberg, Lawrence M. 1987. *Hukbalahap Insurrection*. Washington, D.C.: Analysis Branch, U.S. Army Center of Military History.

Gruzinski, Serge. 1992. *The Aztecs: Rise and Fall of an Empire*. London: Thames and Hudson.

Gutman, Yechiel. 1995. *A Storm in the G.S.S.* Tel Aviv: Yediot Aharonot (Hebrew).

Guttridge, Leonard F. 1992. *Mutiny: A History of Naval Insurrections*. Annapolis, Md.: United States Naval Institute Press.

Gwynn, Denis. 1931. *Traitor or Patriot? The Life and Death of Roger Casement*. New York: Jonathan Cape and Harrison Smith.

Hadar, David. 1971. "The Attitude of the Superpowers to Yoel Brand's Mission." *Molad* 4 (no. 19–20), new series: 112–125 (Hebrew).

Hadas-Lebel, Mireille. 1994. *Flavius Josephus: Eyewitness to Rome's First-Century Conquest of Judea*. Translated by Richard Miller. London: Macmillan.

Hadfield, Robert L. 1979. *Mutiny at Sea*. Stanfordville, New York: E. M. Coleman. Reprint of the 1938 edition published by Dutton, New York.

Hadley, Michael L. 1995. *Count Not the Dead: The Popular Image of the German Submarine*. Montreal and Kingston: McGill-Queen's University Press.

Hagan, Frank. 1989. "Espionage as Political Crime? A Typology of Spies." *Journal of Security Administration* 12 (no. 1):19–36.

———. 1997. *Political Crime: Ideology and Criminality*. Boston: Allyn and Bacon.

Hamerow, Theodore. 1997. *On the Road to the Wolf's Lair: German Resistance to Hitler*. Cambridge: Harvard University Press.

Hammer, Joseph Vaughn. 1835. *The History of the Assassins*. London: Smith and Elder, Cornhill.

Hanser, Richard. 1979. *A Noble Treason: The Revolt of the Munich Students Against Hitler*. New York: G. P. Putnam's Sons.

Harel, Isser. 1985. *The Truth About the Kasztner Murder*. Jerusalem: Edanim Publishers, Yediot Aharonot Edition (Hebrew).

———. 1987. *Soviet Espionage: Communism in Israel*. Tel Aviv: Yedioth Ahronot, Edanim (Hebrew).

———. 1989. *Security and Democracy*. Tel Aviv: Edanim Publishers (Hebrew).

Hassig, Ross. 1988. *Aztec Warfare: Imperial Expansion and Political Control*. Norman: University of Oklahoma Press.

———. 1992. *War and Society in Ancient Mesoamerica*. Berkeley and Los Angeles: University of California Press.

———. 1994. *Mexico and the Spanish Conquest*. London and New York: Longman.

———. 1996. *The Maid of the Myth: La Malinche and the History of Mexico*. Unpublished paper. Department of Anthropology, University of Oklahoma. August.

Haynes, John Earl, and Harvey Klehr. 1999. *Venona: Decoding Soviet Espionage in America*. New Haven and London: Yale University Press.

Heald, Tim. 1997. "Cris Patten and China's Marxists." *Evening Standard*, July 14, p. 24.

Heaps, Willard A. 1969. *Assassination: A Special Kind of Murder*. New York: Meredith Press.

Hedley, Bull, ed. 1986. *The Challenge of the Third Reich*. Oxford: Oxford University Press.

Heilbruner, Oded. 1995. "The Label 'Traitor' Was Accepted with No Appeal." *Ha'aretz*, December 24, p. B2 (Hebrew).

Hewins, Ralph. 1965. *Quisling: Prophet Without Honour*. London: W. H. Allen.

Heymann, David C. 1976. *Ezra Pound, The Last Power: A Political Profile*. New York: Seaver Books.

Hibbert, Christopher. 1978. *Great Mutiny: India, 1857*. New York: Viking Press.

Hickam, Homer H., Jr. 1989. *Torpedo Junction*. Annapolis, Md.: Naval Institute Press.

Hicks, George. 1995. *The Comfort Women: Sex Slaves of the Japanese Imperial Forces*. London: Souvenir Press.

Higham, Charles. 1985. *American Swastika: The Shocking Story of Nazi Collaborators in Our Midst from 1933 to the Present*. Garden City, N.Y.: Doubleday.

———. 1988. *Wallis: Secret Lives of the Duchess of Windsor*. London: Sidgwick and Jackson.

Hilberg, Paul. 1985. *The Destruction of the European Jews*. New York: Holmes and Meier.

Hirschfeld, Gerhard. 1988. *Nazi Rule and Dutch Collaboration: The Netherlands Under German Occupation, 1940–1945*. Translated from the German by Louise Willmot. Oxford, New York, and Hamburg: Berg.

Hirschfeld, Gerhard, and Patrick Marsh, eds. 1989. *Collaboration in France: Politics and Culture During the Nazi Occupation, 1940–1944*. Oxford: Berg.

Hodgson, G. S. 1955. *The Order of Assassins*. The Hague: Mouton. Reprinted in New York by AMS Press.

Hoettl, Wilhelm. 1953. *The Secret Front: The Story of Nazi Political Espionage*. London: Weidenfeld and Nicolson.

Hoffmann, Peter. 1977. *The History of the German Resistance, 1933–1945*. Cambridge: MIT Press.

———. 1988. *German Resistance to Hitler*. Cambridge: Harvard University Press.

Hohne, Heinz. 1979. *Canaris*. Garden City, N.Y.: Doubleday.

Hoidal, Oddvar K. 1989. *Quisling: A Study in Treason*. Oslo: Norwegian University Press.

Hollingsworth, Mark, and Nick Fielding. 1999. *Defending the Realms: MI5 and the Shayler Affair*. London: Deutch.

Horowitz, Varda, and Dalia Ben-Arie. 1998. "Forbidden Relations." *Lai'sha*, July 20 (no. 2675), pp. 14–16 (Hebrew).
Howard, Michael. 1990. *Strategic Deception in the Second World War*. London: Pimlico.
Howe, Russell Warren. 1986. *Mata Hari: The True Story*. New York: Dodd, Mead.
———. 1990. *The Hunt for "Tokyo Rose."* New York: Madison Books.
Hoy, Claire, and Victor Ostrovsky. 1990. *By Way of Deception: A Devastating Insider's Portrait of the Mossad*. Toronto: Stoddart.
Hunter, Nigel. 1990. *The Expedition of Cortés*. East Sussex: Wayland.
Hurst, James Willard. 1983. "Treason." In *Encyclopedia of Crime and Justice*, vol. 4, edited by Sanford H. Kadish, pp. 1559–1562. New York: Free Press.
Hurwood, Bernhardt J. 1970. *Society and the Assassin*. New York: Parents' Magazine Press.

Ichheiser, Gustav. 1970. *Appearances and Realities*. San Francisco: Jossey-Bass.
Ingliss, Brian. 1973. *Roger Casement*. London: Hodder and Stoughton.

Jenkins, Simon. 1997. "The Governor, Treason, and Plot." *The* (London) *Times*, July 12, p. 22.
Johnson, Chambers. 1990. *An Instance of Treason: Ozaki Hotsumi and the Sorge Spy Ring*. Stanford: Stanford University Press.
Johnson, William Weber. 1977. *Cortés*. London: Hutchinson.
Johnson-George, C., and W. Swap. 1982. "Measurement of Specific Interpersonal Trust: Construction and Validation of a Scale to Assess Trust in a Specific Other." *Journal of Personality and Social Psychology* 43:1306–1317.
Johnston, Kenneth R. 1998. *The Hidden Wordsworth: Poet, Lover, Rebel, Spy*. New York: W. W. Norton.

Kaminka, Aharon. 1943–1944. "Rabbi Yochanan Ben-Zakkai and His Students." *Zion* 9:70–83 (Hebrew).
Karpin, Michael. 1999. *Murder in the Name of God: The Plot to Kill Yitzhak Rabin*. New York: Henry Holt.
Katz, Shmuel. 1966. *Inside the Miracle (Day of Fire)*. Tel Aviv: Karni (Hebrew).
Kedar, Binyamin. 1982. "Masada: The Myth and the Complex." *Jerusalem Quarterly* 24:57–63.
Kedward, H. Roderick. 1993. *In Search of the Maquis: Rural Resistance in Southern France, 1942–1944*. Oxford: Clarendon Press.
Kedward, H. Roderick, and Roger Austin, eds. 1985. *Vichy France and the Resistance: Culture and Ideology*. London: Croom Helm.
Kee, H. W., and R. E. Knox. 1970. "Conceptual and Methodological Considerations in the Study of Trust." *Journal of Conflict Resolution* 14:357–366.
Keegan, John, ed. 1978. *Who Was Who in World War II*. New York: Thomas Y. Crowell.
Keenan, Edward L. 1971. *The Kurbskii-Grozni Apocrypha: The Seventeenth-Century Genesis of the "Correspondance" Attributed to Prince A. M. Kurbskii and Tsar Ivan IV*. Cambridge: Harvard University Press.
Kersaudy, François. 1982. *Churchill and De Gaulle*. New York: Atheneum.

Kershaw, Ian. 1987. *The "Hitler Myth."* Oxford: Oxford University Press.

Kersten Krystyna. 1991. *The Establishment of Communist Rule in Poland, 1943–1948.* Berkeley: University of California Press.

Kessler, Leo. 1991. *Betrayal at Venlo.* London: Leo Cooper.

Kilroy, Thomas. 1994. *Double Cross.* Loughcrew, Ireland: Gallery Press.

Kilzer, Louis C. 1994. *Churchill's Deception: The Dark Secret That Destroyed Nazi Germany.* New York: Simon & Schuster.

King, Robert D. 1989. "Treason and Traitors." *Society* 26 (no. 5):39–48.

Klaidman, Daniel, and Kosova Weston. 1998. "A Question of Betrayal." *Newsweek,* January 12, p. 38.

Klaits, Joseph. 1985. *Servants of Satan: The Age of the Witch Hunts.* Bloomington: Indiana University Press.

Klausner, Samuel Z. 1998. "E. Digby Baltzel: Moral Rhetoric and Research Methodology." *Sociological Theory* 16 (no. 2):149–171.

Klement, Frank L. 1984. *Dark Lanterns: Secret Political Societies, Conspiracies, and Treason Trials in the Civil War.* Baton Rouge and London: Louisiana State University Press.

Klemperer, Klemens von. 1994. *German Resistance Against Hitler: The Search for Allies Abroad, 1938–1945.* Oxford: Clarendon Press.

Knightly, Phillip. 1986. *The Second Oldest Profession: Spies and Spying in the Twentieth Century.* New York: W. W. Norton.

Knightley, Phillip, and Caroline Kennedy. 1987. *An Affair of State: The Profumo Case and the Framing of Stephen Ward.* New York: Atheneum.

Knox, Oliver. 1997. *Rebels and Informers: Stirrings of Irish Independence.* London: J. Murray.

Knox, Ronald. 1981. *Death March: The Survivors of Bataan.* New York: Harcourt Brace Jovanovich.

Kobi, Tzvi. 1998. "Betrayals at the Top. You Understand, Mr. Prosecutor, This Is What Everyone Does." *Olam Haisha,* March (no. 173):24–28 (Hebrew).

Koch, H. W. 1989. *In the Name of the Volk: Political Justice in Hitler's Germany.* London: I. B. Tauris.

Kohl, Philip L., and Clare Fawcett, eds. 1995. *Nationalism, Politics, and the Practice of Archaeology.* Cambridge: Cambridge University Press.

Kohn, Alexander. 1986. *False Prophets: Fraud and Error in Science and Medicine.* Oxford: Basil Blackwell.

Kooistra, Paul. 1989. *Criminals as Heroes: Structure, Power, and Identity.* Bowling Green, Ky.: State University Popular Press.

Korn, Marianne. 1985. *Ezra Pound and History.* Orono, Maine: National Poetry Foundation, University of Maine.

Kramarz, Joachim. 1967. *Stauffenberg: The Life and Death of an Officer.* London: Andre Deutch.

Kramer, R., M. Brewer, and B. Hanna. 1996. "Collective Trust and Collective Action: Trust as a Social Decision." In *Trust in Organizations,* edited by R. Kramer and T. Tyler. Thousand Oaks, Calif.: Sage Publications.

Kraus, Clifford. 1997. "After 500 Years, Cortés's Girlfriend Is Not Forgiven." *New York Times,* International, March 26, p. A4.

Ku, Agnes S. 1998. "Boundary Politics in the Public Sphere: Openness, Secrecy, and Leak." *Sociological Theory* 16 (no. 2):172–192.

Kurtzman, Dan. 1997. *Blood and Water: Sabotaging Hitler's Bomb.* New York: Henry Holt.

Ladouceur, David. 1987. "Josephus and Masada." In *Josephus, Judaism, and Christianity,* edited by Louis H. Feldman and Gohei Hata, pp. 95–113. Detroit: Wayne State University Press.

Landa, J. 1994. *Trust, Ethnicity, and Identity.* Ann Arbor: University of Michigan Press.

Laqueur, Walter. 1976. *Fascism: A Reader's Guide.* Berkeley: University of California Press.

———. 1980. *The Terrible Secret: Suppression of the Truth About Hitler's "Final Solution."* Boston: Little, Brown.

———. 1985. *A World of Secrets: The Uses and Limits of Intelligence.* New York: Basic Books.

Lawson, Annette. 1988. *Adultery: An Analysis of Love and Betrayal.* Oxford: Basil Blackwell.

Leach, Robert. 1995. *Turncoats: Changing Party Allegiance by British Politicians.* Aldershot, England: Dartmouth.

Leber, Annedore, collector. 1957. *Conscience in Revolt: Sixty-Four Stories of Resistance in Germany, 1933–1945.* London: Vallentine, Mitchell.

Lees, Michael. 1990. *The Rape of Serbia: The British Role in Tito's Grab for Power, 1943–1944.* San Francisco: Harcourt Brace Jovanovich.

Lentz III, Harris M. 1988. *Assassinations and Executions: An Encyclopedia of Political Violence, 1865–1986.* Jefferson, North Carolina and London: McFarland.

León-Portilla, Miguel, ed. [1962] 1990. *The Broken Spears: The Aztec Account of the Conquest of Mexico.* Boston: Beacon Press.

Lerner, Max. 1930. "Assassination." In *Encyclopedia of the Social Sciences,* vol. 2, edited by Edwin Seligman. New York: Macmillan.

Levack, Brian P. 1987. *The Witch-Hunt in Early Modern Europe.* London: Longman.

Levine, Donald N., ed. 1971. *Georg Simmel on Individuality and Social Forms.* Chicago: University of Chicago Press.

Lewis, Bernard. 1967. *The Assassins: A Radical Sect in Islam.* London: Weidenfeld and Nicolson. (Reprint, London: Al Saqi Books, 1985).

———. 1975. *History: Remembered, Recovered, Invented.* Princeton: Princeton University Press.

Littlejohn, David. 1972. *The Patriotic Traitors: The Story of Collaboration in German-Occupied Europe, 1940–1945.* Garden City, N.Y.: Doubleday.

Lottman, Herbert R. 1985. *Pétain: Hero or Traitor?* Harmondsworth, Middlesex: Penguin Books, Viking.

———. 1986. *The People's Anger in Post-Liberation France.* London: Hutchinson.

Luhmann, Niklas. 1988. "Family, Confidence, Trust: Problems and Alternatives." In *Trust: Making and Breaking Cooperative Relations,* edited by D. Gambetta, pp. 94–107. New York: Basil Blackwell.

———. 1995. *Social Systems.* Stanford: Stanford University Press.

MacDonald, Callum, and Jan Kaplan. 1995. *Prague in the Shadow of the Swastika: A History of the German Occupation, 1939–1945.* London: Quartet Books.

Mackay, James. 1995. *William Wallace: Braveheart.* Edinburgh and London: Mainstream Publishing.

MacWilliam, H. D., ed. 1910. *The Official Records of the Mutiny in the Black Watch: A London Incident of the Year 1743.* London: F. Groom.

Manvell, Roger. 1971. *The Conspirators: 20th July 1944.* New York: Ballantine Books.

Manvell, Roger, and Heinrich Fraenkel. 1969. *The Canaris Conspiracy: The Secret Resistance to Hitler in the German Army.* New York: David McKay.

Margalit, Dan. 1982. "Murder in 6 Emmanuel Blvd." *Ha'aretz*, supplement, April 30, pp. 12–13 (Hebrew).

Marius, Richard. 1995. "A Man for All Seasons." In *Past Imperfect: History According to the Movies*, edited by Mark C. Carne, pp. 70–73. London: Cassell.

Maron, Gideon. 1998a. "Deserted Manbar, Saved the Homeland," *Yediot Aharonot* ("7 Days" Supplement), August 14, pp. 30–34.

———. 1998b. "The Traitors: With the Back to the Country." *Yediot Aharonot*, Simchat Torah Supplement, October 11, pp. 8–11 (Hebrew).

Martin, David, ed. 1978. *Patriot or Traitor? The Case of General Mihailovic.* Stanford: Hoover Institution.

Marx, Gary, and Cyrille Fijnaut, eds. 1995. *Undercover: Police Surveillance in Comparative Perspective.* The Hague: Kluwer Law International.

Mason, Herbert Molloy. 1978. *To Kill Hitler: The Attempts on the Life of Adolf Hitler.* London: Michael Joseph.

Masterman, J. C. 1972. *The Double-Cross System, 1939–1945.* London: Pimlico.

Mastny, Vojtech. 1971. *The Czechs Under Nazi Rule: The Failure of National Resistance, 1939–1942.* New York and London: Columbia University Press.

Maurer, David W. 1940. *The Big Con: The Story of the Confidence Man and the Confidence Game.* Indianapolis, Ind.: Bobbs-Merrill.

———. 1974. *The American Confidence Man.* Springfield, Ill.: Thomas.

Mayer, R. C., J. H. Davis, and D. F. Schoorman. 1995. "An Integrative Model of Organizational Trust." *Academy of Management Review* 20 (no. 3):709–734.

Mayer S. L., ed. 1977. *Encyclopedia of World War II.* London: Hamlyn.

McDonagh, Melanie. 1997. "There's a Place for an Honest-to-God Mistress." *Evening Standard*, August 21, p. 13.

McKale, Donald. 1974. *The Nazi Party Courts: Hitler's Management of Conflict in His Movement, 1921–1945.* Wichita: University of Kansas Press.

Melman, Yossi. 1998. "An Observer of Our Own." *Ha'aretz*, December 10, p. B2 (Hebrew).

———. 1999. "Why Uri Illan Committed Suicide." *Ha'aretz*, February 9, p. B3 (Hebrew).

Melman, Yossi, and Dan Raviv. 1989. *The Imperfect Spies: The History of Israeli Intelligence.* London: Sidgwick and Jackson.

Miethe, Terance D. 1998. *Whistleblowing at Work: Tough Choices in Exposing Fraud, Waste, and Abuse on the Job.* Boulder: Westview Press.

Milazzo, Matteo. 1975. *The Chetnik Movement and the Yugoslav Resistance.* Baltimore: Johns Hopkins University Press.

Miller, Nathan. 1995. *War at Sea: A Naval History of World War II.* New York: Scribner.

Mills, C. Wright. 1970. *The Sociological Imagination.* Harmondsworth: Penguin Books. (Reprint of original edition, Oxford University Press, 1959).

———. 1940. "Situated Actions and Vocabularies of Motives." *American Sociological Review* 5:904–913.

Misztal, Barbara A. 1996. *Trust in Modern Societies.* Cambridge: Polity Press.

Morris, Benny. 1991. *The Roots of British Appeasement: The British Weekly Press and Nazi Germany During the 1930s.* London: Frank Cass.

Muhlbauer, Varda, and Mina Zemach. 1991. *Onesies Twosies.* Tel Aviv: Am Oved (Hebrew).

Muller, Ingo. 1991. *Hitler's Justice: The Courts of the Third Reich.* Translated by Deborah Lucas Schneider. Cambridge: Harvard University Press.

Murphy, Brendan M. 1987. *Turncoat: The Strange Case of British Traitor Sergeant Harold Cole.* New York: Harcourt Brace Jovanovich.

Nachshon, Illan. 2000. "A Study: Every Seventh Child in Britain Does Not Know Who His/Her Real Father Is." *Yediot Aharonot,* January 24, p. 20 (Hebrew).

Nardi, Chen. 1996. *Men and Betrayal.* Tel Aviv: Modan (Hebrew).

Near, Jent P., and Marcia P. Miceli. 1985. "Organizational Dissidence: The Case of Whistleblowing." *Journal of Business Ethics* 4:1–16.

———. 1992. *Blowing the Whistle: The Organizational and Legal Implications for Companies and Employees.* Lexington, Mass.: Lexington Books.

———. 1997. "Whistleblowing as Antisocial Behavior." In *Antisocial Behavior in Organizations,* edited by R. A. Giacalone and J. Greenberg, pp. 130–149. London: Sage Publications.

Nettler, Gwynn. 1982. *Lying, Cheating, Stealing.* Vol. 3 in Criminal Careers Series. Cincinnati: Anderson Publishing.

Neumann, Alfred. 1945. *Six of Them.* Translated from the German by Anatol Murad. New York: Macmillan.

Neusner, Jacob. 1970. *The Life of Yochanan Ben-Zakkai, ca. 1–80 C.E.* Leiden, England: Brill.

Nevo, Amos. 1987. "The Fighter Shmuel." *Yediot Aharonot,* weekend supplement ("7 Days"), November 27, pp. 20–23, 45 (Hebrew).

Newnham, Tom. 1978. *A Cry of Treason.* Palmerton North, New Zealand: Dunmore Press.

Niv, David. 1965–1980. *The Battles of the National Military Organization (Ma'archot Hairgun Hatzvai Haleumi).* Six volumes. Tel Aviv: Mossad Klosner (Hebrew).

Noakes, Jeremy, and Geoffrey Pridham, eds. 1988. *Nazism, 1919–1945: A Documentary Reader.* Exeter: University of Exeter.

Norton, Cherry, and Chris Hastings. 1997. "Telltale Signs That Betray the Adulterer." *Sunday Times,* September 21, p. 10.

Novick, Peter. 1968. *The Resistance Versus Vichy: The Purge of Collaborators in Liberated France.* New York: Columbia University Press.

O'Day, Rosemary. 1974. "Intimidation Rituals: Reactions to Reformers." *Journal of Applied Behavioral Science* 10:373–385.

Ofir-Shacham, Orna. 1998. "Who Betrays Who, and Why?" *Yediot Aharonot,* "Yours" supplement, August 2, pp. 4–5 (Hebrew).

Oliver, Amalya. L. 1997. "On the Nexus of Organizations and Professions: Networking Through Trust." *Sociological Inquiry* 67 (no. 2):227–245.

Ormerod, Captain Gerald J. 1997. "Loyalty Is the Highest Honor." *U.S. Naval Institute Proceedings*, June, vol. 123/6/1,132, pp. 55–56.

O'Toole, J. A. 1991. *Honorable Treachery: A History of U.S. Intelligence, Espionage, and Covert Action from the American Revolution to the CIA.* New York: Atlantic Monthly Press.

Page, Bruce, David Leitch, and Phillip Knightley. 1969. *Philby: The Spy Who Betrayed a Generation.* Harmondsworth, England: Penguin Books.

Pallone, Nathaniel, and James J. Hennessy, eds. 1995. *Fraud and Fallible Judgment: Varieties of Deception in the Social and Behavioral Sciences.* New Brunswick, N.J.: Transaction Publishers.

Parker, John. 1988. *King of Fools.* London: Futura.

Parrish, Thomas, and S. L. A. Marshall, eds. 1978. *The Encyclopedia of World War II.* London: Secker & Warburg.

Paul, Allen. 1991. *Katyn: The Untold Story of Stalin's Polish Massacre.* New York: Scribner's.

Paxton, Don. 1972. *Vichy France: Old Guard and New Order, 1940–1944.* New York: Knopf.

Penkovsky, Oleg. 1965. *The Penkovsky Papers.* Translated by P. Deriabin. London, St. James's Place: Collins.

Penrose, Barrie, and Simon Freeman. 1986. *Conspiracy of Silence: The Secret Life of Anthony Blunt.* London: Grafton Books.

Philby, Kim. 1969. *My Silent War.* London: Panther Books.

Philip, Craig. 1994. *Last Stands: Famous Battles Against the Odds.* London: Grange Books.

Pincher, Chapman. 1987. *Traitors: The Labyrinths of Treason.* London: Sidgwick & Jackson.

Ploscowe, Morris. 1934 "Treason." In *Encyclopaedia of the Social Sciences,* edited by Edwin R. A. Seligman and Alvin Johnson, pp. 93–96. New York: Macmillan.

Polmar, Norman, and Thomas B. Allen. 1997. *Spy Book: The Encyclopedia of Espionage.* New York: Random House.

Pope, Dudley. 1956. *The Battle of the River Plate.* Annapolis, Md.: Naval Institute Press.

Pound, Ezra. 1978. *"Ezra Pound Speaking": Radio Speeches of World War II.* Edited by Leonard W. Doob. Westport, Conn.: Greenwood Press.

Prange, Gordon W. 1984. *Target Tokyo: The Story of the Sorge Spy Ring.* With Donald M. Goldstein and Katherine V. Dillon. New York: McGraw-Hill.

Prescott, William H. 1925. *History of the Conquest of Mexico.* London: George Allen & Unwin.

Pryce-Jones, David. 1976. *Unity Mitford: A Quest.* London: Weidenfeld and Nicolson.

Pu-Yi, H. 1987. *From Emperor to Citizen: The Autobiography of Aisin-Gioro Pu-Yi.* London: Oxford University Press.

Quaife, G. R. 1987. *Godly Zeal and Furious Rage: The Witch in Early Modern Europe.* New York: St. Martin's Press.

Rachum, Ilan. 1990. *The Israeli General Security Service Affair.* Jerusalem: Carmel (Hebrew).
Rajak, Tessa. 1983. *Josephus: The Historian and His Society.* London: Duckworth.
Randall, Willard Sterne. 1990. *Benedict Arnold: Patriot and Traitor.* New York: Quill, William Morrow.
Rapoport, David C. 1971. *Assassination and Terrorism.* Toronto: Canadian Broadcasting Corporation.
————. 1984. "Fear and Trembling: Terrorism in Three Religious Traditions." *American Political Science Review* 78 (no. 30):658–677.
Rapoport, Uriel, ed. 1982. *Josephus Flavius.* Jerusalem: Yad Itzhak Ben-Zvi (Hebrew).
Raviv, Dan, and Yossi Melman. 1990. *Every Spy a Prince.* Boston: Houghton Mifflin.
Redman, Tim. 1991. *Ezra Pound and Italian Fascism.* Cambridge and New York: Cambridge University Press.
Report of the Royal Commission. 1946. Appointed under the Order in Council P.C. 411 of February 5, 1946, and submitted June 27, 1946. Ottawa: Edmond Cloutien, Printer to the King's Most Excellent Majesty Controller of Stationary.
Richelson, Jeffrey T. 1995. *A Century of Spies: Intelligence in the Twentieth Century.* New York: Oxford University Press.
Rings, Werner. 1979. *Life with the Enemy: Collaboration and Resistance in Hitler's Europe, 1939–1945.* Translated by J. Maxwell Brownjohn. London: Weidenfeld and Nicolson.
Ripka, Hubert. 1945. *Fifth Column at Work.* London: Trinity Press.
Roberts, Walter. 1973. *Tito, Mihailovic, and the Allies, 1941–1945.* New Brunswick, N.J.: Rutgers University Press.
Robinson, Peter W. 1996. *Deceit, Delusion, and Detection.* London: Sage.
Rogers, Lois. 2000. "One in Seven Fathers 'Not the Real Parent.'" *Sunday Times,* January 23, p. 7.
Rolef, Hattis Susan. 1988. *Political Dictionary of the State of Israel.* Jerusalem: Keter (Hebrew).
Rosenbloom, Joshua L. 1998. "Strikebreakers and the Labor Market in the U.S.A., 1881–1894." *Journal of Economic History* 58 (no. 1):183–205.
Rosenfeld, Shalom. 1955. *Criminal File No. 124: The Greenwald-Kasztner Trial.* Tel Aviv: Karni (Hebrew).
Roy, Jules. 1967. *The Trial of Marshal Pétain.* Translated by Robert Baldick. New York: Harper and Row.
Rusbridger, James. 1989. *The Intelligence Game: The Illusions and Delusions of International Espionage.* London: Bodley Head.
Rusbridger, James, and Eric Nave. 1991. *Betrayal at Pearl Harbor: How Churchill Lured Roosevelt into World War II.* New York: Summit Books.

Sarbin, Theodore R., Ralph M. Carney, and Carson Eoyang. 1994. *Citizen Espionage: Studies in Trust and Betrayal.* Westport, Conn.: Praeger.

Sawatsky, John. 1984. *Gouzenko: The Untold Story*. Toronto: Macmillan.

Schellenberg, Walter. 1965. *Schellenberg*. Edited and translated by Louis Hagan, introduced by Alan Bullock. London: Mayflower.

Scheppele, Kim Lane. 1988. *Legal Secrets: Equality and Efficiency in the Common Law*. Chicago: University of Chicago Press.

Schiff, Ze'ev, and Ehud Ya'ari. 1984. *War of Deception*. Jerusalem and Tel Aviv: Shocken (Hebrew).

Schiff, Ze'ev, and Eitan Haber, eds. 1976. *Israel, Army and Defence: A Dictionary*. Tel Aviv: Zmora, Bitan, Modan (Hebrew).

Schoenbrun, David. 1990. *Maquis: Soldiers of the Night. The Story of the French Resistance*. London: Robert Hale.

Scott, Janny. 1996. "Alger Hiss, Divisive Icon of Cold War, Dies at 92." *New York Times*, Saturday, November 16, pp. 1, 31.

Sefer Toldot HaHagana (The History of the Hagana). 1954–1973. Eight volumes. First five volumes published by Tel Aviv: Ma'arachot; last three volumes published by Tel Aviv: Am Oved (Hebrew).

Segal, Avi. 1996. "It Is Not Allowed to Die in Defense of the Wailing Wall." *Jerusalem*, October 18, p. 10 (Hebrew).

Segev, Shmuel. 1986. *Alone in Damascus: The Life and Death of Eli Cohen*. Jerusalem: Keter (Hebrew).

Seligman, Adam. 1997. *The Problem of Trust*. Princeton: Princeton University Press.

Sellers, Charles C. 1930. *Benedict Arnold: The Proud Warrior*. New York: Minton, Balch.

Selwyn, Francis. 1987. *Hitler's Englishman: The Crime of "Lord Haw-Haw."* London: Routledge & Kegan Paul.

Seth, Ronald. 1956. *The Undaunted: The Story of Resistance in Western Europe*. New York: Philosophical Library.

———. 1972. *Encyclopedia of Espionage*. London: Book Club Associates.

———. 1973. *Jackals of the Reich: The Story of the British Free Korps*. London: New English Library.

Shemer, Sara. 1992. *An Intimate Report About Women in Israel*. Tel Aviv: Ma'ariv Library (Hebrew).

Shenhar, Mayan. 1988. "Betrayals." *Laisha*, February 23, no. 2654, pp. 12–14 (Hebrew).

Shermer, David. 1971. *Blackshirts: Fascism in Britain*. New York: Ballantine Books.

Shibutani, Tamotsu. 1978. *The Derelicts of Company K: A Sociological Study of Demoralization*. Berkeley: University of California Press.

Shteinberg, Yesha'ayahu. 1996. "Who Else Is Guilty?" *Ha`aretz* (October 21) p. 2B. (Hebrew).

Simmel, Georg. 1950. *The Sociology of Georg Simmel*. Translated, edited, and an introduction by Kurt H. Wolff. New York: Free Press.

———. 1955. *Conflict and the Web of Group Affiliation*. New York: Free Press.

Sinclair, Andrew. 1986. *The Red and the Blue: Intelligence, Treason, and the Universities*. London: Weidenfeld and Nicolson.

Sinel, L. P. 1969. *The German Occupation of Jersey: A Diary of Events from June 1940 to June 1945*. London: Corgi Books.

Smelser, Neil J. 1998. "The Rational and the Ambivalent in the Social Sciences." 1997 Presidential Address. *American Sociological Review* 63 (no. 1):1–16.

Smelser, Ronald. 1975. *The Sudeten Problem, 1933–1938: Volkstumspolitik and the Formulation of Nazi Foreign Policy*. Middletown, Conn.: Wesleyan University Press.

Smith, John Chabot. 1976. *Alger Hiss: The True Story*. New York: Holt, Rinehart and Winston.

Snyder, Louis L. 1976. *Encyclopedia of the Third Reich*. New York: McGraw-Hill.

Sontag, Sherry, and Christopher Drew. 1998. *Blind Man's Bluff: The Untold Story of American Submarine Espionage*. New York: Public Affairs.

Speer, Albert. 1971. *Inside the Third Reich: Memoirs by Albert Speer*. Translated from the German by Richard and Clara Winston. New York: Avon Books.

Sprinzak, Ehud. 1999. *Brother Against Brother: Violence and Extremism in Israeli Politics from Altalena to the Rabin Assassination*. New York: Free Press.

Staples, William J. 1997. *The Culture of Surveillance: Discipline and Social Control in the United States*. New York: St. Martin's Press.

Steinlauf, Michael C. 1997. *Bondage to the Dead: Poland and the Memory of the Holocaust*. Syracuse, N.Y.: Syracuse University Press.

Stern, Menachem. 1987. "Yoseph Ben-Matitiahu, Historian of 'Wars of the Jews.'" In *Studies in Historiography*, edited by Joseph Salmon, Menachem Stern, and Moshe Zimmermann, pp. 41–51. Jerusalem: Zalman Shazar Center for Jewish History (Hebrew).

Stern, Menachem, ed. 1984. *The History of the Land of Israel: The Roman Byzantian Period*, vol. 4. Jerusalem: Yad Yitzhak Ben-Zvi and Keter (Hebrew).

Steven, Stewart. 1980. *The Spymasters of Israel*. New York: Ballantine Books.

Stewart, Sidney. 1956. *Give Us This Day*. New York: W. W. Norton.

Stohl, Clifford. 1989. *The Cuckoo's Egg: Tracking a Spy Through the Maze of Computer Espionage*. New York: Doubleday.

Stokker, Kathleen. 1997. *Folklore Fights the Nazis: Humor in Occupied Norway, 1940–1945*. Madison: University of Wisconsin Press.

Stone, I. F. 1988. "Was There a Witch Hunt in Ancient Athens?" *New York Review of Books* 34 (no. 21–22):37–41.

Stone, Michael Edward, ed. 1984. *Jewish Writing of the Second Temple*. Assen, Netherlands: Van Gorcum.

Sztompka, Piotr. 1999. *Trust: A Sociological Theory*. Cambridge: Cambridge University Press.

Tanaka, Chester. 1997. *Go for Broke: A Pictorial History of the Japanese American 100th Infantry Battalion and the 442d Regimental Combat Team*. San Francisco: Presidio Press.

Teveth, Shabtai. 1992. *Shearing Time: Firing Squad at Beth-Jiz*. Tel Aviv: Ish Dor (Hebrew).

Thackeray, Henry St. John. 1968. *Josephus: The Man and the Historian*. New York: Ktav Publishing.

Thomas, Gwynne. 1995. *King, Pawn, or Black Knight?* Edinburgh and London: Mainstream Publishing.

Thomas, Hugh. 1993. *The Conquest of Mexico*. London: Pimlico.

Tolstoy, Nikolai. 1979. *Victims of Yalta*. London: Corgi Books.

Tomasevich, Jozo. 1975. *War and Revolution in Yugoslavia, 1941–1945: The Chetniks*. Stanford: Stanford University Press.

Toms, Carel. 1967. *Hitler's Fortress Islands: The First Photo-History of the German Occupation of British Soil*. London: Four Square Books.

Tonks, Randall A. R. 1971. *HMS Exeter: Heavy Cruiser, 1929–1942*. Coburg House, Windsor, England: Warship Profile, Profile Publications.

Torrey, E. Fuller. 1984. *The Roots of Treason: Ezra Pound and the Secret of St. Elizabeth's*. New York: McGraw-Hill.

Toscano, Louis. 1990. *Triple Cross: Israel, the Atomic Bomb and the Man Who Spilled the Secrets*. New York: Birch Lasne Press.

Toscano, Mario. 1967. *The Origins of the Pact of Steel*. Baltimore: Johns Hopkins University Press.

Tournoux, Jean-Raymond. 1964. *Sons of France: Pétain and De Gaulle*. Translated by Oliver Coburn. New York: Viking Press.

Trunk, Isaiah. [1972], 1977. *Judenrat*. New York: Stein and Day.

Turner, Jonathan H. 1991. *The Structure of Sociological Theory*, 5th ed. Belmont, California: Wadsworth Publishing.

Tute, Warren. 1989. *The Reluctant Enemies: The Story of the Last War Between Britain and France, 1940–1942*. London: Collins.

Vaillant, George C. [1944] 1962. *Aztecs of Mexico: Origin, Rise, and Fall of the Aztec Nation*. Revised by Suzannah B. Vaillant. London: Allan Lane.

Verner, Simcha. 1992. "The Whistleblowers and the Persecuted." *Nihul* 89:6–11 (Hebrew).

Verrier, Anthony. 1990. *Assassination in Algiers: Churchill, Roosevelt, de Gaulle, and the Murder of Admiral Darlan*. London: Macmillan.

Vinitzky-Seroussi, Vered. 1999. "The Social Reaction to Treason Within a Pluralistic Society: The Pollard Affair." Forthcoming in *Advances in Criminological Theory* 8:389–408.

Volkman, Ernest. 1994. *Spies: The Secret Agents Who Changed the Course of History*. New York: John Wiley & Sons.

Walker, Mark. 1989. *German National Socialism and the Quest for Nuclear Power, 1939–1949*. Cambridge: Harvard University Press.

Wallace, Willard M. 1954. *Traitorous Hero: The Life and Fortunes of Benedict Arnold*. New York: Harper & Brothers.

———. 1978. *Connecticut's Dark Star of the Revolution: General Benedict Arnold*. Hartford, Conn.: American Revolution Bicentennial Commission of Connecticut.

Waller, John H. 1996. *The Unseen War in Europe: Espionage and Conspiracy in the Second World War*. London: I. B. Tauris Publishers.

Warmbruun, Werner. 1963. *The Dutch Under German Occupation, 1940–1945*. Stanford: Stanford University Press.

Wasserstein, Bernard. 1982. "New Light on the Assassination of Lord Moyne." *Zemanim* 7:4–17 (Hebrew).

————. 1998. *Secret War in Shanghai: Treachery, Subversion, and Collaboration in the Second World War*. London: Profile Books.

Wauck, John. 1991. "Ambiguous Defection." *American Scholar* 60:620–622.

Weale, Arian. 1994. *Renegades: Hitler's Englishmen*. London: Weidenfeld and Nicolson.

Weinberg, Gerhard L. 1994. *A World at Arms: A Global History of World War II*. Cambridge: Cambridge University Press.

Weiner, Tim, David Johnston, and Neil A. Lewis. 1995. *Betrayal: The Story of Aldrich Ames, An American Spy*. London: Richard Cohen Books.

Weinstein, Allen. 1978. *Perjury: The Hiss-Chambers Case*. London: Hutchinson.

Weinstein, Allen, and Alexander Vassiliev. 1999. *The Haunted Wood: Soviet Espionage in America—The Stalin Era*. New York: Random House.

Weiss-Rosmarin, Trude. 1966. "Masada and Yavneh." *Jewish Spectator* 31 (no. 9):4–7.

Weitz, Giddi. 1998. "What Is Good for Bibi." *Kol Hair*, August 21, p. 29 (Hebrew).

Weitz, Yechiam. 1995. *The Man Who Was Murdered Twice*. Jerusalem: Keter Publishing (Hebrew).

West, Nigel, ed. 1993. *The Faber Book of Espionage*. London: Faber and Faber.

————. 1995. *The Faber Book of Treachery*. London: Faber and Faber.

West, Rebecca. [1964], 1985. *The New Meaning of Treason*. Harmondsworth, England: Penguin Books.

West, W. J. 1987. *Truth Betrayed*. London: Duckworth.

Weyl, Nathaniel. 1950. *Treason: The Story of Disloyalty and Betrayal in American History*. Washington D.C.: Public Affairs.

Whalen, Robert Weldon. 1993. *Assassinating Hitler: Ethics and Resistance in Nazi Germany*. Selingsrove: Susquehanna University Press (London and Toronto: Associated University Presses).

Wharam, Alan. 1995. *Treason: Famous English Treason Trials*. Phoenix Mill, England: Alan Sutton Publishing.

Wheal, Elizabeth-Ann, Stephen Pope, and James Taylor. 1995. *A Dictionary of the Second World War*, 2nd ed. London: Grafton Books.

Wheeler-Bennett, John W. 1967. *The Nemesis of Power: The German Army in Politics, 1918–1945*. London: Macmillan; and New York: St. Martin's Press.

Whitcomb, Roger S. 1998. *The Cold War in Retrospect: The Formative Years*. Westport, Conn.: Praeger.

White, John Baker. 1957. *Sabotage Is Suspected*. London: Evans Brothers.

Whymant, Robert. 1996. *Stalin's Spy: Richard Sorge and the Tokyo Espionage Ring*. London: I. B. Tauris Publishers.

Williams, Anthony. 1976. "Resistance and Opposition Amongst Germans." In *Resistance in Europe 1939–1945*, edited by Stephen Hawes and Ralph White, pp. 135–169. Harmondsworth, England: Penguin Books.

Williams, Peter, and David Wallace. 1989. *Unit 731: The Japanese Army's Secret of Secrets*. London and Toronto: Hodder and Stoughton.

Williamson, Gordon. 1995. *Loyalty Is My Honor: Personal Accounts from the Waffen-SS*. London: Motorbooks.

Wilson, Colin. 1975. *Order of Assassins*. London: Panther Books.

Winks. Robin W. 1987. *Cloak and Gown: Scholars in the Secret War, 1939–1961*. New York: William Morrow.

Wise, David. 1988. *The Spy Who Got Away: The Inside Story of Edward Lee Howard, the CIA Agent Who Betrayed His Country's Secrets and Escaped to Moscow*. New York: Random House.

Wistrich, Robert. 1984. *Who's Who in Nazi Germany*. New York: Bonanza Books.

Witcover, Jules. 1989. *Sabotage at Black Tom: Imperial Germany's Secret War in America, 1914–1917*. Chapel Hill, N.C.: Algonquin Books.

Wittlin, Thaddeus. 1965. *Time Stopped at 6:30: The Untold Story of the Katyn Massacre*. Indianapolis, Ind.: Bobbs Merrill.

Wolff, Kurt, ed. 1950. *The Sociology of Georg Simmel*. New York: Free Press.

Woodward, Kennet L. 1997. "Sex, Morality, and the Protestant Minister." *Newsweek* (International Edition), July 28, p. 50.

Wright, Esmond. 1986. "A Patriot for Whom? Benedict Arnold and the Loyalists." *History Today* 36:29–35.

Wyman, David S. 1984. *The Abandonment of the Jews: America and the Holocaust, 1941–1945*. New York: Pantheon Books.

Yehezkeli, Tzadok. 1997. "Was There a Traitor Aboard the *Exodus*?" *Yediot Aharonot* ("7 Days" Supplement), March 28, pp. 66–68 (Hebrew).

———. 1998. "They Say That I Betrayed 20 Agents. I Betrayed a Lot More: Aldrich Ames, the Most Destructive Mole in the History of the C.I.A., in a First Interview to an Israeli Newspaper." *Yediot Aharonot* ("7 Days" Supplement), April 24, pp. 16–24 (Hebrew).

Yellin-Mor, Natan. 1974. *Lohamei Herout Israel (LEHI)*. Tel Aviv: Shikmona (Hebrew).

Young, Gordon. 1959. *In Trust and Treason: The Strange Case of Suzanne Warren*. London: Edward Hulton.

Young, Peter. 1981. *The World Almanac Book of World War II*. Englewood Cliffs, N.J.: Prentice-Hall.

Zaslavsky, Victor. 1999. "The Katyn Massacre: 'Class Cleansing' as Totalitarian Praxis." *Telos* 114:67–107.

Zelizer, Barbie. 1999. "Defending the American Dream: Narrative of Espionage in the American Popular Press." Paper presented at the 51st Annual Meeting of the American Society of Criminology, November, Toronto.

Zentner, Christian, and Friedmann Bedurftig, eds. 1997. *The Encyclopedia of the Third Reich*. Translated by Amy Hackett. New York: Da Capo Press.

Zerubavel, Eviatar. 1991. *The Fine Line: Making Distinctions in Everyday Life*. New York: Free Press.

Zerubavel, Yael. 1980. *The Last Stand: On the Transformation of Symbols in Modern Israeli Culture*. Ph.D. dissertation in Folklore and Folklife. University of Pennsylvania, Philadelphia.

———. 1995. *Recovered Roots: Collective Memory and the Making of Israeli National Tradition*. Chicago: University of Chicago Press.

Ziegler, Philip. 1990. *King Edward VIII: The Official Biography*. London: Collins.

Zilberberg, Avi. 1997. "Assaf Hefetz—For Your Treatment." *Ma'ariv* ("Weekend" Supplement), March 14, pp. 58–62 (Hebrew).

Zimmermann, Moshe. 1986. *Opposition to National Socialism*. Jerusalem: Hebrew University, Magness Press (Hebrew).

Index

and collaboration, 136; collective level, 42, 308, 309; in the conquest of Mexico, 273; content of, 307, 310; context of, 24, 307; continuous vs. discrete variable, 25, 37, 308; core of, 25, 27, 196, 307; and crisis, 122; and danger, 9; definition of, 115, 308, 309; as deviance, 25, 28, 127, 310, 311; emotional, 52, 312; encyclopedia of, 127, 307; frequency of, 308; forms of, 25, 312; group, 309; and identity, 311, 312; intellectual, 226; international, 38, 72–75; interpersonal, 309; meaning of, 28, 307; and morality, 28, 41; motivation for, 115, 305; national, 309; organizational, 309; personal level, 18, 27, 37, 42, 125, 126, 308, 309; in politics, 303; and power, 28, 41, 125; professional, 38; reactions to, 37; of the State, 76; and secrecy, 37, 39, 116, 260, 309, 310, 312; and secularism, 294; in society, 52; socially constructed, 23; sociology of, 127; state level, 27, 37; structure of, 23, 27, 37, 196, 228, 273, 306, 307, 309, 310; vs. treason, 17, 312; typology of, 38; universal structure vs. moral content, 310; as violating loyalty, 23, 308; as violating trust, 12, 23, 308; and Weimar, 180, 196; widespread existence of, 101. See also, Loyalty; Stealth; Traitor; Treason; Trust; Turncoating

Betrayers of Truth, 95
Bible, 19, 36, 68; and spies, 316n64
Big Three, 170
Billings, Warren, 119
Binet, Major Meir, 67
Biography, 34, 41, 311; personal and social, 311

Bishop: of Argyll, 21; runaway, 22; traitor, 22
Black, Donald, 310
"Black fuhrer," 121
Black, Ian, 70, 277, 293
Black marketeers, 167
Blackshirts (British), 246
Black Watch Mutiny, 56
Blair, Tony, 83
Blitzkrieg, 241
Bloch, Michael, 237, 240
"Blood for Trucks," 95–96, 292–293
Blue Angel, The, 185
Blunt, Anthony, 42, 63, 113, 256, 257, 260, 338n149
Bohemia and Moravia, 141
Boleyn, Anne, 123
Bomber Command, 146
Bombing: Britain, 137; Jerusalem and Tel Aviv, 195, 330n74
Bomb(s), 67, 77, 291; death camps, 96; in Hitler's airplane, 183
Bonhoeffer, Dietrich, 181, 183–184
Bonnier, Fernand de la Chapelle, 163
Boston: siege of, 35
Boveri, Margaret, 112–114, 116, 162, 164, 165
Bowels, Camilla Parker, 50
Bower, Donald E., 189, 190
Bowyer Bell, J., 95
Boyd, Belle, 118
Bradford, Sarah, 234, 235, 239, 240, 241, 245, 246, 248, 249, 250, 254, 256
Brand, Yoel: mission, 95–96, 97, 290, 292, 293
Brando, Marlon, 65
Brandt, Clare, 30, 31
Brandt, Willy, 41, 138
Brassillach, Robert, 160
Braveheart, 21, 123
Brazil, 77, 85
Brewer M., 10
Bridge at Remagen, The, 20